THEOLOGY OF THE GOSPEL OF MARK

THEOLOGY OF THE GOSPEL OF MARK

A Semantic, Narrative, and Rhetorical Study of the Characterization of God

Paul L. Danove

LONDON • NEW YORK • OXFORD • NEW DELHI • SYDNEY

T&T CLARK
Bloomsbury Publishing Plc
50 Bedford Square, London, WC1B 3DP, UK
1385 Broadway, New York, NY 10018, USA
29 Earlsfort Terrace, Dublin 2, Ireland

BLOOMSBURY, T&T CLARK and the T&T Clark logo
are trademarks of Bloomsbury Publishing Plc

First published in Great Britain 2019
Paperback edition first published 2021

Copyright © Paul L. Danove, 2019

Paul L. Danove has asserted his right under the Copyright,
Designs and Patents Act, 1988, to be identified as Author of this work.

For legal purposes the Acknowledgements on p. xiv constitute
an extension of this copyright page.

Cover design: Tjaša Krivec

All rights reserved. No part of this publication may be reproduced or
transmitted in any form or by any means, electronic or mechanical,
including photocopying, recording, or any information storage or retrieval
system, without prior permission in writing from the publishers.

Bloomsbury Publishing Plc does not have any control over, or responsibility for,
any third-party websites referred to or in this book. All internet addresses given
in this book were correct at the time of going to press. The author and publisher
regret any inconvenience caused if addresses have changed or sites have
ceased to exist, but can accept no responsibility for any such changes.

A catalogue record for this book is available from the British Library.

Library of Congress Cataloging-in-Publication Data
Names: Danove, Paul L., author.
Title: Theology of the Gospel of Mark: a semantic, narrative, and rhetorical study of the
characterization of God / Paul L. Danove.
Description: 1 [edition]. | New York: T&T Clark, 2019. |
Includes bibliographical references and index.
Identifiers: LCCN 2019020063 (print) | ISBN 9780567684066 (hardback)
Subjects: LCSH: God–Biblical teaching. | Bible Mark–Theology.
Classification: LCC BS2398 .D36 2019 (print) | LCC BS2398 (ebook) | DDC 226.3/066–dc23
LC record available at https://lccn.loc.gov/2019020063
LC ebook record available at https://lccn.loc.gov/2019980125

ISBN: HB: 978-0-5676-8406-6
PB: 978-0-5677-0198-5
ePDF: 978-0-5676-8407-3
eBook: 978-0-5676-8410-3

Typeset by RefineCatch Limited, Bungay, Suffolk

To find out more about our authors and books visit
www.bloomsbury.com and sign up for our newsletters.

in memoriam
Rev. Stephen Happel of the Catholic University of America

CONTENTS

Preface	xii
Acknowledgments	xiv
List of Abbreviations	xv

Part I
THE METHODOLOGICAL STUDY

THE SEMANTIC, NARRATIVE, AND RHETORICAL METHODS
OF ANALYSIS AND DESCRIPTION

Chapter 1
THE METHOD OF SEMANTIC ANALYSIS AND DESCRIPTION 3
  1. The Model of Semantic Communication: Semantic Frames 3
  2. Specification of the Content of Semantic Frames 6
  3. The Focus of the Semantic Study: Case Frames 9
  4. Case Frame Analysis and Description: Thematic Roles 10
  5. Specifying the Licensing Properties of Predicators 12
  6. Clarifications Concerning the Semantic Study 13
  7. Clarifications Concerning the Case Frame Descriptions 17
  8. Pre-Existing and Cultivated Semantic Beliefs 18

Chapter 2
THE METHOD OF NARRATIVE ANALYSIS AND DESCRIPTION 19
  1. The Model of Narrative Communication: Narrative Frames 19
  2. Specification of the Content of Narrative Frames 20
  3. The Focus of the Narrative Study: Character Frames 22
  4. Character Frame Analysis and Description: References to God 23
  5. Specifying the Actions and Attributes of God 38
  6. Clarifications Concerning the Narrative Study 40
  7. Clarification Concerning Character Frame Descriptions 41
  8. Pre-Existing and Cultivated Narrative Beliefs Concerning God 41

Chapter 3
THE METHOD OF RHETORICAL ANALYSIS AND DESCRIPTION AND
THE THEOLOGICAL STUDY 43
  1. The Model of Rhetorical Communication: Rhetorical Frames 43
  2. Specification of the Content of Rhetorical Frames 45
  3. The Focus of the Rhetorical Study: Predicator Repetition Frames 47

4.	Predicator Repetition Frame Analysis and Description: Linkages and Emphases	47
5.	Specifying the Rhetorically Organized Content about God	49
6.	Clarifications Concerning the Rhetorical Study	51
7.	Clarifications Concerning Predicator Repetition Frame Descriptions	53
8.	Pre-Existing and Cultivated Rhetorical Beliefs Concerning God	55
9.	Prelude to the Theological Study: The Exegetical Study (Part 2)	55
10.	Statements of God's Actions and Attributes: The Theological Study (Part 3)	56

Part II
THE EXEGETICAL STUDY

THE SEMANTIC AND NARRATIVE ANALYSIS OF THE CONTENT OF RHETORICAL CONTEXTS

Chapter 4
EXEGESIS OF THE RHETORICAL CONTEXTS IN MARK 1–9   63

1.	Mark 1	63
2.	Mark 2	67
3.	Mark 3	68
4.	Mark 4	69
5.	Mark 5	71
6.	Mark 6	72
7.	Mark 7	73
8.	Mark 8	74
9.	Mark 9	77

Chapter 5
EXEGESIS OF THE RHETORICAL CONTEXTS IN MARK 10–15   81

1.	Mark 10	81
2.	Mark 11	84
3.	Mark 12	86
4.	Mark 13	91
5.	Mark 14	94
6.	Mark 15	98

Part III
THE THEOLOGICAL STUDY

THE REPEATED ACTIONS AND ATTRIBUTES OF GOD

Chapter 6
GOD AS AGENT   101

1.	God Tears (*σχίζω [Ap])	101

2. God Will Shorten (*κολοβόω [Ap]) the Days	105
3. God Does/Makes/Acts (*ποιέω [Ap])	106
4. God Says (*λέγω [Ace])	108
5. God Is the Agent by Whom Events Come To Be (*γίνομαι [pA])	109
6. God Will Save (*σῴζω [Ap])	110
7. God Forgives (*ἀφίημι [Apb])	111
8. God Was the Agent of Writing (*γέγραπται [Ace])	112
9. God Sends (*ἀποστέλλω [Aθg])	114
10. God Gives (*δίδωμι [Aθg])	116
11. God the Agent	118

Chapter 7
GOD AS AGENTIVE BENEFACTIVE — 127

1. God Has Forgiveness (*ἄφεσις [Bb])	128
2. God Has a Voice (*φωνή [B])	129
3. God Has Creation (*κτίσις [B]) Which Had a Beginning	130
4. God Has All Possible Things (*δυνατόν [B])	131
5. God Has the Scripture (*γραφή [B])	132
6. God Has the Scripture by Which Events Are Necessary (*δεῖ [vi-iB])	134
7. God Will Have the Elect (*ἐκλεκτός [B])	136
8. God Has the Vineyard (*ἀμπελών [B])	137
9. God Has the Commandments (*ἐντολή [B])	139
10. God Has the Commandments That Do/Do Not Permit (*ἔξεστιν [vi-iB]) Events	140
11. God Has Jesus the Christ (*χριστός [B])	142
12. God Has the Reign (*βασιλεία [B])	143
13. God the Agentive Benefactive	146

Chapter 8
GOD AS INNATE AND ORIGINATING BENEFACTIVE — 149

1. God Has Glory (*δόξα [B])	150
2. God Has a Right [Hand] (*δεξιά [B])	151
3. God Has Power (*δύναμις [B])	151
4. God Has Life (*ζωή [B])	153
5. God Has the Holy Spirit (*πνεῦμα [B])	155
6. God (with Jesus, the Twelve, and Disciples) Has Authority (*ἐξουσία [B])	158
7. God the Innate Benefactive	159
8. God Has the Things (*τά [B])	161
9. God (with Jesus) Has the Way (*ὁδός [B])	162
10. God (with Jesus) Has/Is the Topic of the Gospel (*εὐαγγέλιον [B/T])	163
11. God the Originating Benefactive	165

Chapter 9
GOD AS RECIPIENT AND RECIPROCAL BENEFACTIVE — 167

1. God Has (Recipient Benefaction of) Sinful Actions (*ἁμάρτημα [bB]) — 168
2. God Is/Is Not Blasphemed (*βλασφημέω [acB]) — 169
3. God Has (Recipient Benefaction of) Blasphemies (*βλασφημία [bB]) — 170
4. God Has (Recipient Benefaction of) Sins (*ἁμαρτία [bB]) — 171
5. God Has (Recipient Benefaction of) the House (*οἶκος [bB]) — 172
6. God Has (Recipient Benefaction of) the Sanctuary (*ναός [bB]) — 174
7. God Has (Recipient Benefaction of) the Temple (*ἱερόν [bB]) — 175
8. God the Recipient Benefactive — 177
9. God Has Slaves (*δοῦλος [B]) — 179
10. God Has the Prophets (*προφήτης [B]) — 179
11. God Has Messengers/Angels (*ἄγγελος [B]) — 180
12. God Has Jesus the Son (*υἱός [B]) — 181
13. God the Reciprocal Benefactive — 184

Chapter 10
GOD AS CONTENT, EXPERIENCER, GOAL, AND INSTRUMENT — 185

1. God Is to Be Loved (*ἀγαπάω [eC/apB]) — 186
2. God Is Given Thanks (*εὐχαριστέω [acE]) by Jesus — 188
3. God Is the Experiencer of Prayer (*προσευχή [E]) — 190
4. God Is the Experiencer of Hosanna (*ὡσαννά [aE]) — 190
5. God Loves (*ἀγαπητός [Ec/Apb]) Jesus the Son — 191
6. God Is Blessed (*εὐλογέω [atE]) by Jesus — 192
7. God Is Prayed To (*προσεύχομαι [acE]) — 193
8. God the Experiencer — 196
9. God the Goal — 198
10. God the Instrument — 199

Chapter 11
GOD AS PATIENT, SOURCE, THEME, AND TOPIC; PROPOSALS AND CONCLUSION — 201

1. God Is One (*εἷς [P]) — 202
2. God Is Father (*πατήρ [bP]) — 202
3. God Is God (*θεός [bP]) — 204
4. God the Patient — 205
5. God Is the Source of the Sign (*σημεῖον [S]) — 205
6. God Is the Source from Whom One Receives (*λαμβάνω [gθS]) — 206
7. God the Source — 207
8. God the Theme — 209
9. God Is the Topic of Faith (*πίστις [ecT]) — 209
10. God Is to Be Believed In (*πιστεύω [ecT]) — 210

11.	Proposals for Further Developing the Theological Study	212
12.	Conclusion	216

Appendices 217
   A. Definitions: Thematic Roles 217
   B. References to God by Thematic Role 218
   C. Rhetorical Contexts with References 221

Bibliography 225
Index 233

PREFACE

This study proposes a set of complementary semantic, narrative, and rhetorical methods for investigating characterization (Methodological Study), re-presents the narrative and narratively-interpreted semantic content of the contexts containing the 314 references to the character God in the Gospel of Mark (Exegetical Study), and develops statements of the fifty-six repeated actions and attributes of God within Mark 1:1–16:8 (Theological Study). This study has three goals. The first is to provide narrative biblical scholars with a set of coherent methods that guide the interpretation of biblical narratives from the semantic surface structure of a text to the formulation of statements of characters' actions and attributes and, where applicable, guide the further formulation of statements of characters' repeated actions and attributes. The second is to demonstrate the application of this set of methods in the specification of the repeated and non-repeated actions and attributes of God in the Gospel of Mark. The third is to format and articulate the statements of God's repeated actions and attributes in a manner that readily is usable both by students of the bible and by theologians in general and systematic theologians in particular. The following discussion specifies the order and content of the presentation of the study.

The Methodological Study (Part I) proposes and illustrates the methods of semantic (Chapter 1)/narrative (Chapter 2)/rhetorical (Chapter 3) analysis and description. These discussions specify the model of semantic/narrative/rhetorical communication assumed in the Theological Study, introduce the concepts of semantic/narrative/rhetorical frames, develop and illustrate the interpretive potential of case/character/predicator repetition frames, offer a series of clarifications about the frames introduced and developed, and distinguish pre-existing from cultivated semantic/narrative/rhetorical beliefs. Chapter 3 also incorporates concluding discussions of the presuppositions and format of the Exegetical Study and the Theological Study. The Methodological Study addresses directly only semantic, narrative, and rhetorical considerations and does not interact directly with alternative methodological approaches to the text and its content.

The Exegetical Study (Part II) applies the semantic/narrative methods to the forty rhetorical contexts in Mark 1–9 (Chapter 4) and the thirty-eight rhetorical contexts in Mark 10–15 (Chapter 5) that contain the 314 semantically and narratively-justified references to God. These discussions re-present the content of the rhetorical contexts in a manner that highlights the actions and attributes of God, sets the actions and attributes in their proper semantic and narrative relation to other contextual content, and explains interpretations of specific contextual content. The Exegetical Study reveals that each of the seventy-eight rhetorical contexts incorporates at least one repeated action or attribute of God. As a consequence, the statements of God's fifty-six repeated actions and attributes in the Theological Study incorporate the content associated with all 314 references to God. The footnotes of the Exegetical Study focus on referencing and interacting with biblical scholarship that addresses and clarifies the proposed semantic and narrative interpretation of the text.

The Theological Study (Part III) articulates the statements of God's repeated actions and attributes (Chapters 6–11.10) and offers concluding considerations concerning the study (Chapter 11.11–11.12). Chapters 6–11.10 develop the statements in groups according to the thematic role predicated of God. These discussions develop repeated actions and attributes associated with each thematic role in the order of increasing frequency of occurrence and conclude with a consideration of patterns or progressions of development within each group. For thematic roles not associated with repeated attributes, the discussion considers only patterns in their development.

Within the Theological Study, Chapter 6 presents God's actions (God as Agent). Chapters 7–9 develop what God is attributed with having by virtue of acting (Chapter 7: God as Agentive Benefactive), innately and as origin (Chapter 8: God as Innate and Originating Benefactive), and reception and reciprocal relationships (Chapter 9: God as Recipient and Reciprocal Benefactive). Chapter 10 presents God's attributes as the content of human experience (God as Content), as one who experiences (God as Experiencer), as the destination of motion (God as Goal), and as the means of another's action (God as Instrument). Chapter 11 presents God as the object of predication (God as Patient), as the source of things (God as Source), as in motion or at rest (God as Theme), and as the focus of belief (God as Topic) and offers proposals for further development of the Theological Study and concluding comments about the Theological Study. The Theological Study (Chapters 6–11.10) develops the semantic, narrative, and rhetorical potentialities of the text and references and incorporates only limited coherent content from alternative methodological approaches to the text.

The Appendix defines the thematic roles predicated of God, lists the 314 semantically and narratively-justified references to God by thematic role, their associated Greek word, English translation, and location[s] in the text of Mark, and includes a summary of the rhetorical contexts and the references to God that they contain.

ACKNOWLEDGMENTS

I wish to thank Mr. Jonathan Atkinson (M.A. Villanova) for his assistance collecting library materials, Mr. Patrick Connolly (M.A. Villanova) for proofing the text of Chapters 1–3, Mr. Stephen Purcell (B.A. Villanova) for proofing the entire text, Dr. Anthony Godzieba (Villanova) for his helpful feedback on the outline of the project, and the late Rev. Stephen Happel (Catholic University of America) for his encouragement at the initial stage of developing this project.

ABBREVIATIONS

AB	Anchor Bible
ANTC	Abingdon New Testament Commentaries
ATJ	*Asbury Theological Journal*
BECNT	Baker Exegetical Commentary on the New Testament
BDF	Friedrich Blass, Albert Debrunner and Robert W. Funk, *A Greek Grammar of the New Testament and Other Early Christian Literature* (Cambridge: Cambridge University Press, 1961)
Bib	*Biblica*
BibInt	*Biblical Interpretation: A Journal of Contemporary Approaches*
BibSac	*Biblia Sacra*
BIOSCS	*Bulletin of the International Organization for Septuagint and Cognate Studies*
BIS	Biblical Interpretation Series
BLS	*Berkeley Linguistics Society*
B-TS	Biblisch-Theologische Studien
CBNT	Coniectanea Biblica New Testament
CBQ	*Catholic Biblical Quarterly*
CBQMS	Catholic Biblical Quarterly Monograph Series
CCSS	Catholic Commentary on Sacred Scripture
CGTC	Cambridge Greek Testament Commentary
COQG	Christian Origins and the Question of God
CSL	Current Studies in Linguistics
CSLI	Center for the Study of Language and Information
FN	*Filología Neotestamentaria*
GNC	Good News Commentary
HBT	*Horizons in Biblical Theology*
HtKNT	Herders theologischer Kommentar zum Neuen Testament
JBL	*Journal of Biblical Literature*
JR	*Journal of Religion*
JSNT	*Journal for the Study of the New Testament*
JSNTSup	Journal for the Study of the New Testament, Supplement Series
JTI	*Journal of Theological Interpretation*
JTS	*Journal of Theological Studies*
L&P	*Linguistics and Philosophy*
LB	*Linguistica Biblica*
LBS	Linguistic Biblical Studies
LInq	*Linguistic Inquiry*
LNTS	Library of New Testament Studies
LSJ	H. G. Liddell, Robert Scott, and H. Stuart Jones, *Greek–English Lexicon* (Oxford: Clarendon Press, 9th edn, 1968)

MIT	Massachusetts Institute of Technology
NCBC	New Cambridge Bible Commentary
Neot	*Neotestamentica*
NICNT	New International Commentary on the New Testament
NovT	*Novum Testamentum*
NovTSup	Novum Testamentum, Supplements
NTS	*New Testament Studies*
PNTC	Penguin New Testament Commentary
QS	*Quaderni di Semantica*
S&HBC	Smyth & Helwys Bible Commentary
SBLDS	Society of Biblical Literature Dissertation Series
SCM	Student Christian Movement
SNTG	Studies in New Testament Greek
SNTSMS	Society for New Testament Studies Monograph Series
SPS	Sacra Pagina Series
ST	*Studia Theiologica*
TDNT	Gerhard Kittel and Gerhard Friedrich (eds.), *Theological Dictionary of the New Testament* (trans. Geoffrey W. Bromiley, 10 vols., Grand Rapids: Eerdmans, 1964–)
TNTL	The New Testament Library
TSL	Typological Studies in Language
TrinJ	*Trinity Journal*
UBS	United Bible Societies
UBSGNT	United Bible Societies Greek New Testament
WBC	Word Biblical Commentary
WeBC	Westminster Bible Companion
WUNT	Wissenschaftliche Untersuchungen zum Neuen Testament

Part I

The Methodological Study

The Semantic, Narrative, and Rhetorical Methods of Analysis and Description

Chapter 1

THE METHOD OF SEMANTIC ANALYSIS AND DESCRIPTION

This chapter introduces the method of semantic analysis and description assumed in the following study of the theology of the Gospel of Mark. The initial discussion presents an overview of the study's model of communication and its interpreter. The discussion of the semantic method of analysis and description then introduces the concepts associated with semantic frames, specifies the content of particular semantic frames, develops the analytical and descriptive potential of case frames, offers a series of clarifications about semantic and case frames, and provides a statement of the semantic competencies assumed by the narration. Within the semantic study, "Mark" designates the semantic content of the text of the Gospel of Mark, which is taken to include the text of UBSGNT 4 from 1:1–16:8.[1]

1. The Model of Semantic Communication: Semantic Frames

This discussion introduces the study's model of communication and then specifies the elements of the model of semantic communication that establish the foundation for the semantic study of characterization.

---

1. Barbara Aland et al. eds., *The Greek New Testament*, 4th rev. edn. (Stuttgart: Biblia-Druck, 1993). The following study assumes that the Gospel of Mark ends at 16:8 based on: (1) the textual considerations of Kurt Aland, "Bemerkungen zum Schluss des Markusevangeliums," in *Neotestamentica et Semitica: Studies in Honour of Matthew Black*, ed. E. Earle Ellis and Max Wilcox (Edinburgh: T&T Clark, 1969), 157–80, and Bruce M. Metzger, *A Textual Commentary on the Greek New Testament* (Stuttgart: Biblia-Druck, 1975), 122–8; (2) the literary considerations of Thomas E. Boomershine and Gilbert L. Bartholomew, "The Narrative Technique of Mark 16:8," *JBL* 100, no. 2 (1981): 213–23; (3) the grammatical considerations of Paul L. Danove, *Linguistics and Exegesis in the Gospel of Mark: Applications of a Case Frame Analysis and Lexicon* (JSNTSup 218; SNTG 10; Sheffield: Sheffield Academic Press, 2001), 73–7; and (4) the genre considerations of Elizabeth E. Shively, "Recognizing Penguins: Audience Expectation, Cognitive Genre Theory, and the Ending of Mark's Gospel," *CBQ* 80, no. 2 (2018): 273–92.

a. The Model of Communication

This study attributes to the text the capacity to guide its own interpretation.[2] Thus its model of communication focuses not on historical author(s) and readers or possible applications by contemporary readers but on the author and reader implied by the text.[3]

According to this model, the implied author proposes, structures, and provides guidelines for evaluating the content of the Gospel of Mark; and the implied reader receives this content and interprets it under the guidance provided by the implied author.[4] The narration assumes and evokes particular pre-existing competencies, knowledge, and convictions for the implied reader and cultivates new competencies, knowledge, and convictions for the implied reader.[5] This and following discussions reference these competencies, knowledge, and convictions as "beliefs."

The distinction between pre-existing and cultivated beliefs usually is straightforward. The introduction of words without definitions, concepts without explanations, and named characters without detailed descriptions signal appeals to beliefs assumed for the implied reader. In contrast, definitions for words,

---

2. Discussions of what is implied by textually guided interpretation appear in Elizabeth Struthers Malbon, "Narrative Criticism: How Does the Story Mean?," in *Mark & Method: New Approaches in Biblical Studies*, ed. Janice Capel Anderson and Stephen D. Moore (Minneapolis, MN: Fortress, 1992), 23–49, and in Gabriel Fackre, "Narrative Theology: An Overview," *Interpretation* 37, no. 4 (1983): 340–52.

3. The study assumes the model of narrative communication proposed by Seymour Chatman, *Story and Discourse: Narrative Structure in Fiction and Film* (Ithaca, NY: Cornell University Press, 1978), 28, 149–51, developed by Paul L. Danove, *The End of Mark's Story: A Methodological Study* (BIS 3; Leiden: Brill, 1993), 64–5, and refined by Bastiaan M. F. van Iersel, *Mark: A Reader-Response Commentary*, trans. W. H. Bisscsheroux (JSNTSup 164; Sheffield: Sheffield Academic Press, 1998), 16–22. The implied author and the implied reader receive introduction in Chatman, *Story and Discourse*, 146–51, and in Wayne C. Booth, *The Rhetoric of Fiction*, 2nd edn. (Chicago: University of Chicago Press, 1983), 74–5; cf. Stephen D. Moore, *Literary Criticism and the Gospels: The Theoretical Challenge* (New Haven, CT: Yale University Press, 1989), 180.

4. Further consideration of the proposed construct of the implied reader appears in Bernard C. Lategan, "Coming to Grips with the Reader in Biblical Literature," *Semeia* 48 (1989): 5, and in Hans Robert Jauss, *Toward an Aesthetic of Reception*, trans. Timothy Bahti (Minneapolis, MN: University of Minnesota, 1982). The nature and role of the guidelines for interpretation generally receive discussion under the heading of "point of view": cf. Chatman, *Story and Discourse*, 151–8; and Norman R. Petersen, "'Point of View' in Mark's Narrative," *Semeia* 12 (1978): 97–121.

5. The role of the reader's beliefs, knowledge, and familiarity with literary conventions in the interpretive process receives attention in Booth, *Rhetoric of Fiction*, 157, 177; in Umberto Eco, *The Role of the Reader: Explorations in the Semiotics of Texts* (Bloomington, IN: Indiana University Press, 1979), 7–8; and in Peter J. Rabinowitz, "Truth in Fiction: A Reexamination of Audiences," *Critical Inquiry* 4, no. 1 (1977): 125–33.

explanations for concepts, and detailed introductions for new named characters signal narrative attempts to cultivate beliefs for the implied reader.

The distinction between evoked and cultivated beliefs permits a distinction of two constructs of the implied reader: the authorial audience and the narrative audience.[6] The authorial audience is the construct of the pre-existing beliefs assumed for the implied reader, and the narrative audience is the construct of the beliefs cultivated for the implied reader. The study omits consideration of a third possible construct of the implied reader, the ideal narrative audience, which arises in the context of unreliable narration, because the narrator of the Gospel of Mark is reliable, that is, indicative of the guidelines for interpretation proposed by the implied author.[7]

b. The Model of Semantic Communication: Semantic Frames

The model of semantic communication assumes that the encounter with each word of Mark evokes for the interpreter semantic frames. These semantic frames accommodate the interpretation of the word by making available information about and semantic referents for the words accommodated by the frame; relationships to other semantic frames containing the words and referents; perspectives for evaluating the function of the words; and expectations concerning the semantic content of communication.[8] Each word within a semantic context evokes semantic frames and

---

6. The distinction between the authorial audience and the narrative audience receives development in Peter J. Rabinowitz, *Before Reading: Narrative Conventions and the Politics of Interpretation* (Ithaca, NY: Cornell University Press, 1987), 26–7; cf. Rabinowitz, "Truth in Fiction," 126–33.

7. The ideal narrative audience receives development in Rabinowitz, "Truth in Fiction," 127–8. Discussions of reliability in the Gospel of Mark appear in Robert C. Tannehill, "The Disciples in Mark: The Function of a Narrative Role," *JR* 57, no. 4 (1977): 390–1; Petersen, "Point of View," 105–11; Robert M. Fowler, *Loaves And Fishes: The Function of the Feeding Stories in the Gospel of Mark* (SBLDS, 54; Chico, CA: Scholars Press, 1981), 229; and David Rhoads, Joanna Dewey, and Donald Michie, *Mark as Story: An Introduction to the Narrative of a Gospel*, 2nd rev. edn. (Minneapolis, MN: Fortress, 1999), 39. Although Elizabeth Struthers Malbon, "History, Theology, Story: Re-Contextualizing Mark's 'Messianic Secret' as Characterization," in *Character Studies and the Gospel of Mark*, ed. Christopher W. Skinner and Matthew Ryan Hauge (JSNTSup 483; London: Bloomsbury, 2014), 45–55, demonstrates a subtle distinction in point of view among the implied author, narrator, and Jesus in the characterization of Jesus in the Gospel of Mark, this distinction does not directly impact the characterization of God.

8. Semantic frames receive introduction in Charles J. Fillmore, "The Need for Frame Semantics Within Linguistics," in *Statistical Methods in Linguistics*, ed. Hans Karlgren (Stockholm: Scriptor, 1977), 5–29; cf. Teuen A. van Dijk, "Semantic Macro-Structures and Knowledge Frames in Discourse Comprehension," in *Cognitive Processes in Comprehension*, ed. Marcel Adam Just and Patricia A. Carpenter (Hillsdale, NJ: Lawrence Erlbaum Associates, 1977), 3–32. An overview of the concept, "semantic frame," appears in Charles J. Fillmore, "Frames and the Semantics of Understanding," *QS* 6, no. 2 (1985): 222–54.

the intersection of their content identifies one or more sets of information, relationships, perspectives, and expectations that permit the grammatical interpretation of all the words in the context. The most significant semantic context is the phrase. For example, the words of the verb phrase governed by "lease" (ἐκδίδομαι, 12:1) evoke various semantic frames; and the intersection of their content identifies the contractual commercial transaction semantic frame as the optimal meaningful context for the interpretation of the words of the phrase in that context.[9] This frame provides information about leasing; the relationships among "leasers," "lessees," "properties," and "fees"; perspectives for evaluating these relationships; and expectations for the grammatical use of these words. This semantic frame accommodates the interpretation of "the human being" as leaser, "farmers" as lessees, and "it/vineyard" as the property. This frame also provides the meaningful context for interpreting some of the fruit in 12:2 as the seasonal fee of the leasing contract.

2. Specification of the Content of Semantic Frames

Although the content of the semantic frames evoked by words in one language rarely coincides with that evoked by the translations of the words in another language, the proper selection of English translations for the words in Mark provides sufficient overlap in the content of the semantic frames to make special clarification unnecessary. The following discussion considers those Greek words whose evoked semantic frames differ sufficiently in content from their English translations to impact the study of the characterization of God.

a. Love (ἀγαπάω)

Whereas the English "love" in its contemporary usage gives prominence to the affective and experiential element of relationships, ἀγαπάω in Mark complements the affective focus by also evoking semantic frames that provide information, relationships, perspectives, and expectations concerning covenantal obligations. This is apparent in the fact that, in four of its five occurrences, the verb is introduced in response to a question about the commandments (12:30, 31, 33a, 33b). Significantly, in the remaining occurrence (10:21), Jesus responds to the man who has fulfilled central obligations of the Mosaic covenant (10:19-20; cf. Exod 20:12-16; Deut 5:16-20) by loving him and telling him that, in order to inherit everlasting life, he must also sell what he has, give it to the poor, and follow Jesus.[10] This clarifies that love's affective response to another requires action on behalf of the other.[11]

---

9. A detailed description of the related "commercial transaction frame" appears in Fillmore, "The Need for Frame Semantics," 20.

10. All citations from the Septuagint are taken from Alfred Rahlfs, ed., *Septuaginta* (Stuttgart: Deutsche Bibelstiftung, 1935).

11. Concerning these active or agentive implications, see Ethelbert Stauffer, "ἀγαπάω," *TDNT* 1:44–5.

1. The Method of Semantic Analysis and Description 7

b. Forgive (ἀφίημι)

Unlike the English "forgive," which evokes semantic frames that include many words referencing possible things and persons that may be forgiven, ἀφίημι with the meaning "forgive" in Mark most frequently evokes semantic frames that reference "sins" understood as "covenantal debts."[12] These semantic frames provide the information that, insofar as actions that violate the covenant cannot be undone, the sins/debts incurred by those actions cannot be repaid. As a consequence, ἀφίημι differs from "forgive" in not evoking commercial transaction semantic frames that provide information, relationships, perspectives for evaluation, and expectations concerning various means of repayment.

c. Has Been Written (γέγραπται)

"Write" and γράφω evoke semantic frames that provide references to significantly different information and different words associated with the mechanisms and materials of writing and possible writers. Still, there is sufficient overlap in the content of the semantic frames to accommodate straightforward interpretation in some cases. The situation is different with the third-person singular perfect passive indicative form of the Greek verb, "has been written" (γέγραπται), which, especially in the context of references to scripture, has a technical meaning that designates an action of composition conducted under the authority of God, the instigator and guarantor of what is written. In this context, γέγραπται is deemed to evoke semantic frames that provide the word "god" ([ὁ] θεός) as the expected definite semantic referent of the writer and relate what is written to the semantic frames evoked by "scripture" (γραφή).

d. Be Necessary (δεῖ)

Unlike the English "be necessary," which evokes semantic frames that include many words referencing possible necessitating forces, δεῖ in Mark evokes semantic frames that assume a specific referent for the necessitating force. This is apparent in the proximate statements concerning the suffering of the Son of Man, which are introduced first by "be necessary" (δεῖ, 8:31) and then by "has been written" (γέγραπται, 9:12). The proximate repetition of these statements without intervening narrative developments to explain the referent of the necessitating force indicates that the implied author of Mark assumes for the authorial audience a pre-existing recognition that what is written (γέγραπτα) under God's agency is the referent of

---

12. Paul L. Danove, "The Action of Forgiving in the New Testament," in *Forgiveness: Selected Papers from the 2008 Annual Conference of the Villanova University Theology Institute*, ed. Darlene Fozard Weaver and Jeffrey S. Mayer (Villanova, PA: Villanova University Press, 2008), 41–2.

the necessitating force.¹³ This interpretation receives reinforcement in Jesus' later statement about the Son of Man going as is written about him (14:21).

e. Be Permitted (ἔξεστιν)

Unlike "be permitted," which evokes semantic frames that include a number of typical words for possible licensing entities, ἔξεστιν in Mark evokes semantic frames that identify an expected word and referent for this entity. The most frequently proposed referent, "law" (νόμος), is not viable in Mark where this word never appears.¹⁴ Instead, Mark presents a significant interest in the word "commandment" (ἐντολή, 7:8, 9; 10:5, 19; 12:28, 31); and five of the six occurrences of ἔξεστιν appear in discussions about what specific commandments do or do not permit: what can be done on the Sabbath (2:24; 3:4; cf. Exod 20:8-11; Deut 5:12-15), who can eat the bread of offering (2:26; cf. Lev 24:9), whom a man may not marry (6:18; cf. Lev 18:16; 20:21), and whether one may divorce (10:2; cf. Deut 24:1). Even the sixth occurrence, in the discussion of whether one may pay the census tax (12:14), may be interpreted in relation to what is permitted by the first commandment (Exod 20:2-6; Deut 5:6-10).¹⁵ These considerations indicate that the semantic frames evoked by ἔξεστιν identify "commandment" (ἐντολή) as the specific licensing entity.

---

13. Recent scholarship tends to favor the interpretation of "the plan of God" as the expected referent of the necessitating force: cf. W. R. Telford, *The Theology of the Gospel of Mark* (Cambridge: Cambridge University Press, 1999), 41, 114–15; Francis J. Moloney, *The Gospel of Mark: A Commentary* (Peabody, MA: Hendrickson, 2002), 173; Walter Grundmann, "δεῖ, δέον ἐστί," *TDNT* 2:22; and William L. Lane, *The Gospel According to Mark: The English Text with Introduction, Exposition, and Notes* (Grand Rapids, MI: Eerdmans, 1974), 295–6. Although this interpretation may apply, for example, in the Gospel of Luke, which presents the statement, "The Son of Man goes as has been determined (ὁρίζω)" (Luke 22:22), Mark lacks vocabulary associated with plans. Again, Joel Marcus, *Mark 1–8: A New Translation with Introduction and Commentary* (AB 27A; New York: Doubleday, 2000), 605, identifies "the will of God" as the necessitating force and discusses the link between God's will and being foretold in the scriptures. Such a proposed link, however, cannot be deemed intrinsic to Mark. Rather, Jesus' quotation and application of what has been written, "This people honors me with their lips but their hearts are far from me" (7:6) clarifies that this is not according to God's will for God's people.

14. Recommendations for "the law of God" as the licensing entity appear in Werner Foerster, "ἔξεστιν," *TDNT* 2:560–1; Lane, *The Gospel of Mark*, 114–15; Morna D. Hooker, *The Gospel According to Saint Mark* (Peabody, MA: Hendrickson, 2005), 102–3; and M. Eugene Boring, *Mark: A Commentary* (TNTL; Louisville, KY: Westminster John Knox, 2006), 89–90.

15. See John R. Donahue and Daniel J. Harrington, *The Gospel of Mark* (SPS 2; Collegeville, MN: Liturgical, 2002), 344.

3. The Focus of the Semantic Study: Case Frames

Each semantic frame that accommodates the interpretation of the words in a context evokes a specific case frame for each predicator in that context. Predicators, words that license the presence of other words, include verbs, conjunctions, adjectives, prepositions, and interjections, as well as those nouns, pronouns, and adverbs that either require or permit the completion of their meaning by other phrasal elements.[16] Case frames make available information about the predicator, its relationships to possible required and non-required phrasal elements, perspectives for evaluating the function of these phrasal elements, and expectations concerning the use of the predicator.[17]

Predicators require completion by "arguments," semantic entities that are necessary to complete the meaning of the predicator, and admit to completion by "adjuncts," semantic entities that provide a specification of a predicator's meaning beyond that required for its correct grammatical use.[18] The number of arguments that a predicator requires is equal to the number of semantic entities that must be referenced to relate the predicator's concept or meaning.[19] Among the words that

---

16. The "licensing" of elements is part of the more comprehensive principle of "government": cf. Charles J. Fillmore and Paul Kay, *Construction Grammar* (Stanford: CSLI, 1999), 4:9–12.

17. The original proposal of the case frame appears in Charles J. Fillmore, "The Case for Case," in *Universals in Linguistic Theory*, ed. Emmon Bach and Robert T. Harms (New York: Holt, Rinehart and Winston, 1968), 28, and has received development in various Case Grammatical systems: cf. Wallace L. Chafe, *Meaning and the Structure of Language* (Chicago: University of Chicago Press, 1970), 144–60; and Walter A. Cook, "A Case Grammar Matrix" in *Languages and Linguistics: Working Papers* 6 (1972): 15–47. Simon S. M. Wong, *A Classification of Semantic Case-Relations in the Pauline Epistles* (New York: Peter Lang, 1997), has applied such a Case Grammar in the study of the verbs of the Pauline corpus. The proposed method's linguistic analysis also has affinities with the discussion of thematic relations in generative grammars (Ray S. Jackendoff, *Semantic Structures* [CSL, 18; Cambridge, MA: MIT Press, 1990], 155–66), in the application of Case Grammar within tagmemics (John T. Platt, *Grammatical Form and Grammatical Meaning: A Tagmemic View of Fillmore's Deep Structure Case Concepts* [Amsterdam: North-Holland, 1971], 9–27), and in the representation of event schemas in Cognitive Linguistics (René Dirven and Marjolijn Verspoor, eds., *Cognitive Exploration of Language and Linguistics* [Amsterdam/Philadelphia: Benjamins, 1998], 79–83).

18. The concepts of "argument" and "adjunct" have their origins in the field of logic: cf. Randy Allen Harris, *The Linguistics Wars* (New York: Oxford University Press, 1993), 115–17; James D. McCawley, *Grammar and Meaning: Papers on Syntactic and Semantic Topics* (New York: Academic Press, 1976), 136–9; and Frederick J. Newmeyer, *Linguistic Theory in America: The First Quarter-Century of Transformational Generative Grammar* (New York: Academic Press, 1980), 148–50.

19. The determination of the number of arguments required by predicators is based on the internal logic of the predicator and is confirmed by its characteristic NT usage.

function as predicators, verbs require completion by one, two, or three arguments, conjunctions by two arguments, adjectives and prepositions by one or two arguments, and interjections and specific nouns, pronouns, and adverbs by one argument. "Required complements" realize the arguments of a predicator, and "non-required complements" realize the adjuncts of a predicator.

Case frame analysis describes the licensing properties of predicators and specifies the semantic function of each of the predicator's arguments and adjuncts. For example, the verb predicator "lease" (ἐκδίδομαι, 12:1) requires completion by three arguments that function semantically as a leaser (human being), property (vineyard), and lessee (farmers).

4. Case Frame Analysis and Description: Thematic Roles

Although "leaser," "property," and "lessee" precisely describe the semantic functions of the arguments required by "lease" (ἐκδίδομαι) in 12:1, the semantic study requires a small set of more generalized semantic functions that can describe all arguments and adjuncts. For this purpose, the semantic study uses thematic roles.[20]

The semantic study requires the use of seventeen thematic roles. The semantic functions "leaser," "property," and "lessee" are described respectively by the thematic roles Agent (A), "the animate entity that actively instigates an action and/or is the ultimate cause of a change in another entity," Theme (Θ), "the entity literally or figuratively moving from one place to another or located in a place," and Goal (G), "the literal or figurative entity towards which something moves."[21] In the following

---

20. Thematic roles are similar to the semantic cases originally proposed in Fillmore, "The Case for Case," 24–5. They are used in many formulations of Case Grammar and Generative Semantics under varying designations: "thematic relations" in Ray S. Jackendoff, *Semantic Interpretation in Generative Grammar* (Cambridge, MA: MIT Press, 1972), 29–46, and in Jeffrey S. Gruber, *Lexical Structures in Syntax and Semantics* (Amsterdam: North-Holland, 1976), 37–52; "participant roles" in Keith Allan, *Linguistic Meaning*, vol. 1 (London: Routledge & Keegan Paul, 1986), 383–5; "case roles" in Talmy Givón, *Syntax: A Functional-Typological Introduction*, vol. 1 (Amsterdam/Philadelphia: Benjamins, 1984), 96–145; and "thematic roles" in David R. Dowty, "Thematic Roles and Semantics," *BLS* 12 (1986): 340–54; Dowty, "On the Semantic Content of the Notion 'Thematic Role'," in *Properties, Types and Meaning*, vol. 2, ed. Gennaro Chierchia, Barbara H. Partee, and Raymond Turner (Dordrecht: Kluwer, 1989), 69–130; and in John I. Saeed, *Semantics* (Oxford: Blackwell, 1997), 139–71. The relationships between frame-specific roles and thematic roles is developed in David R. Dowty, "Thematic Proto-Roles and Argument Selection," *Language* 67, no. 3 (1991): 547–619; Saeed, *Semantics*, 150–2; and Farrell Ackerman and John Moore, "Valence and the Semantics of Causativization," *BLS* 20 (1994): 2–4.

21. These and all following definitions of thematic roles receive development and further explanation in Fillmore and Kay, *Construction Grammar* 4:21–2, in Saeed, *Semantics*, 140–1, and in Givón, *Syntax* 1, 126–7.

examples, the required complements that realize arguments appear in brackets, [ ], with their thematic roles in parentheses, ( ), and the Greek predicators appear in parentheses after their English translations.

> [A man (A)] leased (ἐκδίδομαι, 12:1) [it/a vineyard (Θ)] [to farmers (G)].
> [I (A)] send (ἀποστέλλω. 1:2) [my messenger (Θ)] [before your face (G)].
> before (πρό, 1:2) [your face (G)].

These examples permit three clarifications concerning the case frame analysis. First, this analysis describes the licensing properties of each predicator separately. Thus the description of ἀποστέλλω considers only the arguments (and adjuncts) directly licensed by this predicator but not those licensed by its complements. Second, the analysis assumes that predicators impose semantic functions on prepositions, which then impose the same semantic functions on their arguments. This explains the multiple uses of prepositions in English and Greek. Third, the appropriate context for semantic analysis, the phrase, is defined as the predicator with all of its licensed elements: the verb phrase (clause), noun phrase, preposition phrase, etc.

Two further thematic roles always occur in relation to a Theme, Locative (L), "the literal or figurative place in which an entity is situated or an event occurs," and Source (S), "the literal or figurative entity from which something moves."

> [Your Father (Θ)] in (ἐν, 11:25) [the heavens (L)].
> [Their heart (Θ)]...is distant (ἀπέχω, 7:6) [from me (S)].

The semantic study uses the thematic roles Benefactive (B), "the ultimate entity for which an action is performed or for which literally or figuratively something happens or exists," and Topic (T), "the topic of focus of a mental or psychological state, event, or activity." In the following examples, the genitive complement of "gospel" may be interpreted as either subjective (Benefactive) or objective (Topic).[22]

> face (πρόσωπον, 1:2) [of you (B)].
> gospel (εὐαγγέλιον, 1:14) [of/about God (B/T)].
> belief (πίστις, 11:22) [in/concerning God (T)].

Also significant are the thematic roles Content (C), "the content of a mental or psychological state, event, or activity," Experiencer (E), "the animate being that is the locus of a mental or psychological state, event, or activity," and Instrument (I), "the means by which an action is performed or something happens." In the second example, the verb predicator requires completion by Agent, Content, and Experiencer arguments and licenses an Instrument adjunct.

---

22. The subjective (Benefactive)/objective (Topic) genitive distinction receives consideration in BDF, 89–90 (§§162–163). For the appropriateness of this dual interpretation in Mark 1:1, see Moloney, *Mark*, 49; Hooker, *St. Mark*, 54; and Joel Marcus, *Mark 8–16: A New Translation with Introduction and Commentary* (AB 27B; New Haven and London: Yale University Press, 2009), 172.

[In you (C)] [I (E)] delight (εὐδοκέω, 1:11).
[I (A)] compel [you (E)] to swear (ὁρκίζω, 5:7) [by God (I)] [that... (C)].

The semantic study also uses the thematic roles Patient (P), "the entity undergoing an action," and Event (V), "the complete circumstantial scene of an action or event." The Patient thematic role also is imposed on the object of benefaction (what is possessed) and on the subject of predication with "be" (εἰμί). In the second example, "be" (εἰμί) does not function as an independent predicator but joins with another predicator—here the adjective predicator "one" (εἷς)—to form a single complex predicator "be one."[23] Since "be" licenses no arguments and adjuncts, only the conjoined predicator receives notation:

[He (B)] had (ἔχω, 12:6) [one, a Beloved Son (P)].
[He (P)] is one (εἷς, 12:32).
[By the Lord (A)] [this (P)] came to be (γίνομαι, 12:11).
[For you (B)] [to have your brother's wife (V)] is not permitted (ἔξεστιν, 6:18).

The remaining five thematic roles are circumstantial: Cause (Cau), "the circumstantial motivation for an action or event"; Condition (Cnd), "the entity or event required for another event to occur"; Manner (Man), "the circumstantial qualification of an action or event"; Purpose (Pur), "the goal of a complete event"; and Result (Res), "the consequence of a complete event."

[Because of the Elect (Cau)]...[God (A)] shortened (κολοβόω, 13:20) [the days (P)].
[If the Lord did not shorten the days (Cnd)] [no flesh (P)] would be saved (σῴζω, 13:20).
[In truth (Man)] [you (A)] teach (διδάσκω, 12:14) [the way of God (C)].
[He (A)] sent (ἀποστέλλω, 12:2) [to the farmers (G)]...[a slave (Θ)] [in order that that he might take from the farmers some of the fruit of the vineyard (Pur)].
[The crowd (Θ)]...came together (συνέρχομαι, 3:20) [so that they could not even eat bread (Res)].

Within the following study, Agent, Content, Event, Experiencer, Patient, Theme, and Topic thematic roles are restricted to arguments. Benefactive, Goal, Instrument, Locative, and Source thematic roles describe the arguments of some predicators and the adjuncts of others. The Cause, Condition, Manner, Purpose, and Result thematic roles are restricted to adjuncts. Only the Agent and Experiencer thematic roles are restricted to animate entities. The complete list of thematic roles with their definitions appears in the Appendix.

5. Specifying the Licensing Properties of Predicators

The semantic study specifies the licensing properties of predicators in a format that lists the predicator's English translation, the dictionary form of the Greek

---

23. Complex predicators receive introduction in Danove, *Linguistics and Exegesis*, 55–8.

predicator (except for γέγραπται whose inflected form is preserved, §1.2c), the Greek predicator's required arguments, and its chapter and verse location in Mark. The description begins with the English translation and places the remaining information in parentheses. Within the parentheses appear the Greek predicator and, within brackets, the arguments listed according to their small letter abbreviations (e.g., "a" for Agent, "b" for Benefactive) followed by a comma, and, in final position, its location in Mark. When the same predicator appears with the same licensing properties in multiple locations, the locations are combined. These considerations yield the following case frame descriptions for the noted predicators.

lease (ἐκδίδομαι [aθg], 12:1)
tear (σχίζω [ap], 1:10; 15:38)
gift (δῶρον [b], 7:11).

6. Clarifications Concerning the Semantic Study

This discussion presents clarifications concerning three categories of default Benefactive relationships, two further categories of Benefactive relationships, the class of verbs that designate transference, and two categories of permissibly omitted required complements.

a. Default Benefactive Relationships

Three categories of default Benefactive relationships are associated with specific classes of predicators whose arguments reference animate semantic entities. The first category of default Benefactive relationships occurs with classes of verb predicators that require completion by first/subject animate arguments, their cognate nouns, and their cognate adjectives when used as nouns; the second category occurs with verbs of giving when their Goal argument references an animate entity; and the third category occurs with specific noun predicators designating animate entities that are defined in relation to other noun predicators designating animate entities.

The first category of default Benefactive relationships is associated with verb predicators that require completion by an Agent argument and either a Patient or a Theme argument. These verbs most frequently designate actions of making (an Agent makes a Patient) and transferring (an Agent transfers a Theme to a Goal/ from a Source). For such verbs, Greek (like English) grammar imposes the interpretation that the animate Agent entity functions as the default Benefactive of the Patient or Theme entity whenever (1) the Patient or Theme entity is designated by a predicator that requires completion by a Benefactive that is not realized in the text, and (2) the context identifies no alternative referent for this Benefactive. Examples of such default "agentive" Benefactives occur in "A human being planted a vineyard" (12:1) and "He (the human being) sent a slave to the farmers" (12:2). In these verb phrases, "vineyard" and "slave" both require completion by a Benefactive that is not realized; and the contexts identify no specific referent for the Benefactive. As a consequence, Greek grammar imposes the interpretation that the human being planted his own vineyard and sent his own slave to the farmers. When the same verbs have cognate nouns or adjectives that may be used as nouns, these cognates also have the default interpretation of requiring completion by an animate agentive Benefactive. For example, "create" (κτίζω) and "anoint" (χρίω), which require completion by an Agent and a Patient, have the related nouns "creation" (κτίσις) and "anointed" (χριστός), which require completion by an animate agentive Benefactive.

The second category of default Benefactive relationships is restricted to verbs of giving (an Agent gives a Theme to a Goal) and benefaction (an Agent effects a Patient for a Benefactive) and applies whenever (1) the Goal or Benefactive references an animate semantic entity and (2) the Theme or Patient is designated by a predicator that requires completion by a Benefactive.[24] Such default "recipient" Benefactive relationships occur in "Who gave to you this authority?" (11:28) and "I will build [for God] another [sanctuary] not made with hands" (14:58). Here Greek grammar imposes the interpretation that the animate Goal or Benefactive entity is recipient Benefactive of the Theme (has the authority) or Patient (has the sanctuary) at the termination of the action and that the Theme or Patient requires completion by both an agentive Benefactive (whose authority and my sanctuary) and a recipient Benefactive (authority to you and sanctuary for God).[25]

The third category of default Benefactive relationships occurs with noun predicators that designate animate entities defined in reciprocal relation to other noun predicators that designate animate entities. Such reciprocal relationships generally are familial, legal, social, or religious and follow the pattern, "if X is Benefactive of Y, then Y is Benefactive of X." For example, the definition of "father" (πατήρ) logically involves a reference to biological or legal progeny, and the predicator itself requires completion by a Benefactive argument that designates the progeny. As a consequence, if X is father of Y and Y references masculine animate entity, then Y is son of X. The reciprocal Benefactive relationships in Mark most frequently are parent/child, teacher/student, and owner/slave. Thus the human being (12:1) that sends a slave in 12:2 is both reciprocal and agentive Benefactive of the slave.

---

24. Further discussion of the default Benefactive relationships with verbs of giving appears in Paul L. Danove, "A Comparison of the Usages of δίδωμι and δίδωμι Compounds in the Septuagint and New Testament," in *The Language of the New Testament: Context, History, and Development*, ed. Stanley E. Porter and Andrew W. Pitts (LBS 6; Leiden: Brill, 2013), 365–400.

25. When both Benefactives of a noun appear in the same phrase, English grammar realizes the agentive Benefactive by a possessive noun ('s, s') or adjective and the recipient Benefactive by a "to" or "for" prepositional phrase (God's authority to Jesus and their sanctuary for God). When only one of the Benefactives is present, however, English grammar permits its realization by a possessive noun or adjective, which can cause ambiguity (whose authority/your authority and my sanctuary/God's sanctuary).

b. Innate and Originating Benefactive Relationships

In addition to the three categories of default Benefactive relationships imposed by Greek grammar, Mark incorporates two further categories of Benefactive relationships grounded in the relationships provided by semantic frames. Although such relationships may qualify both animate and inanimate entities, only those pertaining to animate entities receive consideration.

The first category of these Benefactive relationships pertains to animate entities and relates them to their inherent attributes whenever these attributes are realized by nouns requiring completion by a Benefactive. Such innate Benefactive relationships pertain to the animate entity's body and its parts, mental faculties, and inherent capacities. For example, "your eye" (ὁ ὀφθαλμός σου, 9:47) attributes innate benefaction of "eye" to "you," and "the will of God" (τὸ θέλημα τοῦ θεοῦ, 3:35) attributes "God" with innate benefaction of "the will."

The second category of Benefactive relationships pertains to animate entities and relates them to other entities as their origin rather than their agentive Benefactive. Such originating Benefactive relationships are realized by nouns requiring completion by a Benefactive, and the exact nature of their originating benefaction need not be specified. For example, in the noun phrase "the way of God" (τὴν ὁδὸν τοῦ θεοῦ, 12:14), the way is proposed to have originated in some fashion from "God." Here the context identifies "Jesus," the referent of the Agent teaching it, as the way's agentive Benefactive without clarifying how the way originates from "God."

c. Verbs of Transference

Verbs of transference require completion by three arguments that function as an Agent, a Theme, and either a Goal or a Source. When they require completion by an Agent, a Theme, and a Goal (aθg) in their most frequent usage, Greek (like English) verbs of transference have the perspective that the Agent and Source are coincident or proximate at the initiation of transference; and, when they require completion by an Agent, a Theme, and a Source (aθs) in their most common usage, they have the perspective that the Agent and Goal are proximate or co-directional at the initiation of transference.[26] When the phrases licensed by verbs of transference contain no countervailing information, their default interpretation is that the Theme moves away from the Agent with the former group (aθg) and that the Theme moves toward the Agent with the latter group (aθs).

> At the proper time he sent (ἀποστέλλω [aθg], 12:2) a slave [from himself (s)] to the farmers.
> Take (ἀποφέρω [aθs], 14:36) this cup from me [towards yourself (g)].

---

26. Further discussion of these verbs and their attending conceptualizations of transference appears in Paul L. Danove, *Grammatical and Exegetical Study of New Testament Verbs of Transference: A Case Frame Guide to Interpretation and Translation* (SNTG 13; LNTS 329; London: T&T Clark, 2009), 25–7.

As these examples illustrate, Greek (like English) grammar interprets the Agent and Source to have the same semantic referent with the former verbs (aθg) and the Agent and Goal to have the same referent with the latter verbs (aθs) unless the semantic context explicitly introduces countervailing content.

d. Permissible Required Complement Omission

Although the grammatical interpretation of a predicator requires that each of its arguments have a semantic referent, Greek (like English) grammar permits arguments of predicators to remain unrealized as required complements in specific situations. This discussion introduces two categories of permissibly-omitted or null-required complements, identifies the conditions that accommodate null complements, and specifies the procedures for retrieving their semantic referents.

Greek grammar permits required complements of predicators to remain null when they have a retrievable definite semantic referent. Most frequently, such definite null complements retrieve their semantic referent from the previous or immediately following context.[27] For example, the noun predicator "gospel" (εὐαγγέλιον) realizes its required Benefactive/Topic complement by "of Jesus Christ" in 1:1 and by "of God" in 1:14 but appears without this complement realized in 1:15. In this context (1:1-15), Greek grammar retrieves both "Jesus Christ" and "God" as the definite semantic referent of the lexically unrealized Benefactive/Topic argument in 1:15.

Greek grammar also permits the Agent or Theme-required complements of verb predicators to remain null in the context of passivization, even when the context provides no definite semantic referent for these arguments.[28] In such circumstances, the verb predicator itself imposes an indefinite but circumscribed interpretation for the unrealized argument based on its licensing properties. An example of such indefinite null complements occurs in the verb phrase, "the heavens being torn." Here the verb predicator "tear" (σχίζω, 1:10) requires

---

27. Definite null complements receive introduction and development in Charles J. Fillmore, "Pragmatically Controlled Zero Anaphora," *BLS* 12 (1986): 95–107, and in his, "Topics in Lexical Semantics," in *Current Issues in Linguistic Theory*, ed. Roger W. Cole (Bloomington, IN: Indiana University Press, 1977), 96–7. They receive further development under various designations: "definite object deletion" in Anita Mittwoch, "Idioms and Unspecified N[oun] P[hrase] Deletion," *LInq* 2, no. 2 (1971): 255–9; "latent object" in Peter Hugoe Matthews, *Syntax* (Cambridge: Cambridge University Press, 1981), 125–6; and "contextual deletion" in D. J. Allerton, *Valency and the English Verb* (London and New York: Academic Press, 1982), 34, 68–70.

28. Indefinite Null Complements receive development in Bruce Fraser and John Robert Ross, "Idioms and Unspecified N[oun] P[hrase] Deletion," *LInq* 1, no. 2 (1970): 264–95, and in Ivan A. Sag and Jorge Hankamer, "Toward a Theory of Anaphoric Processing," *L&P* 7, no. 3 (1984): 325–45. A discussion of the passivization grammatical construction appears in Fillmore and Kay, *Construction Grammar*, 8:20, 30.

completion by an Agent and a Patient but realizes only the Patient argument. Since the context identifies no definite semantic referent for the Agent, the verb itself imposes the indefinite but circumscribed interpretation "by some Agent."

7. Clarifications Concerning the Case Frame Descriptions

This discussion offers clarifications concerning the case frames evoked by the previously discussed words (§1.2), "love" (ἀγαπάω), "forgive" (ἀφίημι), "has been written" (γέγραπται), "be necessary" (δεῖ), and "be permitted" (ἔξεστιν).

a. Love (ἀγαπάω)

With the general meaning of an affective response, ἀγαπάω requires completion by an Experiencer and a Content (ec). With the specialized implication as a covenantal obligation requiring action for another, ἀγαπάω requires completion by an Agent, a Patient, and a Benefactive (apb) and designates the action, "fulfill covenantal obligations to."[29] The following study will list the predicator according to its basic meaning as an affective response (Experiencer, Content) but analyze it according to both interpretations (ἀγαπάω [ec/apb]).

b. Forgive (ἀφίημι)

With the meaning "forgive," ἀφίημι consistently requires completion by an Agent, a Patient, and a Benefactive (apb) with the interpretation, "an Agent forgives sins/covenantal debts for a Benefactive." Although the English "forgive" also may require completion by the same arguments, it more frequently requires completion by an Experiencer, a Content, and a Topic (an Experiencer forgives someone for something), a use that does not occur with ἀφίημι.

c. Has Been Written (γέγραπται), Be Necessary (δεῖ), and Be Permitted (ἔξεστιν)

The licensing properties of these three predicators can be obscured by the fact that their English translations frequently insert "it" as their anticipatory or extraposed subject.[30] This anticipatory subject is not licensed by the predicators but is a function of English grammar, which attempts to avoid overly-complex subject complements. As a consequence, γέγραπται has the same semantic requirements

---

29. With this specialized meaning, ἀγαπάω functions as a verb of benefaction, whose properties receive explication in Danove, "A Comparison of the Usages of δίδωμι and δίδωμι Compounds," 367–8.

30. A discussion of "it" extraposition appears in Laurel J. Brinton, *The Structure of Modern English: A Linguistic Introduction* (Amsterdam/Philadelphia: Benjamins, 2000), 218–20.

as "write" and so requires completion by an Agent, a Content, and an Experiencer (ace); and both δεῖ and ἔξεστιν require completion by an Event and an Instrument (vi). The previous discussion also indicates that the semantic frames evoked by δεῖ identify what is written (the Content licensed by γέγραπτα) as the semantic referent of its Instrument; and those evoked by ἔξεστιν identify "commandment[s]" (ἐντολή) as the semantic referent of its Instrument.

8. Pre-Existing and Cultivated Semantic Beliefs

The semantic study attributes to the pre-existing semantic beliefs of the authorial audience the content of all semantic and case frames evoked by the vocabulary of Mark except for obvious examples of the translation of non-Greek words. The following discussion identifies the formats for the translation of non-Greek words and then considers a possible but rejected candidate for the cultivation of new semantic beliefs.

The only assured examples of the cultivation of new semantic beliefs for the narrative audience appear in the context of the translation or definition of non-Greek words. These translations or definitions have three observed formats: the non-Greek word to be defined followed by "which is" (ὅ ἐστιν) followed by the Greek translation (3:17; 7:11, 34); the phrase to be translated followed by "which is translated" (ὅ ἐστιν μεθερμηνευόμενον) followed by the Greek translation (5:41; 15:22, 34); and the Greek translation followed by "which is" (ὅ ἐστιν) followed by the non-Greek word to be translated (12:42; 15:16, 42). In this regard, the only potential ambiguity in distinguishing pre-existing from cultivated semantic beliefs concerns "abba" in the phrase "abba Father" (αββα ὁ πατήρ, 14:36). Here the introduction of the proposed translation immediately after "abba," without the typical clausal links, is taken to indicate a traditional formulation familiar to the authorial audience. Except for the noted definitions, the content of all other semantic frames evoked by vocabulary are attributed to the authorial audience's beliefs.

Chapter 2

THE METHOD OF NARRATIVE ANALYSIS AND DESCRIPTION

This chapter introduces the method of narrative analysis and description assumed in the study of the theology of the Gospel of Mark. The initial discussion presents an overview of the study's model of narrative communication and its interpreter. The discussion of the narrative method introduces narrative frames, specifies the content of particular narrative frames, develops the analytical and descriptive potential of character frames for identifying references to God, offers a series of clarifications about narrative and character frames, and provides a statement of the narrative beliefs assumed for the authorial audience and cultivated for the narrative audience. Within the narrative study, "Mark" designates the narrative content of the Gospel of Mark within 1:1–16:8.

1. The Model of Narrative Communication: Narrative Frames

The model of narrative communication assumes that the encounter with Mark evokes narrative frames that accommodate the narrative interpretation of the content of the semantic frames evoked by the words within 1:1–16:8.[1] The recognition that a narrative is beginning or is in process evokes narrative frames that make available information about narrative entities, the relationships into

---

1. The narrative frame receives introduction in Menakhem Perry, "Literary Dynamics: How the Order of a Text Creates Its Meaning," *Poetics Today* 1, no. 1–2 (1979): 36; Eco, *Role of the Reader*, 20–1, 37; and Robert Alter, *The Pleasures of Reading in an Ideological Age* (New York: Simon and Schuster, 1989), 122. The narrative frame has affinities with "theme" as used in Gerald Prince, *Narrative as Theme: Studies in French Fiction* (Lincoln, NE: University of Nebraska Press, 1992), 5, and as defined in Russell Brown, "Theme," in *Encyclopedia of Contemporary Literary Theory: Approaches, Scholars, Terms*, ed. Irena R. Makaryk (Toronto: University of Toronto Press, 1993), 643. The narrative study assumes that a close reading of Mark would establish adequate grounds for evoking the narrative frames that receive attention.

which they may enter, perspectives for evaluating their function, and expectations concerning the content of the narration.[2]

Each clause within a narrative context evokes narrative frames, and the intersection of their content typically identifies a number of narrative frames that permit the narrative interpretation of all the semantic content in the context. Although the maximal narrative context for interpretation is the narration as a whole, the narrative study places primary focus on the sentence.[3] For example, the clauses in the sentence constituted by 1:1-3 evoke a series of narrative frames, among the most basic of which are frames that accommodate the narrative interpretation of verbs as specific actions, events, or states; nouns as specific persons, places, or things; and so on.[4] For the clause, "I send (ἀποστέλλω [aθg], 1:2) my messenger before your face," these frames interpret "send" as a particular action of transferring, "I," "my," "messenger," and "your" as having personal character referents, "before" as having a spatial reference, and "face" as having a reference to the human body.

2. Specification of the Content of Narrative Frames

The narrative study makes extensive use of the interpretive potential of three categories of narrative frames: scriptural, overlay, and contextual.

a. Scriptural Narrative Frames

Particular clauses and sets of clauses in the sentences of Mark function as "scriptural parallels" that have the potential to evoke for the authorial audience scriptural narrative frames whose information, relationships, perspectives, and expectations received previous cultivation in the interpretation of specific scriptural passages. The following study accepts as a scriptural parallel a continuous passage in Mark that (1) incorporates at least 50 percent of the vocabulary of a continuous passage from the Septuagint (LXX) and (2) contains at least four words with the same lexical form as words of the passage from the LXX. For example,

---

2. The development of the proposed content of narrative frames appears in Danove, *The End of Mark's Story*, 81-7.

3. The use of the narrative as a whole in the study of the characterization of God within the Gospel of Mark proves advantageous, for example, in the study of the narrative function of characterization: cf. Paul L. Danove, "The Narrative Function of Mark's Characterization of God," *NovT* XLIII, no. 1 (2001): 12-30. The sentence, however, provides the optimal context for developing the content of the characterization of God. Unless otherwise indicated, the sentence divisions assumed in the narrative study are those proposed in UBSGNT 4.

4. This study treats 1:1-3 as a single grammatical sentence: cf. Danove, *Linguistics and Exegesis*, 78-83.

these considerations identify 1:2 as a scriptural parallel capable of evoking for the authorial audience the narrative frames cultivated by the narration of Exod 23:30.

Behold I send my messenger before your face.
ἰδοὺ ἀποστέλλω τὸν ἄγγελόν μου πρὸ προσώπου σου (Mark 1:2)
ἰδοὺ ἐγὼ ἀποστέλλω τὸν ἄγγελόν μου πρὸ προσώπου σου (Exod 23:20)

Although the definition of scriptural parallels excludes many proposed scriptural allusions within Mark, it provides a secure and rigorous basis for the study of characterization.

b. Overlay Narrative Frames

The narrative study assumes that Mark, on occasion, either evokes for the authorial audience or cultivates for the narrative audience specific narrative beliefs that overlay the content of scriptural narrative frames with alternative content. For example, the narration of 1:3 evokes the scriptural narrative frames cultivated by the narration of Isa 40:3. While the scriptural narrative frames interpret "God" as the narrative referent of the Benefactive arguments of "way" and "paths," overlay narrative frames interpret "Jesus" as the narrative referent of these Benefactives.[5]

Prepare the way of the Lord; make straight his paths (1:3).
Prepare the way of the Lord; make straight the paths of our God (Isa 40:3).

Within the following study, narrative overlays primarily interpret scriptural references to God as references to Jesus. The narrative study notes such overlays by stating that narrative frames interpret "God (with Jesus)" as the narrative referent of specific semantic referents within Mark.

c. Contextual Narrative Frames

The narration continually evokes contextual narrative frames that permit the retrieval of the referents of narrative entities within a continuous context. In general, such retrieval becomes necessary when Greek grammar permits the anaphoric reduction of nouns to pronouns or verbal endings or the complete omission of the complements of predicators as definite null complements and indefinite null complements (§1.6d).[6] For example, in 12:29, Jesus states, "The Lord our God is one Lord"; and in 12:32 a scribe responds, "In truth you say that he is one." Here contextual narrative frames ground the retrieval of "the Lord your God" as the narrative referent of "he."

---

5. Hans-Josef Klauck, *Vorspiel im Himmel? Erzähltechnik und Theologie im Markusprolog* (B-TS 32; Neukirchen: Neukirchener, 1997), 87, and Rikki E. Watts, *Isaiah's New Exodus and Mark* (WUNT 2:88; Tübingen: Mohr Siebeck, 1997), 87, confirm that the purpose of such narrative overlays is to ensure that references to God and Jesus are joined.

6. A discussion of the grammatical retrieval of semantic referents appears in Fillmore, "Pragmatically Controlled Zero Anaphora," 95–107.

3. The Focus of the Narrative Study: Character Frames

The narrative interpretation that a semantic entity has a character referent evokes character frames that provide information about characters, the relationships into which characters may enter, perspectives for evaluating characters, and expectations concerning characterization. Narrative frames interpret semantic entities to have character referents whenever they function with Agent or Experiencer thematic roles, which are restricted to animate entities (§1.4). Narrative frames also interpret a semantic entity that functions as an Agent or Experiencer in one context to have the same character referent in all previous and following occurrences, even when they are not functioning as an Agent or an Experiencer. Scriptural narrative frames also may evoke for the interpreter character referents from scriptural narratives.

Character frames interpret all nouns, noun phrases (nouns with all of their modifiers), and adjectives used as nouns that have the same character referent as designations for that character.[7] The narrative study names characters according to their most frequent designation and capitalizes all nouns and adjectives in designations and names of characters. For example, within 11:20-25, narrative frames interpret the noun predicator "god" (θεός [b], 11:22), which previously realized the Agent argument of "join" (συζεύγνυμι [apg], 10:9), and "father (πατήρ [b], 11:25) in the heavens," which realizes the Agent argument of "forgive" (ἀφίημι [apb], 11:25), as character designations (God and Father in the Heavens). Both designations have the same character referent, and the narrative study names this character God because "God" is the character's most frequent designation within Mark. Again, in 1:24, narrative frames interpret the noun "jesus" (ἰησοῦς), which realizes the Agent argument of destroy (ἀπόλλυμι [ap]), and the adjectives "nazarene" (ναζαρηνός [p]) and "holy [one]" (ἅγιος [b]) as designations (Jesus, Nazarene, and Holy One of God) for the same character. The narrative study names this character Jesus, the most frequent designation for this character in Mark.

Since Mark contains stories within stories, the resolution of character referents may require multiple steps and use the content of various frames. Thus the identification of God as the referent of the designation, Lord (κύριος [b], 12:9) of the Vineyard, requires a two-step interpretation, first to identify this as a designation for a character within 12:1-12 and then to identify God as its character referent based on information introduced elsewhere within Mark. For example, only God is the Benefactive of "beloved son" elsewhere in Mark (12:6; cf. 1:11; 9:7).

Character frames permit the identification of both direct and indirect references to God. Direct references arise when narrative frames interpret God as the character referent of the semantic referent of a predicator's realized or unrealized

---

7. See Thomas Docherty, *Reading (Absent) Character: Towards a Theory of Characterization in Fiction* (Oxford: Clarendon, 1983), 74, for a description of the roles of designations and names in characterization.

argument or realized adjuncts.[8] Indirect references arise when a predicator requires completion by an argument that (1) is not realized as a complement and (2) functions as a predicator that requires completion by an argument that has God as its character referent. An example of indirect references appears with "be necessary" (δεῖ [vi]), which requires completion by an Instrument argument that never receives realization as a complement but has "scripture" as its semantic referent (§§1.2d, 1.7c). Since "scripture" (γραφή [b]) requires completion by an agentive Benefactive, "be necessary" is deemed to introduce an indirect reference to God, the character referent of the agentive Benefactive of "scripture."

4. Character Frame Analysis and Description: References to God

This discussion develops and applies six criteria that permit the identification of 314 direct and indirect references to the character God in association with 117 predicators.[9] The discussion first develops and applies the six criteria to the arguments of all predicators, whether realized or unrealized (§1.6d), and all realized adjuncts within 1:1–16:8. The discussion of each criterion begins with its statement. For economy of presentation, the discussion of each criterion provides one or two detailed expositions of its application to specific texts before proceeding with a more summary presentation of the remaining references identified by the criterion. Also for economy of presentation, references that admit to identification by multiple criteria receive discussion under only one criterion. When available, the notes provide further supporting evidence for the proposed references. The discussion of each criterion also uses contextual narrative frames to retrieve further references once a criterion identifies a reference to God in a given context. The concluding discussion briefly considers possible but rejected references and the reasons for their rejection. The complete list of references to God receives tabulation in the Appendix.

The discussion identifies the references by the Greek predicator, its arguments, and location using the method of semantic description of predicators (§1.5) with

---

8. Since predicators require completion by arguments, all unrealized arguments must have a retrievable semantic referent for grammatical interpretation, and narrative frames then interpret this as a narrative referent. In contrast, the inclusion of adjuncts is at the discretion of the implied author, and only those explicitly introduced by the implied author receive narrative interpretation. The exclusion of possible but unrealized adjuncts removes potentially tendentious proposals for references to God and provides a grammatically and narratively justified set of references for the Theological Study.

9. The list of references developed in this discussion differs from that proposed in Paul L. Danove, *The Rhetoric of the Characterization of God, Jesus, and Jesus' Disciples in the Gospel of Mark* (JSNTSup 290; New York: T&T Clark, 2005), 28–33. The differences are due to a rigorous application of the six proposed criteria and reflect in part reconsiderations of passivized verbs as presented in Beniamin Pascut, "The So-Called *Passivum Divinum* in Mark's Gospel," *NovT* 54 (2012): 313–33.

three modifications. First, within the list of arguments of the predicator, the argument that has God as its character referent is capitalized, e.g., send (ἀποστέλλω [Aθg]). Second, when God is the referent of a realized adjunct, the adjunct appears after the list of arguments of the predicator separated by a hyphen, and the abbreviation for the adjunct is capitalized, e.g., make to swear (ὀρκίζω [ace-I]). Third, with indirect references, the notation lists the arguments of the predicator followed by a hyphen followed by a repetition of the argument that licenses the character reference. Only the argument with the character referent is capitalized, e.g., be necessary (δεῖ [vi-iB]).

Statements concerning references omit the phrases "as the character referent of" and "the predicator," the word "complement," and quotation marks, so that the statement, "X identifies God as the Agent of Y," has the interpretation, "X identifies God as the character referent of the Agent complement of the predicator Y." This and following discussions also assume that 1:1-15 constitutes a coherent narrative context for the purpose of contextual retrieval.[10]

a. Criterion 1: Scriptural Parallels

The first criterion, scriptural parallels (§2.2a), uses the content of the scriptural narrative frames that they evoke to ground the identification of eighty-one direct references to God in Mark.

This criterion isolates for 1:2 a scriptural parallel in Exod 23:20, which identifies God as the Agent of send (ἀποστέλλω [Aθg], 1:2) and Benefactive of messenger (ἄγγελος [B], 1:2). Mal 3:1 further identifies God as the Benefactive of face (πρόσωπον [B], 1:2); and narrative overlay frames interpret God (with Jesus) as its Benefactive.

Isa 40:3 identifies God as the Benefactive of way (ὁδός [B], 1:2, 3) and paths (τρίβος [B], 1:3); and the narration overlays these with references to Jesus.

Ps 2:7 identifies God as reciprocal Benefactive of son (υἱός [B], 1:11) and Experiencer/Agent of beloved (ἀγαπητός [Ec/Apb], 1:11), which permits the contextual retrieval of God as the Benefactive of voice (φωνή [B], 1:11) and the Experiencer of delight [in] (εὐδοκέω [Ec], 1:11).

Isa 29:13 identifies God as the Experiencer of honor (τιμάω [aE], 7:6), the Source of be distant (ἀπέχω [θS], 7:6), and the Experiencer of worship (σέβομαι [aE], 7:7).

Gen 1:27 and 5:2 identify God as the Agent of make (ποιέω, [Ap], 10:6).[11]

---

10. Grammatical, narrative, and rhetorical arguments for interpreting 1:1-15 as a coherent context appear in Paul L. Danove, "Mark 1,1-15 as Introduction to Characterization," in *Greeks, Jews, and Christians: Historical, Religious and Philological Studies in Honor of Jesús Peláez del Rosal*, ed. Lautaro Roig Lanzillotta and Israel Muñoz Gallarte (Córdoba: El Almendro, 2013), 127–48.

11. God's action of making in 10:6 does not assert God's agentive Benefaction of "them" because this pronoun does not license a Benefactive argument.

Ps 118:26 identifies God as the Benefactive of name (ὄνομα [B], 11:9). This permits the contextual retrieval of God as the Experiencer of hosanna (ὡσαννά, [aE] 11:9, 10), which is interpreted as an acclamation addressed to God as Experiencer.[12]

Isa 56:7 identifies God as the Benefactive of house (οἶκος [bB], 11:17a) and Experiencer of prayer (προσευχή [E], 11:17).[13] The fact that "Temple" and "house" reference the same entity within the immediate context (11:15-17) permits the contextual retrieval of God as Benefactive of Temple (ἱερόν [bB], 11:15a, 15b, 16).

Isa 5:2 (cf. Isa 5:7 for the contextual identification of God) identifies God as the Agent of plant (φυτεύω [Ap], 12:1), put around (περιτίθημι [Ap], 12:1), dig (ὀρύσσω [Ap], 12:1), build (οἰκοδομέω [Ap], 12:1), and lease (ἐκδίδομαι [Aθg], 12:1), as well as the agentive Benefactive of vineyard (ἀμπελών [B], 12:1), fence (φραγμός [Bb], 12:1), winepress (ὑπολήνιον [Bb], 12:1), and tower (πύργος [Bb], 12:1) and identifies Human Being as a designation for God in this parable.[14] Contextual retrieval then identifies God as the Agent of send (ἀποστέλλω [Aθg], 12:2, 4, 5a, [5b], 6), take (λαμβάνω [Aθs], 12:2), speak (λέγω [Ace], 12:6), give (δίδωμι [Aθg], 12:9), do (ποιέω [Ap], 12:9), and destroy (ἀπόλλυμι [Ap], 12:9); as the Benefactive of have (ἔχω [Bp], 12:6), son (υἱός [B], 12:6a, 6b), heir (κληρόνομος [B], 12:7), slave (δοῦλος [B], 12:2, 4, [5a], [5b]), and vineyard (ἀμπελών [B], 12:2, 8, 9a, 9b); as the Experiencer of beloved (ἀγαπητός [E], 12:6); as the Goal of send (ἀποστέλλω [aθG], 12:3); as the Patient of the vineyard's benefaction of lord (κύριος [bP], 12:9); as the Source of inheritance (κληρονομία [S], 12:7); and as the Theme of go on a journey (ἀποδημέω [Θg], 12:1) and come (ἔρχομαι [Θg], 12:9). These references permit the retrieval of Lord of the Vineyard as a designation for

---

12. If translated literally, "hosanna" would cast God as the Agent of "save"; but its use as an acclamation in 11:9-10 recommends an alternative interpretation: cf. van Iersel, *Mark*, 354; and Hooker, *The Gospel According to Saint Mark*, 359-60. This study follows the interpretation, "praise," which is a noun predicator requiring completion by an Experiencer; cf. Johannes P. Louw and Eugene A. Nida, *Greek-English Lexicon of the New Testament Based on Semantic Domains*, vol. 1, 2nd edn. (New York: UBS, 1988), 430-1 (§33.364).

13. House (οἶκος) and all following nouns requiring completion by a recipient Benefactive with God as its referent (B) also admit to completion by agentive Benefactive with a human beings as its referent (b). The resulting description of licensing properties (bB) receives consideration in §1.6a.

14. For the interpretation of 12:1 as referencing Isa 5:1-7, see Marcus, *Mark 8-16*, 802; Adela Yarbro Collins, *Mark: A Commentary*, ed. Harold W. Attridge (Minneapolis, MN: Hermeneia and Augsburg: Fortress, 2007), 545, 547, and Moloney, *The Gospel of Mark*, 230; cf. David Stern, "Jesus' Parables from the Perspective of Rabbinic Literature: The Example of the Wicked Husbandmen," in *Parable and Story in Judaism and Christianity*, ed. Clemens Thoma and Michael Wyschogrod (New York: Paulist, 1989), 60-1; and Joachim Jeremias, *The Parables of Jesus*, rev. edn., trans. S. H. Hook (London: SCM, 1955; New York: Scribner, 1963), 70. See Telford, *Theology*, 63, for the interpretation of God as the one planting the vineyard.

God. Within this and following discussions, brackets, [ ], around locations clarify that the predicator is permissibly omitted by Greek grammar and must be retrieved for correct contextual interpretation.

Ps 118:22-23 identifies God as the Agent of come to be (γίνομαι [pA], 12:11).

Exod 3:6, 15–16 identifies God (θεός [bP], 12:26b, 26c, 26d) as the Patient of Abraham's, Isaac's, and Jacob's benefaction and permits the contextual retrieval of God as the Agent of say (λέγω [Aec], 12:26a) and God (θεός, [bP] 12:27a, [27b]) as the Patient of benefaction of [the] dead and of [the] living. The first scriptural parallel that explicitly identifies "God" as a designation for God appears in v. 26.

Deut 6:4-5 identifies God (θεός [bP], 12:29, 30) as the Patient of Israel's benefaction, the Patient of one (εἷς [P], 12:29), and the Content/Benefactive of love (ἀγαπάω [eC/apB], 12:30). Contextual retrieval then identifies God as Patient of one (εἷς [P], 12:32) and he (αὐτός [P], 12:32), the Content/Benefactive of love (ἀγαπάω [eC/apB], 12:33), and the Benefactive of burnt offering (ὁλοκαύτωμα [bB], 12:33) and offering (θυσία [bB], 12:33).

Ps 110:1 identifies God as the Agent of say (λέγω [Ace], 12:36), Benefactive of right [hand] (δεξιά [B], 12:36), and Agent of put (τίθημι [Aθg], 12:36).

Ps 22:1 identifies God (θεός [bP], 15:34a, 34b) as the Patient of Jesus' benefaction and Agent of abandon (ἐγκαταλείπω [Ap], 15:34).

b. Criterion 2: The Designation "God"

The second criterion, the designation "God," uses the fact that scriptural parallels (§2.4a) identify "God" as a designation for God on seven occasions (12:26b, 26c, 26d, 29, 30; 15:34a, 34b), that the remaining occurrences of this word similarly function as a designation for a character, and that contexts of their occurrence never propose an alternative referent for this designation to identify "God" as a designation for God in all of its forty-nine occurrences. This designation and contextual retrieval identify fifty-five direct references to God. The discussion groups the occurrences according to the thematic role imposed by the predicators.

God is the Agent of forgive (ἀφίημι [Apb], 2:7), join (συζεύγνυμι [Apg], 10:9), and create (κτίζω [Ap], 13:19). The contextual agency of God in forgiving evokes for "blaspheme" the meaning, "speak something against God or God's attributes," which identifies God as the Benefactive of blaspheme (βλασφημέω [apB], 2:7) and establishes a precedent for the religious interpretation of "blaspheme" and the related noun "blasphemy."[15] God's agency in creating permits the contextual retrieval of God as the agentive Benefactive of creation (κτίσις [B], 13:19). The contextual continuity between "God" (13:19) and "Lord" (13:20) identifies "Lord" as designation for God and permits the contextual retrieval of God as the Agent of shorten (κολοβόω [Ap], 13:20a, 20b), save (σῴζω [Ap], 13:20), and choose (ἐκλέγομαι [Ap], 13:20) and as the agentive Benefactive of elect (ἐκλεκτός [B], 13:20, 22, 27).

---

15. See Joseph H. Thayer, *Thayer's Greek-English Lexicon of the New Testament* (Peabody, MA: Hendrickson, 1996), 102–3 (§§987, 988).

God is the Benefactive of Christ/Anointed (χριστός [B], 1:1), son (υἱός [B], 1:1; 3:11; 5:7; 15:39), holy one (ἅγιος [B], 1:24), house (οἶκος [bB], 2:26), will (θέλημα [B], 3:35), reign (βασιλεία [B], 1:15, 4:11, 26, 30; 9:1, 47; 10:14, 15, 23, 24, 25; 12:34; 14:25; 15:43), commandment (ἐντολή [B], 7:8, 9), word (λόγος [B], 7:13), things (τά [B], 8:33; 12:17b), [not] impossible thing (ἀδύνατον [B], 10:27), possible thing (δυνατόν [B], 10:27), way (ὁδός [B], 12:14), and power (δύναμις [B], 12:24) and the Benefactive/Topic of gospel (εὐαγγέλιον [B/T], 1:14).[16] The context of 9:43-47 sets "life" and "reign" in parallel, which permits the contextual retrieval of God as Benefactive of life (ζωή [B], 9:43, 45). In 10:27, the permissibly omitted subject (what is not impossible for God) is "to save," which identifies God as the Agent of save (σῴζω, [Ap], [10:27]). Jesus teaches and so functions as the agentive Benefactive of "way" in 12:14.

God is the Experiencer of glorify (δοξάζω [aE], 2:12).

God is the Goal of give back (ἀποδίδωμι [aθG], 12:17).

God is the Instrument of compel to swear (ὁρκίζω [aec-I], 5:7).

God is the Patient of most high (ὕψιστος [P], 5:7) and good (ἀγαθός [P], 10:18).

God is the Topic of faith (πίστις [ecT], 11:22), which permits the contextual retrieval of God as the Topic of believe (πιστεύω [ecT], 11:23. 24).

c. Criterion 3: Interpretive Conventions

The third criterion, interpretive conventions, assumes that, whenever the narration introduces either predicators that require completion by arguments with a definite referent or what appears to be a designation for a character and the narration does not explicitly identify the definite narrative referent for the argument or designation, the authorial audience is expected to be able to supply the appropriate definite referent from pre-existing narrative beliefs. Interpretive conventions resolve into two categories, those that draw on general semantic and theological pre-existing beliefs and those that draw on specifically future-oriented/eschatological pre-existing beliefs. Where possible, the discussion notes scholarly arguments or information from the LXX that supports the likelihood of the proposed pre-existing narrative beliefs. Interpretive conventions and contextual retrieval identify seventy-four direct references to God.

(i) Pre-existing Semantic and Theological Beliefs An example of the first category of interpretive conventions appears in the use of "pray." This predicator requires completion by three arguments (Agent, Content, and Experiencer) and permits the Experiencer to remain unrealized only when it has a definite semantic referent. Since the Experiencer complement never receives realization within 1:1–16:8 and the contexts of its occurrences never identify a viable alternative character referent for the Experiencer, this criterion uses the extensive pre-existing Christian beliefs

---

16. This discussion interprets the phrase, "with God" (παρὰ τῷ θεῷ, 10:27), to indicate within God's power or possession and so the preposition "with" (παρά) to require completion by a Benefactive. On the originality of "of God" in 1:1, see Tommy Wasserman, "The 'Son of God' Was in the Beginning (Mark 1:1)," *JTS* (NS) 62, no. 1 (April 2011): 20–50.

of the authorial audience to identify God as the sole appropriate referent of the consistently unrealized Experiencer.[17] This identifies God as Experiencer of pray (προσεύχομαι [acE], 1:35; 6:46; 11:24, 25; 12:40; 13:18; 14:32, 35, 38, 39). The identification of God as the Experiencer of "pray" in 11:24-25 also permits the contextual retrieval of God as Experiencer of ask (αἰτέω [acE], 11:24) and the Source of receive (λαμβάνω [gθS], 11:24) and identifies "Father in the Heavens" (11:25) as a designation for God. This identification then permits the contextual retrieval of God as the Theme of in (ἐν [Θl], 11:25), the Patient of benefaction of father (πατήρ [bP], 11:25), and the Agent of forgive (ἀφίημι [Apb], 11:25b) and specifies the "heavens" as the location of God.

The introduction of "Christ/Anointed," hereafter "Christ," as a designation for Jesus in 1:1 (§2.3) without further explanation, assumes pre-existing beliefs that identify God as the agentive Benefactive of Christ (χριστός [B], 8:29; 9:41; 12:35; 13:21; 14:61; 15:32).[18]

Pre-existing beliefs (§§1.2c, 1.7c) identify God as the Agent of the third person singular perfect passive indicative of write (γέγραπται [Ace], 1:2; 7:6; 9:12, 13; 11:17; 14:21, 27); and, since pre-existing beliefs identify God's agency only with this form of the verb, it is listed according to this form.[19] God's contextual benefaction of Jesus the Christ and Son (1:1) and God's agency in writing (1:2) permit the contextual retrieval of God as the most appropriate Benefactive of prophet (προφήτης [B], 1:2).[20]

Pre-existing beliefs identify "Holy Spirit" as a designation for a character that consistently is attributed with God's benefaction.[21] This identifies God as the

17. See the discussion of the verbs of "praying" in Paul L. Danove, *New Testament Verbs of Communication: A Case Frame and Exegetical Study* (LNTS 520; London: Bloomsbury, 2015), 60–1.

18. This discussion interprets Jesus' statement in 14:62 (ἐγώ εἰμι) as "I am he," which does not introduce an elliptical reference to God the Blessed One (14:61).

19. Gottlob Schrenk, "γράφω," *TDNT* 1:742–9, notes that "[w]hat is quoted as γέγραπται [in the LXX] is normative because it is guaranteed by the binding power of Yahweh the King and Lawgiver" (747). The grammar in the contexts of the first two occurrences of γέγραπται supports this interpretation. Although the Book of Isaiah is cited in both contexts, the preposition ἐν in 1:2 identifies Isaiah either as the Locative (in) or the Instrument (by) of writing; and Isaiah's specifically noted agentive function in 7:6 is limited to prophesying.

20. The use of false prophet (ψευδοπροφήτης, 13:22) to identify prophets that have a character other than God as their Benefactive supports this identification.

21. The likelihood of these pre-existing beliefs is supported by the references to this character in the LXX under the designations, "Holy Spirit" (Ps 51:11; Wis 9:17; Isa 63:10, 11), "Spirit" (Gen 6:3; 2 Chr 24:20; Zech 4:6; 7:12; Isa 63:14; Ezek 3:12, 14a; 11:1; 43:5), "Spirit of the Lord" (Judg 3:10; 11:29; 13:25; 14:6, 19; 15:14; 1 Sam 10:6; 16:13, 14; 2 Sam 23:2; 1 Kgs 22:24; 2 Kgs 2:16; 2 Chr 15:1; 18:23; 20:14; Wis 1:7; Mic 3:8; Isa 61:1; Ezek 11:5), and "Spirit of God" (Gen 1:2; 41:38; Num 23:7; 24:2; Judg 6:34; 1 Sam 10:10; 19:20, 23; 2 Chr 24:20; Isa 11:2). The Holy Spirit also is attributed with speaking through other characters (Mark 13:11; cf. 2 Sam 23:2; 1 Kgs 22:24).

Benefactive of spirit (πνεῦμα [B], 1:8; 3:29; 12:36; 13:11). God's benefaction of "spirit" in 1:8 permits the contextual retrieval of God as the Benefactive of spirit (πνεῦμα [B], 1:10, 12) and identifies "Holy Spirit" as a designation for God's Spirit. Since "Spirit" also functions as the name of other characters, following discussions reference this character as "the Holy Spirit" or "God's Spirit."

Pre-existing beliefs concerning "sin" provide two complementary avenues for identifying references to God. On the one hand, they interpret "sin" in relation to the non-fulfillment of the commandments. This permits the identification of indirect references to God through God's benefaction of the commandments and various attributes (§2.4b).[22] On the other hand, pre-existing beliefs also interpret sin as an offense that incurs covenantal debts owed to God. This permits the identification of direct references to God through God's benefaction of the resulting debts.[23] In order to avoid redundancies of reference, the following study develops only the direct references to God; and the subsequent discussion (§2.4f) develops the implication of these references in relation to the commandments and God's attributes. These considerations identify God as the Benefactive of sinful action (ἁμάρτημα [bB], 3:28, 29), sin (ἁμαρτία [bB], 1:4, 5; 2:5, 7, 9, 10), blasphemy (βλασφημία [bB], 3:28), and trespass (παράπτωμα [bB], 11:25).[24] The occurrences in 3:28-29 also permit the contextual retrieval of God as the Agent of forgive (ἀφίημι [Apb], 3:28), and the agentive Benefactive of forgiveness (ἄφεσις [Bb], 3:29).

Pre-existing beliefs identify God as the Agent of passivized occurrences of forgive (ἀφίημι [Apb], 2:5, 9; 4:12).[25]

---

22. Most commentators ground the discussions of sin in terms of the fulfillment / non-fulfillment of the Law: Gottlob Schrenk, "δίκαιος," *TDNT* 2:186; Gustav Stählin and Walter Grundmann, "The Concept of Sin in Judaism," *TDNT* 1:289. The discussion of "blasphemy" draws on Hermann Wolfgang Beyer, "βλασφημία," *TDNT* 1:622.

23. Gustav Stählin, "The Linguistic Usage and History of ἁμαρτάνω, ἁμάρτημα and ἁμαρατία before and in the NT," *TDNT* 1:295; and Karl Heinrich Rengstorf, "ἁμαρτωλός," *TDNT* 1:333.

24. Note that the Benefactive thematic role encompasses both benefaction (for) and malefaction (against): cf. Seppo Kittilä and Fernando Zúñiga, "Introduction: Benefaction and Malefaction from a Cross-linguistic Perspective," in *Benefactives and Malefactives: Typological Perspectives and Case Studies*, ed. Fernando Zúñiga and Seppo Kittilä (TSL 92; Amsterdam/Philadelphia: Benjamins, 2010), 1–28.

25. The evocation of pre-existing beliefs with the passivized form of this verb receives the support of Collins, *Mark: A Commentary*, 185, and Marcus, *Mark 1–8*, 216, and reflects the verb's use with "sin" in the LXX to designate God's action of forgiving (Lev 4:20, 26, 35; 5:6, 10, 13; Num 15:25; Ps 32:1; Isa 33:24) or not forgiving (Isa 22:14) which seems to be the basis of the scribes' reaction to the initial passivized occurrence in Mark (2:5).

Pre-existing beliefs recommend God as the most appropriate Agent of give (δίδωμι [Aθg], 6:2) and come to be (γίνομαι [pA], 6:2b) and the Benefactive of wisdom (σοφία [B], 6:2).[26]

Pre-existing beliefs recognize that both "bless" and "give thanks" require completion by an Experiencer with a definite referent and that, especially in the context of meals, God is the referent.[27] This identifies God as the Experiencer of bless (εὐλογέω [aE], 6:41; 8:7; 14:22) and give thanks (εὐχαριστέω [acE], 8:6; 14:23).

Scripturally-based pre-existing theological beliefs that recognize God's agency in making or establishing covenants identify God as the agentive Benefactive of covenant (διαθήκη [B], 14:24).[28]

Pre-existing beliefs recognize that the hymns at Passover meals are directed to God, which identifies God as the Experiencer of sing (ὑμνέω [acE], 14:26).[29]

Pre-existing beliefs interpret "sign" as a means for God to authenticate someone's words and/or actions. This identifies God as the Source of sign (σημεῖον [S], 8:11, 12a, 12b), which permits the contextual retrieval of God as the Agent of give (δίδωμι [Aθg], 8:12).[30]

(ii) Pre-existing Future-Oriented / Eschatological Beliefs   This criterion also uses specifically future-oriented and eschatological pre-existing theological beliefs to identify references to God.

The future-oriented pre-existing beliefs concern the mission activities of the disciples of Jesus after his death and resurrection. These beliefs identify God as the

---

26. In the LXX, God is the only Agent that gives (δίδωμι) wisdom (Exod 36:1, 2; 1 Kgs 2:35a; 5:9, 26; 1 Chr 22:12; 2 Chr 1:10, 12; 9:23; 1 Esdr 4:60; Prov 2:6; Eccl 2:26; Job 38:36; Wis 9:4, 17; Sir 6:37; 43:33; 45:26; 51:17; Dan 2:21, 23) and the only noted Source from which wisdom (σοφία) comes (Wis 7:7). The only other "giver" of wisdom, blows and reproofs (Prov 29:15), functions as the Instrument of giving wisdom.

27. The background of these proposed beliefs receives development in Hermann Wolfgang Beyer, "εὐλογέω and εὐλογία," *TDNT* 2:754–65, and in Hans Conzelmann, "εὐχαριστέω, εὐχαριστία, εὐχάριστος," *TDNT* 9:407–15. Conzelmann also recommends the interpretation of εὐχαριστέω and εὐλογέω as synonyms in 8:6–7.

28. God establishes (ἵστημι, Gen 6:18; 9:11; 17:7, 19, 21; Exod 6:4; ἀνίστημι, Gen 9:9), gives (δίδωμι, Gen 9:12), or makes (διατίθημι, Gen 9:17, 15:18; Exod 24:8; τίθημι, Gen 17:2; Exod 34:10, 27) covenants and is attributed with agentive benefaction of these covenants (Gen 6:18; 9:9, 15; 17:2, 4, 7, 9, 13, 14, 19, 21; Exod 2:24; 6:4; 19:5; 23:32).

29. This discussion assumes that the meal is concluded in the traditional fashion, with the singing of the Hallel Psalms (113–118) which are hymns of thanksgiving to God: cf. Donahue and Harrington, *The Gospel of Mark*, 401; Hooker, *The Gospel According to Saint Mark*, 344; Donald Senior, *The Passion of Jesus in the Gospel of Mark* (Passion Series 2; Wilmington, DE: Michael Glazier, 1984), 62; and Hugh Anderson, *The Gospel of Mark* (NCB; London: Oliphants, 1976), 316.

30. See Karl Heinrich Rengstorf, "σημεῖον," *TDNT* 7:234–6.

most appropriate Agent of give (δίδωμι [Aθg], 13:11) in relation to what Peter, Andrew, James, and John will say.

The scriptural parallel in the first sentence of Mark (1:1-3) evokes scriptural narrative frames concerning God's sending of Elijah (Mal 3:1) before the great and terrible day of the Lord (Mal 4:5). These scriptural narrative frames assert an eschatological perspective for interpreting subsequently narrated events, and pre-existing beliefs associated with this eschatological perspective come to the fore especially in contexts that focus on God's end-time evaluation of and response to human actions.[31] These pre-existing beliefs identify God as the most appropriate evaluative Source from which one will receive one's wage (μισθός [S], 9:41).[32] They also recommend God as the most appropriate Agent of measure (μετρέω [Aθg], 4:24), add (προστίθημι [Aθg], 4:24), give (δίδωμι [Aθg], 4:25), and take up (αἴρω [Aθs], 4:25), agentive Benefactive of condemnation (κρίμα [Bb], 12:40), and Source of inherit (κληρονομέω [gθS], 10:17) and receive (λαμβάνω [gθS], 10:30; 12:40).[33]

d. Criterion 4: Narrative Retrieval

The fourth criterion, narrative retrieval, relies on the repeated identification of references to God in relation to a given argument of a predicator to identify subsequent references to God in relation to the same argument of the same predicator. Narrative retrieval becomes possible when the narration identifies at least twice in succession God (sometimes with Jesus) as the sole referent of an argument (never an adjunct) of a predicator and thereafter introduces the predicator without its argument realized as a complement. Since the predicator

---

31. This discussion accepts the proposal by Adela Yarbro Collins, *Is Mark's Gospel a Life of Jesus?: The Question of Genre* (Milwaukee, WI: Marquette University Press, 1990), that the Gospel of Mark may be interpreted as a narration of the course of eschatological events (46) and that the narration evinces an overarching eschatological perspective (58). As such Mark is designed to elicit specific pre-existing eschatological beliefs.

32. Marcus, *Mark 8–16*, 88, interprets "wage" specifically as the reward of God's eschatological blessing.

33. The interpretation of God's agency in the occurrences in 4:24-25 receives the support of Marcus, *Mark 1–8*, 320, and George Martin, *The Gospel According to Mark: Meaning and Message* (Chicago: Loyola, 2005), 91. Most frequently these occurrences receive evaluation as "theological" or "divine" passives as introduced in Joachim Jeremias, *New Testament Theology: The Proclamation of Jesus*, trans. John Bowden (New York: Scribner, 1971), 10–13, and developed in John R. Donahue, "A Neglected Factor in the Theology of Mark," *JBL* 101, no. 4 (1982): 566. The eschatological interpretation of the occurrences in 4:24-25 assumes that the repetition of "the one having ears to hear, let him/her hear" (4:9, 23) demarcates 4:1-23 as the narrative unit concerning the proper interpretation of Jesus' teachings and that 4:24 begins a new narrative unit (4:24-34) concerning the reign of God and its consummation (4:29, 32). The passivized form of "prepare" in 10:40 is excluded from this list because, elsewhere in Mark, preparing is an action imposed on subordinates (1:2, 3; 14:12, 15, 16).

requires completion by an argument with a definite referent, subsequent occurrences with the argument unrealized evoke the same referent unless the narration proposes an alternative referent for the argument. Narrative retrieval identifies twenty-two direct references to God.

Within 1:1-15, the Benefactive/Topic of "gospel" is "Jesus Christ" (1:1), then "God" (1:14; cf. §1.6d), and then unrealized in its third occurrence (1:15). Greek grammar then retrieves both of the two previous referents as the semantic referent in the third occurrence, which permits the retroactive reinterpretation of both "Jesus Christ" and "God" as its semantic referent in the previous occurrences (1:1, 14), so that God (with Jesus) is the Benefactive/Topic of gospel (εὐαγγέλιον [B/T], 1:1, 14, 15). Since this predicator never occurs again with its Benefactive/Topic realized and the contexts never propose for it an alternative referent, narrative retrieval identifies God (with Jesus) as Benefactive/Topic of gospel (εὐαγγέλιον [B/T], 8:35; 10:29; 13:10; 14:9).

God's explicit benefaction of "commandment" in its first two occurrences (7:8, 9; cf. §2.4b) permits the subsequent narrative retrieval of God as its Benefactive except in 10:5, in which Jesus rejects the commandment on divorce and notes that Moses, and not God, is the actual agentive Benefactive of its writing. Since no further objections appear in the contexts of its following occurrences, narrative retrieval identifies God as the Benefactive of commandment (ἐντολή [B], 10:19; 12:28, [29], [31a], 31b).

In the previous discussion (§2.4a), scriptural parallels identify the first occurrence of "Lord" (1:3) as a designation for God (with Jesus); and the contextual retrieval of "Lord" as the referent attributed with benefaction with "paths" (1:3) repeats this reference. This permits the narrative retrieval of God (with Jesus) as the referent of "Lord," which identifies God (with Jesus) as the Agent of do (ποιέω [Ap], 5:19) and Experiencer of be merciful (ἐλεέω [Eb], 5:19).[34] Further narrative retrieval is impossible because the next two occurrences of "Lord" reference only Jesus (7:28; 11:3), which disrupts the narrative retrieval of God.

God's benefaction of "life" in 9:43 and 45 (§2.4b) permits the narrative retrieval of God as the Benefactive of [everlasting] life (ζωή [B], 10:17, 30).

God's saving in [10:27] and 13:20 permits the narrative retrieval of God as the Agent of save (σῴζω [Ap], 13:13).

God's benefaction of the Temple in 11:15a, 15b, and 16 (§2.4a) permits the subsequent narrative retrieval of God as Benefactive of Temple (ἱερόν [bB], 11:11, 27; 12:35; 13:1, 3; 14:49).

---

34. Since the intervening occurrence of "Lord" (2:28) appears in a designation, "Lord of the Sabbath," it does not participate in or interrupt this development. Further discussion of the dual reference of "Lord" in 1:3 and 5:19 appears in Daniel Johansson, "*Kyrios* in the Gospel of Mark," *JSNT* 33, no. 1 (2010), 104–6. The dual reference in 5:19 also receives consideration in Boring, *Mark*, 154, and in John Paul Heil, *The Gospel of Mark as Model for Action: A Reader-Response Commentary* (New York/Mahwah, NJ: Paulist, 1992), 121, who interprets God to act through Jesus in 5:19.

e. Criterion 5: Narrative Precedents

The fifth criterion, narrative precedents, uses the identification of God (sometimes with Jesus) as the referent of the consistently unrealized argument of a repeated predicator to identify God as the referent of that predicator's argument in other contexts whenever the other contexts identify no alternative referent. As a consequence, the use of precedents is excluded for any predicator that identifies distinct referents of the same unrealized argument of a predicator in different contexts. Narrative precedents and contextual retrieval identify twenty-six direct references to God.

Since God is the Benefactive of "messenger/angel" in 1:2 (§2.4a) and the narration subsequently identifies no alternative referent for its Benefactive, the occurrence in 1:2 provides a precedent for the subsequent identification of God as the Benefactive of messenger/angel (ἄγγελος [B], 1:13; 8:38; 12:25; 13:27, 32).

God's benefaction of "prophet" in 1:2 (§2.4a) and the absence of alternative referents in following contexts identify subsequent occurrences of God as the Benefactive of prophet (προφήτης [B], 6:4, 15a, 15b; 8:28; 11:32).

God as the recipient Benefactive of "blaspheme" in 2:7 (§2.4b) identifies God as the Benefactive of blaspheme (βλασφημέω [apB], 3:28, 29) and of blasphemy (βλασφημία [bB], 7:22; 14:64).[35]

God's benefaction of "forgiveness" in 3:29 (§2.4c) retroactively identifies God as the agentive Benefactive of forgiveness (ἄφεσις [Bb], 1:4).

God as the Experiencer of "prayer" in 11:17 (cf. §2.4a) serves as a precedent for the retroactive retrieval of God as the Experiencer of prayer (προσευχή [E], 9:29).

God as the Topic of "faith" in 11:22 and of believe in 11:23-24 (§2.4b) permits the retroactive retrieval of God as the Topic of faith (πίστις [ecT], 2:5; 4:40; 5:34; 10:52) and believe (πιστεύω [ecT], 5:36; 9:23, 24).

God's agency in sending Jesus the Beloved Son in 12:6 (§2.4a) retroactively identifies God as the Agent of send (ἀποστέλλω [Aθg], 9:37), which permits the contextual retrieval of God as the Theme of receive (δέχομαι [gΘs], 9:37d).

God's agentive Benefaction of "creation" in 13:19 (§2.4b) retroactively identifies God as the Benefactive of creation (κτίσις [B], 10:6).

f. Criterion 6: Convergence

The sixth criterion, convergence, uses two or more complementary considerations to identify God (sometimes with Jesus) as the sole or most probable referent of arguments or adjuncts. This criterion, which relies heavily on previously identified references and contextual retrieval, identifies fifty-six references, forty-three direct and thirteen indirect.

---

35. Although Adela Yarbro Collins, "The Charge of Blasphemy in Mark 14.64," *JSNT* 26, no. 4 (2004): 396, would interpret the occurrence of βλασφημία in 7:22 to concern only the relations between human beings, the prior focus on blasphemy against God is taken to introduce a similar focus in this context.

(i) Direct References from Convergence This discussion uses convergence to identify forty-three direct references to God.

The previously identified references to God and God's agency within 1:1-15 converge with the pre-existing theological beliefs that God made the heaven (Gen 1:6-8) to identify God as the most appropriate Agent of the heavens' tearing (σχίζω [Ap], 1:10).

Pre-existing theological beliefs recognize that God created human beings (10:6; cf. Gen 1:26, 27; 2:7, 8) and that God blessed and sanctified the Sabbath (Gen 2:3). In this light, Jesus' statement about the coming to be of the Sabbath and the human being would evoke pre-existing theological beliefs that interpret God as Agent by whom these come to be (γίνομαι [pA], 2:27a, [27b]).

Jesus' use of a passivized form of "give" in 4:11 recommends against identifying him as the verb's Agent, and the context explicitly identifies no alternative candidate for reference. Since what is given is the secret of God's reign and has the potential to culminate in God's action of forgiving (4:12), God is the most appropriate Agent of give (δίδωμι [Aθg], 4:11).[36]

The translation of "corban" by "gift" indicates that "corban" is not expected to evoke pre-existing beliefs to assist in its interpretation (§1.8). This singular occurrence of "gift," however, can assist in interpretation only if it evokes pre-existing beliefs that recognize its use in vows to God, which identifies God as the Benefactive of gift (δῶρον [bB], 7:11).

God as the Agent of "save" in contexts that concern the ultimate disposition of human beings at the end of this age and the similar implication of "save life" join to recommend God as the Agent (and the one destroying one's life for the sake of Jesus and the gospel as the Instrument) of save (σῴζω [Ap], 8:35b).

The identification of God as the Benefactive of "son" and Experiencer of "beloved" in 1:11 and 12:6, the use of "son" as a designation for Jesus in 1:11, 9:7, and 12:6, and the repetition of "voice," "son," and "beloved" in 1:11 and 9:7 converge to identify God as the Benefactive of voice (φωνή [B], 9:7) and son (υἱός [B], 9:7), and Experiencer of beloved (ἀγαπητός [Ec], 9:7).

The context of Jesus' interaction with the Chief Priests, Scribes, and Elders (11:27–12:12) identifies Jesus as God's Son (§2.4a) whom God sent (12:6) to take some of the fruit of the vineyard (12:2). The contextual identification of Jesus as God's delegate recommends God as the most appropriate referent of the Agent of give (δίδωμι [Aθg], 11:28), which permits the contextual retrieval of God as the Benefactive of authority (ἐξουσία [B], 11:28a, 28b, 29, 33). These occurrences serve as a narrative precedent for the retrieval of God (with Jesus) as the Benefactive of authority (ἐξουσία [B], 1:22, 27; 2:10) and God (with Jesus and the Twelve) as the Benefactive of authority (ἐξουσία [B], 3:15; 6:7) as well as the subsequent retrieval of God (with Jesus, the Lord of the Household) as the Benefactive of authority (ἐξουσία [B], 13:34).

---

36. The interpretation of God as the Agent of "give" in 4:11 receives the support of Moloney, *Mark*, 91; Collins, *Mark: A Commentary*, 249; and Marcus, *Mark 1–8*, 216.

Technically, God's agency in giving in 11:28 simultaneously identifies God as the Source from which the authority moves (§1.6c).³⁷ Jesus' statement in 11:30 then asserts a parallel between "authority" and "the baptism of John" and asks for the Source of that baptism. These considerations converge with the identification in 11:25 of the location of God as the heavens (§2.4c(i)) to recommend God as the Source of John's baptism (βάπτισμα [S], 11:30).³⁸

The recognition of God's agency in what has been written (§2.4c(i)) joins with the discussion of default Benefactive relationships (§1.6a) to identify God as the agentive Benefactive of what is written, scripture (γραφή [B], 12:10, 24; 14:49).

Although "son" appears in a number of designations for Jesus, it functions independently as a designation for Jesus only in "my Son" (1:11; 9:7; 12:6b), with God as the sole Benefactive, and Son (12:6a; 13:32).³⁹ The use of "son" as a designation for Jesus in contexts in which God is its Benefactive converges with the meaning of "blessed one" (14:61) to identify "Blessed One" as a designation for God, God as the Benefactive of son (υἱός [B], 14:61) and right [hand] (δεξιά [B], 14:62), and "Power" as a designation for God.

The use of "son" as a designation for Jesus in contexts in which God is its Benefactive also permits the formulation of Jesus' reciprocal benefaction of God, which would be realized by a phrase in the pattern, "my Father" (§1.6a). This pattern is realized in 8:38 in the phrase "his Father," where Jesus the Son of Man references the Benefactive. These considerations converge to identify "Father" as a designation for God, God as the Patient of Jesus the Son of Man's benefaction with father (πατήρ [bP], 8:38), and God as the Benefactive of glory (δόξα [B], 8:38). The latter occurrence then serves as a narrative precedent for the subsequent identification of God as the Benefactive of glory (δόξα [B], 13:26), which permits the contextual retrieval of God as Benefactive of power (δύναμις [B], 13:26). God's repeated benefaction of power (12:24; 13:26) then serves as a precedent for retrieving God as the Benefactive of power (δύναμις [B], 9:1).

Jesus' benefaction with "father" in 8:38 also establishes a narrative precedent for the direct use of "Father" as a designation for God. This identifies God as the Benefactive of son (υἱός [B], 13:32), Experiencer of know (οἶδα [Et], 13:32), Patient of Jesus' benefaction with father (πατήρ [bP], 14:36), Agent of [not] take away (παραφέρω [Aθs], 14:36), Benefactive of possible thing (δυνατόν [B], 14:36), and Experiencer of want (θέλω [Ec], [14:36]).

---

37. Discussion of the co-referentiality of the Agent and Source of give (δίδωμι) appears in Paul L. Danove, "Verbs of Transference and Their Derivatives of Motion and State in the New Testament: A Study of Focus and Perspective," *FN* 19 (2006): 53–5.

38. Marcus, *Mark 8–16*, 796, 799, identifies "Heaven" as a circumlocution for "God" in this context: cf. Helmut Traub, "οὐρανός," *TDNT* 5:514, who deems "Heaven" as a synonym for God.

39. Son of God (1:1; 3:11; 5:7; 15:39); Son of Man (2:10, 28; 8:31, 38; 9:9, 12, 31; 10:33, 45; 13:26; 14:21a, 21b; 41, 62); Son of Mary (6:3); and Son of David (10:47, 48).

The previous use of "has been written" to introduce statements attributed to God (1:2; 7:6; 11:17) and the interpretation of God as the referent of the first person singular subject of the verb in the statement in 1:2 converge to recommend the interpretation of God as the Agent of strike (πατάσσω [Ap], 14:27).[40]

Pre-existing semantic beliefs that identify "sanctuary" as a designation for the Temple converge with God's benefaction of the Temple (§§2.4a, 2.4d) to identify God as the Benefactive of sanctuary (ναός, [bB], 14:58a; 15:29, 38) and its permissibly omitted occurrence with "another" (ναός, [bB], [14:58b]).[41]

The context of the tearing of the sanctuary's curtain (15:38) identifies no referent for the Agent, and God's agency in tearing the sky (1:10) is not sufficient to establish a precedent for retrieving God because the referent of the Patient is different. The tearing of this quite tall curtain "from top to bottom," however, excludes possible human agency; and God's benefaction of the sanctuary itself identifies God as the most likely candidate for acting with respect to the sanctuary and its contents.[42] These considerations propose God as the most probable Agent of tear (σχίζω [Ap], 15:38).[43]

(ii) Indirect References from Convergence The thirteen indirect references derived from convergence are associated with the Benefactive arguments of unrealized Instrument arguments of three predicators.

The contextual interpretation of "prophesy" in 7:6 as "speak the message of God" joins with the recognition that David spoke a psalm by the Holy Spirit (12:36; cf. Ps 110:1), which has God as its Benefactive (§2.4c(i)), to identify an indirect reference to God as Benefactive of the Instrument of prophesy (προφητεύω [aci-iB], 7:6).[44]

The recognition of "scripture" as the expected referent of the Instrument of "be necessary" (§§1.2d, 1.7c) and God as the agentive Benefactive of "scripture" (§2.4c(i)) converge to identify God as the Benefactive of the Instrument of be necessary (δεῖ [vi-iB], 8:31; 9:11; 13:7, 10, 14; 14:31).

---

40. Collins, *Mark: A Commentary*, 670, and Marcus, *Mark 8–16*, 969, support this interpretation.

41. O. Michel, "ναός," *TDNT* 4:882.

42. R. T. France, *The Gospel of Mark: A Commentary on the Greek Text* (Grand Rapids, MI: Eerdmans, 2002), 657, Collins, *Mark: A Commentary*, 763; and Marcus, *Mark 8–16*, 1066, interpret the tearing from the top to bottom to indicate divine agency. An implication of the Benefactive relationship is that the entity attributed with benefaction of another entity is assumed to have the capacity to act with respect to the other entity: cf. Paul L. Danove, "The Usages of δίδωμι in the Septuagint: Its Interpretation and Translation," *BIOSCS* 43 (2010): 26.

43. Further arguments for the interpretation of God's agency in the tearing of the curtain appear in Harry L. Chronis, "The Torn Veil: Cultus and Christology in Mark 15:37-39," *JBL* 101, no. 1 (1982): 109–11.

44. Gerhard Friedrich, "Prophets and Prophecies in the New Testament," *TDNT* 6:829.

The recognition of "commandment" as the expected referent of the Instrument of "be permitted" (§§1.2e, 1.7c) and God as the Benefactive of "commandment" (§§2.4b, 2.4d) converge to identify God as the Benefactive of the Instrument of be permitted (ἔξεστιν [vi-iB], 2:24, 26; 3:4; 6:18; 10:2; 12:14).

g. Rejected References

This discussion explains the reasons for limiting references to God to only particular occurrences of specific predicators.

Although the repetition of God (with Jesus) as Benefactive of the way (ὁδός) in 1:2, 3 (§2.4a) is sufficient to permit the narrative retrieval of their benefaction in subsequent occurrences, the third occurrence of "way" in 2:23 presents Jesus' disciples making a way and so identifies them as its agentive Benefactive. This disrupts the continuity of reference to God, which is not explicitly reasserted until 12:14 (§2.4b).

"Save" (σῴζω) requires completion by an Agent and Patient or an Instrument and Patient. God is assumed to be the Agent only when the action concerns the ultimate disposition of the human being and no other character is proposed as Agent (8:35b; [10:27]; 13:13, 20). Although the occurrence in 8:35a also concerns the ultimate disposition of the human being, the Agent wishing to save one's life but destroying it is human. Elsewhere the verb designates the action of restoring physical integrity to a human being and has as Agent Jesus (5:23; 15:30, 31a, 31b) or human beings (3:4; 10:26) and as Instrument touching Jesus (5:28; 6:56) or faith (5:34; 10:52).

The previous discussions (§§2.4b, 2.4f(i)) identified God as the Benefactive of power (δύναμις [B], 9:1; 12:24; 13:26) and recognized its use as a designation for God (14:62). Elsewhere "power" has Jesus (5:30; 6:2, 5) or other characters (9:39) as its agentive Benefactive or designates human characters (6:14) or heavenly beings other than God (13:25).

Although the previous discussion (§2.4f(i)) identified God as the Source of John's baptism (11:30), this occurrence does not permit the narrative retrieval of God as its Source in its three remaining occurrences (1:4; 10:38, 39), where "baptism" has different referents. The baptism of repentance proclaimed by John (1:4) is interpreted to reference not the baptism effected by John but the baptism to be effected by Jesus as agentive Benefactive. The baptism in 10:38-39 references the coming suffering, rejection, and death of Jesus the Son of Man which, in this context (10:32-40), has as the referent of its agentive Benefactive the Chief Priests, Scribes, and Gentiles and the unspecified characters who hand over Jesus to them.

This study interprets the occurrence of a participle of "say" (λέγω) after a finite form of "say" as a narrative convention that highlights the verbatim nature of the following Content complement (quote).[45] This excludes consideration of the

---

45. The grammatical constraints on the use of λέγω in this narrative convention receive consideration in Paul L. Danove, "Λέγω Melding in the Septuagint and New Testament," *FN* 16 (2003): 23–4.

participle of "say" in 12:26b after the finite form of "say" with God as the Agent in 12:26a.

5. Specifying the Actions and Attributes of God

The narrative study uses character frames and the transformational capacities of English grammar to reformulate the semantic content of the predicators, arguments, and adjuncts with God as their character referent into narrative statements of the actions (Agent) and attributes (all other thematic roles) of God. These statements consist of a main clause that reformulates the narrated content about God in the phrase licensed by a predicator and a qualification that clarifies the contextual relationship between the licensing predicator and other contextual predicators.

a. The Main Clause

The main clause reformulates the content of the phrase containing the reference to God so that "God" becomes the subject of the verb predicators or complex predicators ("be" plus a non-verb predicator).[46] In this reformulation, the Greek form of the licensing predicator and its location in the text appear in parentheses after the verb or complex predicator. The main clause then introduces other complements of the predicator in their proper grammatical relationship to God and specifies characters by name and, if present, designation (which follows the name without the intrusion of commas). The constraints of English grammar require three distinct procedures for formulating main clauses.

The first procedure applies when God is the referent of the Agent, Benefactive, Content, Patient, or Theme arguments of a verb or participle predicator, the Experiencer or Goal arguments of specific verb predicators, or the Benefactive argument of noun predicators. This procedure produces main clauses governed by verb predicators in English. The main clause uses the verb predicators or converts participle predicators to their corresponding verb predicators. When necessary to place "God" in the subject position, verb predicators may be passivized. The main clauses retrieve all pertinent narrative referents from the semantic context. In the following illustrations, the second example interprets the content of the text as a covenant obligation that requires obedience, and the third reflects that the reference is in a command. These and following examples note the text and the action (act.) or attribute (attr.) on the left. The tense of verbs in these and following examples receives explanation in the next section.

---

46. The properties of complex predicators receive elaboration in Danove, *Linguistics and Exegesis*, 55–8.

2. The Method of Narrative Analysis and Description   39

 text: [I (A)] send [my messenger (Θ)] [before your face (G)].
 act.: God sends (ἀποστέλλω, 1:2) John the Messenger before the face of God (with Jesus).

 text: [You (E)] shall love [the Lord your God (C)] [with . . .].
 attr.: God the Lord of Israel is to be loved (ἀγαπάω, 12:30) by Israel with. . . .

 text: Pay back [the things of God (Θ)] [to God (G)].
 attr.: God is to be paid back (ἀποδίδωμι, 12:17) the things of God.

God appears as the referent of Benefactive arguments with the verb predicator "have" (ἔχω) and with noun predicators. English grammar has a transform that permits a clausal formulation of the Benefactive relationship with noun predicators by making the Benefactive complement the subject complement of "have" and the noun predicator (Patient) the object of "have" (X of Y → Y has X).

 text: [He (B)] had [one, a beloved son (P)].
 attr.: God has (ἔχω, 12:6) one, Jesus the Beloved Son.

 text: son [of me (B)]
 attr.: God has Jesus the Son (υἱός, 12:6).

The second procedure applies whenever God is the referent of Patient or Theme arguments of complex and non-verb predicators. The procedure uses the complex predicators or makes non-verb predicators complex through the addition of "be," so that the main clauses in English consistently have complex predicators. The notation of the Greek predicator omits the "be" (εἰμί) component (§1.4). Although both the passivized verb predicators of the first procedure and complex predicators of the second procedure use "be," there is no confusion because the predicators noted in the former statements are verbs or participles and those noted in the latter statements are not verbs or participles.

 text: [He (P)] is one.
 attr.: God is one (εἷς, 12:32).

 text: [Father (Θ)] in [the heavens (L)]
 attr.: God the Father is in (ἐν, 11:25) the heavens.

 text: [God (P)] of me
 attr. God is the God (θεός, 15:34a) of Jesus.

The third procedure applies when God is the referent of Experiencer or Goal arguments of specific verb predicators, Instrument adjuncts, and Source or Topic arguments. Since English has no consistent transform for raising entities with these thematic roles as the subject of verb or complex predicators, the third procedure constructs paraphrases on the pattern, "God is the Instrument of/by whom," "God is the Source of/from whom," "God is the Topic of/about whom," "God is the Experiencer of/to whom," and "God is the Goal of/to whom," followed by the licensing predicator. In the second example, double brackets identify the permissibly omitted but required Source complement.

> text: [I (A)] make [you (E)] swear [by God (I)] [that you ... (C)].
> attr.:   God is the Instrument by whom Legion compels Jesus to swear (ὁρκίζω, 5:7) that Jesus....

> text: [I (G)] to inherit [everlasting life (Θ)] [[from someone (S)]]
> attr.:   God is the Source from whom one inherits (κληρονομέω, 10:17) everlasting life.

> text: gospel [of/about God (B/T)]
> attr.:   God (with Jesus) has/is the Topic of the gospel (εὐαγγέλιον, 1:14).

> text: prayer [[to God (E)]]
> attr.:   God is the Experiencer of prayer (προσευχή, 9:29).

b. Qualification

The statements of actions and attributes introduce a qualification after the main clause whenever another predicator licenses the predicator of the action or attribute. The qualification, which clarifies the relationship between the predicators, appears in a restrictive relative clause or participial phrase.

> text: [He (A)] will baptize [by the Holy Spirit (I) [[of God (B)]]].
> attr.:   God has the Holy Spirit (πνεῦμα, 1:8) by which Jesus will baptize.

> text: [[You (B)]] have [faith (P)] [in God (T)].
> attr.:   God is to be the Topic of faith (πίστις, 11:22) which disciples are to have.

6. Clarifications Concerning the Narrative Study

This discussion presents three clarifications concerning narrative frames and their contributions to the formulation of statements of the actions and attributes of God.

Temporal narrative frames accommodate the formulation of statements of actions and attributes using the simple past, simple present, or future tense depending on whether the action or attribute is applicable to God before, during, or after the story time which runs from God's sending of John the Messenger (1:2) to the women's flight from the tomb (16:8).

Reliability narrative frames accommodate an evaluation of the applicability of actions and attributes based on the reliability of the narrator making claims about God and the contextual narrative content that attends the claims. These frames identify God, Jesus, John the Messenger, prophets, demons, and all unclean spirits except Legion as consistently reliable narrators, which permits the straightforward use of the content of their claims in statements of actions and attributes. Claims by all other characters require validation through contextual confirmation or coherence with otherwise established reliable assertions. For example, since the drowning of the pigs into which Legion enters (5:13) may be construed as destructive of Legion, the previously discussed attribute (§2.5a), "God is the Instrument by whom Legion makes Jesus swear (ὁρκίζω, 5:7) that ...," proves to contain an inaccurate claim about God. As a consequence, reliability narrative frames require the restatement of this attribute as "God is *not* the Instrument by whom Legion compels Jesus to swear (ὁρκίζω, 5:7) that ...".

Semantic relation narrative frames interpret the circumstantial semantic relations Cause, Condition, Purpose, and Result as narrative causes, conditions, purposes and results. Other categories of narrative frames accommodate the interpretation of similar relationships by proper narrative means. For example, the sequencing of events may interpret the statement of one character to be the result of a previous statement or action by another character. The narrative study clarifies the origin of these relationships by retaining the capitalized forms for relationships based on thematic roles and using non-capitalized forms of the same words for narratively motivated relationships.

7. Clarification Concerning Character Frame Descriptions

Character frames suppress the licensing properties of noun and adjective predicators that function as designations (e.g., God and Holy One), except when the noun predicator licenses a reciprocal Benefactive argument (e.g., Father, Son) or the narration explicitly realizes an argument or adjunct for the predicator (e.g., my God, Holy One of God).

8. Pre-Existing and Cultivated Narrative Beliefs Concerning God

The narrative study identifies no evidence of the cultivation of new information about God for the narrative frames evoked by the narration. This implies that the authorial audience's pre-existing narrative beliefs already recognize the content of the main clause of every action and attribute proposed for God in Mark. An example of the breadth and depth of beliefs about God assumed for the authorial audience appears in 1:1-3, which evinces no strategy to introduce or cultivate new narrative beliefs.[47] For these verses to be meaningful, the authorial audience must

---

47. Chaïm Perelman, *The Realm of Rhetoric*, trans. William Kluback (Notre Dame, IN: University of Notre Dame Press, 1982), 21, notes that the process of interpretation must begin with what is accepted by the interpreter. The significance of such pre-existing beliefs for the interpretive process receives attention in Booth, *Rhetoric of Fiction*, 157, 177, and in Eco, *Role of the Reader*, 7-8.

recognize why "Christ" is adequate to distinguish the noted Jesus from other possible characters with that name, what "Christ" implies, which god is being referenced, in which sense Jesus can be understood to be God's Son, who Isaiah the prophet is, how Isaiah as prophet is related to God, and why the words written in/by Isaiah are authoritative and significant.[48] The authorial audience also must have sufficient pre-existing beliefs to recognize God as the referent of "I," John the Baptist as the referent of "messenger," and God as the scriptural referent of "you" and "lord" in 1:2–3.[49] These considerations indicate that the authorial audience of the Gospel of Mark is attributed with extensive pre-existing Christian beliefs about God.[50] In particular, since these verses place all other characters in relation to God (Jesus is God's son, Isaiah is God's prophet, the messenger is God's) and attribute all action directly (send) or ultimately (writing, crying out, preparing, making straight) to God's initiative, pre-existing beliefs concerning God form the primary basis for asserting the initial reliability of the narration.

The only possible but rejected instance of the cultivation of new information for narrative frames from the content of main clauses appears in the explanation of the term "corban" (κορβάν). Its explanation by a single Greek word (7:11), however, indicates at least some pre-existing familiarity with such gift pledges (§§1.8, 2.4f).

The narrative study attributes to pre-existing narrative beliefs the relationships, perspectives, and expectations of the narrative frames evoked by the content of main clauses (§2.5a) and to the cultivated narrative beliefs the relationships, perspectives, and expectations of the narrative frames cultivated by the content of qualifications (§2.5b).[51]

---

48. Even if the authenticity of "Son of God" in 1:1 is rejected, the straightforward narration of "You are my beloved son" in 1:11 would evoke similar pre-existing beliefs about God, Jesus, and their relationship.

49. Further elaboration of the pre-existing narrative beliefs concerning God appears in Danove, *Rhetoric of the Characterization*, 33–5.

50. This sketch coheres with the more detailed proposals concerning the authorial audience's pre-existing beliefs in Ernest Best, "Mark's Readers: A Profile," in *The Four Gospels*, ed. F. Van Segbroeck et al., vol. 2 (Leuven: Leuven University Press, 1992), 839–55; and Bastiaan M. F. van Iersel, "The Reader of Mark as Operator of a System of Connotations," *Semeia* 48 (1989): 83.

51. Studies in the redactional activity in Mark 1:4–16:8 reveal numerous instances of the introduction of references to God into traditional material and of the cultivation of narrative-specific relationships, perspectives, and expectations in connection with traditional references to God: cf. E. J. Pryke, *Redactional Style in the Marcan Gospel: A Study of Syntax and Vocabulary as Guides to Redaction in Mark* (Cambridge: Cambridge University Press, 1978).

Chapter 3

THE METHOD OF RHETORICAL ANALYSIS AND DESCRIPTION AND THE THEOLOGICAL STUDY

This chapter introduces the method of rhetorical analysis and description assumed in the following study of the theology of the Gospel of Mark and then describes the application of the semantic/narrative/rhetorical method. The initial discussion presents an overview of the study's model of rhetorical communication and its interpreter. The discussion of the rhetorical method introduces rhetorical frames, specifies the content of particular rhetorical frames, develops the analytical and descriptive potential of predicator repetition rhetorical frames, offers a series of clarifications about rhetorical and predicator repetition frames, and provides a statement of the rhetorical beliefs assumed for the authorial audience and cultivated for the narrative audience. Within the rhetorical study, "Mark" designates the perceived rhetorical strategies of the Gospel of Mark. The concluding discussions describe the application of the semantic/narrative/rhetorical method of analysis and description in the Exegetical Study (Chapters 4–5) and Theological Study (Chapters 6–11).

1. The Model of Rhetorical Communication: Rhetorical Frames

The model of rhetorical communication assumes that the encounter with Mark evokes rhetorical frames that link the content of specific semantic and narrative frames within 1:1–16:8.[1] The recognition that a narrative is augmenting the content of previously evoked or cultivated semantic and/or narrative frames evokes rhetorical frames that make available information about the previously evoked or cultivated and current semantic and/or narrative content, relationships between the previously evoked or cultivated content of frames and the current augmentation of this content, perspectives for evaluating the function of the augmentation, and expectations concerning the further augmentation of content.

---

1. The proposed characteristics of rhetorical frames are projected from the corresponding characteristics of semantic and narrative frames.

Each rhetorical context that augments the content of previously evoked or cultivated semantic and/or narrative frames has the potential to evoke rhetorical frames. Although the maximal rhetorical context for interpretation is the narrative as a whole, the rhetorical study places primary focus on continuous passages containing the interaction of a set of characters concerning a specific topic.[2] The Appendix provides the complete list of rhetorical contexts that include references to God.

For example, 13:18-20 constitutes a rhetorical context insofar as it sets in direct relationship a novel set of characters (God, Disciples of Jesus, the Elect, and human beings) and, in distinction from the surrounding material, focuses on God's direct end-time actions for Disciples of Jesus, the Elect, and human beings. The encounter with this rhetorical context has the potential to evoke rhetorical frames for a number of reasons. For example, God's action of shortening (κολοβόω [Ap], 13:20b) the days is attributed to a Cause (the Elect, whom God will choose). Recognition of this has the potential to evoke rhetorical frames that link the content of the semantic and narrative frames in this rhetorical context to that of the previous rhetorical context in which God's action is attributed to a Cause. These rhetorical frames provide the information that God previously was attributed with the action by which the human being came to be (γίνομαι [pA], [2:27b]), which was identified as the Cause of God's action by which the Sabbath came to be (γίνομαι [pA], 2:27a).

These rhetorical frames would accommodate the linkage of the information of the semantic and narrative frames in the two rhetorical contexts (2:23-28 and 13:18-20); relate the two caused actions, their consequences, and any other content associated in a similar manner with the two caused actions and their consequences; provide perspectives for evaluating this resulting linked content; and establish expectations concerning any subsequently narrated actions of God attributed to a Cause. These rhetorical frames would accommodate the information that specific human beings are the Cause of God's actions, as well as the relationship between the primordial human being because of whom the Sabbath came to be and the end-time Elect because of whom the days will be shortened. The same frames would accommodate the perspective that God's caused actions consistently are for the benefit of specific human beings and the expectation that subsequently narrated caused actions of God, if such occur, will concern specific human beings and be for their benefit.

The discussion of the rhetorical context constituted by 13:18-20 highlights the distinctiveness of rhetorical frames. Like the previously considered categories of frames, rhetorical frames accommodate the interpretation of semantic and/or narrative content by supplying information, relationships, perspectives, and

---

2. The entirety of more tightly crafted intercalations receives interpretation as a discrete rhetorical context, despite changes in characters and topic. For an introduction to intercalations, see John R. Donahue, *Are You the Christ? The Trial Narrative in the Gospel of Mark* (SBLDS 10; Missoula, MT: Scholars, 1973), 58-9.

expectations. Unlike those categories of frames, however, rhetorical frames offer no intrinsic information, relationships, perspectives, and expectations to assist in interpretation. Instead, they link the content of other categories of frames in ways that accommodate the abstraction of linked information, relationships, perspectives, and expectations. As a consequence, rhetorical frames provide a very convivial vehicle for developing narrative-specific content and thereby cultivating the beliefs of the narrative audience.

2. Specification of the Content of Rhetorical Frames

Among the categories of rhetorical frames, semantic coordination frames and narrative coordination frames occur with sufficient frequency to make significant, albeit subsidiary, contributions in the rhetorical study.

a. Semantic Coordination Rhetorical Frames

The introduction of a predicator that is cognate to a previously occurring predicator evokes semantic coordination frames that link the content of the semantic and narrative frames in the rhetorical contexts of the cognate predicator to the content of the semantic frames in the rhetorical contexts of the previously occurring predicator. This has significance for the rhetorical study whenever God is the referent of the same arguments (e.g., Experiencer/Experiencer with pray/prayer), parallel arguments (e.g., Agent/agentive Benefactive with create/creation), and, to a lesser degree, differing arguments (e.g., Benefactive/Experiencer with will/want) of cognate predicators. The rhetorical study assumes that semantic coordination rhetorical frames ultimately link the content of all semantic and narrative frames in the rhetorical contexts of the occurrences of cognate predicators.

For example, the narration initially evokes and strengthens pre-existing beliefs about the predictive potential of what has been written (γέγραπται [Ace]) under God's agency by demonstrating that what was written in the past of the story world about God sending God's Messenger/Angel (Exod 23:20; Mal 3:1) and this People honoring God only with their lips (Isa 29:13 LXX) is realized in the present of the story world when God sends John the Messenger (1:2) and the Pharisees and Scribes from Jerusalem are described as honoring God only with their lips (7:6). The initial occurrence of the cognate "scripture" (γραφή [B], 12:10), for which God is the agentive Benefactive, then evokes semantic coordination rhetorical frames that make available these strengthened beliefs about the predictive potential of what was written and apply them to the scripture quote about the rejected stone becoming the cornerstone (12:10; cf. Ps 118:22), thereby strengthening the assurance that the content of this quote will be realized with respect to Jesus. The same rhetorical frames are evoked by the first occurrence of "be necessary" (δεῖ [vi-iB], 8:31), for which God's scripture is the necessitating Instrument, and provide a strong warrant for the narrative audience's acceptance of the inevitability of the apparently novel and discordant content concerning the Son of Man's coming suffering, being rejected, being killed, and rising.³ In this way, semantic coordination rhetorical frames ground the introduction of narrative clarifications dependent on a predicator into the content of its cognate predicator. These frames also accommodate various subsidiary developments like those considered in the following example.

When the semantic relationships with cognates are not exact or parallel, as with God as innate Benefactive of will (θέλημα [B], 3:35) and as Experiencer of want (θέλω [Ec], [14:36]), only subsidiary developments that focus on the linkages of content between two rhetorical contexts are possible. In the former context, Jesus states that those doing God's will are Jesus' brother and sister and mother. In the latter context, Jesus affirms his filial relationship with God as Abba Father when he chooses what God wants rather than what he wants. At this point, semantic coordination rhetorical frames accommodate the recognition that those doing God's will enact their filial relationship with God on the pattern of Jesus and that this filial relationship grounds the resulting familial relationship as brother, sister, and mother to Jesus.

b. Narrative Coordination Rhetorical Frames

The introduction of two non-cognate predicators that reference the same narrative entity or event in a rhetorical context evokes narrative coordination rhetorical frames that link the content of the semantic and narrative frames in all rhetorical contexts of both predicators. Narrative coordination signals either that the narrative referents of non-cognate predicators are identical or overlap in significant characteristics, or that the narrative referent of one predicator incorporates that of the other predicator. The rhetorical study restricts its focus to the narrative coordination of non-cognate predicators that have God as the referent of the same or parallel arguments.

For example, the rhetorical context constituted by 9:42-48 sets in parallel two assertions about entering life (ζωή [B], 9:43, 45) with one assertion about entering God's reign (βασιλεία [B], 9:47).⁴ This parallel evokes narrative coordination rhetorical frames that link the content of the semantic and narrative frames in 9:42-48 to that of the semantic and narrative frames in the rhetorical contexts of subsequent occurrences of "life" with God as the referent of the Benefactive (10:17, 30) and previous and subsequent occurrences of "reign" with God as the referent of the Benefactive (1:15, 4:11, 26, 30; 9:1; 10:14, 15, 23, 24, 25; 12:34; 14:25; 15:43). The rhetorical study interprets "life" and "reign" to have distinct narrative referents that overlap in significant characteristics.

An example of the incorporation of the narrative referent of one non-cognate by another appears in the rhetorical context constituted by 11:15-17, which

---

3. Paul L. Danove, "The Rhetoric of the Characterization of Jesus as the Son of Man and Christ in Mark," *Bib* 84 (2003): 23–5.

4. Donahue and Harrington, *Mark*, 287–8, interpret "life" and "the reign of God" in this context as either equivalent or parallel; cf. Telford, *Theology*, 80.

references the same narrative entity first by "Temple" (ἱερόν [bB], 11:15a, 15b, 16) and then by "house" (οἶκος [bB], 11:17). This parallel evokes narrative coordination rhetorical frames that link the content of the semantic and narrative frames 11:15-17 to those in the rhetorical contexts of the previous occurrence of "house" with God as Benefactive (2:26) and the previous and subsequent occurrences of "Temple" (11:11, 27; 12:35; 13:1, 3; 14:49) which consistently have God as the referent of the Benefactive. These frames ground the interpretation that "house" is the general term for an edifice dedicated to God and "Temple" is the specific designation for this edifice in Jerusalem.

3. The Focus of the Rhetorical Study: Predicator Repetition Frames

The recognition that a predicator is being repeated evokes predicator repetition rhetorical frames that link and establish emphases within the information, relationships, perspectives for evaluation, and expectations of the semantic and narrative frames in the rhetorical contexts of the predicator's occurrences.[5] The rhetorical study uses the linking and emphasizing potential of predicator repetition rhetorical frames to organize and describe the semantic and narrative content associated with God's repeated actions and attributes. As with the previously considered categories of rhetorical frames, predicator repetition rhetorical frames offer no intrinsic information to assist in interpretation but link and emphasize the content of previously evoked or cultivated and current semantic and narrative frames.

4. Predicator Repetition Frame Analysis and Description: Linkages and Emphases

Predicator repetition rhetorical frames accommodate the linkage of the semantic and narrative content of the rhetorical contexts of repeated predicators that have God as the character referent of an argument or adjunct. These frames also accommodate the recognition of relative emphasis of repeated actions and attributes in relation to each other. The following discussion develops the linking

---

5. The contributions of repetition in narratives receives consideration in Neil. R. Leroux, "Repetition, Progression, and Persuasion in Scripture," *Neot* 29, no. 1 (1995): 8–10; Bastiaan M. F. van Iersel, "Locality, Structure, and Meaning in Mark," *LB* 53 (1983): 45–54; Rabinowitz, *Before Reading*, 53; David Rhoads and Donald Michie, *Mark as Story: An Introduction to the Narrative of a Gospel* (Philadelphia: Fortress, 1982), 46-7; Meir Sternberg, *The Poetics of Biblical Narrative: Ideological Literature and the Drama of Reading* (Bloomington, IN: Indiana University Press, 1985), 365–440; and Robert C. Tannehill, *The Sword of His Mouth* (Philadelphia: Fortress, 1975), 39–51: cf. H. Porter Abbott, *The Cambridge Introduction to Narrative*, 2nd edn. (Cambridge: Cambridge University Press, 2008), 75–6.

and emphasizing potentials of predicator repetition rhetorical frames for the repeated predicator "send" (ἀποστέλλω).

a. Linkages

Predicator repetition rhetorical frames link the content of all semantic and narrative frames in the rhetorical contexts of the occurrences of a repeated predicator. For example, these frames link the semantic and narrative content of the contexts of the one permissibly omitted and twenty realized occurrences of "send." This linkage accommodates an investigation of the manner in which this linked content relates the character referents of any of its three arguments. Thus a study of the Agents of sending would consider the relationships among God (1:2; 9:37; 12:2, 4, 5a, [5b], 6), Jesus (3:14; 5:10; 6:7; 8:26; 11:1, 3; 13:27; 14:13), the mother, brothers, and sisters of Jesus (3:31), a human being casting seed on the earth (4:29), Herod (6:17, 27), and the Chief Priests, Scribes, and Elders (12:3, 13). The following discussion develops two categories of contributions of the linkages accommodated by predicator repetition rhetorical frames to the rhetorical study.

The primary contribution of predicator repetition rhetorical frames is to link the semantic and narrative content of the rhetorical contexts of each repeated predicator that has God as the referent of the same argument on multiple occasions.[6] These frames link and organize the semantic and narrative content of the four rhetorical contexts (1:1-3; 9:33-37; 12:1-5; 12:6-8) in which God sends (1:2; 9:37; 12:2, 4, 5a, [5b], 6). The resulting organization sets all other contextual actions and attributes of God in their proper narrative relationships to God's action[s] of sending and relates to each other all whom God sends (Theme), all to whom God sends (Goal), and all noted semantic and narrative causes, conditions, purposes, or results of God's sending. These relationships, in turn, become the basis for linking all other content about those sent (Theme) by God, those to whom (Goal) God sends, and the content of all repeated circumstantials (whether semantically or narratively based) to God as the Agent of sending. Thus God's actions of sending link to each other John the Messenger (1:2), Jesus (9:37; 12:6), and God's Slaves (12:2, 4, 5a, [5b]), link the purpose for God's sending of John (to prepare the way, 1:2) and the Purpose for God's sending of God's Slaves and Jesus (to take some of the fruit of the vineyard, 12:2), and propose John, the Slaves, and Jesus as the instruments by which God would accomplish these purposes.

The linkage of content also accommodates the recognition of secondary parallels, both complementary and contrasting, between God and other characters with respect to an action or attribute. For example, God sends Jesus, who proclaims (1:14, 38, 39) and casts out demons (1:34, 39; 7:30; 9:25), and Jesus, in turn, intends to/does send the Twelve, who are constituted to (Purpose)/do proclaim (3:14/6:12) and cast out demons (3:15/6:13). The rhetorical study introduces such secondary

---

6. The previous discussion (§2.4) identified no repeated predicator for which God is the referent of an adjunct on more than one occasion.

observations only when they clarify or support claims about God's actions or attributes derived from the primary category of linkages.

b. Relative Emphasis

After its introduction with God as the referent of an argument, each subsequent occurrence of a predicator with God as the referent of the same argument evokes predicator repetition rhetorical frames. Since each such evocation calls attention to the predicator and the semantic and narrative content of its rhetorical context, predicator repetition rhetorical frames grant greater relative emphasis to God's more frequently occurring actions and attributes. Thus the six evocations of predicator repetition rhetorical frames by the second and following occurrences of "send" with God as the referent of the Agent grant relatively greater emphasis to God's action of sending than the single evocation of these frames by the second (and final) occurrence of "tear" (σχίζω [Ap], 1:10; 15:38) grants to God's action of tearing.

5. Specifying the Rhetorically Organized Content about God

The rhetorical study uses predicator repetition rhetorical frames in conjunction with the content of semantic, case, narrative, character, and other categories of rhetorical frames to reformulate the semantic and narrative content of the rhetorical contexts containing God's repeated actions and attributes into statements of those actions and attributes. The rhetorical statements address the linked content of the narrative statements of the repeated action or attribute, the linked content related to the repeated action or attribute in the various rhetorical contexts, and the patterns of and progressions in the development of the linked content associated with the repeated action or attribute. In general, this requires a simultaneous address of the content of two, several, or all of the rhetorical contexts, although, on occasion, the full exposition of a complex development introduced in one rhetorical context requires a preliminary detailed discussion focused exclusively on that introductory context. Predicator repetition rhetorical frames provide a host of avenues for development, some straightforward and others less so. For economy of presentation, the following discussion develops two straightforward and complementary avenues of inquiry and provides two examples of each. For each avenue of approach, the first example illustrates the broad range of potentialities afforded by repeated verb predicators; and the second example illustrates the more circumscribed potentialities afforded by repeated non-verb predicators.

The most straightforward contribution of predicator repetition rhetorical frames is the progressive linkage of God to other characters, things, and events. Verb predicators are most prodigious in this regard because, on average, they require completion by more arguments and license more adjuncts than other predicators. The following example illustrates the most direct potentialities for development afforded by the repetition of "send" (ἀποστέλλω) with God as the referent of the Agent. Among the direct relationships with God are those to the character referents of the Theme, John the Messenger (1:2), Jesus (9:37; 12:6), and God's Slaves (12:2, 4, 5a, [5b]). Predicator repetition rhetorical frames accommodate the recognition that, chronologically, God's sending of God's Slaves occurs in the past of the story world, while God's sending of John the Messenger and Jesus occurs in the present. God's actions of sending always are purposive, and the linkage of these Purposes is open to the type of development previously introduced (§3.4a). Although all those sent are depicted in a positive relationship with God, Jesus is unique in having co-benefaction of God's face, way, paths, and designation as Lord (1:2-3) and in being identified as the one whom God loves (12:6). These considerations contribute to developments concerning the fact that only the reception of Jesus (and not God's Slaves or John) accomplishes the reception of God (9:37). God's action of sending always sets those sent in contact with other characters, which engenders mediated relationships for God with those characters and related things and events. Among the characters, those contributing to God's purpose in sending (those preparing the way and straightening the paths, 1:2-3) also are set in a positive relationship with God, whereas those frustrating the Purpose of God's sending (the farmers of the vineyard, 12:2-9) are set in opposition to God and are evaluated negatively. As these few observations begin to illustrate, repeated verb predicators accommodate a variety of possibilities for development.

More restricted but still significant are the potentialities afforded by the repetition of non-verb predicators with God as the character referent of an argument or as the referent of the predicator itself. For example, God's repeated benefaction of Angels/Messengers (ἄγγελος) links the referents of these characters to God and each other (1:2, 13; 8:38; 12:25; 13:27, 32) and extends positive evaluations to the characters so designated. God's Angels/Messengers perform specific actions of preparing and crying out (1:2-3), ministering to Jesus (1:13), and being sent by Jesus the Son of Man in his gathering of God's Elect (13:27). They also are attributed with being sent by God (1:2) and by Jesus the Son of Man (13:27), having a voice (1:3), coming with Jesus the Son of Man (8:38), being compared to the dead who rise and being in the heavens (12:25), and not knowing that day or hour (13:32). Significantly, they are related to Jesus in some fashion in each occurrence and to other characters, things, and events in most occurrences. As a consequence they provide further content concerning God's relationship with Jesus and relate God positively or negatively to other characters, things, and events. Each of these observations is open to further specification and development concerning God.

The linkages afforded by predicator repetition rhetorical frames also have the potential to ground the recognition of patterns and progressions in the development of specific relationships or topics. For example, repetition of "save" (σῴζω), when designating action pertaining to the ultimate disposition of a human being, first occurs in the statement, "Whoever wishes to save one's life will destroy it; but whoever destroys one's life for the sake of Jesus and the gospel will save it" (8:35).

"Save" requires completion by an Agent or an Instrument first/subject complement (§2.4g), and the context does not clarify whether the character referents of the subjects are to be interpreted as an Agent or an Instrument. The next rhetorical context of the occurrence of "save" with this meaning then presents the statement, "For human beings [to save a human being] is impossible; but for God [to save a human being is] not [impossible]" (10:27). Linkage of these two passages retroactively interprets the occurrences of "save" in 8:35a to identify the one wishing to save one's life but destroying as the one attempting but failing to function as the Agent of "save" and the one destroying one's life for the sake of Jesus and the gospel as the one succeeding in functioning as the Instrument of "save" (8:35b). The following occurrences of "save" then present further opportunities for development.

Again, in the second occurrence of "power" (δύναμις), contextual repetition of "come" establishes a tenuous relationship between the end-time coming of Jesus the Son of Man with/by God's glory (8:38) and the proximate coming of God's reign with/by God's power (9:1). The fourth occurrence of "power" then asserts that the Son of Man will come with/by much power and glory (13:26). This progression solidifies the relationships between God's power and God's glory and between the end-time coming of Jesus the Son of Man and the proximate coming of God's reign. The same progression simultaneously specifies Jesus the Son of Man's end-time coming as the occasion of the definitive (in comparison to the proximate coming of God's reign) manifestation of God's power and glory. These recognitions and the content associated with the further repetition of "power" then open further avenues for developing the associated statements of God's repeated attributes.

As noted at the beginning of this discussion, the potentialities afforded by predicator repetition rhetorical frames are vast, and this discussion attempted to demonstrate only a few of their more straightforward contributions and point to possible others. When more fully developed and augmented by less straightforward (and not previously considered) potentialities, predicator repetition rhetorical frames provide in most cases an overabundance of avenues for developing the characterization of God.

6. Clarifications Concerning the Rhetorical Study

Although predicator repetition rhetorical frames are the primary means of linking and organizing the semantic and narrative content concerning God's actions and attributes, semantic and narrative coordination frames also play a subsidiary role in the formulation of select statements of repeated actions and attributes.

a. Semantic Coordination Frames

As previously discussed (§3.2a), the rhetorical study assumes that semantic coordination rhetorical frames ultimately link the content of all semantic and narrative frames in the rhetorical contexts of the occurrences of cognate predicators. As a consequence, these frames are able to coordinate the content of narrative statements of non-repeated actions and attributes and/or the rhetorical statements of repeated actions and attributes. On occasion, a previously formulated statement may contain information about a subsequently discussed action or attribute dependent on a cognate predicator. When this occurs, the rhetorical study introduces a summary of this clarifying information into the subsequent statement with a notation referencing the previously formulated statement. For example, clarifying information from the statement about God's agency in writing (γέγραπται) may be introduced in summary fashion into the subsequently formulated statement concerning God's repeated benefaction of the scriptures (γραφή) with a reference to the previously formulated statement concerning God's action of writing. When the information, linkages, or emphases in the rhetorical contexts of repeated cognate predicators differ significantly from that of its cognate, the statement of the subsequently considered repeated cognate provides a brief discussion of the difference[s]. Semantic coordination frames have the potential to contribute to the statements incorporating actions and attributes dependent on the following cognates, with repeated cognates noted by a preceding asterisk (*).[7]

will (θέλημα [B]) / want (θέλω [Ec])
inherit (κληρονομέω [gθS]) / inheritance (κληρονομία [S])
forgive (*ἀφίημι [Apb]) / forgiveness (*ἄφεσις [Bb])
sin (*ἁμαρτία [bB]) / sinful action (*ἁμάρτημα [bB])
blasphemy (*βλασφημία [bB]) / blaspheme (*βλασφημέω [apB])
write (*γέγραπται [Ace]) / scripture (*γραφή [B])
pray (*προσεύχομαι [acE]) / prayer (*προσευχή [E]).

b. *Narrative Coordination Frames*

As previously discussed (§3.2b), narrative coordination frames link the content of the semantic and narrative frames in the rhetorical contexts of non-cognate

---

7. Among the potential but rejected cognate candidates for semantic coordination are love (*ἀγαπάω [eC/apB]) and beloved (*ἀγαπητός [Ec/Apb]), glorify (δοξάζω [aE]) and glory (*δόξα [B]), authority (*ἐξουσία [B]) and be permitted (*ἔξεστιν [vi-iB]), heir (κληρόνομος [B]) and inherit (κληρονομέω [gθS]) / heir (κληρόνομος [B]), and Prophet (*προφήτης [B]) and prophesy (προφητεύω [aci-iB]), for which God references different and non-parallel arguments. Also rejected are cognates, power (*δύναμις [B]) and possible thing (*δυνατόν [B]) / [not] impossible thing (ἀδύνατον [B]), speak (*λέγω [Ace]) and word (λόγος [B], 7:13), which have significantly different contextual meanings. Three viable sets of candidates, possible thing (*δυνατόν [B]) and [not] impossible thing (ἀδύνατον [B]), elect (*ἐκλεκτός [B]) and choose (ἐκλέγομαι [Ap]), and creation (*κτίσις [B]) and create (κτίζω [Ap]), are omitted because the non-repeated references appear in the rhetorical contexts of their cognate repeated references and so automatically are incorporated into their statements.

predicators that are set in parallel or that reference the same narrative entity within a rhetorical context. As a consequence, these frames coordinate the content of the statements of non-repeated and/or repeated actions and attributes. Narrative coordination frames accommodate the linkage of the content of the statements of God's repeated benefaction of life (*ζωή [B]) and the reign (*βασιλεία [B]) through a parallel in 9:43-47 and the statements of God's repeated benefaction of the house (*οἶκος [bB]) and the Temple (*ἱερόν [bB]) through their reference of the same edifice in 11:15-17. They also link the narrative statement of God's benefaction of the word (λόγος [B]) and the rhetorical statement of God's repeated benefaction of the commandments (*ἐντολή [B]).

7. Clarifications Concerning Predicator Repetition Frame Descriptions

This discussion provides clarifications concerning the application of the content accommodated by predicator repetition rhetorical frames in formulating statements of God's repeated actions and attributes and concerning four further contributions of predicator repetition rhetorical frames to specifying content about God.

a. Revisiting the Content of Rhetorical Contexts Repetitively (Not Redundantly)

The repeated evocation of the content of the same rhetorical context in the discussions of different repeated actions and attributes need not and should not produce redundancies or mere duplications in the content of rhetorical statements. This is the case because the formulations of these statements develop the content of the rhetorical context from the differing perspectives of each repeated action or attribute under consideration. This can be illustrated from the previously considered examples (§3.5). Although the statements for God's sending (ἀποστέλλω) and God's Angels/Messengers (ἄγγελος) address the content of the same rhetorical context (1:1-3), the former is concerned with an action and the latter with an attribute. A review of the illustrative examples associated with the action and attribute reveals no redundancies. The same is true of the illustrative examples provided in the discussions of God's action of saving (σῴζω) and God's power (δύναμις). Although both address progressions initiated in the same rhetorical context (8:31–9:1), they present minimal overlap and no redundancies in content.

b. Four Further Contributions of Repetition Frames

To this point, the discussion of the rhetorical study has placed primary focus on predicator repetition rhetorical frames and their contributions to formulating statements of God's repeated actions and attributes. The repetition of semantic, case, narrative, and character frames associated with repeated predicators also has the potential to evoke repetition rhetorical frames that make subsidiary contributions to the formulation of statements of God's repeated actions and attributes.

Repeated semantic frames in the rhetorical contexts of the occurrences of repeated predicators with God as the referent of an argument evoke repetition rhetorical frames that permit the identification of subsidiary linkages among the predicators. These linkages are subsidiary because the narration never explicitly draws attention to them. For example, the semantic frames evoked by "sanctuary" (ναός [bB]) provide information that this predicator may reference the same entity as "Temple".[8] This has implications for the rhetorical statements concerning both repeated attributes.

Repeated case frames within the rhetorical contexts of the occurrences of predicators with God as the referent of an argument evoke repetition rhetorical frames that link and emphasize the narrated content concerning other predicators. On occasion, this information is salient to the study of the actions and attributes of God. For example, the repeated evocation of the same case frames for predicators in the context of "reign" identifies a novelty concerning God's reign and verbs of motion. In one rhetorical context (1:14-15), the reign of God as Theme moves (draws near) toward human beings as Goal (1:15), and, in another rhetorical context (9:42-47), human beings as Theme move (come) toward and into the reign of God as Goal (9:47). This has implications for describing God's benefaction of the reign.

Repeated narrative frames in the rhetorical contexts containing actions or attributes of God have the potential to evoke repetition rhetorical frames whose content receives development in relation to another character (usually Jesus). For example, Jesus' interactions with other characters have the potential to cultivate for narrative frames content identifying particular characters and groups as speaking and/or acting in opposition to Jesus. This content concerning Jesus then would be evoked and linked to God in the narrative statement of God's action of putting (τίθημι, 12:36), which depends on the scriptural quote, "Sit at my right [hand] until I put your enemies under your feet" (Ps 110:1). At this point, God's action for Jesus the Lord of David places the enemies opposed to Jesus in opposition to God.

Repeated character frames in the rhetorical contexts incorporating actions and attributes of God evoke repetition rhetorical frames that link to God all narrative content concerning God, establish emphases within this narrated content, and ultimately provide the basis for the coherent characterization of God.[9] These frames are foundational to the following study because they provide the overarching linkage of the content of all statements of God's repeated actions and attributes.

---

8. Such subsidiary contributions complement those introduced in §1.2.

9. The rhetorical implications of the sequential organization of content about God accommodated by the repetition of character frames receives development in Danove, "The Narrative Function of Mark's Characterization of God," 23–9.

8. Pre-Existing and Cultivated Rhetorical Beliefs Concerning God

Although the narrative study attributes all of the information, relationships, perspectives, and expectations of the narrative frames derived from the main clause of the narrative statements of God's actions and attributes to the pre-existing beliefs of the authorial audience (§2.8), the rhetorical study attributes all of the information, relationships, perspectives, and expectations of rhetorical frames to the cultivated beliefs of the narrative audience. This is the case because rhetorical frames have no innate content but link and emphasize the content of other frames in specific ways, and the resulting linkages and emphases are novel to the Gospel of Mark.

9. Prelude to the Theological Study: The Exegetical Study (Part 2)

The following study applies the methods of semantic, narrative, and rhetorical analysis and description (Part I: Chapters 1–3) to develop statements of God's repeated actions and attributes (Part III: Chapters 6–11). Development of each of these statements requires a careful review of the narrative and narratively interpreted semantic content of each rhetorical context of a repeated predicator. Incorporation of such a review into the statement of each repeated action or attribute, however, would introduce numerous duplications and greatly lengthen the resulting statements. For economy of presentation, the review of the content of each rhetorical context appears only once in the Exegetical Study (Part II: Chapters 4–5) prior to the formulation of the theological statements of God's repeated actions and attributes and the concluding discussion concerning their possible further development (Part III: Chapters 6–11). The following discussion specifies the format and extent of—and scholarly resources for—the exegesis of the content of rhetorical contexts containing references to God and then clarifies the order of the presentation of the Exegetical Study.

a. The Format of the Exegetical Study

The review of the narrative and narratively interpreted semantic content of the rhetorical contexts containing references to God provide the full narrative statements of all actions and attributes of God and set all other contextual content in its proper relationship with God's actions and attributes. The reviews introduce clarifications concerning the semantic and narrative content of each context and consider the contribution of semantic, case, narrative, character, and various categories of rhetorical frames either in context or after all salient semantic and narrative information receives introduction. On occasion, the reviews incorporate diagrams to assist in interpretation. Where appropriate, the reviews introduce brief discussions of proposed interpretations and/or offer references to scholarly works offering more detailed justifications for proposed interpretations. Contextual content not contributing in a significant way to the following Theological Study receives summary treatment. The Exegetical Study maintains the distinction between semantic (capitalized) and narrative (non-capitalized) causes, conditions, purposes, or results. Within the Exegetical Study, "Mark" variously references the semantic, narrative, and rhetorically organized content of the text of the Gospel of Mark within 1:1–16:8.

b. The Extent of the Exegetical Study

The reviews of the content of rhetorical contexts aim to be comprehensive but not exhaustive, providing complete narrative statements of God's actions and attributes, careful attention to all contextual relationships that are salient to the Theological Study, and summary treatment of all other contextual content. At the same time, the reviews make no claim to be exhaustive. This is unavoidable for two reasons. First, references to God appear in a majority of the rhetorical contexts of Mark, and an exhaustive review of all possible exegetical considerations pertaining to the content of the contexts is beyond the scope of any single manuscript. Second, although the Gospel of Mark admits to analysis and description according to a variety of methods, the Exegetical Study restricts itself primarily to developing the potentialities of the previously introduced semantic, narrative, and rhetorical frames and, on occasion, to the contribution of other categories of narrative and rhetorical frames. Thus the Exegetical Study makes only very limited use, typically in the footnotes, of the contributions of historical and other methods.

c. The Scholarly Resources for the Exegetical Study

The paucity of scholarship specifically focused on the narrative study of the characterization of God in the Gospel of Mark severely limits the opportunities to enter into dialogue with other scholarship. As a consequence, the scholarly resources available for citation in the Exegetical Study are limited, and frequently provide only the opportunity to note areas of convergence and divergence with respect to proposed interpretations.

d. The Order of the Presentation of the Exegetical Study

The Exegetical Study develops the content of the seventy-eight rhetorical contexts containing references to God in the order of their occurrence. The rhetorical contexts in each chapter of the Gospel of Mark appear under separate sectional headings, Mark 1–9 (Chapter 4.1–9) and Mark 10–15 (Chapter 5:1–6) and each rhetorical context receives a subsection heading.

10. Statements of God's Actions and Attributes: The Theological Study (Part 3)

The Theological Study (Part III: Chapters 6–11) employs the methods of semantic, narrative, and rhetorical analysis and description (Part I: Chapters 1–3) and

3. *The Method of Rhetorical Analysis and the Theological Study* 57

assumes the content of the exegesis of the rhetorical contexts (Part II: Chapters 4–5) to formulate statements of God's fifty-six repeated actions and attributes. The remaining sixty-two non-repeated actions and attributes of God occur within the rhetorical contexts of the fifty-six repeated actions and attributes and receive consideration in the statements of the repeated actions and attributes and in concluding summaries of actions and the various categories of attributes. The statements of repeated actions and attributes are formulated for a general audience, avoid technical semantic, narrative, and rhetorical concepts and terms except as noted in the following discussion, and do not maintain the distinction between semantic and narrative causes, conditions, purposes, or results, which appear non-capitalized throughout. The following discussion specifies the format and extent of—and scholarly resources for—the theological statements of God's repeated actions and attributes and the order of the presentation of the Theological Study.

(i) The Format of the Statements of God's Repeated Actions and Attributes The statements of God's repeated actions and attributes consist of an identifying heading, an abbreviated rehearsal of the narrative statements for each occurrence of the repeated action or attribute under consideration, and an elaboration of the content of their rhetorical contexts that identifies and develops linked and emphasized content. Since statements and their parts (heading, rehearsal, and elaboration) frequently are lengthy, the following discussion is limited to a description of the procedure for generating them and provides examples only of those elements that admit to brief illustration.

The heading The heading of the statement consists of an identifying label and an explanatory observation.

The label incorporates the words common to all the individual narrative statements of the repeated action or attribute, followed in parentheses by the Greek predicator and the abbreviated notation of its licensing properties. When the verbs of the narrative statements of the repeated action or attribute differ in tense, the heading uses the present, which is always one of the tenses in such statements. The label places an asterisk before the repeated Greek predicator. These conventions yield the labels, "God sends (*ἀποστέλλω [Aθg])" for God's repeated action of sending because no other words in the individual narrative statements are repeated and the tenses vary, and "God will shorten (*κολοβόω [Ap]) the days" for God's repeated action of shortening because both individual narrative statements use the future tense and have the same referent for the Patient, the days.

The explanatory observation presents the repeated predicator of the action or attribute, the locations of its occurrences, and the locations of the rhetorical contexts containing the occurrences. When all of the rhetorical contexts of the repeated action or attribute either incorporate or are incorporated into the rhetorical contexts of another repeated action or attribute of God, the explanatory observation notes this information together with the heading[s] for the incorporated or incorporating repeated predicator[s], as in the following explanatory observations for God's actions of shortening the days and sending.

> God's shortening (*κολοβόω [Ap], 13:20a, 20b) the days occurs in a single rhetorical context (13:18-20) that is incorporated into those of God saving (*σῴζω [Ap], §6.6), having the Elect (*ἐκλεκτός [B], §7.7), and being prayed to (*προσεύχομαι [acE], §10.7).
>
> God's sending (*ἀποστέλλω [Aθg], 1:2; 9:37; 12:2, 4, 5a, [5b], 6) occurs in four rhetorical contexts (1:1-3; 9:33-37; 12:1-5, 6–8) that incorporate that of God having Slaves (*δοῦλος [B], §9.9).

Where appropriate, the explanatory observations introduce clarifications concerning the semantic (§1.2) and narrative (§2.2) frames evoked by the repeated predicator and information about specific topics introduced in the rhetorical contexts under consideration.

The rehearsal As an aid for recollection, the rehearsal appears in subsection "a" of the statement of the repeated action or attribute. The rehearsal re-presents the main clause (§2.5a) of the narrative statements derived from each occurrence of the repeated action or attribute and, when available, incorporates at least one piece of information from the qualification (§2.5b) or context that accommodates distinctions among the occurrences. When the action or attribute is applicable to God in more than one time (past, present, future), the rehearsal presents these in separate sentences in chronological order; and, when practicable, the rehearsal for each time appears in a single sentence. For economy of presentation, the rehearsal condenses similar material, as in the following rehearsals of God's actions of shortening (*κολοβόω [Ap]) and sending (*ἀποστέλλω [Aθg]).

> God the Lord will shorten the days of the tribulation, which is the condition for God to save some human beings (13:20a), and has as its cause God's Elect (13:20b).
>
> God sent Slaves to the Farmers (the Chief Priests, Scribes, and Elders) for the purpose of taking some of the fruit of the vineyard (God's people) of God (12:2, 4, 5a, [5b]).
>
> God sends John the Messenger before God's (with Jesus') face to prepare God's (with Jesus') way (1:2; cf. Mal 3:1; Exod 23:20), Jesus (9:37), and Jesus the Beloved Son last of all to the Farmers for the purpose of taking some of the fruit of the vineyard (12:6).

The elaboration The elaboration begins in subsection "b" of the statement of the repeated action or attribute. The elaboration uses the information, relationships, perspectives for evaluation, and expectations accommodated by predicator repetition rhetorical frames to identify and develop in one or more sub-sections various elements of linked and emphasized content. The elaborations develop repetitions of content within the narrative statements, repetitions of relationships between the action or attribute and other content within the rhetorical contexts, and subsidiary considerations, especially concerning instances of narrative coordination (§3.2b) or the repetition of other words in two or more of the rhetorical contexts. When the rhetorical contexts of semantically coordinated actions and attributes (§3.2a) do not overlap, the discussion of their semantic coordination appears only in the concluding sub-section of the statement of the second-occurring action or attribute. This permits a consideration of all the content associated with both statements. When the rhetorical contexts of semantically coordinated actions and attributes overlap, the implications of the semantic coordination receive development in context, and a concluding discussion, if required, considers the content of their non-overlapping rhetorical context[s]. Since the sub-sections of elaborations require recourse to the content of the Exegetical Study, no example can be provided.

(ii) The Extent of the Statements of God's Repeated Actions and Attributes The statements of God's repeated actions and attributes are neither comprehensive nor exhaustive. The sheer volume of content for consideration afforded by predicator repetition rhetorical frames prohibits anything more than the presentation of a few of the more emphasized developments for a majority of the repeated actions and attributes. On occasion, the contribution of other categories of narrative and rhetorical frames requires its own consideration, providing further constraints on the topics for elaboration. As a consequence, the elaborations of repeated actions and attributes with three or more occurrences typically do not address all significant developments, especially those pertaining to half or fewer of the rhetorical contexts. Thus the elaborations, in general, stand ready for further development.

(iii) The Scholarly Resources for the Statements of God's Repeated Actions and Attributes The extreme paucity of critical scholarship specifically concerning the rhetoric of the characterization of God in the Gospel of Mark limits the possibilities of citation and dialogue. When such scholarship is available, it focuses primarily on specific repeated actions and occasionally on specific attributes of God. As a consequence, the Theological Study provides only limited citations of scholarship, and, in most cases, these are constrained to notices of similar or dissimilar interpretations.

(iv) The Order of the Presentation of the Theological Study The Theological Study presents the fifty-six statements of God's repeated actions and attributes grouped in alphabetical order according to the thematic role referenced by God (first Agent, then Benefactive, then Content, and so on) and, within each group, in the order of the increasing relative emphasis according to predicator repetition rhetorical

frames.[10] Because God's repeated Benefactive attributes account for thirty of the fifty-six statements and because the statements associated with each of the five categories of the Benefactive role (§§1.6a, 1.6b) exhibit distinctive patterns of development, the presentation resolves the statements of God's benefaction into five groups arranged alphabetically according to the type of benefaction (agentive, innate, originating, recipient, and reciprocal) and, within each sub-group, in the order of increasing relative emphasis. The presentation incorporates a discussion of all occurrences, both repeated and non-repeated, with God as the referent of the same thematic role and of each category of benefaction. When the thematic role is associated with one or more statements of God's repeated actions and attributes, the discussion of all occurrences with that thematic role appears after the statement of the repeated action or attribute with the greatest relative emphasis. The discussion of all occurrences of that thematic role identifies significant patterns of development for all or many of the actions or attributes in that group. When no predicators with God as the referent of a thematic role are repeated (God as Goal, Instrument, and Theme), the discussion of all occurrences constitutes the only focused presentation on that category of attribute. The Theological Study concludes with a consideration of the possibilities for its further development. This yields the following order of presentation: God as Agent (Chapter 6), Agentive Benefactive (Chapter 7), Innate and Originating Benefactive (Chapter 8), Recipient and Reciprocal Benefactive (Chapter 9), Content, Experiencer, Goal, and Instrument (Chapter 10), and Patient, Source, Theme, and Topic, Proposals, and Conclusion (Chapter 11).

---

10. As the Theological Study demonstrates, other categories of rhetorical frames have the potential to accommodate developments that permit less frequently occurring predicators with God as the referent of the same argument to evoke rhetorical contexts that play a more significant role in the characterization of God than rhetorical contexts evoked by more frequently repeated predicators with God as the referent of the same argument. This is readily apparent when less frequently occurring actions and attributes receive more lengthy and detailed statement than more frequently repeated actions and attributes. Although rhetorical frames provide numerous alternative means of asserting relative emphasis, the Theological Study's primary dependence on the potentialities of predicator repetition rhetorical frames recommends their use in determining relative emphasis and presenting repeated actions and attributes in the their proposed order of increasing relative emphasis.

Part II

THE EXEGETICAL STUDY

THE SEMANTIC AND NARRATIVE ANALYSIS OF THE CONTENT OF RHETORICAL CONTEXTS

Chapter 4

EXEGESIS OF THE RHETORICAL CONTEXTS IN MARK 1-9

This chapter provides an exegetical study of the forty rhetorical contexts containing references to God in Mark 1-9. These rhetorical contexts present 128 actions and attributes of God.

1. Mark 1

a. 1:1-3

God (with Jesus the Christ and Son) has/is the Topic of the gospel (εὐαγγέλιον [B/T], 1:1) that has its beginning with the sending of John the Messenger. God has Jesus the Christ (*χριστός [B], 1:1) and Son (*υἱός [B], 1:1). God was the Agent of writing (*γέγραπται [Ace], 1:2), "Look, I send my Messenger before your face ..." (Mal 3:1; Exod 23:20; Isa 40:3 LXX). God has Isaiah the Prophet (*προφητής [B], 1:2) in/by (Locative/Instrument) whom God wrote. God sends (*ἀποστέλλω [Aθg], 1:2) John the Messenger before the face of God (with Jesus). This sending initiates the present of the story time. Narrative overlays interpret God's sending of Elijah before God's face (Mal 3:1) prior to the coming of the great and terrible day of the Lord (Mal 4:5) in terms of God's sending of John the Messenger before Jesus' face (1:2) prior to God's initiation of the end times (1:10).[1] The realization in the present of what God was the Agent of writing in the past highlights the predicative capacity of what was written (§1.2c). God has John the Messenger (*ἄγγελος [B], 1:2) whom God sends to prepare the way of God (with Jesus). God (with Jesus) has the face (πρόσωπον [B], 1:2) before which God sends John the Messenger. Jesus' co-benefaction of face (v. 2) ensures that what God wrote is addressed specifically

---

1. Although what was written is constituted by a series of scripture quotes from both the Pentateuch (Exod 23:20) and the Prophets (Isa 40:3; Mal 3:1), the following context (1:4-8) develops only the Prophetic references in relation to John as Messenger fulfilling Elijah's role (Mal 4:5). The following context's (1:4-8) depiction of John wearing Elijah's clothing (1:6; cf. 2 Kgs 1:8) and Jesus' subsequent reference to John as Elijah (9:11-13) confirm the identification of John the Messenger with Elijah the Prophet.

to Jesus, thereby establishing a direct communication relationship from God to Jesus.[2] God (with Jesus) has the way (*ὁδός [B], 1:2; cf. Mal 3:1; Exod 23:20) that John the Messenger prepares. God (with Jesus) the Lord has the way (*ὁδός [B], 1:3) that John's addressees are to prepare, and God (with Jesus) has the paths (τρίβος [B], 1:3) that John's addressees are to make straight (Isa 40:3). "Way" evokes its association to the eschatological restoration of Israel proclaimed by Isaiah, which again anticipates God's initiation of the end-times in relation to the advent of Jesus.[3] Narrative overlays that assert God's and Jesus' co-benefaction of face (1:2), way (1:2, 3), and paths (v. 3) and co-use of the designation "Lord" associate these divine attributes with Jesus. What was written places the actions of John (preparing, calling out) and of his addressees (preparing, making straight) under God's direction. This context associates God's (with Jesus') benefaction of the gospel (εὐαγγέλιον [B]) with content about God and Jesus as Topic (εὐαγγέλιον [T]).

b. 1:4-8

God has the forgiveness (*ἄφεσις [bB], 1:4) of sins, which is the Purpose of the baptism of repentance proclaimed by John. "Repentance" receives interpretation as a change in mindset that accommodates the recognition of one's sins and sinfulness. Such repentance is the condition for God's forgiveness. God has recipient benefaction of the sins (*ἁμαρτία [bB], 1:4) requiring God's forgiveness. God has recipient benefaction of the sins (*ἁμαρτία [bB], 1:5) confessed by those whom John baptizes. "Confessing" receives interpretation as an appropriate consequence of repentance and its recognition of sins. John's action of baptizing and the people's action of confessing are contemporaneous, which further identifies repentance as the condition for being baptized by John.[4] God has the Holy Spirit (*πνεῦμα [B], 1:8) by which Jesus will baptize. Repetition of "proclaim" relates the Content of John's statements about the baptism of repentance for the forgiveness of sins with those about the contrast between John who baptizes by (Instrument) water and Jesus the Mightier One who will baptize by (Instrument) God's Holy Spirit. This identifies God's Holy Spirit as the Instrument of God's forgiveness. Whereas Mark never links God and water, God's necessary involvement in Jesus' action of baptizing by God's Spirit will accomplish the baptism of repentance for the forgiveness of sins proclaimed by John.

---

2. The contribution of the direct communication relationships in 1:1-3 to the overall narrative development of Mark receives development in Danove, "Mark 1,1-15 as Introduction," 127–48.

3. Timothy C. Gray, *The Temple in the Gospel of Mark: A Study in Its Narrative Role* (Grand Rapids, MI: Baker Academic, 2008), 14.

4. Boring, *Mark*, 42, proposes that John proclaims a baptism that offers God's forgiveness of sins and calls the recipient to repentance. Although there is nothing in Mark that would deny the interpretation of this baptism as a call for further repentance, God's forgiveness (3:29) and forgiving (2:5, 7, 9; 3:28; 4:12; 11:25b) elsewhere in Mark consistently is conditioned; and the proposed condition in this context is repentance.

c. 1:9-11

God tears (*σχίζω [Ap], 1:10) the heavens, which Jesus sees immediately on coming up from the water after being baptized by John. God's tearing of the heavens, which undoes in part God's making of the heavens (Gen 1:1, 6-8), begins the dissolution of the present created order and initiates the end times, as anticipated in the opening scripture quote (1:2-3; cf. Mal 3:1; 4:5; Isa 40:3).[5] God has the Spirit (*πνεῦμα [B], 1:10) that Jesus sees coming down onto him like a dove after being baptized by John. The coming of God's Spirit, a primary characteristic of the end times, strengthens the proposed eschatological significance of God's tearing.[6] God has the voice (*φωνή [B], 1:11) from the heavens that addresses Jesus with the statement, "You are my beloved Son; in you I delight" (1:11; cf. Ps 2:7; Isa 42:1). God has Jesus the Son (*υἱός [B], 1:11) and loves (*ἀγαπητός [Ec/Apb], 1:11) and delights (εὐδοκέω [Ec], 1:11) in Jesus the Son. This statement by God's voice, which establishes a direct communication relationship from God to Jesus, receives interpretation as God's affirmation of Jesus' status as God's Son.[7] The absence of an explicit statement that other characters see these events or hear God's voice is taken to indicate that Jesus is their sole Experiencer. The sequence of events accommodates the interpretation that God's tearing of the heavens is the condition for the coming of God's Spirit onto Jesus and for God's voice to address Jesus from the heavens.[8]

---

5. God's tearing develops Mark's overarching eschatological perspective concerning the narrated events of the Gospel as introduced in the overlay of John in the scripture quote concerning Elijah (1:2; cf. Mal 3:1) whom God intends to send before the great and terrible day of the Lord (Mal 4:5). According to Moloney, *Mark*, 36, "in those days" also highlights the eschatological nature of Jesus' coming.

6. The pouring out of God's Spirit is a characteristic of God's future salvation (Joel 2:28-29; Isa 44:3; Ezek 36:26-27; Zech 12:10; 13:1).

7. Rudolf Bultmann, *The History of the Synoptic Tradition*, trans. John Marsh, rev. edn. (New York: Harper & Row, 1968), 247-9, interprets the voice's statement as the consecration of Jesus as the Messiah: cf. Wilfrid Harrington, *Mark* (Wilmington, DE: Michael Glazier, 1979), 6. Collins, *Mark: A Commentary*, 150, interprets God's voice as appointing Jesus as Messiah when the Spirit comes onto him. The proposed interpretation of the statement as an affirmation, however, recognizes that by 1:11 Jesus already has been attributed with fulfilling the role previously reserved to God (1:2; cf. Mal 3:1), having God's face and way (1:2; cf. Exod 23:20; Mal 3:1) and way, paths, and title "Lord" (1:3; cf. Isa 40:3 LXX), and being stronger than John (1:7): cf. C. Clifton Black, *Mark* (ANTC; Nashville, TN: Abingdon, 2011), 60; R. Alan Culpepper, *Mark* (S&HBC; Macon, GA: Smyth & Helwys, 2007), 50; M. Eugene Boring, "Markan Christology: God-Language for Jesus?," *NTS* 45 (1999), 463; and Robert H. Gundry, *Mark: A Commentary on His Apology for the Cross* (Grand Rapids, MI: Eerdmans, 1993), 49, 53.

8. Marcus, *Mark 1-8*, 165, interprets the tearing of the heavens as the condition for the pouring out of the Spirit; and Moloney, *Mark*, 36, states that the tearing of the heavens promises a communication from above: cf. C. E. B. Cranfield, *The Gospel According to St. Mark* (CGTC; Cambridge: Cambridge University Press, 1959), 53; and Morna D. Hooker, *The Message of*

d. 1:12-13

God has the Spirit (*πνεῦμα [B], 1:12) that casts Jesus out into the desert where Satan tests Jesus for forty days. This action by God's Spirit is interpreted to reflect God's intent for Jesus to be tested in preparation for his ministry.[9] God has the Angels (*ἄγγελος [B], 1:13) that serve Jesus in the desert.

e. 1:14-15

God (with Jesus) has/is the Topic of the gospel (*εὐαγγέλιον [B/T], 1:14) that Jesus proclaims after John is handed over. God has the reign (*βασιλεία [B], 1:15) that has drawn near, that is, has completed its approach and, as a consequence, is at hand.[10] God (with Jesus) has/is the Topic of gospel (*εὐαγγέλιον [B/T], 1:15) in/by (Topic/Instrument) which human beings are to believe. The fulfilling of the time and the drawing near of God's reign are proposed as the propitious environment for human beings to repent and believe in/by the gospel of/about God (with Jesus). This context associates God's (with Jesus') benefaction of the gospel (εὐαγγέλιον [B]) with content about God and Jesus as Topic (εὐαγγέλιον [T]).

f. 1:21-28

God (with Jesus, 11:28) has the authority (*ἐξουσία [B], 1:22) apparent in Jesus' teaching. The context contrasts Jesus who teaches as one having God's authority and the Scribes who do not teach as ones having God's authority. God has Jesus the Holy One (ἅγιος [B], 1:24) who has God's authority. The designation "Holy One of God" receives interpretation as a messianic title highlighting Jesus' exercise of God's authority over demonic spirits.[11] God (with Jesus) has the authority (*ἐξουσία [B], 1:27) associated with Jesus' new teaching and manifest when Jesus commands unclean spirits and they obey him. The context associates God's (with Jesus') authority both with Jesus' teaching and with Jesus' action of commanding unclean spirits.

Mark (London: Epworth, 1983), 11. Abbott, *Introduction to Narrative*, 41, discusses the manner in which the sequencing of events in narratives gives the impression of a sequencing of cause and effect.

9. See Larry W. Hurtado, *Mark* (GNC; Cambridge: Harper & Row, 1983), 6.

10. This interpretation follows that of Aloysius M. Ambrozic, *The Hidden Kingdom: A Redaction-Critical Study of the References to the Kingdom of God in Mark's Gospel* (CBQMS 2; Washington, D.C.: Catholic University of America Press, 1972), 7. Similar interpretations from various approaches appear in Werner H. Kelber, *The Kingdom in Mark: A New Place and a New Time* (Philadelphia: Fortress, 1974), 9; and Dan O. Via, Jr., *Kerygma and Comedy in the New Testament: A Structuralist Approach to Hermeneutic* (Philadelphia: Fortress, 1975), 82.

11. Max Botner, "The Messiah Is 'the Holy One': ὁ ἅγιος τοῦ θεοῦ as a Messianic Title in Mark 1:24," *JBL* 136, no. 2 (2017): 417–33.

g. 1:35-38

God is prayed to (*προσεύχομαι [acE], 1:35) by Jesus in a deserted place the morning after Jesus heals many having illnesses and casts out many demons (1:34) and before Jesus goes elsewhere to proclaim. Jesus identifies proclaiming as the Purpose for his coming forth (1:38).

2. Mark 2

a. 2:1-12

God is the Topic of the faith (*πίστις [ecT], 2:5) of the paralyzed man and those carrying him. The apparent Content of their faith concerning God is that Jesus is able to enact God's healing of the paralyzed man. Jesus interprets the actions of the paralyzed man and those carrying him as demonstrations of their faith. God forgives (*ἀφίημι [Apb], 2:5) the sins of the paralyzed man. God has recipient benefaction of these sins (*ἁμαρτία [bB], 2:5) as covenantal debts owed to God (§1.2b). The actions of the paralyzed man and those carrying him are the apparent basis for Jesus to state that God forgives the paralyzed man's sins. God is not blasphemed (*βλασφημέω [apB], 2:7) by Jesus when Jesus tells the paralyzed man that his sins are forgiven. God (with Jesus the Son of Man, 2:10-11) is able to forgive (*ἀφίημι [Apb], 2:7) sins for human beings. God has recipient benefaction of these sins (*ἁμαρτία [bB], 2:7). Jesus' recognition that the Scribes are discussing in their hearts that Jesus is blaspheming by (Instrument) his spirit specifies "spirit," when licensing a Benefactive, as the means of cognition and discernment.[12] God forgives (*ἀφίημι [Apb], 2:9) the sins of the paralyzed man. God has recipient benefaction of these sins (*ἁμαρτία [bB], 2:9). God (with Jesus, 11:28) has the authority (*ἐξουσία [B], 2:10) by which God (with Jesus the Son of Man) forgives sins on the earth. This identifies Jesus the Son of Man as the instrument of God's forgiveness. God has recipient benefaction of these sins (*ἁμαρτία [bB], 2:10). God is glorified (δοξάζω [aE], 2:12) by all for the man's healing and the forgiveness of his sins. Glorifying God is the appropriate response insofar as Jesus heals the man by God's authority.

b. 2:23-28

God has the commandments about the Sabbath (Exod 34:21; cf. Exod 20:10; 23:12; 31:14, 15; 35:2; Lev 23:3; Deut 5:14) that permit (*ἔξεστιν [vi-iB], 2:24) the making of a way and the plucking of heads of grain on the Sabbath. God had the house (*οἶκος [bB], 2:26) which David entered when he and his companions were hungry and in which David ate the bread of offering and gave it to his companions. God has the commandments about the bread of offering (Lev 24:5-9) that permitted (*ἔξεστιν [vi-iB], 2:26) David to do these things. This statement interprets Jesus'

---

12. Marcus, *Mark 1-8*, 217, interprets Jesus' spirit as Instrument.

assertion that it is not permitted for anyone but the Priests to eat the bread to summarize the literal interpretation attributed to the Pharisees. The context draws a parallel between Jesus' Disciples making a path and plucking heads of grain on the Sabbath and David entering God's house and eating the bread when he was hungry.[13] The point of contention is not whether God has the commandments about the Sabbath and bread of offering but how these commandments are to be interpreted and applied. While the Pharisees interpret the commandments about the Sabbath to prohibit the actions of Jesus' Disciples, scripture apparently interpreted the commandments about the bread of offering to condone David's actions (1 Sam 21:2-7).[14] God is the Agent by whom the Sabbath came to be (*γίνομαι [pA], 2:27a) and the human being [came to be] (*γίνομαι [pA], [2:27b]). These were among God's actions in creating (Gen 1:26-27; 2:2-3). The human being is the Cause of the Sabbath coming to be, whereas the Sabbath is not the Cause of the human being coming to be. Thus the Cause of God's action in the coming to be of the Sabbath ultimately is God's previous action in the coming to be of the human being (Gen 1:262:3). The Result of the human being's status as Cause of the Sabbath is that Jesus as the Son of Man is Lord of the Sabbath. The parallel between the Disciples and David has three implications: God's commandments pertaining to the Sabbath are to be interpreted and applied in a manner that accommodates the exigencies of human need; Jesus as Son of Man has dominion over the interpretation and application of the Sabbath regulations; and Jesus' interpretation and application of God's commandments is consonant with scriptural precedents and so, implicitly, with God's intended interpretation and application of the commandments. The relationship between Jesus' Disciples and David proposes Jesus as superior to both.

3. Mark 3

a. 3:1-6

God has the commandments (Exod 20:10; 31:14, 15; 35:2; Lev 23:3; Deut 5:14) that permit (*ἔξεστιν [vi-iB], 3:4) the doing of good rather than evil and the saving of life rather than killing on the Sabbath. The evoked commandments recall Jesus' previous dispute about what is permitted on the Sabbath (2:23–28), and Jesus' assertion about doing good and saving life provides a general statement of his principle for interpreting and applying God's commandments.

---

13. Although Mary Healy, *The Gospel of Mark* (CCSS; Grand Rapids, MI: Baker Academic, 2008), 65, finds in Jesus' statement an implied comparison of Jesus to David who also was anointed (1 Sam 16:13), the primary comparison concerns the actions of Jesus' Disciples and the actions of David.

14. 1 Sam 21:2-7 does not condemn David's actions as violations of the law: cf. Sherman E. Johnson, *A Commentary on the Gospel According to St. Mark* (London: Adam & Charles Black, 1960), 67.

b. 3:7-12

God has Jesus the Son (*υἱός [B], 3:11) before whom unclean spirits fall down when they see him and who commands the unclean spirits that they not make him known.

c. 3:13-19

God (with Jesus, 11:28) has the authority (*ἐξουσία [B], 3:15) to cast out demons, which Jesus intends the Twelve to have as well.

d. 3:20-35

God forgives (*ἀφίημι [Apb], 3:28) for human beings all the sins and blasphemies that they may blaspheme. The use of the present tense in this and following occurrences of "forgive" reflects the interpretation that God's offer to forgive sins and blasphemies is perennial. God has recipient benefaction of all sinful actions (*ἁμάρτημα [bB], 3:28) and all blasphemies (βλασφημία [bB], 3:28) against God as debts owed to God. God (with others) is blasphemed (*βλασφημέω [apB], 3:28) by human beings. God (with the Holy Spirit) is blasphemed (*βλασφημέω [apB], 3:29) insofar as God has the Holy Spirit (*πνεῦμα [B], 3:29) that human beings may blaspheme. God has the forgiveness (*ἄφεσις [Bb], 3:29) that those blaspheming the Holy Spirit never have. God has the everlasting (into the coming age) recipient benefaction of the sinful action (*ἁμάρτημα [bB], 3:29) of human beings who blaspheme the Holy Spirit. Although God forgives all sinful actions and blasphemies for human beings (v. 28), those blaspheming God's Holy Spirit never have God's forgiveness (v. 29) because they blaspheme and so reject the Holy Spirit, the Instrument of God's forgiveness (1:8; cf. §4.1b). The accusation by the Scribes from Jerusalem that Jesus has an unclean spirit/Beelzebul (3:22) is the Cause of Jesus' teaching about God's action of forgiving. Since Jesus has the Holy Spirit (1:10) and not an unclean spirit, these Scribes blaspheme both Jesus and the Holy Spirit and so will not have God's forgiveness as long as they hold to their blasphemy against the Holy Spirit. God has the will (θέλημα [B], 3:35) whose enactment makes one Jesus' brother and sister and mother.

4. Mark 4

a. 4:10-12

God gives (*δίδωμι [Aθg], 4:11) the secret of God's reign to those around Jesus with the Twelve. The action is deemed to begin in the present and continue into the future for those committed to Jesus' teaching. God's action of giving does not establish but recognizes the distinction between the "insiders" (those around Jesus with the Twelve) and the "outsiders" (those for whom everything happens in/by parables). Both the insiders and the outsiders hear Jesus' parable about the sower

(4:1-9), but only the insiders pursue its interpretation by asking Jesus (4:10).[15] God has the reign (*βασιλεία [B], 4:11), of/about (Benefactive/Topic) which there is a secret. This secret qualifies the reign as mysterious, hidden, and requiring revelation; and it grants recipients the capacity to perceive and understand its presence, especially in the actions and teachings of Jesus.[16] Those perceiving Jesus' actions, understanding his teachings, and turning satisfy the condition for God's forgiveness.[17] God does not forgive (*ἀφίημι [Apb], 4:12; cf. Isa 6:9-10) for those seeing but not perceiving, hearing but not understanding, and so not turning. The greater context (4:1-16) clarifies that God's giving of the secret opens the possibility for insiders to perceive and understand that the one sowing sows the seed/word on all types of soil/people, that the ultimate production of the seed/word depends not on the one sowing or the seed/word but on the soil/people into which it is sown, and that the instances of abundant production (thirty-, sixty-, and a hundredfold) are manifestations of God's reign which grows despite many occasions of failure.

b. 4:24-25

God will measure out (μετρέω [Aθg], 4:24) to human beings according to the measure by which they measure out, that is, employ the secret of God's reign to perceive and understand Jesus' teachings and action, turn, and receive forgiveness (4:11). God will add (προστίθημι [Aθg], 4:24) to human beings according to the measure by which they measure out. God will give (*δίδωμι [Aθg], 4:25) to those having, that is, having employed the secret. God will take up (αἴρω [Aθs], 4:25) from those not having the little that they have. This and the related contextual actions of God will occur at the end of the present age and are associated with God's end-time judgment of human beings.[18] Thus God's end-time judgment will

---

15. Robert H. Stein, *Mark* (BECNT; Grand Rapids, MI: Baker Academic, 2008), 207, states that those around Jesus with the Twelve are self-selected.

16. Suzanne Watts Henderson, *Christology and Discipleship in the Gospel of Mark* (SNTSMS 135; Cambridge: Cambridge University Press, 2006), 117, proposes that the secret of God's reign "provides an interpretive lens for viewing [all things]."

17. Here "turning" is interpreted to designate the same action as "repenting" in relation to the forgiveness of sins (1:4).

18. God's actions in 4:24-25 typically receive interpretation as focusing specifically on the implications of attentiveness to Jesus' teachings in the present: cf. Stein, *Mark*, 227; Healy, *Mark*, 90; Martin, *Mark*, 91; and Harrington, *Mark*, 60-1. Although the entirety of 4:1-34 focuses on Jesus' teachings about God's reign, the repetition of "has ears to hear, let him/her hear" (ἔχει ὦτα ἀκούειν ἀκουέτω) at the end of Jesus' first statement of the parable of the sower (4:9) and at the end of the parable's explanation and further comments (4:23) is taken to signal the conclusion of Jesus' teaching about the need for disciples to apply the secret of God's reign to perceive, understand, and turn (4:1-23): cf. Robert A. Guelich, *Mark 1–8:26* (WBC 34A; Dallas: Word Books, 1989), 232. The command to be careful and its associated comments using the future tense of verbs (4:24-25) that introduce parables

respond to (measure out) and exceed (add) what human beings do with the secret that God gives to them (4:11).

c. 4:26-29

God has the reign (*βασιλεία [B], 4:26) that is like the seed growing slowly and steadily until the harvest without the sower understanding how it does so.

d. 4:30-32

God has the reign (*βασιλεία [B], 4:30) that is like the seed of the mustard plant which, when sown on the earth, is the smallest of seeds but becomes the largest of plants so that birds may dwell under its shadow.

e. 4:35-41

God is the Topic of the faith (*πίστις [ecT], 4:40) that Jesus' Disciples do not yet have. The apparent Content of the faith that the Disciples are lacking is that God is able to command even the wind and the sea through Jesus as instrument (4:41).[19] A further element of this faith is that Jesus is concerned about the welfare of his Disciples and is able to act decisively for their welfare. The context contrasts being characterized by this faith and being cowardly.

5. Mark 5

a. 5:1-13

God the Most High has Jesus the Son (*υἱός [B], 5:7) who tells Legion to come out of the man. God is most high (ὕψιστος [P], 5:7). God is not the Instrument by whom Legion compels Jesus to swear (ὁρκίζω [aec-I], 5:7) that he will not torment Legion. This, the only attempt by a character in Mark to use God as Instrument, fails.

---

focusing on the consummation of God's reign (4:26-34) then are taken to concern the implications of properly perceiving, understanding, and turning (measuring out) for the end-time disposition of human beings: cf. Ben Witherington III, *The Gospel of Mark: A Socio-Rhetorical Commentary* (Grand Rapids, MI: Eerdmans, 2001), 170; and Culpepper, *Mark*, 147. Hurtado, *Mark*, 62, relates the present and end-time implications of these statements.

19. Bastiaan M. F. van Iersel and A. J. M. Linmans, "The Storm on the Lake, Mk iv 35–41 and Mt viii 18–27 in the Light of Form-Criticism, 'Redaktionsgeschichte' and Structural Analysis," in *Miscellanea Neotestamentica*, ed. T. Baarda, A. F. J. Klijn, and W. C. van Unnik, vol. 2 (NovTSup; Leiden: Brill, 1978), 32, would interpret Jesus' actions in calming the storm as an exercise of his own divine authority.

b. 5:18-20

God (with Jesus) the Lord does (*ποιέω [Ap], 5:19) for the former demoniac many things. The realization of the Benefactive (for you/the former demoniac) grants it special emphasis. The many things include the going forth of Legion from the man (5:8, 13) and his resultant state of being clothed and in his right mind (5:15). God (with Jesus) is merciful (ἐλεέω [Eb], 5:19) to the former demoniac in relation to these many things. The coordination of "doing" and "being merciful" (5:19) interprets the actions of God (with Jesus) as acts of mercy. The man responds to Jesus' command to announce what God (with Jesus) the Lord has done for him by proclaiming what Jesus has done for him.

c. 5:25-34

God is the Topic of faith (*πίστις [ecT], 5:34) of the woman with the flow of blood. The apparent Content of her faith concerning God is that God is able to heal her from her affliction through Jesus as instrument, even if she only touches Jesus' garment. Jesus' statement that the woman's faith has saved her identifies her faith and resulting action as the further Instrument of her healing.

d. 5:35-43

God is to be believed in (*πιστεύω [ecT], 5:36) by Jairus. The apparent Content that Jairus is to believe concerning God is that God is able to save his daughter through Jesus as instrument, even though others deem his daughter dead.

6. Mark 6

a. 6:1-6a

God has the wisdom (σοφία [B], 6:2) given to Jesus and apparent in Jesus' teachings. God gives (*δίδωμι [Aθg], 6:2) this wisdom to Jesus. God is the Agent by whom the powerful deeds come to be (*γίνομαι [pA], 6:2b) through Jesus' hands. This identifies Jesus' hands (and so Jesus himself) as the Instrument of God's action. God has the Prophet (*προφήτης [B], 6:4) dishonored in his hometown, among his own kin, and in his own house. The context proposes that Jesus is one such Prophet, that his teachings manifest God's wisdom and his actions manifest God's powerful deeds, and that God's benefaction of a Prophet can be verified by the wisdom of God in his teachings and the powerful deeds that can only come to be by God. Jesus' efficacy as Instrument of God's action, however, can be limited by unbelief.

b. 6:6b-13

God (with Jesus, 11:28) has authority (*ἐξουσία [B], 6:7) over unclean spirits, which Jesus gives to the Twelve. The Twelve exercise this authority in casting out many demons (6:13), which establishes their (with Jesus') recipient benefaction of God's authority and identifies them (with Jesus) as the instrument of God's action.

4. Exegesis of the Rhetorical Contexts in Mark 1–9   73

c. 6:14-16

God has a Prophet (*προφήτης [B], 6:15a) whom some say Jesus is. God has the Prophets (*προφήτης [B], 6:15b) of whom Jesus is said to be one.

d. 6:17-20

God has the commandments about marriage to a living brother's wife (Lev 18:16; 20:21) that do not permit (*ἔξεστιν [vi-iB], 6:18) Herod to have as his wife Herodias, the wife of his brother.

e. 6:35-44

God is blessed (*εὐλογέω [aE], 6:41) by Jesus for the five loaves of bread that Jesus takes, breaks, and gives to his Disciples to distribute to the five thousand men to eat and for the two fish that Jesus divides for all.

f. 6:45-52

God is prayed to (*προσεύχομαι [acE], 6:46) by Jesus on the mountain after Jesus bids farewell to his Disciples and dismisses the crowd participating in the miraculous meal (6:41-44) and before he walks on the sea (6:48-50).

7. Mark 7

a. 7:6-13

God has the Holy Spirit by which (Instrument) Isaiah prophesied (προφητεύω [aci-iB], 7:6). God was the Agent of writing (*γέγραπται [Ace], 7:6), "This people honors me with their lips …" (Isa 29:13). Narrative overlays identify "this people" as the Pharisees and some Scribes from Jerusalem (7:1). God's action of writing is associated with Isaiah's prophesying. Jesus' statement of what God wrote establishes a direct communication relationship of condemnation from God to these Pharisees and Scribes. Since what God wrote expresses God's displeasure with these Pharisees and Scribes, it does not admit to interpretation as God's intent for them. It does confirm, however, the predicative capacity of what was written. God is honored (τιμάω [aE], 7:6) by this people with their lips. God is the Source from which this people's heart is distant (ἀπέχω [θS], 7:6). God is worshipped (σέβομαι [aE], 7:7) by this people to no effect. The Pharisees and Scribes honor only with their lips, have their heart distant, and worship to no effect when they teach as teachings the commands of human beings.

"Teachings" has the potential to evoke scriptural antecedents that concern instruction in God's law that should not be abandoned (Prov 2:17), what God pours out like prophecy (Sir 24:33), and what is to be exhibited (Sir 39:8). Thus teaching as teachings the commands of human beings constitutes a direct assault on God's action and intent.

God has the commandment (ἐντολή [B], 7:8) that the Pharisees and Scribes leave behind when they cling to the tradition of human beings. God has the commandment (ἐντολή [B], 7:9) that the Pharisees and Scribes reject so that their tradition (i.e., the tradition of the Elders, 7:5) may stand. Jesus' example of such leaving behind and rejecting contrasts what Moses said about honoring one's parents (7:10; cf. Exod 20:12; Deut 5:16) and not speaking ill of them (7:10; cf. Exod 21:17; Lev 20:9), and what the Pharisees and Scribes say about the gift. God has recipient benefaction of the gift (δῶρον [bB], 7:11) that the Pharisees and Scribes say precludes its use for the benefit of one's parents. God has the word (λόγος [B], 7:13) that the teaching of the Pharisees and Scribes renders null. The context interprets God's word as synonymous with God's commandments.

b. 7:17-23

God has recipient benefaction of the blasphemies (*βλασφημία [bB], 7:22) that come out of human beings. The context associates these blasphemies with improper thoughts, immorality, theft, murder, adultery, greed, wickedness, deceit, sensuality, envy, arrogance, and foolishness (7:21-22).

8. Mark 8

This discussion of the rhetorical contexts within Mark 8 includes content concerning 9:1, which is a constituent of the concluding rhetorical context (8:31–9:1).

a. 8:1-9

God is given thanks (*εὐχαριστέω [acE], 8:6) by Jesus for the seven loaves of bread that Jesus takes, breaks, and gives to his Disciples to distribute to the four thousand to eat. God is blessed (*εὐλογέω [aE], 8:7) by Jesus for the few fish that Jesus says to distribute.

b. 8:11-14

God is the Source of the sign (*σημεῖον [S], 8:11) from heaven, which the Pharisees seek from Jesus, testing him, and to which Jesus responds with a sigh. Scriptural antecedents interpret the requested sign as God's validation that Jesus' statements and actions are of God.[20] God is the Source of the sign (*σημεῖον [S], 8:12a,) that

---

20. Such validating signs may be found in Deut 13:2; 1 Sam 2:34; 10:1-8; Isa 7:1-14. A discussion of their significance appears in Evald Lövestam, *Jesus and "this Generation": A New Testament Study*, trans. Moira Linnarud (CBNT 25; Stockholm: Almqvist & Wiksell, 1995), 21–3; cf. Guelich, *Mark 1–8:26*, 414; and Olof Linton, "The Demand for a Sign from Heaven (Mk 8,11-12 and Parallels)," *ST* 19 (1965): 112-29.

this generation seeks from Jesus. God does not give (*δίδωμι [Aθg], 8:12) the requested sign to this generation, which Jesus asserts in the form of a prophetic statement.²¹ God is the Source of the sign (*σημεῖον [S], 8:12b) that God does not give to this generation. Jesus' statements identify the Pharisees with "this generation" which is portrayed as adulterous and sinful (8:38), unbelieving (9:19), and not passing away until Jesus' predictions of the end times happen (13:30).²² The apparent reason for God not giving the requested sign is that the Pharisees do not recognize that Jesus' previous teachings (2:17, 25-28; 3:4; 7:6-13) and actions (2:16; 3:5) in their presence are God's validating signs, which obviates the need for a further sign.

c. 8:27-30

God has the Prophets (*προφήτης [B], 8:28) one of whom is said to be Jesus. God has Jesus the Christ (*χριστός [B], 8:29).

d. 8:31–9:1

God has the scriptures by which it is necessary (*δεῖ [vi-iB], 8:31) that Jesus the Son of Man suffer much, be rejected by the Elders, the Chief Priests, and the Scribes, be killed, and after three days rise. There is no specific scriptural antecedent for this statement.²³ Subsequent events (14:43–16:6) confirm the predictive potential of what was written in God's scriptures about Jesus the Son of Man. God has the things (*τά [B], 8:33), which are the Content that Peter does not think. "Thinking the things of God" receives two complementary interpretations. On the one hand, Peter's rebuke of Jesus indicates that Peter (Experiencer) is refusing to

---

21. Rudolf Pesch, *Das Markusevangelium*, 2 vols (HtKNT II/1-2; Freiburg: Herder, 1976–77), 1:408, discusses the prophetic characteristics of Jesus' sign and following statement.

22. "This generation" has as its scriptural referent the sinful children of God and the bent and perverted generation that deals falsely with God (Deut 32:5) and the perverted generation and faithless children from whom God will hide God's face (Deut 32:20).

23. Anderson, *Mark*, 216, founds this necessity on the various scriptures "concerning the persecution of God's prophets and ambassadors by an impenitent people"; and Ira Brent Driggers, "God as Healer of Creation in the Gospel of Mark," in *Character Studies and the Gospel of Mark*, ed. Christopher W. Skinner and Matthew Ryan Hauge (JSNTSup 483; London: Bloomsbury, 2014), 96, in his discussion of the "low" elements of Mark's Christology states:

> [T]he Son dies, not because the Father wills his death, but rather because the Son remains uncompromisingly faithful to the Father's intentions in sending him (14.32-42). The passion is necessary (δεῖ, 8.31) and "of God" (τοῦ θεοῦ, 8.33) insofar as it is the inevitable result of a divine mission that elicits hostility and that refuses to deviate in the face of that hostility.

grant assent to what was written in God's scriptures concerning Jesus the Son of Man (Content).²⁴ On the other hand, the expression as a whole also has the interpretation of "enacting one's commitment to God," and Peter's rebuke of Jesus, instead, enacts his commitment to those set in opposition to God.²⁵ Peter's failure to think the things of God and enact his commitment to God places him in opposition to God and Jesus, enacts his commitment to those opposed to God, and makes him like Satan.

God will save (*σῴζω [Ap], 8:35b) the life of the one destroying one's life because of Jesus and the gospel. In contrast, the one wanting and attempting to act as Agent in saving one's life ultimately will destroy it. This contrast proposes God as the Agent and the human being as Instrument of God's saving action for that human being.²⁶ God (with Jesus) has/is the Topic of the gospel (*εὐαγγέλιον [B/T], 8:35). Jesus and the gospel of/about God (with Jesus) may be the Cause of one destroying one's life to save one's life. The context relates Jesus the Son of Man's necessary suffering, being rejected, and being killed as the condition for his rising and the Disciple's required destroying one's life because of Jesus and the gospel of/about God (with Jesus) as the condition for saving one's life.²⁷ This relationship interprets Jesus' hard teachings about discipleship as further content of the things of God.

God the Father of Jesus the Son of Man has the glory (*δόξα [B], 8:38) with/by (Manner/Instrument) which Jesus the Son of Man will come. As such, Jesus the Son of Man's end-time coming will manifest God's glory. God is the Father (*πατήρ [bP], 8:38) of Jesus the Son of Man in his end-time coming. God has the holy Angels (*ἄγγελος [B], 8:38) in the company of whom Jesus the Son of Man will come. God has the reign (*βασιλεία [B], 9:1) that comes with/by (Manner/Instrument) God's power before some of Jesus' addressees die.²⁸ God has the power (*δύναμις [B], 9:1) with/by (Manner/Instrument) which God's reign comes. The

---

24. "Think" (φρονέω, 8:33) introduces Jesus' focus in the following hard teaching about discipleship on verbs that require completion by a first argument Experiencer: want (θέλω, 8:34, 35), be ashamed (ἐπαισχύνομαι, 8:38a), taste (γεύομαι, 9:1), and see (ὁράω, 9:1).

25. On the interpretation of τὰ τοῦ X φρονεῖν as "enact one's commitment to X," see Gerald Wheaton, "Thinking the Things of God? The Translation and Meaning of Mark 8:33c," *NovT* 57 (2015): 42–56.

26. Heil, *Mark*, 183, interprets Jesus' endurance of what is necessary as Jesus' way of accomplishing God's salvation for himself.

27. Further discussion of the development of this relationship and its implications appears in Danove, "The Rhetoric of the Characterization of Jesus as Son of Man and Christ," 16–34; cf. Narry F. Santos, "Jesus' Paradoxical Teaching in Mark 8:35; 9:35; and 10:43–44," *BibSac* 157 (2000): 15–25.

28. As the Theological Study will demonstrate, Mark uses both the Manner and the Instrument interpretations of ἐν (with/by) in 9:38 and 9:1 to ground distinctive developments concerning God's glory (*δόξα [B], §8.1) and God's power (*δύναμις [B], §8.3).

coming of God's reign is going to manifest God's power. Repetition of "come" and "with/by" relates the end-time coming of Jesus the Son of Man with/by God's glory in the company of God's holy Angels and the proximate (within the lifetime of some of Jesus' addressees) coming of God's reign with/by God's power.

The one denying one's self, taking up one's cross, and following Jesus and destroying one's life for the sake of Jesus and the gospel thinks the things of God, enacts one's commitment to God, acts as the Instrument of God's salvation of one's life, is not ashamed of Jesus and his words, will be a beneficiary of Jesus the Son of Man's end-time coming with God's glory, and may see God's reign come with/by God's power in one's lifetime. Jesus the Son of Man's suffering, being rejected, being killed, and rising, as enacted in Mark 14–16, is interpreted to demonstrate that he thinks the things of and enacts his commitment to God, acts as the Instrument of God's salvation of his life, and, in so doing, allows God to reign to be manifest in his life.[29] As a consequence, the coming of God's reign with power, which is to occur within the lifetime of some of Jesus' addressees, is apparent in Jesus the Son of Man's suffering, being rejected, being killed, and rising as predicted by God's scriptures.[30] This context associates God's (with Jesus') benefaction of the gospel (εὐαγγέλιον [B]) with content about God and Jesus as Topic (εὐαγγέλιον [T]).

9. Mark 9

The content of 9:1 appears in the discussion of rhetorical content (8:31–9:1) of which it is a constituent.

a. 9:2-9

God has the voice (*φωνή [B], 9:7) from the cloud that addresses Peter, James, and John with the statement, "This is my beloved Son; listen to him!" (Ps 2:7). God has Jesus the Son (*υἱός [B], 9:7) and loves (*ἀγαπητός [Ec/Apb], 9:7) Jesus the Son.

---

29. This interpretation coheres with those that propose Jesus the Son of Man's fidelity to his mission from God as the necessitating force by which he will suffer much, and be rejected, be killed, and ultimately rise: cf. van Iersel, *Mark*, 283; Hugh M. Humphrey, *He Is Risen!': A New Reading of Mark's Gospel* (New York/Mahwah, NJ: Paulist, 1992), 75–6; Terrence J. Keegan, *A Commentary on the Gospel of Mark* (New York: Paulist, 1981), 103; and Anderson, *Mark*, 216.

30. Some commentators propose the crucifixion of Jesus as the event that manifests God's reign with power: cf. N. T. Wright, *Jesus and the Victory of God* (COQG 2; Minneapolis, MN: Fortress, 1996), 651; Ched Myers, *Binding the Strong Man: A Political Reading of Mark's Story of Jesus* (Maryknoll, NY: Orbis, 1988), 391–2; and Kent Brower, "Mark 9:1: Seeing the Kingdom in Power," *JSNT* 6 (1980): 17–41. Jesus' statement, however, situates his death at the end of a series of necessary events that together are the prerequisite for his rising, which also is a powerful manifestation of God's reign.

God's voice establishes a direct communication relationship from God to Peter, James, and John, reveals God's reciprocal benefaction of Jesus (Father of Son), and imposes on them the obligation to be in a direct communication relationship not from God, Elijah, or Moses but from Jesus.

b. 9:11-13

God has the scriptures (Mal 3:1; 4:5) by which it is necessary (*δεῖ [vi-iB], 9:11) that Elijah/John come first. The previously established coming of Elijah/John (1:2) verifies the predictive potential of these scriptures. God was the Agent of writing (*γέγραπται [Ace], 9:12) about Jesus the Son of Man that he would suffer much and be scorned. There is no specific scriptural antecedent for this statement. Subsequent events (14:43–15:37) confirm the predictive potential of what was written in God's scriptures about Jesus the Son of Man. Jesus' statement of what God wrote again (9:12) establishes a direct communication relationship from God to Peter, James, and John. "Suffer much" evokes Jesus' earlier statement that it is necessary that the Son of Man suffer much (8:31), which similarly assumes the predictive potential of what was written in God's scriptures about Jesus the Son of Man. God was the Agent of writing (*γέγραπται [Ace], 9:13) about Elijah/John that they would do to him whatever they wish. There is no specific scriptural antecedent for this statement. Those doing whatever they wish to Elijah/John include the one handing over John (1:14) and Herod, Herodias, and Herodias' daughter (6:17-29). Their actions confirm the predictive potential of what was written in God's scriptures.

c. 9:14-27

God is to be believed in (*πιστεύω [ecT], 9:23) that (Content) God is able to accomplish good works through human beings as instrument. Since the statement of Jesus on which this attribute is based lacks a specific semantic referent for the one believing in/concerning God, the attribute is taken to assert a general truth. Jesus' statement includes the claim that all things are possible for one so believing in/concerning God (9:23). Jesus makes this statement in response to the request by a man whose son is possessed by an unspeaking spirit, "If you are able, help us, having compassion for us" (9:22), where "us" references the man and his son. Jesus' response proposes himself as one so believing and so having all possible things (δυνατός) and able (δύναμαι) to help the man and his son. God is believed in (*πιστεύω [ecT], 9:24) by the man that (Content) God is able to accomplish good works through human beings as instrument. The man's further request that Jesus help his unbelief (9:24), however, indicates that his faith in/concerning God is not sufficient to serve as instrument in exorcising the unspeaking spirit from his son. Jesus grants the man's initial request by commanding the unspeaking spirit to come out of the man's son (9:25), which it does (9:26). Whether Jesus' action for the son addresses the man's second request, to help the man's unbelief, remains unspecified.

d. 9:28-29

God is Experiencer of prayer (*προσευχή [E], 9:29) which is the only efficacious Instrument by which the unspeaking and deaf-making spirit (9:14-27) and those like it are able to come out of human beings. This indicates that only those in a direct communication relationship to God (like Jesus, 1:35; 6:46; 14:32, 35, 39) are able to order such spirits out of human beings.

e. 9:33-37

God is received (δέχομαι [gΘs], 9:37d) by the one receiving Jesus, while Jesus is received by the one receiving a child in reference to/concerning (Topic) Jesus' name. This proposes the reception of the most dependent and vulnerable out of one's commitment to Jesus as the means of receiving Jesus and ultimately God.[31] Since the reception of Jesus accomplishes the reception of God, Jesus functions as God's delegated emissary.[32] God sends (*ἀποστέλλω [AΘg], 9:37) Jesus. Since this dynamic of receiving would be impossible without God (Agent) sending Jesus (Theme), the reception of God (Theme) ultimately depends on God's agency.

f. 9:38-48

God has Jesus the Christ (*χριστός [B], 9:41) by (Instrument) whose name one may give Disciples a cup of water to drink because (Cause) the Disciples are of Jesus. God will be the Source of the wage (μισθός [S], 9:41) that the one so giving will not destroy. God has the life (*ζωή [B], 9:43) into which it is better to enter lacking a hand than, having two hands, go away into Gehenna. God has the life (*ζωή [B], 9:45) into which it is better to enter lacking a foot than, having two feet, be cast into Gehenna. God has the reign (*βασιλεία [B], 9:47) into which it is better to enter with one eye than, having two eyes, be cast into Gehenna where the worm does not die and the fire is not extinguished (Isa 66:24). These statements narratively coordinate God's life and God's reign and contrasts them with corruption (worm) and annihilation or disintegration (fire). Repetition of "if your," "causes you to stumble," "enter into," "having," "than having two," and "be cast into Gehenna" (9:43, 45, 47) asserts a common referent for "life" and "reign" when they function as the Goal of future motion, and the context relates not destroying one's wage from God and entering God's life and reign in the future. At the same time, the context relates present actions for the benefit of fellow believers (giving a drink) and for the benefit of oneself (cutting off, casting out); and the triple contrast between life/reign and Gehenna (9:43, 45, 47) establishes that what one does (give a drink of water by Jesus' name, cut off, cast out) or does not do in the present functions as a condition for maintaining one's wage from God and entering the life/reign of God or Gehenna in the future.

---

31. Harrington, *Mark*, 146.
32. Healy, *Mark*, 186.

Chapter 5

EXEGESIS OF THE RHETORICAL CONTEXTS IN MARK 10–15

This chapter provides an exegetical study of the thirty-eight rhetorical contexts containing references to God in Mark 10–15. These exegetical contexts present 186 actions and attributes of God. The study identifies no references to God in 16:1-8.

1. Mark 10

a. 10:1-9

God does not have the commandments that permit (*ἔξεστιν [vi-iB], 10:2) a husband to divorce his wife. God has creation (*κτίσις [B], 10:6) which had a beginning. God makes (*ποιέω [Ap], 10:6) human beings male and female from the beginning of creation (Gen 1:27; 5:2). The use of the present tense (makes) interprets "from the beginning of creation" to indicate that God's creative action, begun in the past, continues into the present and presumably the future. God joins (συζεύγνυμι [Apg], 10:9) the man and woman in marriage, a further perennial creative action that human beings ought not undo. Jesus appears to deduce God's action of joining using the interpretive principle that, if God's action functions as the Cause of a Result, then the Result also is of God. In this case, God's making human beings male and female is the Cause for a human being to leave his father and mother and cling to his wife (Gen 2:24), and the Result of this leaving and clinging is that the two become one flesh.[1] Jesus then applies the further interpretive principle that God's actions and attributes cannot be in conflict. Since God's action of joining would be in conflict with having a commandment that permits the dissolution of that joining, God does not have this commandment. Thus the answer to the Pharisees' question about the permissibility of divorce is "no." Rather, the commandment that authorizes divorce (Deut 24:1) is of Moses and not of God

---

1. Frederick W. Schmidt, "Loyal Opposition and the Law in the Teaching of Jesus: The Ethics of a Restorative and Utopian Eschatology," *ATJ* 56, no. 1 (2001): 37, correctly notes that Jesus' statements in 10:9 and 2:27 make a direct appeal to God's intent in creating.

as agentive Benefactive, and the Cause of Moses writing it was the hardness of human hearts.[2] This highlights the opposition between God's action as Cause and human hardness of heart as Cause.

b. 10:13-16

God has the reign (*βασιλεία [B], 10:14) that the children brought to Jesus for his touch have and those like these children also have. These children and those like them may not be prevented from coming to Jesus. The bringing of children to Jesus for his touch highlights the dependence of children on the benevolent action of others. God has the reign (*βασιλεία [B], 10:15) that one is to receive as one receives a child.[3] The implication is that, just as the reception of a child imposes on the receiver the obligation to nurture and protect the child and, within this context, to bring the child to Jesus for his touch, the reception of God's reign imposes on the receiver the obligation to nurture and protect it. Receiving God's reign as one receives a child is the Condition for entrance into it (10:15).

c. 10:17-22

God is the Source from whom one may inherit (κληρονομέω [gθS], 10:17) everlasting life. The proposed conditions for inheriting everlasting life are keeping God's commandments and selling what one has, giving to the poor, and following Jesus. Jesus' statement identifies keeping God's commandments as the necessary but not sufficient condition for inheriting everlasting life. God has everlasting life (*ζωή [B], 10:17). God alone is good (ἀγαθός [P], 10:18). Since God alone is good, the one recognizing Jesus as good recognizes Jesus' likeness to God. God has the commandments (*ἐντολή [B], 10:19), "You shall not kill (Exod 20:13; Deut 5:17); you shall not commit adultery (Exod 20:14; Deut 5:18); you shall not steal (Exod 20:15; Deut 5:19); you shall not bear false witness (Exod 20:16); you shall not defraud; honor your father and your mother (Exod 20:12; Deut 5:16)," which are known and claimed to be observed by the man asking Jesus what he may do to inherit everlasting life.

d. 10:23-27

God has the reign (*βασιλεία [B], 10:23) that those having possessions enter with [how] much difficulty. A near contextual example of the difficulty posed by having possessions is the man claiming to keep God's commandments (10:19-20) but

---

2. Note that 10:5 presents the first occurrence of "write" (γράφω) in Mark for which the scribe (Moses) functions as the Agent.

3. Detailed discussion of this interpretation appears in Peter Spitaler, "Welcoming a Child as a Metaphor for Welcoming God's Kingdom: A Close Reading of Mark 10.13-16," *JSNT* 31, no. 4 (2009): 430–4.

lacking in selling his possessions, giving to the poor, and following Jesus (10:21-22) and ultimately declining Jesus' invitation to follow him. God has the reign (*βασιλεία [B], 10:24) that human beings enter with [how] much difficulty. God has the reign (*βασιλεία [B], 10:25) that a rich person enters less easily than a camel passes through the eye of a needle. While the first statement identifies having possessions as a hindrance to entering God's reign and the third specifies being rich as an insurmountable hindrance to entering God's reign, the second clarifies the great difficulty of entering God's reign for all people. God has the thing impossible (ἀδύνατον [B], 10:27) for human beings, that is, the ability to save human beings. God has all things able [to be done]/possible things (*δυνατόν [B], 10:27) including the ability to save human beings. God can save (*σῴζω [Ap], [10:27]) human beings, which human beings cannot do.[4] God's unique agency in saving human beings relegates the human being destroying and saving one's life (8:35b) to the status of Instrument.

The greater context (10:17-31) identifies this context (10:23-27) as a continuation of Jesus' response to the question (10:17) about the required actions for inheriting everlasting life. The prior context (10:17-22) presents everlasting life (Theme) as moving (inheriting) to the human being (Goal), this context presents the human being (Theme) as moving (entering) to the reign (Goal), and the following context (10:28-31) again presents everlasting life (Theme) as moving (receiving) to the human beings (Goal). These contrasting views of motion receive interpretation as two perspectives on the same event. This context also relates human beings (Theme) entering God's reign (Goal) and God (Agent) saving human beings (Patient) as a third perspective on the same event.[5] These three perspectives (inheriting/receiving everlasting life, entering God's reign, being saved by God) restrict all agency in human salvation to God.

e. 10:28-31

God (with Jesus) has/is the Topic of the gospel (*εὐαγγέλιον [B/T], 10:29). Jesus and the gospel of/about God (with Jesus) may be the Cause of one leaving house, brothers, sisters, mother, father, children, and fields. God will be the Source from whom the one leaving family and possessions because of Jesus and the gospel will receive (*λαμβάνω [gθS], 10:30) in this time a hundredfold houses, brothers, sisters, mothers, children, and fields and, in the coming age, life everlasting. God, however, will not be the Source of the persecutions that will accompany these or of a hundredfold fathers insofar as leaving one's father because of Jesus and the gospel

---

4. Although save (σῴζω) is not stated in the text, it must be retrieved as the complement of "impossible" for the grammatical interpretation of the verb phrase in 10:27a: "saving someone is impossible with human beings but [saving someone] is not impossible with God," where the implied Agent of "save" is first "human beings" and then "God." This statement interprets "is not impossible" to mean "is able/can."

5. Stein, *Mark*, 473.

affirms one's filial relationship with God as Father (11:25). God has the everlasting life (*ζωή [B], 10:30) that the one leaving family and possessions because of Jesus and the gospel will receive. This identifies leaving family and possessions as the condition for receiving from God a hundredfold in this time and life everlasting in the coming age. This context associates God's (with Jesus') benefaction of the gospel (εὐαγγέλιον [B]) with content about God and Jesus as Topic (εὐαγγέλιον [T]).

f. 10:46-52

God is the Topic of the faith (*πίστις [ecT], 10:52) of the blind Bartimaeus. The apparent Content of his faith is that God is able to save (heal) his blindness through Jesus the Son of David as Instrument. Jesus' statement that the man's faith has saved him identifies his faith and action based on it as the further Instrument of his healing.

2. Mark 11

a. 11:1-11

God is the Experiencer of hosanna (*ὡσαννά [aE], 11:9) which is interpreted as an acclamation of praise (§2.4a) directed to the most high place and is associated with Jesus the Blessed One coming in/by (Manner/Instrument) the name of the Lord (Ps 118:26). Narrative overlays identify the Blessed One as Jesus. God has the name (ὄνομα [B], 11:9) in/by which Jesus comes. Coming in/by God's name receives interpretation as coming at God's behest as God's representative.[6] God is the Experiencer of hosanna (*ὡσαννά [aE], 11:10) which is directed to the most high place and is associated with the coming reign of the people's father David. The two acclamations and their associated Contents are related. Although the identification of Jesus as the Blessed One indicates a proper understanding of Jesus' identity, relating Jesus to David and David's reign rather than to God and God's reign, of which Jesus is the proclaimer (1:14-15), indicates a faulty understanding of Jesus and his relationships and so a faulty understanding of God and God's relationships. God has the Temple (*ἱερόν [bB], 11:11) which Jesus enters, in which Jesus looks around at everything, and from which Jesus departs. None of these portray Jesus as Agent. Although Jesus' departure is attributed explicitly to the lateness of the hour, the faulty understanding of Jesus, God, and their relationship has the potential to engender a faulty interpretation of any actions of Jesus in God's Temple in this context. Thus Jesus' departure removes a contextual basis for misinterpreting his subsequent actions in God's Temple.

---

6. Thayer, *Lexicon*, 447.

b. 11:15-19

God has the Temple (ἱερόν [bB], 11:15a) which Jesus enters. God has the Temple (ἱερόν [bB], 11:15b) from which Jesus casts out those selling and buying and in which Jesus overturns the tables of the moneychangers and seats of those selling doves. God has the Temple (ἱερόν [bB], 11:16) through which Jesus does not allow the carrying of vessels. God was the Agent of writing (*γέγραπται [Ace], 11:17), "My house shall be called a house of prayer for all the nations but you have made it a den of thieves" (Isa 56:7; Jer 7:11). Jesus' statement of what God wrote establishes a direct communication relationship of condemnation from God to those buying, selling, changing money, selling doves, and carrying vessels in God's house. God has this house (οἶκος [bB], 11:17) which is to be called a house of prayer for all the nations but which those condemned make a den of thieves. God's house receives contextual interpretation as God's Temple. God is to be the Experiencer of the prayer (προσευχή [E], 11:17) of all the nations, highlighting the intended universality of the direct communication relationship from human beings to God. The Chief Priests and Scribes respond to Jesus' Temple actions and statements by seeking to destroy Jesus, which aligns them with those condemned without incorporating them into God's direct communication relationship to those condemned.

c. 11:20-25

God is to be the Topic of the faith (*πίστις [ecT], 11:22) that the Disciples are to have. The apparent Content of this faith concerning God is that God acts for believing Disciples just as God acts for Jesus in his injunction that no one ever eat of the fig tree's fruit (11:14) by having the fig tree wither (11:20). God is to be believed in (*πιστεύω [ecT], 11:23) by Jesus' Disciple that (Content) what the Disciple speaks happens for the Disciple and is the Disciple's. God may be prayed to (*προσεύχομαι [acE], 11:24) and asked (αἰτέω [acE], 11:24) by Disciples. God is to be believed in (*πιστεύω [ecT], 11:24) by Disciples that (Content) they receive what they pray for and ask of God and that it is theirs. God is the Source from whom Disciples receive (*λαμβάνω [gθS], 11:24) what they pray for and ask of God on the condition that they believe that they have it. God is to be prayed to (*προσεύχομαι [acE], 11:25) by Jesus' Disciples. God is the Father (*πατήρ [bP], 11:25) of Jesus' Disciples, especially in the context of Disciples forgiving what they hold against another and God forgiving their trespasses. God the Disciples' Father is in (ἐν [Θl], 11:25) the heavens. God the Disciples' Father in the Heavens forgives (*ἀφίημι [Apb], 11:25b) trespasses for Jesus' Disciples who, when they stand praying, forgive for others whatever they hold against them. This proposes forgiving what one holds against others as the condition for God to forgive one's trespasses.[7] God has recipient benefaction of the trespasses (παράπτωμα [bB], 11:25) of Jesus' Disciples.

---

7. As Stein, *Mark*, 521, observes, the forgiveness of what is held against another comes before God's forgiveness of trespasses.

d. 11:27-33

God has the Temple (*ἱερόν [bB], 11:27) in which Jesus is walking when the Chief Priests, Scribes, and Elders ask him, "By which authority do you do these things?" or "Who gave to you this authority that you do these things?" God (with Jesus) has the authority (*ἐξουσία [B], 11:28a) by which (Instrument) Jesus does the things that he does. God gives (*δίδωμι [Aθg], 11:28) to Jesus this authority so that (Purpose) he does the things that he does. God (with Jesus) has the authority (*ἐξουσία [B], 11:28b). God (with Jesus) has the authority (*ἐξουσία [B], 11:29), which Jesus agrees to confirm if (condition) the Chief Priests, Scribes, and Elders state the Source of John's baptism. Jesus' counter-question uses the fact that their second question about who gave him his authority asks about both the Agent and Source of Jesus' authority (§1.6b). God is the Source of John's baptism (*βάπτισμα [S], 11:30), which the Chief Priests, Scribes, and Elders do not state. Thus Jesus' question indicates that God is the Source of John's baptism and the Agent/Source of Jesus' authority. God has John the Prophet (*προφήτης [B], 11:32), as held by all.[8] God (with Jesus) has the authority (*ἐξουσία [B], 11:33) by which Jesus does the things that he does but which Jesus does not confirm because his condition is not met.

3. Mark 12

a. 12:1-5

God planted (φυτεύω [Ap], 12:1) a Vineyard. As a consequence, God has agentive benefaction of the Vineyard (*ἀμπελών [B], 12:1). A scriptural antecedent identifies the Vineyard as the house of Israel/God's people (Isa 5:7). The use of the present tense (has) indicates that God's benefaction of the Vineyard, although begun in the past, continues into the present and future. God put around (περιτίθημι [Ap], 12:1) the Vineyard a fence and so has this fence (φραγμός [Bb], 12:1). God dug (ὀρύσσω [Ap], 12:1) a winepress for the Vineyard and so has this winepress (ὑπολήνιον [Bb], 12:1). God built (οἰκοδομέω [Ap], 12:1) a tower for the Vineyard and so has this tower (πύργος [Bb], 12:1). Again, the use of the present tense (has) indicates that God is assumed to have continuing agentive benefaction of fence, winepress, and tower. This proposes that the Vineyard has continuing recipient benefaction of the fence, winepress, and tower which are interpreted to provide all that is required for the Vineyard to be productive. God leased (ἐκδίδομαι [Aθg], 12:1) the Vineyard to Farmers whom the greater context identifies as the Chief Priests, Scribes, and Elders of Jesus' day (12:12; cf. 11:27). God left on a journey (ἀποδημέω [Θg], 12:1). God sent (*ἀποστέλλω [Aθg], 12:2) a Slave to the Farmers at the proper time for the Purpose of taking some of its fruit. God has this Slave (*δοῦλος [B], 12:2). The

---

8. This discussion accepts the crowd's estimation of John to be God's Prophet as reliable based on John's previous enactment of the role of Elijah the Prophet (1:2) and Jesus' previous reference to John as Elijah (9:13).

use of the present tense (has) indicates that God's benefaction of this and following Slaves, although begun in the past, continues into the present and future. God intended to take (λαμβάνω [Aθs], 12:2) some of the fruit of the Vineyard through this Slave, which was God's Purpose in sending the Slave. God has the Vineyard (*ἀμπελών [B], 12:2) to which God sent the Slave. The Purpose clause identifies the Slave (and future representatives sent to the Vineyard) as God's delegated emissary and instrument for taking some of the Vineyard's fruit. God was sent (ἀποστέλλω [aθG], 12:3) this Slave, whom the Farmers took and beat, without any of the fruit of the Vineyard. God sent (*ἀποστέλλω [Aθg], 12:4) another Slave to the Farmers for the same Purpose. God has this Slave (*δοῦλος [B], 12:4), whom the Farmers beat over the head and dishonored. God sent (*ἀποστέλλω [Aθg], 12:5a) another [Slave] to the Farmers for the same Purpose. God has this [Slave] (*δοῦλος [B], [12:5a]), whom the Farmers killed. God [sent] (*ἀποστέλλω [Aθg], [12:5b]) many other [Slaves] to the Farmers for the same Purpose. God has these [Slaves] (*δοῦλος [B], [12:5b]), whom the Farmers beat or killed. Throughout this process of sending, God never took any of the fruit of God's Vineyard.

b. 12:6-8

God has (ἔχω [Bp], 12:6) Jesus left to send to the Farmers (the Chief Priests, Scribes, and Elders, 12:12; cf. 11: 27) of the Vineyard (house of Israel/God's people, 12:1; cf. Isa 5:7). God has Jesus the Son (*υἱός [B], 12:6a) and loves (*ἀγαπητός [Ec/Apb], 12:6) Jesus the Son. God sends (*ἀποστέλλω [Aθg], 12:6) Jesus the Beloved Son last of all to the Farmers for the Purpose of taking some of the fruit of the Vineyard (12:2). "Last of all" indicates that God intends to send no further emissaries to the Farmers. God says (*λέγω [Ace], 12:6) to an unidentified Experiencer that the Farmers are to respect Jesus God's Son. What God says receives interpretation as an injunction.[9] Since the context identifies no referent for the addressee (Experiencer) of God's statement, the statement establishes a direct communication relationship from God to its sole interpreter, the implied reader, enjoining respect for Jesus God's Beloved Son. God's saying and sending are contemporaneous. God has Jesus the Son (*υἱός [B], 12:6b) whom God sends to the Farmers last of all. This verse (v. 6) presents the greatest density of references to God's reciprocal benefaction (have, Son [twice]) of Jesus in Mark. God has Jesus the Heir (κληρονόμος [B], 12:7). God is the Source of the inheritance (κληρονομία [S], 12:7), the Vineyard, which is for Jesus the Heir but which the Farmers seek to have by taking and killing Jesus the Heir. Repetition of "take" (λαμβάνω) in the greater context establishes a contrast between God, who as agentive Benefactive of the Vineyard rightly would take (12:2) some of its fruit, and the Farmers, who as God's lessees wrongfully take God's Slave (12:3) and Son (12:8). God has the Vineyard (*ἀμπελών [B], 12:8), out of which the Farmers cast Jesus God's Beloved Son and Heir after killing him.

---

9. On the use of the future for injunctions, see BDF, 183 (§362).

c. 12:9-12

God is Lord (κύριος [bP], 12:9) of the Vineyard (the House of Israel/God's People, 12:1; cf. Isa 5:7) and has the Vineyard (*ἀμπελών [B], 12:9a). As such, God the Lord and the Vineyard are in a relationship of reciprocal benefaction. God the Lord of the Vineyard will act (*ποιέω [Ap], 12:9) in response to the killing of God's Beloved Son (12:8) and Heir (12:7) whom God sends last of all to the Farmers (12:6) for the Purpose of taking some of the fruit of the Vineyard (12:2). God will come (ἔρχομαι [Θg], 12:9), destroy (ἀπόλλυμι [Ap], 12:9) the Farmers (the Chief Priests, Scribes, and Elders, 12:12; cf. 11:27), and give (*δίδωμι [AΘg], 12:9) the Vineyard to others. The expected consequence of God's actions apparently is that the "others" will render some of the fruit of the Vineyard that is due to God.[10] God has agentive benefaction of the Vineyard (*ἀμπελών [B], 12:9b). This establishes a contrast in the nature of the relationship between God and the Farmers, which is commercial (12:1), and between God and the Vineyard, which is both agentive (12:9b) and reciprocal (12:9a) and, therefore, intimate. Whereas God responded to the killing of God's Slaves (12:5) by sending God's Son (12:6), God responds to the killing of God's Son (12:8) by acting directly (12:9), which highlights the uniqueness of God's reciprocal relationship with Jesus (12:6). God has the scripture (*γραφή [B], 12:10) stating that the rejected stone will become the cornerstone. God will be the Agent by whom Jesus the Rejected Stone becoming the Cornerstone will come to be (*γίνομαι [pA], 12:11). Within the greater context (12:1-12), the Farmers are the ones rejecting Jesus and so are the Ones Building; and repetition of "build" contrasts God, who built a tower for the Vineyard (12:1) and the Farmers/the Ones Building, who reject (12:10) God's Beloved Son and Heir by killing (12:7, 8) and casting (12:8) him out of the Vineyard.[11] Jesus' ultimate status as Cornerstone, which comes to be by God, constitutes God's further response to the rejecting, killing, and casting out of Jesus.

d. 12:13-17

God (with Jesus) has the way (*ὁδός [B], 12:14) that Jesus teaches in truth. This attribute, proposed by the unreliable Pharisees and Herodians, is deemed ironic but valid. God has the commandments that permit (*ἔξεστιν [vi-iB], 12:14) the

---

10. John R. Donahue, "The Revelation of God in the Gospel of Mark," in *Modern Biblical Scholarship: Its Impact on Theology and Proclamation*, ed. Francis A. Eigo (Villanova, PA: Villanova University Press, 1984), 165, identifies the "others" as Mark's community.

11. "Rejected" evokes its former occurrence (8:31) which identifies Jesus the Son of Man as the Rejected Stone and the Ones Building as the Chief Priests, Scribes, and Elders, the present Farmers of God's Vineyard and the ones rejecting Jesus. Douglas R. A. Hare, *Mark* (WeBC; Louisville, KY: Westminster John Knox, 1996), 151–2, proposes the same evocation as the basis of linking the resurrection of the Son of Man (8:31) to Jesus the Beloved Son becoming the Cornerstone (12:11).

giving of the census tax to Caesar. There is no specific scriptural antecedent for these commandments. God is to be given back (ἀποδίδωμι [aθG], 12:17) the things of God. God has these things (*τά [B], 12:17b). Jesus' statement contrasts the actions of giving back to Caesar the coins with his image (εἰκών) and giving back to God the things of God. "Image" has the potential to evoke the fact the scripture attributes God with agentive benefaction of human beings insofar as God makes human beings and does so in God's image (Gen 1:26). This evocation would ground the recognition that the things to be given back to God include human beings themselves as God's creation and bearing God's image.

e. 12:18-27

God has the scripture (*γραφή [B], 12:24) that is not known by the Sadducees who are misled in not acknowledging the resurrection. God's scripture incorporates the commandment concerning a brother taking his dead brother's wife (12:19; cf. Deut 25:5-6) and God's statement to Moses (12:26; cf. Exod 3:6, 14-16). God has the power (*δύναμις [B], 12:24) that the Sadducees also do not know. Not knowing God's scripture and God's power is the Cause that misleads the Sadducees into rejecting the truth of the resurrection and asking Jesus about which of the seven brothers married to the same woman will have her as wife in the resurrection. The Sadducees' lack of knowledge of the scripture is apparent in their question's appeal to the Levirate marriage law (Deut 25:5) that itself assumes that the covenantal bond between a husband and wife ceases at the death of the husband, thereby legally permitting a brother to take the woman as his wife. God has the Angels (*ἄγγελος [B], 12:25) in the heavens. God said (*λέγω [Ace], 12:26a) to Moses, "I am the God of Abraham and the God of Isaac and the God of Jacob" (Exod 3:6, 14-16), which is the other scripture that the Sadducees do not know. This is the sole occurrence of God's direct communication relationship to Moses in Mark. God (*θεός [bP], 12:26b, 26c, 26d) has Abraham, Isaac, and Jacob. God (*θεός [bP], 12:27a) does not have the dead, but [God] (*θεός [bP], [12:27b]) does have the living, which explains God's continuing benefaction of Abraham, Isaac, and Jacob at the time of God's speaking to Moses. Jesus' initial statement proposes God's power as the instrument by which the dead rise. The Sadducees' lack of knowledge of the power of God is apparent in the fact that God's reference to Abraham, Isaac, and Jacob (12:26; cf. Exod 3:6) originally appeared in the context of assurances to Moses (Exod 3:6-17) of God's intent to fulfill for these patriarchs covenantal promises that would no longer be binding if they were not still living by God's power.[12] The Sadducees do not recognize that those rising from the dead neither take wives nor are taken as wives but are like the Angels in the heavens. The likeness

---

12. These observations reflect the discussion of Bradley R. Trick, "Death, Covenants, and the Proof of Resurrection in Mark 12:18-27," *NovT* 49, no. 3 (2007), 232–56, concerning the coherence of Jesus' argument for the resurrection.

to Angels specifies the life in the resurrection as not merely rising from the grave but a new reality sustained by God's power.[13]

Jesus' statements identify the proposed but invalid marriage relationship between the seven brothers and the same woman as both redundant and superfluous in the resurrection. Since the seven brothers take the same wife to ensure that the name of a brother not be wiped out of Israel (Deut 25:6), their action is redundant because those who rise by God's power, whether male or female, live forever and so cannot have their names wiped out.[14] It is superfluous because the only Benefactive relationships that pertain in the resurrection are God's benefaction of the human beings that rise and so continue in existence (as do the Angels) by God's power and God's reciprocal benefaction of the living as their God.

Jesus' statement assumes that God's benefaction of human beings endures only as long as they are living. This distinguishes human beings into the living who rise from the dead and whom God continues to have and the dead who do not rise and whom God does not continue to have. This distinction accommodates the interpretation that the dead who do not rise do not exist past their death.

f. 12:28-34

God has the commandments (*ἐντολή [B], 12:28) of which one is first. God has the first [commandment] (*ἐντολή [B], [12:29]), "Hear, O Israel, the Lord our God is one Lord; and you shall love the Lord your God with all your heart, with all your life, with all your mind, and with all your strength" (12:29-30; cf. Deut 6:4-5). God (*θεός [bP], 12:29) is the Lord of Israel (God's people) and Jesus. God is one (*εἷς [P], 12:29). God is to be loved (*ἀγαπάω [eC/apB], 12:30) by Israel with all of their heart, life, mind, and strength. God (*θεός [bP], 12:30) is the Lord of Israel. God has the second [commandment] (*ἐντολή [B], [12:31a]), "You shall love your neighbor as yourself" (Lev 19:18). God has the other commandments (*ἐντολή [B], 12:31b) of which none are greater than these two. God is one (*εἷς [P], 12:32). God is he (αὐτός [P], 12:32) in relation to whom there is no other god. God is to be loved (*ἀγαπάω [eC/apB], 12:33) by Israel with all their heart, understanding, and strength. God has the burnt offerings (ὁλοκαύτωμα [bB], 12:33) and offerings (θυσία [bB], 12:33) that are not as great as loving God and neighbor. God has the reign (*βασιλεία [B], 12:34) from which the one recognizing the primacy of loving God and neighbor over burnt offerings and offerings is not distant. Although recognizing God's uniqueness and the primacy of loving God and neighbor over burnt offerings and offerings makes one not distant from God's reign, it does not engender contact with or entrance into God's reign. The context proposes enactment of the love commandments in the manner stated (God with all one's heart, life,

---

13. Donahue, "The Revelation of God," 164.
14. Matthew Thiessen, "A Buried Pentateuchal Allusion to the Resurrection in Mark 12:25," *CBQ* 76, no. 2 (2014): 273-90, proposes numerous scriptural references equating Angels with celestial bodies that are assumed to be eternal.

mind, and strength/with all one's heart, understanding, and strength; and neighbor as oneself) as the manner of contact with or entrance into God's reign.¹⁵

g. 12:35-37

God has the Temple (*ἱερόν [bB], 12:35) in which Jesus teaches and quotes David. God has Jesus the Christ (*χριστός [B], 12:35) who the Scribes say is David's Son. God has the Spirit (*πνεῦμα [B], 12:36) by which (Instrument) David said, "The Lord said to my Lord, 'Sit at my right [hand] until I put your enemies under your feet'" (Ps 110:1).¹⁶ God the Lord will say (*λέγω [Ace], 12:36) this statement to the risen Jesus the Lord, thereby establishing a direct communication relationship to him. God the Lord has the right [hand] (*δεξιά [B], 12:36) at which the risen Jesus will be commanded to sit. Being seated at God's right hand receives interpretation as being located in the position of honor with respect to God.¹⁷ This is also the location of the one delegated by God to act by God's power.¹⁸ God will put (τίθημι [Aθg], 12:36) the enemies of Jesus under Jesus' feet.

h. 12:38-40

God is prayed to (*προσεύχομαι [acE], 12:40) as a pretext at length by the Scribes. Jesus commands his Disciples to be wary of the Scribes who want to walk around in robes, want greetings in markets, the first seats in synagogues, and seats of honor at dinners, and devour the houses of widows. God is the Source from whom these Scribes will receive (*λαμβάνω [gθS], 12:40) greater condemnation. God has this greater condemnation (κρίμα [Bb], 12:40) for the Scribes. This identifies wanting to walk around in robes, wanting greetings in markets, the first seats in synagogues, and seats of honor at dinners, and devouring the houses of widows as against God's intent for human beings.

4. Mark 13

a. 13:1-2

God has the Temple (*ἱερόν [bB], 13:1) from which Jesus departs as one of his Disciples expresses admiration for its stones and buildings and Jesus responds that

---

15. David J. Neville, "Moral Vision and Eschatology in Mark's Gospel: Coherence or Conflict?," *JBL* 127, no. 2 (2008): 369, equates entering God's reign with living in accordance with the two commandments to love.

16. Jesus interprets "my Lord" in David's statement from Ps 110:1 as a reference not to David himself but to the one whom David deemed his own Lord and then proposes himself as that someone.

17. Walter Grundmann, "δεξιός," *TDNT* 2:37-40.

18. Hurtado, *Mark*, 196.

not one stone will be left on another. The following context (13:3-8) situates the razing of these stones with events before the end.

b. 13:3-8

God has the Temple (*ἱερόν [bB], 13:3) opposite which Jesus is sitting when he makes the statement about what will be necessary. God has the scripture by which it will be necessary (*δεῖ [vi-iB], 13:7) that wars and reports of war happen. There is no specific scriptural antecedent for this statement. The confirmation of the predictive potential of what was recorded in God's scriptures about Jesus the Son of Man (8:31; cf. 14:43–16:6) and John (9:11; cf. 1:2-3) recommends that these predicted events similarly will occur. Jesus' Disciples are not to be alarmed when they hear about these and are to realize that they do not signal the end.

c. 13:9-13

God has the scripture by which it will be necessary (*δεῖ [vi-iB], 13:10) that the gospel be proclaimed first (before the end) to all the nations. There is no specific scriptural antecedent for this statement. The confirmation of the predictive potential of what was written in God's scriptures about Jesus the Son of Man (8:31; cf. 14:43–16:6) and John (9:11; cf. 1:2-3) recommends that this predicted event will occur. God (with Jesus) has/is the Topic of the gospel (*εὐαγγέλιον [B/T], 13:10) that must be proclaimed by Peter, James, John, and Andrew (13:3, 9) and, by implication, all members of the Twelve to all the nations first (before to the end). God will give (*δίδωμι [Aθg], 13:11) to the Twelve what they will say when they are led and handed over. God has the Holy Spirit (*πνεῦμα [B], 13:11) that will speak when the Twelve are led and handed over. When this occurs, the Twelve will become the instrument of the Holy Spirit's speaking. Those undertaking the necessary proclaiming of the gospel of/about God (with Jesus) will be hated by all because of Jesus' name. God will save (*σῴζω [Ap], 13:13) the Disciple of Jesus persevering to the end. This context associates God's (with Jesus') benefaction of the gospel (εὐαγγέλιον [B]) with content about God and Jesus as Topic (εὐαγγέλιον [T]).

d. 13:14-17

God has the scriptures (Dan 9:27; 11:31; 12:11) by which it will be necessary (*δεῖ [vi-iB], 13:14) that the abomination of desolation stand where he (masculine: ἑστηκότα) is not to stand (Dan 11:31; 12:11). The present confirmation of the predictive potential of what was recorded in God's scriptures about Jesus the Son of Man (8:31; cf. 14:43–16:6) and John (9:11; cf. 1:2-3) recommends that this predicted event similarly will occur, even as it recognizes that the presence of the abomination of desolation defiles the sanctuary (1 Macc 1:54). Those in Judea are to flee when they see this event occur.

5. Exegesis of the Rhetorical Contexts in Mark 10–15   93

e. 13:18-20

God is to be prayed to (*προσεύχομαι [acE], 13:18) by Jesus' Disciples that the tribulation not occur in winter because (Cause) it will be unlike anything in the past (from the beginning of creation that God creates), present (until now), or the future (may not be, 13:19). God is attributed with no role in effecting the tribulation. God has creation (*κτίσις [B], 13:19) that had a beginning and that God creates (κτίζω [Ap], 13:19). The use of the present tense (has, creates) interprets "from the beginning of creation" to indicate that God's creative action, begun in the past, continues into the present and presumably the future. God the Lord will shorten (*κολοβόω [Ap], 13:20a) the days of the tribulation. God will save (*σῴζω [Ap], 13:20) some human beings, which has as its Condition that God shorten the days.[19] God will have the Elect (ἐκλεκτός [B], 13:20) whom God will choose (ἐκλέγομαι [Ap], 13:20). God will shorten (*κολοβόω [Ap], 13:20b) the days because of (Cause) the Elect. All of God's future actions in this context (choosing, shortening [twice], saving) will benefit the Elect; and the context associates Jesus' Disciples who are to pray to God and the Elect whom God will choose. In this, the second and final assertion of the Cause of God's action, God's antecedent action (choosing the Elect) is the ultimate cause of God shortening the days. The noted circumstantial relationships resolve the content of this context into six concentrically arranged constituents that receive labeling by the verse, relationship, predicators, and thematic roles of the arguments referenced by God.

v. 18	result		pray	E
v. 19	↑ Cause		creation/create	B/A
v. 20a		Condition	shorten	A
v. 20b		consequence	save	A
v. 20c	↓ Cause		Elect/choose	B/A
v. 20d	Result		shorten	A

f. 13:21-23

God will not have the Christ (*χριστός [B], 13:21) that someone will say is here or there before the end. God will have the Elect (*ἐκλεκτός [B], 13:22) whom false Christs and false Prophets will attempt to mislead by signs and wonders. This accommodates the interpretation that the signs and wonders associated with Jesus the Christ in the present no longer will be valid proofs of Jesus' identity as the Son of Man in the future.[20]

---

19. This statement interprets the negation of "all flesh would not be saved" (13:20) to indicate that some flesh would be saved.
20. Danove, "Jesus as the Son of Man and Christ in Mark," 16–34.

g. 13:24-29

God has the great power (*δύναμις [B], 13:26) and glory (*δόξα [B], 13:26), with/by (Manner/Instrument) which Jesus the Son of Man will be seen coming at the end.[21] Those alive after the tribulation will see this event. God has the Angels (*ἄγγελος [B], 13:27) whom Jesus the Son of Man will send, apparently as the instruments of his gathering of God's Elect. God will have the Elect (*ἐκλεκτός [B], 13:27) whom Jesus the Son of Man will gather from the four winds, from the end of the earth to the end of heaven after the tribulation. These events, as part of God's end-time action of saving the Elect (13:20), introduce the only two actions of Jesus (gathering, sending) after his resurrection and being seated at God's right and identify Jesus the Son of Man as God's instrument of these saving events.[22]

h. 13:32-37

God alone knows (οἶδα [Et], 13:32) about the day and hour of the culminating events of this age. God has the Angels (*ἄγγελος [B], 13:32) and Jesus the Son (*υἱός [B], 13:32) who do not know about the day and hour of the culminating events of this age. God (with Jesus, 11:28) has the authority (*ἐξουσία [B], 13:34) that Jesus the Human Being gives to his Disciples the Slaves who are to remain alert because they do not know the time of the coming of Jesus the Lord of the Household. This context associates the day and hour known only by God and the time of the coming of Jesus the Head of the Household and contrasts God who knows about the day and hour both with God's Angels and God's Son who do not know about the day or hour and with Jesus' Disciples the Slaves who do not know when Jesus the Lord of the Household is coming.

5. Mark 14

a. 14:3-9

God (with Jesus) has/is the Topic of the gospel (*εὐαγγέλιον [B/T], 14:9) that, when proclaimed into the whole word, will include the account of the action done by the woman who anointed Jesus' body for burial. This context associates God's

---

21. The interpretation of "with/by (μετά) glory" as a Manner/Instrument adjunct depends on the evocation of the previous conjunction of "glory," "come," and "Son of Man" (8:38), where "with (ἐν) glory" functioned as a Manner/Instrument adjunct. The μετά [+gen] realization of Manner adjuncts occurs also in 3:5; 4:16; 6:25; 10:30; 13:26; 14:43a, 43b, 48, 54, 62, 67: cf. Danove, *Linguistics and Exegesis*, 220.

22. As Mary Ann Tolbert, *Sowing the Gospel: Mark's World in a Literary-Historical Perspective* (Minneapolis, MN: Fortress, 1989), 265–6, points out, God's action associated with the coming of Jesus the Son of Man is "a saving, protective, and totally positive event for Mark, it carries with it no threat of divine anger on the Christian community."

(with Jesus') benefaction of the gospel (εὐαγγέλιον [B]) with content about Jesus (εὐαγγέλιον [T]) and what the woman does for Jesus.

b. *14:17-21*

God was the Agent of writing (*γέγραπται [Ace], 14:21) about Jesus the Son of Man's going. There is no specific scriptural antecedent for this statement. Jesus' statement of what God wrote establishes a direct communication relationship from God to the Twelve. The Son of Man's going receives interpretation as the Son of Man's being handed over through (διά) one of the Twelve (Judas Iscariot) as Instrument (14:17-18; cf, 3:19; 14:10, 11). The previous context with Jesus as Theme of "hand over" identifies the Chief Priests and Scribes (10:33) as the Agent handing over Jesus.

c. *14:22-26*

God is blessed (*εὐλογέω [aE], 14:22) by Jesus for the bread that Jesus takes, breaks, and gives to his Disciples/the Twelve (14:14/14:17) while they are eating. Jesus states that this bread is his body. God is given thanks (*εὐχαριστέω [acE], 14:23) by Jesus for the cup that Jesus gives to his Disciples/the Twelve (14:14/14:17) and from which Jesus commands them to drink. Jesus states that his blood is of the covenant and is shed for many (14:24). God has the covenant (διαθήκη [B], 14:24) in/by Jesus' blood. This covenant governs the relationship between God and Jesus' Disciples. The phrase, "blood of the covenant," recalls Moses' statement in reference to God's making the covenant with God's people in the desert (Exod 24:8). This establishes a distinction between that covenant in/by the blood of calves (Exod 24:5) and the present covenant in/by the blood of Jesus. The condition for participation in this covenant is eating Jesus' body and drinking the cup of Jesus' blood. God has the reign (*βασιλεία [B], 14:25) in which Jesus will drink the fruit of the vine new after the shedding of his blood. Repetition of "drink" relates the Disciples' present drinking of the cup of Jesus' blood, and Jesus' future drinking of the fruit of the vine in God's reign and places both within the context of the covenant in/by his blood. God is sung (ὑμνέω [acE], 14:26) a hymn at the conclusion of this meal.

d. *14:27-31*

God was the Agent of writing (*γέγραπται [Ace], 14:27) "I will strike the shepherd and the sheep will be scattered" (Zech. 13:7).[23] Jesus' statement of what God wrote establishes a direct communication relationship from God to the Twelve (14:17). God strikes (πατάσσω [Ap], 14:27) Jesus the Shepherd, with the consequence that

---

23. This quote has significant vocabulary parallels to Zech. 13:7 but has been reformulated to make God the Agent of striking.

Jesus' Disciples the Sheep are scattered. The only action proposed for God between the statement of God striking the Shepherd (Jesus) and the scattering (flight) of the sheep (Jesus' Disciples) at Jesus' arrest (14:50) is God's not taking away the cup from Jesus (14:36).²⁴ This interprets God's striking as God's non-intervention in the events of Jesus' passion. Subsequent events (14:43–15:37) confirm the predictive potential of what was written about God striking Jesus the Shepherd. God has the scriptures by which it may be necessary (*δεῖ [vi-iB], 14:31) that Peter die with Jesus. There is no specific scriptural antecedent for this statement. Since Peter does not die with Jesus, Peter's assertion is invalid in relation to the present of the story time. Jesus' previous statement to Peter (13:10-12), however, acknowledges the possibility that Peter may be among those who will be killed for their proclamation of the gospel. Thus this assertion remains potentially valid.

e. 14:32-42

God is prayed to (*προσεύχομαι [acE], 14:32) by Jesus. God is prayed to (*προσεύχομαι [acE], 14:35) by Jesus that this hour may pass by him. God is Abba Father (*πατήρ [bP], 14:36) of Jesus and so has reciprocal benefaction of Jesus. God Jesus' Abba Father has all things able [to be done]/all possible things (*δυνατόν [B], 14:36) including the capacity to take away this cup from Jesus. This cup references the Son of Man's coming betrayal, condemnation to death, and resurrection (10:33-34).²⁵ God does not take away (παραφέρω [Aθs], 14:36) this cup from Jesus. God does not want (θέλω [Ec], [14:36]) what Jesus wants, to take away this cup from Jesus. Jesus chooses not what he wants but what God wants. God is to be prayed to (*προσεύχομαι [acE], 14:38) by Peter, James, and John that they not come into temptation, but they do not do so. God is prayed to

---

24. As Raymond E. Brown, *The Death of the Messiah: From Gethsemane to the Grave* (New York: Doubleday, 1994), 1:166–7, observes, Jesus' request for God to take away the cup is "not [a prayer] of rebellion but of confidence in God's love and justice. God will listen and will grant the request if it is reconcilable with overall Providence." In this case, however, it is not reconcilable. On the propriety of this prayer and the possibility of its success, see Sharyn Echols Dowd, *Prayer, Power, and the Problem of Suffering: Mark 11:22-25 in the Context of Markan Theology* (SBLDS 105; Atlanta: Scholars, 1988), 57; and Heil, *Model for Action*, 300.

25. If "cup" evokes scriptural antecedents that associate this word with suffering that has to be endured (Isa 51:17, 22; Jer 25:15; 49:12; 51:7; Lam 4:21; Ezek 23:31-32; Hab 2:16), then the cup also would be related to Jesus the Son of Man's necessary suffering (8:31) and predicted suffering much (9:12). Jack Dean Kingsbury, "'God' within the Narrative World of Mark," in *The Forgotten God: Perspectives in Biblical Theology*, ed. A. Andrew Das and Frank J. Matera (Louisville, KY: Westminster John Knox, 2002), 80, further develops the link between 14:36 and 8:31.

(*προσεύχομαι [acE], 14:39) by Jesus who apparently reiterates his request about this cup and his statement of commitment to what God wants.

f. 14:48-52

God has the Temple (*ἱερόν [bB], 14:49), the location of Jesus' teaching day after day, but those arresting Jesus choose, instead, to come out as onto a thief to arrest him with swords and clubs. God has the scriptures (*γραφή [B], 14:49) that are fulfilled at the arrest of Jesus. There is no specific scriptural antecedent for the events narrated in this context. The actions of those with swords and clubs (14:48) from the Chief Priests, Scribes, and Elders (14:43) fulfill God's scriptures, confirming the scriptures' predictive potential.

g. 14:55-59

God has recipient benefaction of the sanctuary (*ναός [bB], 14:58a) made with hands that some falsely accuse Jesus of *saying* that he is going to raze. God has recipient benefaction of the sanctuary (*ναός [bB], [14:58b]) not made with hands that some falsely accuse Jesus of *saying* that he is going to build over a period of three days. The falseness of this dual accusation resides neither in God's recipient benefaction of the sanctuary made/not made with hands nor in Jesus' actions of razing and building but in the claim that Jesus actually spoke this statement.[26]

h. 14:60-64

God the Blessed One has Jesus the Christ (*χριστός [B], 14:61) and Son (*υἱός [B], 14:61), which is the Content of the Chief Priest's question to Jesus. God the Power has the right [hand] (*δεξιά [B], 14:62) at which the Chief Priest and whole Sanhedrin (14:55) will see Jesus the Son of Man sitting when he comes in the company of the clouds of heaven. God does not have recipient benefaction of the blasphemy (*βλασφημία [bB], 14:64) attributed by the Chief Priest to Jesus when Jesus acknowledges that he is the Christ, the Son of the Blessed One, and asserts that he is the Son of Man. As a consequence, the Chief Priest's claim that Jesus has committed blasphemy itself is blasphemy both against Jesus who is the Christ and Son of God the Blessed One and the Son of Man and against God who has Jesus as Christ and Son and at whose right [hand] Jesus the Son of Man will sit when he comes.

---

26. This discussion accepts the validity of the content of the false accusation based on the discussion of van Iersel, *Mark*, 446, who develops the manner in which the false accusers "lie the truth" about Jesus: cf. Donald Juel, *Messiah and Temple: The Trial of Jesus in the Gospel of Mark* (SBLDS 31; Missoula, MT: Scholars, 1977), 57. Senior, *The Passion of Jesus*, 91–92, discusses the irony of the accusation. Heil, *Mark*, 321–22, interprets the accusation as "developing Jesus' statement in 13:2 into a true and more profound prophecy."

6. Mark 15

a. 15:29-32

God has recipient benefaction of the sanctuary (*ναός [bB], 15:29) that Jesus is going to raze and in three days build. Although this attribute is drawn from an accusation that is false insofar as Jesus never explicitly says this, it is deemed valid. God has Jesus the Christ (*χριστός [B], 15:32) the King of Israel. The Chief Priests' statement about Jesus the Christ is ironic but valid.

b. 15:33-36

God is the God (*θεός [bP], 15:34a) of Jesus. God is the God (*θεός [bP], 15:34b) of Jesus. God abandons (ἐγκαταλείπω [Ap], 15:34) Jesus at his death. Narrative overlays interpret the quote containing these references (Ps 22:1) in terms of Jesus. Jesus' experience of abandonment by God coheres with the previously established interpretation of God striking Jesus the Shepherd (14:27; cf. Zech 13:7) as God's non-intervention in the events of Jesus' passion and death (14:36).

c. 15:37-39

God has recipient benefaction of the sanctuary (ναός [bB], 15:38) that has a curtain. God tears (*σχίζω [Ap], 15:38) the curtain of the sanctuary into two from top to bottom immediately after Jesus expires. God's tearing of the sanctuary's curtain is interpreted to remove a barrier between God and human beings.[27] God has Jesus the Son (*υἱός [B], 15:39). The centurion is the first human being in Mark to recognize this fact. The sequence of events accommodates the interpretation of Jesus' expiring and God's tearing of the curtain/barrier between God and human beings as the condition for recognizing Jesus as God's Son.

d. 15:42-47

God has the reign (*βασιλεία [B], 15:43) that is awaited by Joseph of Arimathea, a respected counselor, who made bold to go to Pilate and ask for the body of Jesus after Jesus' death. The context proposes Joseph's expectation (as Experiencer) of God's reign as the motivation (cause or condition) for Joseph making bold (as Experiencer).

---

27. For the interpretation of the curtain as a barrier, see Moloney, *Mark*, 328–9. Donald Senior, "The Death of God's Son and the Beginning of the New Age (Matthew 27:51-54)," in *The Language of the Cross*, ed. Aelred Lacomara (Chicago: Franciscan Herald, 1977), 41, views the veil as a "wall of separation" between God and God's people.

Part III

THE THEOLOGICAL STUDY
THE REPEATED ACTIONS AND ATTRIBUTES OF GOD

Chapter 6

GOD AS AGENT

This chapter develops the statements for God's ten repeated actions and then considers the chronology of God's ten repeated and seventeen non-repeated actions. The discussion addresses the repeated actions in the order of their increasing frequency of occurrence and, for repeated actions with the same number of occurrences, in the order of their introduction. The statement of each repeated action includes a Heading that identifies the references to God, the contexts of their occurrence, and, where appropriate, further information that assists in interpretation, a Rehearsal of the specific narrative information associated with the references (subsection "a"), and an Elaboration of two or more salient characteristics developed through repetition in the contexts of occurrences (beginning with subsection "b"). The statements of actions in the Rehearsals and Elaborations use past, present, and future verb forms depending on whether the actions occur before, during, or after the story time, with perennial actions, as well as actions in the present and past or future, using present verb forms. The concluding discussion develops a chronological summary of God's actions.

1. God Tears (*σχίζω [Ap])

God's tearing (*σχίζω [Ap], 1:10; 15:38) occurs in two contexts (1:9-11; 15:37-39) that are incorporated into those of God having Jesus the Son (*υἱός [B], §9.12).

a. God's Agency in Tearing

God tears the heavens immediately after Jesus is baptized by John (1:10) and the curtain of the sanctuary into two from top to bottom immediately after Jesus expires (15:38).

b. God's Tearing of the Heavens Initiates the End Times

Although God's sending the messenger (1:2) has two possible scriptural antecedents (Exod 23:20; Mal 3:1), the following narrative context (1:4-8) highlights God's sending of Elijah (Mal 3:1) by placing John the Messenger in Elijah's clothing (1:6; cf. 2 Kgs 1:8); and Jesus subsequently confirms John's identification with Elijah (9:13). As a consequence, God's sending of John fulfills the expected sending of Elijah before the great and terrible day of the Lord (Mal 4:5) and introduces the expectation of the coming of the end times. This expectation interprets God's next recorded action, tearing (1:10) the heavens, with its partial dissolution of God's original creative action of making the heavens (Gen 1:7-8), as God's initiation of the end times. The following descent of the Spirit onto Jesus (1:10) strengthens this interpretation insofar as the outpouring of God's Spirit on God's people is a primary characteristic of the end times (Isa 44:3; Ezek 36:26-27; Zech 12:10; 13:1).

As previously discussed (§4.1c), the sequence of events within 1:10-11 accommodates the interpretation of God's tearing the heavens as the condition for the descent of the Holy Spirit and the statement by God's voice. This condition portrays the heavens as a barrier between God, specifically God's Spirit and God's voice, and Jesus.

The sequence of events within 1:10-11 also proposes a relationship between Jesus seeing the descent of the Spirit onto himself and the statement by God's voice affirming that Jesus is God's Beloved Son. The context, however, offers no immediate clarification of the nature of this relationship. That Jesus properly interprets the statement about his identity is apparent in his subsequent use of "Abba," a term of endearment, in an address to God his Father (14:36).[1] God's voice subsequently affirms Jesus' identity as God's Beloved Son to Peter, James, and John (9:7), but neither the context nor following developments offer any indication that these Disciples recognize the implications of this statement. In fact, Jesus' command that they not narrate these events until the Son of Man rises from the dead (9:9) suggests that these Disciples will not recognize the implications of the statement of God's voice until after Jesus' death. At this point, the relationship between the descent of the Spirit onto Jesus before the first statement by God's voice and the absence of the Spirit from the context of the second statement is taken to indicate that Jesus is able to recognize the implications of the first statement because he already possesses the Holy Spirit and that the Disciples do not recognize the implications of the second statement because Jesus has not yet baptized them by the Holy Spirit (1:8). These considerations identify both God's tearing of the heavens—the condition for the descent of the Holy Spirit onto Jesus—and Jesus' reception of the Spirit as the linked conditions for Jesus to recognize the implications of the statement of God's voice. This clarifies that having the Holy Spirit is the condition for the proper recognition of Jesus' identity as God's Son.

---

1. The implication of intimacy in Jesus' use of "Abba" to address God receives development in Stein, *Mark*, 662.

c. The Inclusio of 1:9-11 and 15:37-39

The narration of 1:9-11/15:37-39 introduces/concludes the direct portrayal of Jesus in the present (Jesus comes and is baptized, 1:9/Jesus expires, 15:37) and presents a series of parallels in the sequence of events and vocabulary. Immediately after Jesus comes and is baptized/expires, God tears the heavens (1:10)/the curtain (15:38); Jesus sees the Holy Spirit (1:10)/the centurion sees Jesus expire (15:39); and God's voice identifies Jesus as God's Beloved Son (1:11)/the centurion identifies Jesus as God's Son (15:39). These considerations identify 1:9-11 and 15:37-39 as an *inclusio*.[2]

1:9-11	15:37-39
Jesus comes and is baptized (1:9)	Jesus expires (15:37)
God tears (*σχίζω [Ap], 1:10) the heavens	God tears (*σχίζω [Ap], 15:38) the curtain
Jesus sees (ὁράω, 1:10) the Holy Spirit (πνεῦμα, 1:10) descends	the centurion sees (ὁράω, 15:39) Jesus expires (ἐκπνέω, 15:39)
Jesus is (εἰμί, 1:11) God's Beloved Son (*υἱός [B], 1:11)	Jesus was (εἰμί, 15:39) God's Son (*υἱός [B], 15:39)

In the former context, God's tearing of the heavens, which initiates the end times, establishes an eschatological perspective for interpreting Jesus' coming and baptism, Jesus seeing the descent of the Holy Spirit onto Jesus, and the statement affirming Jesus' identity. The linkage of the parallel events within the two contexts then proposes eschatological significance for God's tearing of the curtain and an eschatological perspective for interpreting Jesus' expiring, the centurion seeing Jesus expire, and the centurion's statement affirming Jesus' identity.

d. God's Tearing of the Curtain Initiates a New Stage in the End Times

Whether the curtain separates the Holy of Holies from the rest of the sanctuary (inner curtain) or the sanctuary from what is outside (outer curtain), God's tearing

---

2. For the contribution of πνεῦμα (1:10) and ἐκπνέω (15:37) to the *inclusio* in 1:9-11 and 15:37-39, see Frank J. Matera, *The Kingship of Jesus: Composition and Theology in Mark 15* (SBLDS 66; Chico, CA: Scholars, 1982), 132–5. Further supporting the relationship between "Spirit" and "expire" is the fact that repetition of ἐκπνέω (15:37, 39) in the latter context ensures that "tear" and "Son" bracket and highlight the occurrences of these words and permit the recognition of the parallel sequence "tear-Spirit/expire-Son" (σχίζω-πνεῦμα/ἐκπνέω-υἱός) in the contexts.

(15:38) of it removes a barrier between God and human beings.³ Then, on seeing that Jesus expires as he does, the centurion affirms Jesus' identity as God's Son (15:39). The centurion is the first human being to recognize this.

As previously discussed (§6.1b), the recognition of Jesus' identity as God's Son requires antecedent reception of the Holy Spirit. The precedent of Jesus receiving the Holy Spirit between God's tearing the heavens (1:10) and the statement of his identity (1:11) proposes that the centurion's reception of the Holy Spirit occurs between God's tearing the curtain (15:38) and the centurion's affirmation of Jesus' identity (15:39). This precedent highlights the sole intervening event, the centurion seeing that Jesus expires as he does. At this point, the second notice of Jesus' expiring (ἐκπνέω, 15:39), which shares the same root as Spirit (πνεῦμα, 1:10), recommends the interpretation that Jesus expires the Holy Spirit.⁴ In this light, Jesus' expiring is the occasion of the centurion's reception of the Holy Spirit.⁵ Thus Jesus' expiring initiates Jesus' baptizing by the Holy Spirit (1:8).

These considerations interpret God's tearing of the curtain, with its consequent removal of the barrier between God and human beings, as the condition for the Spirit expired by Jesus to go forth not in ascent back to God but out into the world of human beings. As a consequence, both God's action of tearing and Jesus' expiring of the Spirit function as the conditions for the centurion to recognize Jesus' identity as God's Son. The reception of the Holy Spirit by the centurion, whose identification through a Latinism (κεντυρίων) that highlights his association with Rome and not with God's people, realizes the further expectation of the end times, the outpouring of God's Spirit not only onto God's people (as after the first tearing) but onto all flesh (Joel 2:28-29).⁶

---

3. For the relation between the heavens and the curtain of the sanctuary in antecedent literature, see Daniel M. Gurtner, "The Rending of the Veil and Markan Christology: 'Unveiling' the ΥΙΟΣ ΘΕΟΥ' (Mark 15:38-39)," *BibInt* 15 (2007), 302-3. If, as David Ulansey, "The Heavenly Veil Torn: Mark's Cosmic *Inclusio*," *JBL* 110, no. 1 (1991), 124-5, suggests, the outer curtain presented a depiction of the night sky, God's tearing of it would echo God's initial tearing (1:10) of the heavens and recall the initiation of the end times. Further discussion of the interpretation of the curtain appears in Timothy J. Geddert, *Watchwords: Mark 13 in Markan Eschatology* (JSNTSup 26; Sheffield: Sheffield Academic Press, 1989), 144.

4. José Enrique Aguilar Chiu, "A Theological Reading of ἐξέπνευσεν in Mark 15:37, 39," *CBQ* 78, no. 4 (2016), 682-705; Gundry, *Mark*, 449; and Howard M. Jackson, "The Death of Jesus in Mark and the Miracle from the Cross," *NTS* 33, no. 1 (1987): 16-37.

5. Aguilar Chiu, "ἐξέπνευσεν," 695, 698-9, 710, develops the relationship between Jesus' expiring of the Holy Spirit and the Holy Spirit's role in the centurion's statement about Jesus; cf. S. Motyer, "The Rending of the Veil: A Markan Pentecost?," *NTS* 33, no. 1 (1987), 155-7.

6. Stein, *Mark*, 57, views both of God's actions of tearing as eschatological events; and Moloney, *Mark*, 36, 328, proposes that these actions initiate distinct stages in the end times.

e. The Two Stages in the End Times

The contexts of God's first/second tearing establish a series of parallels between Jesus God's Son and human beings. God's first/second tearing removes the barrier between God and Jesus/human beings after Jesus' baptism/death. These actions of tearing permit Jesus/human beings to receive the Holy Spirit. Reception of the Holy Spirit enables Jesus/human beings to recognize the identity of Jesus as God's Beloved Son/Son.

The events associated with God's first tearing, the coming of God's Spirit and the affirmation of Jesus' identity, are interpreted to equip Jesus for his coming ministry, insofar as the first action of Jesus after his baptism and reception of the Holy Spirit is proclaiming repentance and belief in the gospel (1:15).[7] In a similar fashion, the events associated with God's second tearing, the availability of God's Spirit to human beings and the affirmation of Jesus' identity, are interpreted to equip human beings to undertake the continuation of Jesus' ministry, insofar as the first action proposed by Jesus for the Twelve after his death is proclaiming the gospel to all the nations (13:10).

These considerations indicate that, just as God's first tearing initiates the end times, God's second tearing initiates a new stage in the end times during which Jesus' Disciples, fully equipped with God's Spirit, recognition of Jesus' identity, and the example of Jesus' teachings and actions, are to continue his ministry.

2. God Will Shorten (*κολοβόω [Ap]) the Days

God's shortening (*κολοβόω [Ap], 13:20a, 20b) the days occurs in a single context (13:18-20) that is incorporated into those of God saving (*σῴζω [Ap], §6.6), having the Elect (*ἐκλεκτός [B], §7.7), and being prayed to (*προσεύχομαι [acE], §10.7).

a. God's Agency in Shortening the Days

God the Lord will shorten the days of the tribulation, which is the condition for God to save some human beings (13:20a), and has as its cause God's Elect (13:20b).

b. God's Shortening the Days Is Directed to Saving Human Beings

God's shortening the days is the condition for God to save some human beings. The cause of God shortening the days, the Elect whom God will choose, identifies the Elect as the beneficiaries of God's end-time saving action. The greater context, however, also specifies the Disciple of Jesus that perseveres to the end as a

---

7. France, *Mark*, 77–8, notes that the Spirit equips Jesus for his mission and for his baptizing by the Holy Spirit.

beneficiary of God's end-time saving action (13:13). This proposes that the Elect whom God will choose will incorporate perseverant Disciples of Jesus.[8]

c. God's Shortening the Days and Jesus' Disciples' Praying

The context presents two concentrically arranged caused actions (§5.4e): Jesus' Disciples' praying to God because of the severity of the end-time tribulation and God's shortening the days because of the Elect. The Disciples' praying is the last action predicated of human beings in this age, and God's shortening the days is the last action predicated of God before God's end-time action of saving. The contrast between these end-time actions is stark: praying will place Jesus' Disciples in a receptive stance toward God, whereas God's shortening the days will be an autonomous creative action. The Disciples' praying will make them the beneficiaries of God's requested action (ensuring that the tribulation not occur in winter), and God will make the Elect the beneficiaries of God's shortening the days. Since Disciples are to believe that they have what they pray for (11:23-24), believing Disciples that continue to pray to God at the end are associated both with the Disciple of Jesus that perseveres to the end (13:13) and the Elect (13:20) as co-beneficiaries of God's end-time saving action.

d. God's Shortening the Days Is a Caused Action

God's shortening the days has as its cause God's Elect. This is the second of only two caused actions of God. In the former occurrence, the human being that came to be by God ([2:27b]) was the cause of the Sabbath coming to be by God (2:27a); and, in this occurrence, the Elect whom God will choose (13:20) will be the cause for God shortening the days. In both occurrences, God's previous actions, the coming to be of the human being and the choosing of the Elect, are the ultimate causes of God's actions. These considerations highlight two characteristics of God's actions. First, nothing external to God is the ultimate cause of God's actions. Second, these caused actions, which bracket the entirety of God's activity from the primordial past to the end of this age, are portrayed as beneficial, first to all human beings and then to all human beings whom God will save, that is, the Elect and the perseverant and praying Disciples associated with the Elect.

3. God Does/Makes/Acts (*ποιέω [Ap])

God's doing/making/acting (*ποιέω [Ap], 5:19; 10:6; 12:9) occurs in three contexts (5:18-20; 10:1-9; 12:9-11). God's action of making human beings male and female (10:6) is deemed perennial (§5.1a).

---

8. The association of Jesus' perseverant Disciple and God's Elect receives development in Charles B. Cousar, "Eschatology and Mark's Theologia Crucis: A Critical Analysis of Mark 13," *Interpretation* 24, no. 3 (1970): 324.

a. God's Agency in Doing/Making/Acting

God the Lord does (with Jesus) many things for the former demoniac (5:19), makes human beings male and female from the beginning of creation (10:6). God will act by destroying the Farmers (Chief Priests, Scribes, and Elders) and giving the Vineyard (God's people) to others (12:9).

b. God's Doing/Making/Acting Is For (or Against) Human Beings

Specification in the first context that what God (with Jesus) does is for the demoniac (5:19) calls attention to those for (benefaction) and against (malefaction) whom God acts in this and the following contexts. This emphasis on beneficiaries encourages the recollection that God's making human beings male and female (10:6) was for Adam, who lacked a helper like himself (Gen 2:20-23). God's future acting is for the Vineyard, which will be able to fulfill its obligation to render some of its fruit to God (12:2). God's actions also are against the demon that keeps the demoniac in isolation from the local people and his family and against the Farmers who prevent God's people from rendering their fruit to God and kill God's Beloved Son. The lack of an object of God's malefaction in making human beings male and female highlights the utter beneficence of this action. The first context identifies all of these beneficial acts as acts of mercy.

c. God's Doing/Making/Acting [Re]establishes Proper Relationships

God's actions for human beings establish the condition for proper relationships between the demoniac and other human beings, between the man and the woman, and between God's people and God. In like manner, God's actions remove impediments to such relationships: the demon, the lack of a helper, and the Farmers frustrating the rendering of fruit to God.

d. God's Doing/Making/Acting Is For All Without Distinction

God's actions are for all human beings (male and female), for a group (God's people), and (with Jesus) for an individual (the demoniac). The universality of God's beneficial actions is especially clear in the case of the demoniac who dwells across the sea (5:1) where pigs are kept (5:11) and so cannot be assumed to be among God's people.

e. God's Doing/Making/Acting As Merciful

The coordination of God (with Jesus) doing and God (with Jesus) being merciful and the generic use of "do" in 12:9 to designate various specific actions of God (destroy, give) invites the interpretation of all that God does as merciful acts for one, some, and all human beings lacking appropriate relationships with God and each other.

4. God Says (*λέγω [Ace])

God's saying (*λέγω [Ace], 12:6, 26a, 36) occurs in three contexts (12:6-8, 18-27, 35-37). "Say" establishes a direct communication relationship from the speaker to the interpreter.

a. God's Agency in Saying

God said to Moses, "I am the God of Abraham and the God of Isaac and the God of Jacob" (12:26a; cf. Exod 3:6, 15-16). God says, "They (Chief Priests, Scribes, and Elders) will respect my Son (Jesus)" to the implied reader (12:6; cf. §5.3b). God the Lord will say to the risen Jesus the Lord of David, "Sit at my right [hand] until I put your enemies under your feet" (12:36; cf. Ps 110:1).

b. What God Says Confirms Jesus' Identity and the Resurrection

God's saying is addressed to an unspecified addressee in the present, to Moses in the past, and to the risen Jesus in the future. God's present saying enjoins respect for Jesus God's Beloved Son on the Chief Priests, Scribes, and Elders who, instead, kill Jesus (12:7-8). God's past saying confirms the resurrection, which demonstrates that the Sadducees know neither the scriptures nor the power of God (12:24). God's future saying occurs in the context of David's acknowledgment of the risen Jesus as his Lord and God's command to the risen Jesus to sit at God's right (12:36) as God's agent (§5.3g) and so provides further confirmation of both Jesus' identity and the resurrection. Repetition associates the Chief Priests, Scribes, and Elders and the Sadducees with the enemies whom God will place beneath the feet of the risen Jesus. This placing will begin when God comes and destroys the Chief Priests, Scribes, and Elders (12:9) and when the Temple complex, the seat of the Sadducees' power, has no stone left on another (13:2). In contrast, David's recognition of the risen Jesus as his Lord appropriately respects Jesus and places David in the proper relationship with God and Jesus.

c. God's Speaking Relates Moses, the Implied Reader of Mark's Gospel, and Jesus

God's actions of saying establish direct communication relationships from God to Moses (12:26a), the implied reader (12:6), and the risen Lord Jesus (12:36). This associates Moses, the implied reader, and Jesus the Lord, with the qualification that only Jesus is able to interpret for the implied reader the implications of what God said to Moses and what David said of Jesus.

d. God's Speaking Emphasizes God's Reciprocal Benefaction of Those Who Will Rise

Repetition of "say" places emphasis on God's reciprocal benefaction. God has explicit reciprocal benefaction of Jesus (have, Son, Son, 12:6), Abraham, Isaac, and

Jacob (God, 12:26), and the living (God, 12:27) and implicit reciprocal benefaction of Jesus (Heir, 12:7; Christ, 12:35) and David (Lord, 12:36). Repetition relates these characters to each other and associates them with those who will rise in the resurrection and be like God's Angels (12:25).[9] In contrast, God is not attributed with reciprocal benefaction of the Chief Priests, Scribes, and Elders who kill God's Beloved Son (12:6-8), the Sadducees who know neither the scriptures nor the power of God and are greatly misled (12:18-27), the dead (12:27), and Jesus' enemies whom God will place under Jesus' feet (12:36). Repetition similarly relates these characters to each other and invites the interpretation that they will neither rise nor be like God's Angels.

5. God Is the Agent by Whom Events Come To Be (*γίνομαι [pA])

God's agency in what comes to be (*γίνομαι [pA], 2:27a, [27b]; 6:2b; 12:11) occurs in three contexts (2:23-28; 6:1-6a; 12:9-12).

a. God's Agency in What Comes to Be

God was the one by whom the Sabbath (2:27a) and the human being ([2:27b]) came to be. God is the one by whom the powerful deeds through Jesus' hands come to be (6:2b). God will be the one by whom it will come to be that the stone rejected by the builders becomes the cornerstone (12:11).

b. God's Agency in What Comes to Be Is for Human Beings

God's actions in what comes to be in the past and present clearly are for the benefit of human beings. The coming to be of the human being benefits all human beings. The coming to be of the Sabbath, specifically with respect to the observance of the Sabbath commandments as interpreted and applied by Jesus the Son of Man and Lord of the Sabbath, is for the benefit of God's people. The coming to be of powerful deeds through Jesus' hands is for the benefit of those to whom Jesus ministers. This pattern proposes that the rejected stone becoming the cornerstone also has beneficiaries. At this point, God's contextually parallel responses to the killing of Jesus the Beloved Son, destroying the Farmers and giving the Vineyard to others (12:9) and the rejected stone becoming the cornerstone (12:10–11), join with God's designation of Jesus God's Beloved Son as God's final and definitive emissary to the Vineyard (12:6) to recommend both the Vineyard and the others newly set over the Vineyard as the beneficiaries. The "others" are taken to be the Twelve who are established and equipped with authority by Jesus in the first stage of the end times (3:15; 6:7) and will remain the only human beings with authority in the

---

9. Donahue, "The Revelation of God," 164, observes that the resurrection is not a return from the grave but enduring life in the power of God.

second stage of the end times.[10] As a consequence, the coming to be of Jesus the Cornerstone will establish Jesus as the mediator of God's relationship with the Vineyard and the Twelve entrusted with its oversight for the remainder of this age.

c. God's Agency in What Comes to Be Specifies Jesus' Identity

God's agency in what comes to be establishes and relates designations for Jesus. Insofar as the Sabbath came to be because of the human being/powerful deeds come to be through Jesus' hands/the rejected stone becoming the cornerstone will come to be, Jesus is Lord of the Sabbath (as Son of Man)/Prophet/Cornerstone. As Lord of the Sabbath, Jesus the Son of Man has dominion over the interpretation and application of Sabbath commandments. As Prophet, Jesus manifests to human beings God's wisdom in his teachings and God's authority in his actions. As Rejected Stone Become Cornerstone, Jesus mediates God's relationship with God's people and the Twelve entrusted with their oversight. The second context's identification of Jesus the Prophet as the instrument of powerful deeds also encourages the recognition of Jesus the Lord of the Sabbath as the instrument of the proper interpretation and application of Sabbath regulations and Jesus the Cornerstone as the instrument of God's relationship with God's people and the Twelve. Thus God's actions make Jesus God's instrument *par excellence* for interpreting and applying what God did in the past, enacting what God does in the present, and mediating what God will do in the future for human beings.

6. God Will Save (*σῴζω [Ap])

God's future saving (*σῴζω [Ap], 8:35b; [10:27]; 13:13, 20) occurs in four contexts (8:31-9:1; 10:23-27, 13:9-13, 18-20) that incorporate that of God shortening (*κολοβόω. [Ap], §6.2) the days.

a. God's Agency in Saving

God will save the one destroying one's life for the sake of Jesus and the gospel (8:35b), will save human beings, something human beings cannot do ([10:27]), will save the Disciple of Jesus persevering to the end (13:13), and will save some human beings, which has as its condition that God shorten the days (13:20).

b. God's Unique Saving Action Is For Specific Human Beings

God, who alone is able to save human beings ([10:27]), will do so at the end of this age (13:13, 20). God's saving action relates the one destroying one's life for the sake of Jesus and the gospel (8:35), the one keeping God's commandments, selling one's

---

10. The same interpretation by different means appears in van Iersel, *Mark*, 368.

possessions, giving to the poor, and following Jesus (10:18–21), the Disciple of Jesus persevering until the end (13:13), and the Elect chosen by God (13:20) and associates to these the Disciples of Jesus who will pray to God before the end (13:18; cf. §6.2c). God's saving action will not be for the one wishing to save one's life but actually destroying it (8:35), the one not keeping God's commandments, selling what one has, giving to the poor, and following Jesus (10:22), and the Disciple of Jesus not persevering to the end (13:13).

c. *The Human Being as Instrument of God's Saving Action for Oneself*

The human being destroying one's life because of Jesus and the gospel (8:35) acts as the instrument of God's saving action for oneself (§4.8d). This interprets the one keeping God's commandments, selling one's possessions, giving to the poor, and following Jesus (10:18-21) and the Disciple of Jesus persevering until the end (13:13) as the instruments of God's saving for themselves.

d. *Two Perspectives on God's Action of Saving*

The contexts place in tension two perspectives on God's saving action: God will save those whom God will choose; and God will save those acting as the instruments of God's saving action for themselves. This tension, which acknowledges God's unique agency in choosing and saving even as it highlights the indispensable role of human action, proposes that those serving as the instruments of God's saving action for themselves will be among those whom God will choose as the Elect.

7. *God Forgives (*ἀφίημι [Apb])*

God's forgiving (*ἀφίημι [Apb], 2:5, 7, 9; 3:28; 4:12; 11:25b) occurs in four contexts (2:1-12; 3:20-35; 4:10-12; 11:20-25) that incorporate those of God being blasphemed (*βλασφημέω [apB], §9.2) and of God having recipient benefaction of sinful actions (*ἁμάρτημα [bB], §9.2). This discussion interprets forgiving as the act of canceling (sending away of) covenantal debts owed to God (§1.2b). Since such debts result from actions that cannot be undone, the only recourse for the debtor is to ask God to cancel them. God's offer of forgiving is deemed perennial (§4.3d).

a. *God's Agency in Forgiving*

God forgives the sins of the paralyzed man (2:5, 9), (with Jesus the Son of Man) is able to forgive sins for human beings (2:7), forgives for human beings all the sinful actions and blasphemies that human beings may blaspheme (3:28), does not forgive for those seeing and not perceiving, hearing and not understanding, and so not turning (4:12; cf. Isa 6:9-10), and, as Father in the Heavens, forgives trespasses for Jesus' Disciples who forgive for others whatever they hold against them (11:25b).

b. God's Action of Forgiving Is Universally Available but Conditioned

God's action of forgiving extends to all sins (2:5, 7, 9), sinful actions (3:28), blasphemies (3:28), and trespasses (11:25), is available to human beings at all times (§4.3d), but benefits only those human beings characterized by specific antecedent actions. Jesus states that the paralyzed man's sins are forgiven on seeing the faith-based action of the man and those carrying him (2:5). Those to whom God gives the secret of God's reign become beneficiaries of God's forgiving once they apply this secret to perceive Jesus' actions, understand his teachings, and turn (4:12). Disciples who pray and forgive what they hold against another have God's forgiveness (11:25). In each case, the antecedent actions affirm and strengthen one's relationship with God concerning whom one believes (2:5), who gives the secret (4:11), and who experiences prayer (11:25). Such actions conform one to the role of the beneficiary of God's action of forgiving. In contrast, actions against one's faith, failing to apply what God gives, and holding things against another undermine one's relationship with God and so one's status as beneficiary of God's forgiveness. In particular, blaspheming God's Holy Spirit (3:29), the instrument of God's forgiveness (§4.1b), can render one unable to have God's forgiveness forever.

c. Jesus' Roles in God's Action of Forgiving

Although forgiving covenantal debts is reserved to God, God delegates to Jesus the Son of Man the authority to forgive covenantal debts on earth. Jesus also contributes to God's action of forgiving through his teachings, which serve as the means by which God gives the secret of God's reign, and his command to his Disciples, by which God imposes the obligation to forgive what is held against another.

d. God's Forgiving as the Origin of All Forgiving

Repetition establishes a series of comparisons and contrasts among God, Jesus, and Jesus' Disciples. God forgives all sins, sinful actions, blasphemies, and trespasses, that is, all covenantal debts. Jesus the Son of Man also forgives all covenantal debts with the dual qualification that his action of forgiving is done by the authority given to him by God and that the forgiving, the sins, or both occur on the earth. The Disciples, in contrast, are attributed with the capacity to forgive only what they hold against another. Both God and Jesus forgive by the Holy Spirit, which recommends a role for the Holy Spirit in the Disciples' forgiving. Both God and Jesus forgive without compulsion, whereas Jesus' Disciples are under obligation to do so. This recommends a different, or at least expanded, role for the Holy Spirit of moving and empowering Disciples to forgive. In all cases, God's action of forgiving is the origin and paradigm for all other actions of forgiving.

8. God Was the Agent of Writing (*γέγραπται [Ace])

God's agency in writing (*γέγραπται [Ace], 1:2; 7:6; 9:12, 13; 11:17; 14:21, 27) occurs in six contexts (1:1-3; 7:6-13; 9:11-13; 11:15-19; 14:17-21, 27-31).

Pre-existing beliefs (§§1.2c, 1.7b) associate God's agency in writing with the third-person singular perfect passive indicative of write (γέγραπται). "Write," like "say" (*λέγω [Ace], §6.4), establishes a direct communication relationship to the interpreter.

a. God's Agency in the Writing of the Scriptures

God was the agent of writing "Look, I send my Messenger before your face..." (1:2; cf. Mal 3:1; Exod 23:20; Isa 40:3 LXX), "This people honors me with their lips..." (7:6; cf. Isa 29:13), "My house shall be called a house of prayer for all the nations but you have made it a den of thieves" (11:17; cf. Isa 56:7; Jer 7:11), and "I will strike the shepherd and the sheep will be scattered" (14:27; cf. Zech. 13:7). God also was the agent of writing that Jesus the Son of Man would suffer much and be scorned (9:12), that they would do to Elijah/John whatever they wish (9:13), and that Jesus Son of Man goes (14:21).

b. God's Agency in Writing Is Focused on Predictive Prophetic Texts

God's actions of writing primarily concern prophetic texts, and only the content of prophetic texts receives development. Although the first half of the quote in 1:2 has as possible antecedents both a prophetic (Mal 3:1) and a non-prophetic (Exod 23:20) text, only the prophetic text receives contextual development through the following overlays that identify John the Messenger with Elijah (1:4-6). The continuation of this quote again references a prophetic text (1:3; cf. Isa 40:3). Thereafter all occurrences of God's action of writing with identifiable antecedents are from prophetic texts: 7:6-13 (Isa 29:13); 11:17 (Isa 56:7; Jer 7:11); and 14:27 (Zech. 13:7). Given this pattern of development, Jesus' statements concerning what was written about the Son of Man (9:12; 14:21) and Elijah/John (9:13), which have no specific discernible scriptural antecedents, are taken to represent Jesus' own distillation of the predictions of prophetic texts. These prophetic texts are interpreted to have recorded in the past what happens in the present and so to have the capacity to predict, not cause, present events (§1.2c). The only noted scribe of God's writing is Isaiah (1:2; 7:6), God's Prophet.

c. What Was Written Is about Jesus, John the Messenger, and Those Opposed to God

God's actions of writing concern most frequently Jesus (1:2-3; 9:12; 14:21, 27), then John the Messenger (1:2-3; 9:13), and then characters opposed to God (with Jesus): the Pharisees and Scribes (7:6-7) and those selling, buying, changing money, selling doves, and carrying vessels in the Temple and making God's house a den of thieves (11:17). All of the referenced content of what God wrote in the past has application in the present, highlighting its predictive capacity. Although what is predicted necessarily happens, God acts directly only in the first predicted event, the sending of John the Messenger, and in the last, the striking of Jesus the Shepherd. In the intervening predicted events, only human beings act and their actions are directed against God and either Jesus or John and place them in opposition to God.

d. Jesus As the Mediator of What Was Written

God's actions of writing establish direct communication relationships from God to Jesus (1:2-3), Pharisees and some Scribes (7:6-7), those selling, buying, changing money, selling doves, and carrying vessels in the Temple and making it a den of thieves (11:17); Peter, James, and John (9:12-13); and the Twelve (14:21, 27). There is a progression in the establishment of these relationships: God's first noted action of writing (1:2-3) directly makes Jesus the interpreter of God's written communication and thereafter Jesus makes others the interpreters of God's written communications. This establishes Jesus as the mediator of what was written to human beings. The proposed means for human beings to respond to God's direct written communication to them is for human beings to establish a direct communication relationship to God through prayer (11:17).

e. Clarifications Concerning Jesus

What was written relates a series of clarifications about Jesus. Jesus God's Son and Christ uniquely has co-benefaction of God's face, way, paths, and title "Lord" (1:2-3). Only Jesus is able to prioritize among God's commandments and interpret and apply them in a manner that does not leave behind, reject, or nullify them (7:6-13). Jesus is the Son of Man who is going to suffer much (9:12) and go (14:21). Jesus is able to evaluate, critique, and regulate Temple practices (11:15-18). Jesus is the Shepherd to his Disciples the Sheep (14:27). God's two direct actions present further clarifications. God's sending of John initiates the present of the story time, prepares for Jesus' ministry, and anticipates God's initiation of the first stage in the end times after Jesus is baptized (1:9). God's striking of Jesus the Shepherd, interpreted as not taking away Jesus' cup (§5.5d), does not prevent Jesus the Son of Man's suffering, being rejected, and being killed, and, most importantly, rising, and anticipates God's initiation of the second stage in the eschatological times after Jesus's death (§6.1d).

9. God Sends (*ἀποστέλλω [Aθg])

God's sending (*ἀποστέλλω [Aθg], 1:2; 9:37; 12:2, 4, 5a, [5b], 6) occurs in four contexts (1:1-3; 9:33-37; 12:1-5, 6-8) that incorporate that of God having Slaves (*δοῦλος [B], §9.9).

a. God's Agency in Sending

God sent Slaves to the Farmers (the Chief Priests, Scribes, and Elders) for the purpose of taking some of the fruit of the Vineyard (God's people) of God (12:2, 4,

5a, [5b]). God sends John the Messenger before God's (with Jesus') face to prepare God's (with Jesus') way (1:2; cf. Mal 3:1; Exod 23:20), Jesus (9:37), and Jesus the Beloved Son last of all to the Farmers for the purpose of taking some of the fruit of the Vineyard (12:6).

b. God's Sending Is Purposive

God sends (1:2) John for the purpose of preparing the way before God (with Jesus), and God sent (12:2-5) Slaves and sends Jesus (12:6) for the purpose of taking some of the fruit of God's people. This places God's sending of John and its purpose in the service of God's sending Jesus and its purpose. The Chief Priests, Scribes, and Elders consistently act in opposition to God's purposes in sending by not believing John (11:31), mistreating and killing God's Slaves (12:3-5), and killing Jesus (12:8). Since God's actions of sending ultimately are directed to the same purpose, Jesus' sending of the Twelve (3:14; 6:7) receives interpretation as having that same purpose. Although the Twelve will continue to experience opposition (13:9-13), it will not be from the same opposition as God's Slaves, John, and Jesus because God will destroy the Farmers (12:9).

c. God's Sending Establishes a Hierarchy among Those Sent

God's action of sending links those sent, John God's Messenger, God's Slaves, and Jesus God's Beloved Son. God sends John to prepare God's (with Jesus') way (1:2), whereas God sent Slaves (12:2-5) and sends Jesus (12:6) for the purpose of taking some of the fruit of God's people. John is executed by command of Herod but God's Slaves (12:4-5) and Jesus (12:8) are killed by the Chief Priests, Scribes, and Elders.[11] Despite the parallels between the Slaves and Jesus, there are differences. God makes no preparation for the sending of the Slaves, but God sends John before Jesus. God's reciprocal benefaction of Slaves is that of owner to property and of John is that of sender to messenger, but God's reciprocal benefaction of Jesus is that of Father to Son and Heir. God sends John and numerous Slaves but sends no further representative after Jesus. Thus God's sending asserts a hierarchy among those sent, with all others either preparing for (John) or anticipating (Slaves) the definitive sending of Jesus God's Beloved Son and Heir.

d. God's Sending Establishes the Contexts for Accepting and Rejecting God

God's sending also relates and draws distinctions among those to whom God sends. God sends John before God (with Jesus) to call his addressees to prepare the way and make straight the paths (1:3). God sends Jesus to an unspecified locale

---

11. John, in contrast, garners only the ambivalence of the Chief Priests, Scribes, and Elders (11:30-33) and endures the deadly hostility of Herod, Herodias, and her daughter (6:17-29).

where he teaches his Disciples to receive a child in reference to his name (9:37). God sent Slaves and sends Jesus God's Beloved Son to the Chief Priests, Scribes, and Elders for the purpose of taking (λαμβάνω) some of the fruit of God's people. This contrasts those heeding John's call and Jesus' teaching with the Chief Priests, Scribes, and Elders who respond by taking (λαμβάνω) first God's Slave whom they beat and sent back empty-handed (12:3) and then Jesus whom they kill (12:8). God's sending of Jesus takes on special significance, given that the only noted way for a human being to receive God is to receive Jesus (9:37), which establishes Jesus as the intermediary between God and Jesus' Disciples.[12] Those preparing the way, making straight the paths, receiving the child in reference to Jesus' name, and rendering the fruit due to God accept and fulfill the role of the one to whom God sends and so receive God. The Chief Priests, Scribes, and Elders, in contrast, choose to take (λαμβάνω) rather than receive (δέχομαι) Jesus and so do not receive God.

10. God Gives (*δίδωμι [Aθg])

God's giving (*δίδωμι [Aθg], 4:11, 25; 6:2; 8:12; 11:28; 12:9; 13:11) occurs in seven contexts (4:10-12, 24-25; 6:1-6a; 8:11-14; 11:27-33; 12:9-12; 13:9-13) that incorporate that of God being the Source of signs (*σημεῖον [B], §11.5). "Give" requires completion by a giver, what is given, and a recipient. Unless the context specifically states otherwise, the giver has agentive benefaction of what is given and the receiver comes to have recipient benefaction of what is given (§1.6a).[13]

a. God's Agency in Giving

God gives the secret of God's reign to those around Jesus with the Twelve (4:11), wisdom to Jesus (6:2), and authority to Jesus so that (purpose) he does the things that he does (11:28), but does not give the requested sign to this generation/the Pharisees (8:12). God will give the Vineyard (God's people) to others (the Twelve) than the Farmers (Chief Priests, Scribes, and Elders, 12:9), what they will say to the Twelve when they are led and handed over (13:11), and, at the end, in abundance to those having (4:25).

b. God's Giving Equips, Introduces New Possibilities, and Prepares

God's giving equips Jesus, the Twelve, and God's people for their assigned tasks, introduces the possibility for a proper relationship with God, and prepares those who will receive everlasting life.

---

12. God's sending of Jesus also establishes Jesus as intermediary between God and Jesus' Disciples insofar as God sends Jesus to perform specific tasks and Jesus in turn sends the Twelve (3:14; 6:7) and Disciples (11:1; 14:13) to perform specific tasks.

13. A discussion of the relationships of benefaction assumed and imposed by "give" appears in Danove, "The Usages of δίδωμι," 23–40.

God's giving equips Jesus for his ministry by giving him the wisdom by which he teaches and the authority by which he acts and will equip the Twelve for their ministry by giving them what they will say. God will equip God's people by giving them to the Twelve who are to render the Vineyard's fruit due to God.

God's giving the secret of God's reign to those who pursue Jesus' teaching introduces the possibility for them to apply the secret to perceive, understand, turn, and become beneficiaries of God's forgiveness (§4.4a) and so enter a proper relationship with God. In contrast, the Pharisees who do not recognize Jesus' previous teachings and actions as God's validating signs (§4.8b) exclude themselves as candidates for being given a further sign.

God's end-time giving prepares those measuring out properly by applying the secret of God's reign to perceive, understand, turn, and receive God's forgiveness (§4.4b) for a life of abundance in the coming age.

c. Jesus as the Paradigm for Receiving and Utilizing What God Gives

God's action of giving relates the recipients, Jesus, those seeking to perceive and understand, the Twelve, and those measuring out properly. God's action of giving contrasts these recipients with the non-recipients, the Pharisees and those having little at the end. God's giving also introduces a distinction between Jesus who actually employs God's wisdom in his teaching and God's authority in his actions and all remaining recipients who are given the secret but not seen as acting on it or whose actions are predicted for the future (future seekers, the Twelve). God's end-time abundant giving functions as a promise for those who employ productively what God gives on the pattern of Jesus.

d. The Implications of God Giving the Secret of God's Reign

God's giving the secret of God's reign introduces a distinction between those perceiving, understanding, and turning and those not doing so. The former have the capacity to recognize the manifestation of God's reign in events: Jesus' present teaching by God's wisdom and acting by God's authority; the future destruction of the Chief Priests, Scribes and Elders and giving of God's people to the Twelve; the future speaking of the Holy Spirit through the Twelve; and the present and future actions of those measuring out properly.[14] God's action of giving initiates, sustains, and completes all of these manifestations of God's reign. Human beings, however, may not respond properly to God's giving, and improper responses have negative consequences. Those given the secret of God's reign but not perceiving, understanding, and turning do not have God's forgiveness. The Twelve given God's

---

14. As Sharyn Echols Dowd, *Reading Mark: A Literary and Theological Commentary on the Second Gospel* (Macon, GA: Smyth & Helwys, 2000), 59–60, observes, those in the synagogue correctly recognize that Jesus has wisdom but their unbelief resides in not recognizing that God gives the wisdom to Jesus.

people will have the warning example of God's action against the Chief Priests, Scribes, and Elders. The Pharisees hearing Jesus' teachings and seeing his actions but not understanding, perceiving, and turning are given no further sign. Repetition links those with improper responses and proposes that they are among those for whom God's present and future action will not be forgiving and God's end-time action will be taking away what little they have (4:25).

11. God the Agent

This discussion develops the chronology of God's sixty-two repeated and non-repeated actions by resolving them into three groups, God's twenty-four pre-eschatological actions, God's first tearing and the subsequent eighteen actions during the first stage of the end times, and God's second tearing and the subsequent eighteen actions in the second stage of the end times. The discussion further resolves each group of actions into four subgroups and investigates the characteristics of each subgroup. Since God's repeated actions already received investigation, their discussion proceeds in summary fashion. The following tables place God's initiating actions on top and indent the sequential subgroupings of actions, with roughly contemporaneous actions separated by commas. The concluding discussion clarifies the relationship between God's pre-eschatological, first stage and second stage actions, and the past, present, and future of the story world.

a. God's Pre-eschatological Actions

God's twenty-four pre-eschatological actions resolve into (i) God's primordial creative actions that initiate this age, (ii) God's actions in establishing and equipping the Vineyard and the Farmers entrusted with its oversight, (iii) God's interactions with the Farmers through Slaves as God's emissaries, and (iv) God's concluding action that prepares for the initiation of the end times.

> create (κτίζω [Ap], 13:19), human beings come to be (*γίνομαι [pA], [2:27b]), Sabbath comes to be (*γίνομαι [pA], 2:27a), make (*ποιέω [Ap], 10:6), join (συζεύγνυμι [Apg], 10:9)
>
>> plant (φυτεύω [Ap], 12:1), put around (περιτίθημι [Ap], 12:1), dig (ὀρύσσω [Ap], 12:1), build (οἰκοδομέω [Ap], 12:1), lease (ἐκδίδομαι [Aθg], 12:1), say (*λέγω [Ace], 12:26), write (*γέγραπται [Ace], 1:2; 7:6; 9:12, 13; 11:17; 14:21, 27)
>>
>>> send (*ἀποστέλλω [Aθg], 12:2, 4, 5a, [5b]), [not] take (λαμβάνω [Aθs], 12:2)
>>>
>>>> send (*ἀποστέλλω [Aθg], 1:2)

(i) God's Primordial Initiating Actions God's primordial initiating actions are the condition for all subsequent developments in this age. Creating (13:19) creation, a perennial action (§5.1a), benefits all of creation including human beings, and the

coming to be ([2:27b]) of the human beings benefits human beings in particular by giving them a helpmate. God's subsequent joining (10:9) of the male and female into one flesh, a further perennial action (§5.1a), overcomes the resulting separation of male and female and reconstitutes the human being (Gen 5:2). The coming to be of the human being ([2:27b]) is the cause for the coming to be (2:27a) of the Sabbath, and Jesus' compassionate interpretation and application of the commandments governing the Sabbath ensure its benefit for human beings.

(ii) God's Establishing and Equipping Actions God's planting (12:1) establishes the Vineyard and God's putting around (12:1), digging (12:1), and building (12:1) provide it with what is required for its productivity. God's leasing (12:1) establishes the Farmers as lessees. What was said (12:26) to Moses and what was written (1:2; 7:6; 9:12, 13; 11:17; 14:21, 27) further equip the Vineyard and equip the Farmers. God's establishing of the Vineyard proposes a relationship of intimacy between God as artisan and the Vineyard as artifact, whereas God's establishing the Farmers proposes a commercial relationship between God as lessor and the Farmers as lessees. Although Isaiah's story attributed a lack of proper productivity to the Vineyard (Isa 5:2, 7), Jesus' story proposes no such lack. There is no report of any past response to what was said and written.

(iii) God's Interactions God interacts with the Farmers exclusively through God's Slaves as emissaries. God's sending (12:2) the first Slave for the purpose of taking (λαμβάνω, 12:2) some of the fruit of the Vineyard elicits hostility from the Farmers who take (λαμβάνω), beat, and send the Slave back empty-handed (12:3). Thereafter God's sending (12:4, 5a, [5b]) Slave after Slave elicits ever-increasing hostility from the Farmers; and God never takes any of the fruit due to God.

(iv) God's Preparatory Action God's final pre-eschatological action is sending (1:2) John the Messenger whose explicit charge is preparation. God's sending of Elijah was to prepare Israel (Mal 4:6) before the coming of God (Mal 3:1-2) and the great and terrible day of the Lord (Mal 4:5). In fulfillment of this, God sends John who addresses his command to prepare to God's people (Isa 40:3) before the coming of Jesus (1:9), who has God's face, way, paths, and title "Lord" (1:2-3), and the initiation of the end times (1:10). John's mission directly to God's people prepares for the broadening of God's interactions from an exclusive focus on the Farmers.

b. God's Actions in the First Stage of the End Times

God's tearing the heavens and eighteen further actions in the first stage of the end times resolve into (i) God's initiating action, (ii) God's actions in establishing and equipping Jesus as God's emissary to the Vineyard and Farmers and in equipping the implied reader, (iii) God's interactions with the Vineyard, Farmers, others, and the Twelve through Jesus as emissary, and (iv) God's concluding actions that prepare for the initiation of the second stage in the end times.

tear (*σχίζω [Ap], 1:10) heavens

    send (*ἀποστέλλω [Aθg], 9:37; 12:6) Jesus, say (*λέγω [Ace], 12:6), give (*δίδωμι [Aθg], 11:28) authority, give (*δίδωμι [Aθg], 6:2) wisdom, powers come to be (*γίνομαι [pA], 6:2b)

        forgive (*ἀφίημι [Apb], 2:5, 7, 9) for paralytic, forgive (*ἀφίημι [Apb], 3:28) all sins and blasphemies, give (*δίδωμι [Aθg], 4:11) the secret, not forgive (*ἀφίημι, 4:12) for those not turning, do (*ποιέω [Ap], 5:19), not give (*δίδωμι [Aθg], 8:12) a sign, forgive (*ἀφίημι [Apb], 11:25b) for Disciples

            strike (πατάσσω [Ap], 14:27), [not] take away (παραφέρω [Aθs], 14:36), abandon (ἐγκαταλείπω [Ap], 15:34)

(i) God's Initiating Action of the End Times   God tearing (1:10) the heavens is the condition for all subsequent narrated events in the first stage of the end times. This action removes a barrier between God and Jesus and permits the Holy Spirit to descend onto Jesus and God's voice to address Jesus. The descent of the Holy Spirit onto Jesus (1:10) fulfills the expectation for the eschatological outpouring of God's Spirit on God's people, is the condition for Jesus to recognize his identity as God's Beloved Son in whom God delights, and explains how Jesus will be able to baptize by the Holy Spirit (1:8). God's tearing directly benefits Jesus.

(ii) God's Establishing and Equipping Actions   God's sending (9:37; 12:6) of Jesus establishes Jesus as God's final and definitive emissary to the Vineyard and Farmers (12:6) insofar as the one receiving Jesus receives God (9:37). God equips Jesus by giving (6:2) Jesus the wisdom by which he teaches and giving (11:28) Jesus the authority by which he does what he does. At this point, Jesus' commissioning of the Twelve, which twice links sending and authority (3:14-15; 6:7), recommends a similar linkage for God's sending of and giving authority to Jesus. This authority is manifest in the powers that come to be (6:2b) by God through Jesus' hands. The effectiveness of these powers, however, is limited by the faith of the recipients of Jesus' teachings and action (6:5-6). God's saying (12:6), "They will respect my Son," which is contemporaneous with God's sending (12:6), equips the implied reader with God's guidance concerning the appropriate response to Jesus (§5.3b). God's actions establishing and equipping Jesus benefit Jesus by providing him with all that is required for his ministry and potentially benefit those responding to Jesus with faith. God's equipping benefits the implied reader and, through the implied reader, all who respond with respect for Jesus.

(iii) God's Interactions   God's interactions are direct or mediated through Jesus, are actual or only potential, and are directed to the Vineyard, Farmers, Twelve, and demoniac.

    God directly forgives (2:5, 7, 9) the sins of the paralyzed man. Jesus states the potential for God to forgive (3:28) all sins and blasphemies, to forgive (4:12) for those given the secret of God's reign, and to forgive (11:25b) the trespasses of Disciples. Although forgiving all sins and blasphemies for human beings (3:28) is a perennial offer of God, the remaining occurrences of this action indicate that God's forgiving has antecedent conditions: the faith-based action of the paralyzed man and those carrying him (2:5), the perceiving, understanding, and turning of those given the secret of God's reign (4:12), and the forgiving of what Disciples hold against another (11:25). In contrast, God does not give (8:12) a sign to the Pharisees, whose association with the Scribes (2:16; 7:1, 5) relates them to the Farmers, because of their continuing failure to recognize Jesus' previous teachings and actions as God's validating signs. God's withholding of further action for the Pharisees, who clearly do not respect Jesus as God's Son, marks a new development in God's relationship with the Farmers.

God's mediated interactions occur through Jesus by whose teaching God gives (4:11) the secret of God's reign to those around Jesus and the Twelve and by whom God acts (5:19) to have Legion depart from the demoniac. This secret accommodates the recognition that God's reign is apparent in Jesus' teachings and actions.[15] God's action for the demoniac, which receives contextual interpretation as God (with Jesus) being merciful (5:19), extends God's interactions to the demoniac and marks a new development, the extension of God's interaction beyond the Vineyard and Farmers.

Jesus' address to his contemporaries of what was said and written extends God's mediated interactions. After the direct address to Jesus of what was written about the sending of John the Messenger (1:2), Jesus addresses the remaining six occurrences of what was written to others. Jesus addresses what was written about "this people" (7:6-7) to the Pharisees and Scribes to condemn their insincere worship of God and nullification of God's commandments. Jesus addresses what was written about the Son of Man (9:12; 14:21) and the Shepherd (14:27) to his Disciples to instruct them about what will befall him as the Son of Man. Jesus addresses what was written about Elijah/John (9:13) to Peter, James, and John to draw a parallel between what happened to John and what will happen to the Son of Man. Jesus addresses what was written about God's house to those making it a den of thieves (11:17) to inform them of the Temple's proper function. Jesus also addresses what God said to Moses to the Sadducees (12:26) to correct their error in stating that there is no resurrection (12:18). The only reported response to these addresses comes from those permitting God's house to become a den of thieves, the Chief Priests and Scribes, who want to destroy Jesus (11:18). Thus God's attempts to interact with the Pharisees, Scribes, Chief Priests, and Sadducees through Jesus fare no better than God's former attempts to interact with the Farmers through God's Slaves.

God also interacts through Jesus with the Twelve, whom Jesus appoints for the purpose of sending them (3:14; 6:7) and giving them authority (6:7) on the pattern of God's sending and giving authority to Jesus. Jesus' actions make the Twelve emissaries of Jesus and interpret the ministry of the Twelve as an extension of the ministry of Jesus.

---

15. Further discussion of this interpretation appears in Frank J. Matera, "Ethics for the Kingdom of God: The Gospel According to Mark," *Louvain Studies* 20 (1995), 193.

(iv) God's Preparatory Actions   God's last three actions in the first stage of the end times, striking (14:27; cf. Zech 13:7) Jesus the Shepherd, not acting to take away (14:36) the cup from Jesus, and abandoning (15:34; cf. Ps 22:1) Jesus, receive interpretation as linked actions directed to preparing Jesus for his role in the second stage of the end times. As developed in 8:31-38, Jesus' necessary suffering, being rejected, and being killed as Son of Man in the first stage of the end times are required for his necessary rising (8:31), which is the condition for his coming as Son of Man in his Father's glory with the holy Angels at the end of the second stage of the end times (8:38).

God striking Jesus (14:27) and God not taking away the cup from Jesus (14:36) receive interpretation as two perspectives on the same event, God's non-intervention in Jesus the Son of Man's necessary (8:31) suffering, being rejected, being killed, and rising (§5.5d).[16] Then, as the bystanders' reaction to Jesus' question about God's abandonment indicates (15:35-36), it is still possible for God to intervene. But God does not do so. Thus God's abandoning Jesus completes God's striking Jesus and not taking away the cup from Jesus. This interprets the "why" of God's abandoning Jesus as God ensuring that Jesus completes the necessary events that culminate in his rising as Son of Man.

Although the events about to befall Jesus make his life very sorrowful to the point of death (14:34; cf. Ps 42:6, 11; 43:5) and Jesus does not want to undergo what awaits him as the Son of Man (14:36a), Jesus undergoes not what he wants but what God wants (14:36b). Thus God's linked actions and inaction ensuring that nothing intervenes in the necessary events that culminate in Jesus' rising ultimately prove beneficial, albeit extremely difficult, to Jesus the Son of Man and prepare him for his role in the second stage of the end times.

c. God's Actions in the Second Stage of the End Times

God's tearing the curtain and eighteen further actions in the second stage of the end times resolve into (i) God's initiating action, (ii) God's actions in establishing and equipping Jesus as God's eschatological agent and Cornerstone and the Twelve

---

16. "Cup" recalls its three previous occurrences (10:38, 39; 14:23) and their association with what is about to befall Jesus the Son of Man. The occurrences in 10:38-39 are bracketed by Jesus' prediction of the Son of Man being handed over, being killed, and rising (10:33-34) and Jesus' statement that the Son of Man came to serve and give his life as a ransom for many (10:45). The occurrence in 14:23 appears after Jesus' statement that the Son of Man goes as was written about him and is to be handed over (14:21). The conjunction of "Son of Man" and "what was written" in 14:21 recalls that what was written about the Son of Man concerns his great suffering (9:12), which in turn recalls that the Son of Man's suffering much/many things, being rejected, being killed, and rising are necessary (8:31). These considerations interpret Jesus' request for God to take away the cup as a request for God to take away the necessary chain of events that culminates in Jesus' rising as Son of Man.

as God's emissaries through Jesus to the Vineyard and all the nations, (iii) God's interactions, and (iv) God's preparatory actions for the coming age.

tear (*σχίζω [Ap], 15:38) the curtain

say (*λέγω [Ace], 12:36), do (*ποιέω [Ap], 12:9), destroy (ἀπόλλυμι [Ap], 12:9), give (*δίδωμι [Aθg], 12:9) Vineyard, come to be (*γίνομαι [pA], 12:11), put (τίθημι [Aθg], 12:36), give (*δίδωμι [Aθg], 13:11) what to say

choose (ἐκλέγομαι [Ap], 13:20) the Elect, shorten (*κολοβόω [Ap], 13:20a, 20b) the days

measure out (μετρέω [Aθg], 4:24), add (προστίθημι [Aθg], 4:24), give (*δίδωμι [Aθg], 4:25) more, take up (αἴρω [Aθs], 4:25), save (*σῴζω [Ap], 8:35b; [10:27]; 13:13, 20)

(i) God's Initiating Action of the Second Stage of the End Times God's tearing (15:38) the curtain of the sanctuary is the condition for all subsequent narrated events in the second stage of the end times. This tearing removes a barrier between God and human beings. Jesus' expiring, which initiates Jesus' baptizing by the Holy Spirit (1:8), fulfills the expectation for the eschatological outpouring of God's Spirit not only on God's people but on all flesh and satisfies the condition for the centurion and all human beings to recognize the identity of Jesus as God's Son. Thus God's second tearing benefits the centurion and potentially benefits all human beings.

(ii) God's Establishing and Equipping Actions God saying (12:36) to the risen Jesus to sit at God's right (κάθημαι ἐκ δεξιῶν), the location of the one delegated to exercise God's power, both establishes and equips Jesus as God's eschatological agent. Jesus is to remain seated in this location until God places (12:36) Jesus' enemies under Jesus' feet. That Jesus remains seated at God's right (ἐκ δεξιῶν κάθημαι) in his end-time coming as Son of Man (14:62) indicates that God's placing of Jesus' enemies under his feet continues throughout the second stage of the end times. God's acting (12:9) by destroying (12:9) the Farmers and giving (12:9) the Vineyard to the Twelve begins God's action of placing Jesus' enemies under his feet and establishes the Twelve as the Vineyard's overseers. God's action in the coming to be (12:11) of Jesus, the stone rejected by the Farmers (11:27; 12:12; cf. 8:31), as the Cornerstone establishes the already fully equipped Jesus as God's definitive emissary to the Vineyard for the remainder of this age and equips the Twelve with their emissary from God. God giving (13:11) what they will say to those proclaiming the gospel to all the nations (13:10) further equips the Twelve previously established and equipped by Jesus to proclaim (3:14).

God's establishment of Jesus as the Cornerstone confirms God's previous selection of Jesus as God's definitive emissary in the first stage of the end times (12:6). God's further equipping of the Twelve, Jesus' emissaries in the first stage of the end times (3:13-16), confirms them as God's indirect (through Jesus) emissaries to all the nations. Thus Jesus' relationship with the Twelve as emissaries parallels God's relationship with Jesus as emissary.

God's actions of establishing and equipping are beneficial to Jesus, who is fully equipped as God's eschatological agent and the Cornerstone, to the Vineyard, whose new overseers, the Twelve, are to permit its rendering of what is due to God, and to the Twelve, who are equipped with Jesus as their intermediary and with what they will say. The same actions are potentially beneficial to those served by Jesus God's agent and Cornerstone, to the Vineyard, and to those who respond positively to the Twelve's proclamation of the gospel.

(iii) God's Interactions God interacts directly with specific human beings by choosing (13:20) them as God's Elect and with creation by shortening (13:20a, 20b) the days. God's direct interactions apparently also extend to Jesus' enemies, whom God continues to place under Jesus' feet. God interacts indirectly through the Twelve with all those who respond positively to their proclamation. This interaction will confirm the continuation and expansion (to all the nations) of Jesus' ministry and conform the Twelve to Jesus insofar as proclaiming the gospel is the first action attributed to Jesus in the first stage of the end times (1:15) and to the Twelve in the second stage of the end times (13:10). Since the Elect are the cause of God's shortening the days and shortening the days is the condition for God to save some (13:20), God's choosing the Elect receives interpretation as choosing those whom God will save. The Elect include Disciples persevering to the end and praying to God concerning the tribulation and all serving as the instrument of God's saving action for themselves. God's shortening the days effectively concludes God's interaction with creation as a whole. These interactions directly benefit the Elect and those responding positively to the gospel.

(iv) God's Preparatory Actions God's remaining future actions occur at the end of this age and concern only human beings. God's end-time preparatory actions begin through Jesus who, as God's delegated agent and the Son of Man, sends God's Angels and gathers God's Elect. God's measuring out (4:24) by the measure by which human beings perceive, understand, and turn and adding (4:24) are for all human beings. God's giving (4:25) is for those having, that is, those perceiving, understanding, and turning; and God's taking up (4:25) what little they have is for those not perceiving, understanding, and turning. This proposes an end-time division of human beings into two groups based on human actions.

God's saving (8:35b; [10:27]; 13:13, 20) concludes God's actions in this age. God will save some human beings (13:20), the Elect, whom God will choose. This again proposes an end-time division of human beings into two groups (Elect and not Elect), but this time the division is based on God's action of choosing. Whereas God's unique capacity to save human beings ([10:27]) highlights God's sovereignty, Jesus' assurances that God will save the life of the one destroying one's life for the sake of Jesus and the gospel (8:35b) and the Disciple persevering to the end (13:13) propose that God's sovereign saving action also is a response to human action. The division of human beings into two groups both by human action and by God's action (choosing) and God's saving as both a sovereign and responsive action maintains God's unique capacity to save while emphasizing the essential role of human actions.

The greater context that asserts God's unique agency in saving (10:17-31) compares being saved by God to entering God's reign (10:23-25), inheriting everlasting life (10:17), and receiving life in the coming age (10:30); and entering God's reign also is compared to entering life (9:43-47). These comparisons situate God's end-time actions of measuring out, adding, and giving for those perceiving, understanding, and turning within God's end-time saving action that prepares the Elect for entrance into God's reign and life in the coming age. The same comparisons interpret God's end-time measuring out, adding, and taking away for those not perceiving, understanding, and turning as the absence of God's saving action, which issues in entering Gehenna (9:48) which is characterized by corruption (worm) and ultimate dissolution (fire).

d. God's Actions Past, Present, and Future

All of God's pre-eschatological actions except sending John the Messenger (1:2) belong to the past of the story world, and all of God's actions in the second stage of the end times except tearing the curtain (15:38) belong to the future of the story world. Thus the present of the story world incorporates God's concluding action in the pre-eschatological times, God's initiating and subsequent actions in the first stage of the end times, and God's initiating action of the second stage of the end times. God's initiation of the first and second stages of the end times immediately after Jesus is baptized and expires links Jesus' baptism and death, brackets and proposes an eschatological significance for Jesus' present actions, and sets the stage for God to set all whom God will save in relation to Jesus God's Beloved Son and the Son of Man by having him send God's Angels to gather God's Elect.

Chapter 7

GOD AS AGENTIVE BENEFACTIVE

This chapter develops the statements for God's agentive benefaction of ten repeated persons, things, or events (hereafter, entities) and then considers the characteristics of God's agentive benefaction of these ten repeated and six further non-repeated entities. The discussion addresses the repeated entities in the order of increasing frequency of occurrence and, for those with the same number of occurrences, in the order of their introduction. Each statement of God's agentive benefaction includes a Heading that identifies the references to God, the contexts of their occurrence, and, where appropriate, further information that assists in interpretation, a Rehearsal of the specific narrative information associated with the references (subsection "a"), and an Elaboration of two or more salient contributions developed through repetition in the contexts of occurrences (beginning with subsection "b"). The concluding discussion identifies commonalities and patterns of development in God's agentive benefaction of the repeated and non-repeated entities.

In eight cases of God's repeated agentive benefaction, the nouns that reference the entities have cognate verbs for which God references the Agent. Four of these cognate verbs appear in Mark: God has agentive benefaction of forgiveness (*ἄφεσις [Bb]), creation (*κτίσις [B]), the Elect (*ἐκλεκτός [B]), and the scripture (*γραφή [B]) precisely because God forgives (*ἀφίημι [Apb], 2:5, 7, 9; 3:28; 4:12; 11:25b), creates (κτίζω [Ap], 13:19), will choose (ἐκλέγομαι [Ap], 13:20), and was the Agent of writing (*γέγραπται [Ace], 1:2; 7:6; 9:12, 13; 11:17; 14:21, 27). In the other four cases, the cognate verb remains implicit: God has a voice (*φωνή [B]), Jesus the Christ (*χριστός [B]), the commandments (*ἐντολή [B]), and the reign (*βασιλεία [B]) because God is assumed to produce sound (φωνέω), anoint (χρίω) Jesus, command (ἐντέλλομαι), and reign (βασιλεύω). In the remaining two cases, God has the Vineyard (*ἀμπελών [B]) insofar as God planted (φυτεύω [Ap], 12:1) it; and God has all things able [to be done]/all possible things (*δυνατόν [B]) insofar as God is able (δύναμι) to do/make them.

The discussion also incorporates the two statements of God's repeated agentive benefaction derived from indirect references to God. For ease of reference, the statements for God having the scripture by which events are necessary (δεῖ [vi-iB]) and God having the commandments that do/do not permit (ἔξεστιν [vi-iB]) events appear immediately after the associated statements for God having the scripture and God having the commandments. Except for these intrusions, all other statements of God's repeated agentive benefaction appear in the order of increasing frequency.

The Headings of the statements of God's repeated agentive benefaction use the present tense of "have" to signal God's perennial benefaction of forgiveness (*ἄφεσις [Bb]), creation (*κτίσις [B]) and, presumably, the reign (*βασιλεία [B]) and possible things (*δυνατόν [B]), God's past, present, and assumed future benefaction of scripture (*γραφή [B]), the Vineyard (*ἀμπελών [B]), and commandments (*ἐντολή [B]), God's present and future benefaction of Jesus the Christ (*χριστός [B]), and God's present benefaction of the voice (*φωνή [B]). Since God's choosing of the Elect (*ἐκλεκτός [B]) is a future event, its statement uses the future tense of "have." The forms of verbs in the Headings of statements derived from indirect references use present forms because they reference what is necessary (δεῖ [vi-iB]) and permitted or not permitted (ἔξεστιν [vi-iB]) in the present and future.

1. God Has Forgiveness (*ἄφεσις [Bb])

God having forgiveness (*ἄφεσις [Bb], 1:4; 3:29) occurs in two contexts (1:4–8; 3:20–35) that are incorporated into those of God having the Holy Spirit (*πνεῦμα [B], §8.5). The one forgiving has agentive benefaction of forgiveness, and the one for whom debts are forgiven has recipient benefaction of forgiveness. The concluding discussion develops the implications of the semantic coordination of forgive (*ἀφίημι [Apb], §6.7) and forgiveness (*ἄφεσις [Bb]).

a. The Attributes of God's Forgiveness

God's forgiveness is of sins and the purpose of the baptism of repentance proclaimed by John (1:4) and never is the possession of the one blaspheming God's Holy Spirit (3:29).

b. The Extent and Limit of God's Forgiveness

God's forgiveness extends to all sins and blasphemies but is not for the one blaspheming God's Holy Spirit. Although God forgives all sins and blasphemies for human beings, those blaspheming the Holy Spirit never have God's forgiveness because they speak against and so reject the Holy Spirit, the instrument of God's forgiveness (§4.1b).

c. God's Forgiveness Is Conditioned

Although God has agentive benefaction of the forgiveness of all sins and blasphemies for human beings at all times, the sinner has recipient benefaction of God's forgiveness only if the condition for its reception is met. The first context specifies antecedent repentance as the condition for receiving God's forgiveness

(1:4). When this condition is not met, the relationships of benefaction are reversed: God continues to have recipient benefaction of and the sinner continues to have agentive benefaction of the debts owed to God.

d. The Semantic Coordination of God's Forgiving and God's Forgiveness

The semantic coordination of "forgive" (*ἀφίημι [Apb], §6.7b) and "forgiveness" links confessing sins (1:4), faith-based action (2:5), application of the secret of God's reign to perceive, understand, and turn (4:12), and forgiving what one holds against another (11:25) as conditions for becoming a beneficiary of God's forgiveness.

2. God Has a Voice (*φωνή [B])

God having a voice (*φωνή [B], 1:11; 9:7) occurs in two contexts (1:9–11; 9:2–9) that are incorporated into those of God having Jesus the Son (*υἱός [B], §9.12) and God loving (*ἀγαπητός [Ec], §10.5) Jesus the Son. God's voice establishes direct communication relationships from God to those addressed.

a. The Attributes of God's Voice

God's voice is from the heavens and addresses Jesus with the statement, "You are my beloved Son; in you I delight" (1:11; cf. Ps 2:7; Isa 42:1), and is from the cloud and addresses Peter, James, and John with the statement, "This is my beloved Son; listen to him!" (9:7; cf. Ps 2:7).

b. God's Voice Recognizes and Affirms Jesus' Identity as God's Beloved Son

Prior to Jesus' first action (proclaiming, 1:14), what has been written asserts Jesus' co-benefaction of God's face (1:2), way (1:2, 3), and paths (1:3) and Jesus' use of God's designation "Lord" (1:3); and John asserts that Jesus is stronger than he (1:8). Since both assertions make claims about who and what Jesus already is, God's voice is deemed to recognize and affirm (and not institute or establish) Jesus' status as God's Beloved Son (§4.1c) first to Jesus (1:11) and then to Peter, James, and John (9:7).[1]

c. God's Voice from Above Consistently Speaks about Jesus

Repetition emphasizes God's reciprocal benefaction of Jesus as Son, God's love of Jesus the Son, and the location of God's voice as "from above" (heaven, cloud).

---

1. The interpretation that God's voice affirms Jesus' status as Son receives the support of Culpepper, *Mark*, 50, and Darrell L. Bock, *Mark* (NCBC; Cambridge: Cambridge University Press, 2015), 116–17.

God's voice consistently speaks about God's relationship with Jesus, and its location is consonant with the heavens (11:25) as the locale of God the Disciples' Father.

d. God's Voice Establishes and Commands Communication Relationships

Although God's voice establishes direct communication relationships from God to Jesus and then to Peter, James, and John and so relates them as addressees, the communications draw a distinction between Jesus and these Disciples: whereas the voice affirms to Jesus his status as God's Son and goes on to express God's delight in Jesus, the voice informs the Disciples of Jesus' status and goes on to command that they listen to Jesus.[2] That is, God's voice commands Peter, James, and John to be in a direct communication relationship not from God (or Moses or Elijah) but from Jesus! The intimacy of God's relationship with Jesus, Father to Beloved Son, explains the propriety of this commanded communication relationship.[3] These considerations confirm Jesus as God's delegated mediator of God's communications to human beings (*γέγραπται [Ace], §6.8d).

3. God Has Creation (*κτίσις [B]) Which Had a Beginning

God having creation (*κτίσις [B], 10:6; 13:19) occurs in two contexts (10:2–9; 13:18–20) that incorporate that of God shortening (*κολοβόω [Ap], §6.2) the days.

a. The Attributes of God's Creation

God's creation had a beginning at which God began to make human beings male and female (10:6) and at which God began to create (13:19).

b. God's Actions from the Beginning of Creation Are Beneficial for Human Beings

Repetition of "from the beginning of creation" emphasizes that creation had its beginning and continues by God's sovereign action and links God's initial and continuing creating (13:19), making human beings male and female (10:6), and joining them into one flesh (10:9) to God's concluding actions of choosing the

---

2. Armand Puig i Tàrrech, "The Glory on the Mountain: The Episode of the Transfiguration of Jesus," *NTS* 58, no. 2 (2012): 169–70, would limit the command of God's voice to Peter, James, and John to listen specifically to Jesus' prediction of his death and resurrection (8:31). While Jesus' statements in 8:31–9:1 are in the foreground at 9:7, the coherence of their content with Jesus' teachings elsewhere is taken to indicate that the command to listen to Jesus extends to all his teachings.

3. C. Drew Smith, "'This Is My Beloved Son; Listen to Him:' Theology and Christology in the Gospel of Mark," *HBT* 24 (2002): 75–83, presents a detailed analysis of Jesus as the Speaker of God.

Elect, shortening the days, and saving some human beings (13:19-20). The two contexts develop these creative actions specifically in relation to their benefit for human beings (§§6.11a, 6.11c). The bracketing of all of God's other actions by these creative actions proposes that all of God's actions in this age are beneficial for human beings and are directed to a single goal, saving some human beings.

c. Human Responses to God from the Beginning of Creation

The contexts link the hardness of human hearts as the cause for Moses to write a commandment that attempts to undo God's beneficial creative action of joining male and female (10:5) and the tribulation as the cause for the Disciples' future praying to God (13:19). This linkage contrasts the inappropriate hardness of heart that results in action (writing a commandment) that opposes God's intent and the appropriate recognition of incapacity that results in action (praying) that fulfills God's intent for human beings (11:17).

4. God Has All Possible Things (*δυνατόν [B])

God having all things able [to be done]/all possible things (*δυνατόν [B], 10:27; 14:36) occurs in two contexts (10:23–27; 14:32–42). The phrase, "with God" (10:27), is interpreted to indicate God's agentive benefaction of all possible things (§2.4b).

a. The Attributes of All God's Possible Things

God's things able [to be done]/possible things include the ability to save human beings (10:27) and to take away the cup from Jesus (14:36).

b. God Has All Possible Things but Enacts Only Those Benefitting Human Salvation

Repetition relates two of God's possible things, saving human beings and taking away Jesus' cup, and asserts a contrast between saving human beings, which God will do, and taking away Jesus' cup, which God does not want to do and does not do. The apparent rationale for God's action and inaction is that God acts only to the benefit of human beings: saving human beings is wholly to the benefit of those saved, whereas taking away Jesus' cup, while wanted by Jesus in the present, would be to the ultimate detriment of Jesus the Son of Man insofar as taking away his passion and death would take away the necessary (8:31) condition for his resurrection (§6.11b). That is, God is unwilling to take away the circumstance for Jesus to destroy his life for the sake of the gospel and so to save it (8:35) and, in so doing, to act as the instrument of God's saving action for himself (*σῴζω [Ap], §6.2d).[4] Thus God who

---

4. This interpretation receives further development in David Rhoads, *Reading Mark, Engaging the Gospel* (Minneapolis, MN: Fortress, 2004), 51–3.

has all possible things is willing to enact only those possible things that serve human salvation.

c. Commitment to and Trust in the God Having All Possible Things

God who has all possible things does not grant what Jesus prays for and asks (14:36). At this point, the repetition of "all things" (πάντα, 10:27; 11:24; 14:36) interprets Jesus' statement to his Disciples, "All things that you pray for and ask, believe that you have them and they will be yours," to apply only to all things that benefit human salvation. Jesus' acceptance of and obedient submission to what God wants, even in the face of his impending death, provides a model for his Disciples' proper response to God when one does not receive from God what one prays for and asks.[5]

5. God Has the Scripture (*γραφή [B])

God having the scripture (*γραφή [B], 12:10, 24; 14:49) occurs in three contexts (12:9–12, 18–27; 14:48–52). The concluding discussion considers the semantic coordination of God's agency in what was written (*γέγραπται [Ace], §6.8) and God's benefaction of the scripture (*γραφή [B]).

a. The Attributes of God's Scripture

God's scripture is read by the Chief Priests, Scribes, and Elders (12:10) and states that the stone rejected by the ones building (Chief Priests, Scribes, and Elders) becoming the cornerstone will come to be by God the Lord (12:10–11; cf. Ps 118:22–23), incorporates the command concerning the brother taking his dead brother's wife (12:19; cf. Deut 25:5–6) and God's statement to Moses (12:26; cf. Exod 3:6, 14-16) but is not known by the Sadducees who also do not know God's power and are misled in not acknowledging the resurrection (12:24), and is fulfilled in the events of the arrest of Jesus (14:49).

b. God's Scripture as Proof of the Resurrection

God's scripture directly or indirectly asserts proofs of the resurrection. Jesus the Rejected Stone becoming the Cornerstone (12:10; cf. Ps 118:22–23) will occur after the Chief Priests, Scribes, and Elders kill Jesus (12:8). God's statement to Moses (12:26; cf. Exod 3:6) confirms that Abraham, Isaac, and Jacob were among the living in the time of Moses. Jesus' statement that the events of his arrest fulfill the scripture (14:49) joins with the notice that those arresting him are from the Chief

---

5. Kingsbury, "Narrative World of Mark," 80; cf. Culpepper, *Mark*, 502; and Donahue and Harrington, *Mark*, 408–9.

Priests, Scribes, and Elders (14:43) to evoke God having the scripture by which it is necessary that Jesus the Son of Man suffer much, be rejected by the Elders, Chief Priests, and Scribes, be killed, and rise (8:31).

c. Not Only Reading But Knowing God's Scripture Is Essential

Jesus' questions recognize that the Chief Priests, Scribes, and Elders (12:10) and the Sadducees (12:26) read God's scripture, but neither group is attributed with knowing or understanding its content.[6] Although the Chief Priests, Scribes, and Elders recognize that Jesus addressed the parable about the Vineyard to them and have read the quote about the Rejected Stone becoming the Cornerstone (12:10-11; cf. Ps 118:22-23), they do not recognize that Jesus is the Rejected Stone who will become Cornerstone. Again, although the Sadducees read the Book of Moses (12:24; cf. Exod 3:6, 14-16), they do not recognize that it confirms the resurrection. Lacking knowledge and understanding of God's scripture, the Chief Priests, Scribes, and Elders fulfill the scripture by sending a crowd to arrest Jesus (14:48; cf. 14:43) and killing Jesus God's Beloved Son and Heir (12:8); and the Sadducees do not acknowledge the resurrection (12:18), do not know the power of God (12:24), and remain in error even after Jesus' explanation of the scripture (12:27). Their failure to learn from Jesus' interpretations of God's scripture places both groups in opposition to God, elicits God's response of coming and destroying the Chief Priests, Scribes, and Elders (12:9), and results in the Sadducees remaining ignorant of the resurrection and of God's power and, by implication, not being among those rising and living (§5.3e). These considerations propose Jesus as the definitive interpreter of God's scripture and confirm that reading and knowing the scripture as interpreted by Jesus are vital for having a proper relationship with God and for being a beneficiary of God's power as manifest in the resurrection.

d. The Prophetic, Prescriptive, and Didactic Potential of God's Scripture

God's scripture predicts God's action for Jesus the Rejected Stone (12:10-11), prescribes the actions of a brother for his dead brother and his wife (12:19), proves that the dead rise (12:26), and predicts the events of Jesus' arrest (14:49). Thus God's scripture incorporates the Law that has prescriptive (12:19; cf. Deut 25:5-6) and didactic (12:26; cf. Exod 3:6, 14-16) potential and the Writings (12:10-11; cf. Ps 118:22-23) and unspecified prophetic texts (*γέγραπται [Ace], §6.8b) that have predictive potential (14:49). Fulfillment of the scripture that predicts the events of Jesus' arrest (14:49) also encourages the recognition that God will enact the scripture concerning Jesus the Rejected Stone becoming the Cornerstone (12:10-11).

---

6. The use of οὐδέ (12:10) and then οὐκ (12:26) to introduce Jesus' questions to the Chief Priests, Scribes, and Elders and then the Sadducees indicates the expectation for a positive response; cf. Herbert Weir Smyth, *A Greek Grammar for Colleges* (New York: American Book, 1920), 598 (§2651a).

e. The Semantic Coordination of God's Action in Writing and God's Scripture

Although God's scripture and what was written logically have the same referent, they present both similarities and differences in development. God's scripture has predictive potential (*γραφή [B], §7.5d), as does what was written (*γέγραπται [Ace], §6.8b). The events of Jesus' arrest (14:43–48) that fulfill the scripture (14:49) evoke Jesus' prediction of necessary events about to befall the Son of Man (8:31), indicating that the scripture that is fulfilled is the same set of prophetic texts on which the prediction is based. The differences concern the texts referenced as scripture, their proposed potentialities, and how Jesus applies them. Whereas what has been written (*γέγραπται [Ace], §6.8) places primary emphasis on prophetic texts, God's scripture encompasses the entirety of the scriptural corpus: the Law (12:24; cf. Exod 3:6, 14–16), the Writings (12:10–11; cf. Ps 118:22–23), and the Prophets (14:49). Whereas what has been written has predictive potential, God's scripture has prescriptive, didactic, and predictive potential. As a consequence, Jesus' application of God's scripture extends beyond its predictive potential to include support for claims in his argument concerning the resurrection (12:26). Thus, while the primary contribution of what was written and the scripture is their predictive potential, the scripture as a whole also provides a foundation for theological argument, which coheres with Jesus' use of the content of scripture elsewhere (10:1–9).

6. God Has the Scripture by Which Events Are Necessary(*δεῖ [vi-iB])

God having the scripture by which events are necessary (*δεῖ [vi-iB], 8:31; 9:11; 13:7, 10, 14; 14:31) occurs in six contexts (8:31–9:1; 9:11–13; 13:3–8, 9–13, 14–17; 14:27–31). This statement assumes the content of the statement for God having the scripture (*γραφή [B], §7.5).

a. The Attributes of What God's Scripture Makes Necessary

God's scripture predicts and so necessitates that Jesus the Son of Man suffer much, be rejected by the Elders, the Chief Priests, and the Scribes, be killed, and after three days rise (8:31) and that Elijah/John the Messenger come first (9:11; Mal 3:1; 4:5). God's scripture predicts and will necessitate that wars and reports of war happen (13:7), that the gospel be proclaimed to all nations before the end (13:10), and that the abomination of desolation stand where he (masculine: ἑστηκότα) is not to stand (13:14; cf. Dan 9:27; 11:31; 12:11). God's scripture may predict and necessitate that Peter die with Jesus (14:31).

b. The Scripture by Which Events Are Necessary Makes Reliable Predictions

God's scripture relates what is necessary in the present for Jesus the Son of Man (8:31) and Elijah/John (9:11) and in the future for Jesus' Disciples (13:7, 10), the people of Judea (13:14), and, perhaps, Peter (14:31). The only identifiable scriptural antecedents by which events are/will be necessary are prophetic texts (Mal 3:1; 4:3; Dan 9:27; 11:31; 12:11). Repetition of "suffer much" (8:31; 9:12) relates the scripture by which it is necessary that Jesus the Son of Man suffer much, be rejected, be killed, and rise and the predictions in what was written about Jesus the Son of Man's suffering much and being treated with contempt (9:12) and going as he does (14:21). Repetition of "Elijah" and "come" also relates the scripture by which it is necessary that Elijah/John come first (9:11) and the predictions in what was written about doing to him whatever they wish (9:13). The realization in the present of what is necessary for and was written about Jesus the Son of Man (14:43–16:7) and Elijah/John (1:2; 6:17–29) confirms the predictive potential and reliability of the scripture by which present events are necessary and proposes the future reliability of the scripture by which events will or may be necessary.

c. God's Action in Realizing the Necessary Events Is Limited

Although God's scripture predicts (8:31; 9:11; 13:7, 10), may predict (14:31), and prescribes (13:14) necessary events, God's action in realizing these events is limited. God enacts Elijah/John coming first by sending him (9:11; cf. 1:2), and God will give to the Twelve what they will say and God's Spirit will speak through the Twelve in their necessary proclamation of the gospel (13:10; cf. 13:11). In contrast, God does not intervene in the necessary events concerning Jesus the Son of Man (8:31, cf. §6.11b) and will play no noted role in the wars and reports of wars (13:7) or in Peter's potential dying (14:31). Since God's attributes cannot be in conflict (§5.1a) and God's scripture contains the commandments (Num 18:3, 7) that make necessary that the abomination not stand where he will, God has no role in this event; and the predictive potential of what was written about the abomination (13:14; cf. Dan 9:27; 11:31; 12:11) cannot be interpreted to reflect God's plan or will (§1.2d). All others enacting the events necessitated by God's scripture are human beings who receive negative evaluation: those causing Jesus the Son of Man's suffering and going and then rejecting and killing him, those engaging in wars, the abominating desolation standing where he will, and those who may cause Peter to die.

d. What Is Necessary Need Not Happen

The most curious fact concerning what is necessary is that it need not happen. The scripture that prescribes and so necessitates that non-priests not draw near the altar (Num 18:1–7) will be violated when the desolating abomination stands where he does (13:14).[7] The scripture that predicts and so necessitates the things befalling Jesus the Son of Man (8:31), wars and reports of war (13:7), and the proclamation of the gospel to all nations (13:10) are contingent respectively on Jesus choosing to do not what he wants but what God wants, on the actions of human beings, and on

---

7. In this regard, the Levirite regulation cited by the Sadducees (12:19; cf. Deut 25:5–6) also recognizes that its prescriptions need not be enacted (Deut 25:7–10).

the Twelve fulfilling their mission. In fact, the only predicted and so necessitated event not contingent on human beings and so sure to occur is the coming of Elijah/ John first (9:11, cf. 1:2).

7. God Will Have the Elect (*ἐκλεκτός [B])

God's future having of the Elect (*ἐκλεκτός [B], 13:20, 22, 27) occurs in three continuous contexts (13:18–20, 21–23, 24–29) that incorporate that of God shortening (*κολοβόω [Ap], §6.2) the days.

a. The Attributes of God's Elect

God's Elect will be chosen by God and be the cause of God shortening the days (13:20), will endure the attempts of false Christs and false Prophets to mislead them by signs and wonders (13:22), and will be gathered from the four winds, from the end of the earth to the end of heaven by Jesus the Son of Man after the tribulation (13:27).

b. All of God's Actions During the Tribulation and at the End Are Saving Actions

During the tribulation, God will choose the Elect who will be the cause of God shortening the days. Shortening the days is the condition for God to save some human beings. Although the Elect are the focus of God's future saving action, repetition of "save" in the greater context links the Disciple of Jesus that perseveres to the end (13:13) to God's Elect (13:20); and the first context associates the Disciples of Jesus that pray to God during the tribulation (13:18) with the Elect (13:20). During the tribulation, some will attempt to mislead God's Elect by claiming that Jesus God's Christ is present and by giving signs and wonders that apparently are similar to those in the ministry of Jesus in the present of the story time (§5.4f). Such false Christs and false Prophets are not to be believed because the only apparition of Jesus after the choosing of the Elect will be at his end-time coming as Son of Man (13:26). At that time Jesus the Son of Man will accomplish God's saving action by sending God's Angels and gathering God's Elect (13:27) who will include Jesus' perseverant and praying Disciples. Thus God's direct actions during the tribulation and indirect (through Jesus the Son of Man) action after the tribulation are saving actions.

c. Proper Identification of Jesus the Christ in the Future

The proper identification of Jesus the Christ in the future will be exclusively by the events preceding and attending the coming of Jesus the Son of Man: the sun will be darkened, the moon will not give its light, the stars will be falling from the sky, and the powers in the heaven will be shaken (13:24–25; cf. Isa 13:10; 34:4) prior to his definitive coming in the clouds with much power and glory (13:26; cf. Dan 7:13-14). Since the celestial events that precede the coming of Jesus the Son of Man are unique and not repeatable by human beings and the sight of the coming of Jesus the Son of Man will be readily apparent to all, God's Elect and Jesus' perseverant and praying Disciples are not to be misled by the signs and wonders that can be enacted by false Christs and false Prophets or by reports claiming that Jesus already is present.

8. God Has the Vineyard (*ἀμπελών [B])

God having the Vineyard (*ἀμπελών [B], 12:1, 2, 8, 9a, 9b) occurs in three continuous contexts (12:1–5, 6–8, 9–12) that incorporate that of God having Slaves (*δοῦλος [B], §9.9).

a. The Attributes of God's Vineyard

God's Vineyard (God's people) was planted and leased to the Farmers (the Chief Priests, Scribes, and Elders) by God (12:1) and had the fruit which God sent God's Slaves to take (12:2-5). God's Vineyard is the locale to which God sends Jesus God's Beloved Son (12:6) and out of which the Farmers cast Jesus God's Beloved Son and Heir after killing him (12:8). God's Vineyard has God as its Lord (12:9a) and will be given to others (the Twelve) by God after God comes and destroys the Farmers (12:9b).

b. The Vineyard Is the Focus of God's Actions in Mark

The twelve verses (12:1-12) of the three continuous contexts concerning the Vineyard contain the greatest density of God's actions (sixteen of sixty-two) in Mark. In the past, God established God's people (plant, v. 1), equipped them with all that is required for them to be productive (put around, dig, build, v. 1), set Farmers over the Vineyard (lease, v. 1), and attempted to interact with the Farmers (send, [not] take, v. 2; send, vv. 4, 5a, [5b]) who responded with escalating and finally deadly hostility to God's actions. In the present, God continues to attempt to interact with the Farmers (send, say, v. 6), but the Farmers again respond with deadly hostility, this time against Jesus God's Beloved Son and Heir. In the future, God will respond to the Farmers' hostility (do, destroy, give, v. 9) and establish Jesus as the Cornerstone (come to be, v. 11). The most consistent characteristic of these actions is that they are directed to the benefit of God's people (§6.11).

c. The Chronology of the Parable and Its Implications

The parable of the Vineyard admits to interpretation as providing a synopsis of the narrated events of Mark from the perspective of God's interaction with God's people and those set over them.[8] "Beloved Son" (12:6) has the potential to evoke its

---

8. Further discussion of this appears in Culpepper, *Mark*, 408, and Tolbert, *Sowing the Gospel*, 232.

occurrence in the context (1:9–11) of God's initiation of the first stage of the end times and, through the *inclusio* of 1:9–11 and 15:37–39 (§6.1c), God's initiation of the second stage of the end times. These evocations propose a series of parallels in the chronologies of the narration as a whole and the Parable of the Vineyard.

Prior to God's initiation of the first stage in the end times in God's first action of tearing (1:10)/prior to the present in the parable (12:1–5), God's last recorded action is sending John the Messenger (1:2)/Slaves (12:2, 4, 5). Immediately after the initiation of the first stage of the end times (1:10)/immediately after the initiation of the present of the parable (12:6), God identifies Jesus as God's Beloved Son (1:11/12:6) and, as previously developed (§6.11b), sends Jesus (9:37/12:6). Immediately prior to God's initiation of the second stage of the end times by God's second tearing (15:38)/immediately prior to God's future responding action (12:9), Jesus expires (15:37)/is killed (12:8). After Jesus expires/is killed, the Twelve undertake his ministry (13:10)/God gives God's Vineyard to others (12:9); and Jesus the Lord is seated at God's right [hand] (12:36)/Jesus the Rejected Stone becomes the Cornerstone (12:10). The following diagram separates the Times, pre-eschatological (pre.), first eschatological stage (St. 1), and second eschatological stage (St. 2) and the past, present (pres.), and future (fut.) events of the parable by slashes (/).

	Mark	/	Vineyard
pre./past	God sends God's Messenger	/	God sends God's Slaves
St. 1/pres.	God sends God's Beloved Son	/	God sends God's Beloved Son
	↓	/	↓
	Jesus God's Son expires	/	Jesus God's Heir is killed
St. 2/fut.	the Twelve's ministry	/	God gives Vineyard to others
	risen Jesus the Lord seated	/	Jesus becomes the Cornerstone

These parallels confirm the Twelve as the others to whom God gives God's people (12:9) and the Chief Priests, Scribes, and Elders (12:12; cf. 11:27) as among the enemies whom God places under the resurrected Lord Jesus' feet (12:36) and relate God's stationing of the risen Jesus the Lord of David at God's right (12:36) and God's agency in Jesus the Rejected Stone becoming the Cornerstone (12:11).

d. *God's Relationship with Jesus: A Further Focus of the Vineyard*

At the center of the three contexts (vv. 6-8) appears the densest concentration in Mark of God's reciprocal benefaction of Jesus, whom God has (v. 6) and who is God's Son (v. 6a, 6b) and Heir (v. 7). The same verses assert God's love for Jesus (v. 6), present God speaking an injunction to respect Jesus (v. 6), and specify Jesus' co-benefaction of God's people as Heir (v. 7). The uniqueness of God's relationship with Jesus is apparent in the fact that, whereas God responded to the killing of God's Slaves (v. 5a, 5b) by sending God's Son (v. 6), God responds to the killing of God's Son (v. 8) by acting directly (v. 9).

e. God's Dual Response to the Killing of Jesus

The parable's dual focus on God's interaction with God's People and on God's relationship with Jesus is reflected in God's dual future response to the killing of Jesus, first of destroying the Farmers and giving the Vineyard to others (v. 9) who are to render some of the fruit due to God and then of Jesus becoming the Cornerstone which will come to be by God (vv. 10-11). As previously discussed (*γίνομαι [pA], §6.5), this action is interpreted to indicate that Jesus, the one sent last of all and the Stone rejected by those formerly entrusted with oversight of God's people, will become the Cornerstone of God's future relationship with God's people and the Twelve newly given their oversight.

9. God Has the Commandments (*ἐντολή [B])

God having the commandments (*ἐντολή [B], 7:8, 9; 10:19; 12:28, [29], [31a], 31b) occurs in three contexts (7:6-13; 10:17-22; 12:28-34) that incorporate that of God being loved (*ἀγαπάω [eC/apB], §10.1).

a. The Attributes of God's Commandments

God's commandments are left behind by the Pharisees and Scribes when they cling to the tradition of human beings (7:8), are rejected by the Pharisees and Scribes so that their tradition (i.e., the tradition of the Elders, 7:3) may stand (7:9), are claimed to be known and observed by the man asking Jesus what he may do to inherit everlasting life (10:19), include one that is first (12:28), include the first, "Hear, O Israel, the Lord our God is Lord alone; and you shall love the Lord your God from all your heart and from all your life and from all your mind and from all your strength" ([12:29]; cf. Deut 6:4-5), include the second, "You shall love your neighbor as yourself" ([12:31a]; cf. Lev 19:18), and include others that are not greater than the first and second (12:31b).

b. Impediments for, Complements to, and Priorities among God's Commandments

God having the commandments relates considerations of the impediments for (first context), complements to (second context), and priorities among (third context) God's commandments. Although the Pharisees and Scribes hold to human traditions/the tradition of the Elders as the appropriate complement to God's commandments, Jesus' example of the gift (7:11) demonstrates that these human traditions render null the actual commandments of God and so are impediments to their proper observance. Jesus then proposes selling what one has, giving to the poor, and following Jesus (10:21) as the proper complement to observing God's commandments. Recognition that the love of God is the greatest commandment and that the love of neighbor is its second (12:29-34) clarifies that the tradition of the Elders is an impediment precisely because it prioritizes the gift over the parents.

Selling what one has, giving to the poor, and following Jesus, in contrast, both accomplishes the second commandment and associates one with Jesus. Together these contexts assert a strong claim that only Jesus is able to prioritize properly among God's commandments and interpret accurately their proper observance.

c. The Perfect Complement to Observing God's Commandments: Following Jesus

All of God's once-cited commandments except "You shall not defraud" have specific scriptural antecedents (10:19; cf. Exod 20:12–16; Deut 5:16–20). Repetition emphasizes loving God (12:30, 33; cf. Deut 6:5), loving neighbor (12:31, 33; cf. Lev 19:18), honoring one's parents (7:10; 10:19; cf. Exod 20:12; Deut 5:16), and God's uniqueness (12:29, 32; cf. Deut 6:4; Isa 45:21). Loving God and neighbor is more significant than all of the commandments concerning Temple sacrifices, and honoring one's parents is greater than all human traditions to the contrary. The one merely observing the commandments concerning relationships among human beings does not inherit everlasting life; and the one merely knowing the supremacy of the love of God and neighbor remains in only a static relationship with God's reign. Rather, loving God and neighbor is paramount; and the one selling what one has, giving to the poor, and following Jesus is proposed as the perfect way to observe all God's commandments, to inherit everlasting life, and to remain in a dynamic relationship of motion into God's reign (*βασιλεία [B], §7.12b).

d. Jesus' Criteria for Evaluating the Authenticity of Commandments

In 10:2–9, Jesus asserts that the commandment sanctioning divorce is not of God. This assertion appears to be the conclusion drawn from a three-step process of reasoning. The process begins with an appeal to God's action in creating: making human beings male and female (v. 6). The process continues through a discernment of God's intent in creating: since the man clinging to his wife is the consequence of God making human beings male and female, the result, the joining of the man and woman (10:9) also is God's action and according to God's original intent in making human beings male and female. The process concludes with the premise that God's actions and attributes cannot be in conflict: God cannot both join the man and woman and have agentive benefaction of the commandment permitting divorce.

10. God Has the Commandments That Do/Do Not Permit (*ἔξεστιν [vi-iB]) Events

God having the commandments that do/do not permit (*ἔξεστιν [vi-iB], 2:24, 26; 3:4; 6:18; 10:2; 12:14) events occurs in five contexts (2:23-28; 3:1-6; 6:17-20; 10:1-9; 12:13-17). This statement assumes the content of the statement for God having the commandments (*ἐντολή [B], §7.9).

a. The Attributes of the Commandments that Do/Do Not Permit Events

God's commandments permitted David to enter the house of God when he and his companions were hungry, to eat the bread of offering, and give it to his companions (2:26; cf. Lev 24:5-9). God's commandments permit Jesus' Disciples to make a way and pluck heads of grain on the Sabbath (2:24; cf. Exod 20:10; 31:14, 15; 35:2; Lev 23:3; Deut 5:14), the doing of good rather than of evil and the saving of life rather than killing on the Sabbath (3:4), and the giving of the census tax to Caesar (12:14). God's commandments do not permit Herod to have as his wife Herodias, the wife of his brother (6:18; Lev 18:16; 20:21), or a husband to divorce his wife (10:2; cf. Deut 24:1).

b. Jesus the Definitive Interpreter, Applier, and Evaluator of the Commandments

God having the commandments that do/do not permit events receives development in five contexts containing one statement by John the Baptist and five statements of Jesus. John's statement that God's commandments do not permit Herod to have as wife Herodias, his brother's former wife, is a straightforward application of the marriage commandments (6:18; cf. Lev 18:16; 20:21). Jesus' statements, in contrast, present carefully reasoned arguments about and syntheses of what God's commandments permit and even a proof establishing that one commandment is not of God (10:5-9).

Jesus' arguments that interpret and apply the commandments concerning the Sabbath to permit his Disciples to make a way and pluck heads of grain on the Sabbath (2:24) appeal to the scripture's apparent approval of the interpretation and application of the commandments concerning the bread of offering to permit David and his companions to eat this bread when they were hungry and in need (2:24-25). These arguments in the first context then receive summary statement in the second: the Sabbath commandments are to be interpreted and applied in a manner that does good and saves life (3:4).

The third and fourth contexts then are linked in their attention to commandments concerning marriage. John's statement of Herod's blatant violation of the commandments concerning marriage (6:18) is followed by Jesus' arguments (§5.1a) concerning God's intent and actions in creating and joining human beings (10:5-9). These arguments establish that God does not and cannot have the commandment permitting divorce (10:4).

In the fifth context, Jesus appears to draw on a synthetic appropriation of God's commandments to argue for the rendering to Caesar what is Caesar's and to God what is God's (12:17).

c. Jesus' Guidelines for Interpreting What the Commandments Permit

Jesus' arguments concerning the application of Sabbath commandments (§4.2b) and the authenticity of the divorce commandment (§5.1a) have in common an appeal to God's intent in creating: the coming to be of the Sabbath (2:27a) and the making of human beings male and female (10:6) and joining them (10:9). Since the Sabbath came to be because of the human being and not the human being because of the Sabbath (2:27), God's Sabbath commandments are to be interpreted and applied in a way that recognizes human need and so does good and saves life. Since God creates human beings male and female and joins them (10:6-9), God does not and cannot have the commandment permitting divorce. These arguments provide general guidelines for interpreting, applying, and evaluating the applicability of all God's commandments: God's intent in creating supersedes all other considerations; the interpretation of God's commandments already present in God's scriptures supersedes all other considerations; if God's action (making human beings male and female) causes a result (the man and woman joining), then the result also is of God; proper interpretation and application of the commandments does good and saves life; and God's perceived actions and attributes cannot be in conflict (joining the man and woman and having the commandment permitting divorce).

d. Interpreting and Applying God's Commandments in 12:13-17

Jesus' repeated appeals to God's creative actions in his arguments about what is/is not permitted encourages the evocation of God's creative action of making human beings in God's image (εἰκών, Gen 1:26) in 12:13-17. This evocation interprets the things of God that human beings are to give back to God to include human beings themselves as those bearing God's image (εἰκών, 12:16).

e. A Further Clarification Concerning What God's Commandments Permit

The discussion of impediments to observing God's commandments (*ἐντολή [B], §7.9b) clarifies that human legal casuistry (tradition of the Elders, human traditions and teachings) that leaves behind, rejects, and renders null God's commandments and fails to maintain the supremacy of the love of God and neighbor ought not intrude in the interpretation and application of God's commandments to permit or not permit events.

11. God Has Jesus the Christ (*χριστός [B])

God having/not having the Christ (*χριστός [B], 1:1; 8:29; 9:41; 12:35; 13:21; 14:61; 15:32) occurs in seven contexts (1:1-3; 8:27-30; 9:38-48; 12:35-37; 13:21-23; 14:60-64; 15:29-32) that incorporate those of God having a right [hand] (*δεξιά [B], §8.2).

a. The Attributes of God's Christ (Jesus)

God's Christ is Jesus the Son of God (1:1), is Jesus (8:29), is Jesus by whose name one may give his Disciples a cup of water to drink because the Disciples are his (9:41), is said by the Scribes to be David's Son (12:35), is Jesus the Son of the Blessed One (14:61), is Jesus the King of Israel (15:32). God's Christ will not be the one (false Christ) who someone will say is here or there before the end (13:21).

b. The Absence of Direct Developments Concerning Jesus as Christ

A striking feature of the noted attributes is that Jesus as Christ is not associated with the actions and experiences that define a character (§2.3). Rather, in all six occurrences in reference to Jesus, "Christ" functions merely to identify Jesus.[9]

c. God's Relationship with Jesus the Christ

God's benefaction of Jesus the Christ most frequently is linked to various designations for God and to other designations for Jesus and grants emphasis to Jesus the Christ's future location with respect to God. God is referenced as Lord (1:3; 12:26), Blessed One (14:61), and Power (14:62); and Jesus the Christ is referenced as Son of God (1:1), Lord (1:3), Prophet (8:28), Son of David (12:35), Lord of David (12:36), Son of the Blessed One (14:61), Son of Man (14:62), and King of Israel (15:32). Among these, God (with Jesus) is Lord (1:3). The contexts grant emphasis to the location of Jesus who as risen Christ and Lord will sit at the right hand of God (12:36) and as Christ and Son of Man will sit at the right hand of God the Power (14:62).

d. The Proper Identification of Jesus the Christ in the Future

Jesus' teaching about false Christs and false Prophets warns his Disciples that their correct identification of Jesus the Christ in the future and at the end will be by celestial events and his coming as the Son of Man in the clouds at God's right hand and not be by the signs and wonders that may resemble the powerful deeds (6:2) associated with Jesus the Christ in the present (*ἐκλεκτός [B], §7.7c).

12. God Has the Reign (*βασιλεία [B])

God having the reign (*βασιλεία [B], 1:15, 4:11, 26, 30; 9:1, 47; 10:14, 15, 23, 24, 25; 12:34; 14:25; 15:43) occurs in eleven contexts (1:14-15; 4:10-12, 26-29, 30-32; 8:34–9:1; 9:38-48; 10:13-16, 23-27; 12:28-34; 14:22-26; 15:42-47). Narrative coordination of God having the reign (*βασιλεία [B]) and life (*ζωή [B], §8.4) occurs in the sixth context (9:38–48).

a. The Attributes of God's Reign

God's reign has drawn near/is at hand (1:15), has a secret given by God (4:11), is like the seed growing slowly and steadily until the harvest (4:26), is like a seed of mustard,

---

9. This predicative use of "Christ" is attributed to Mark's attempt to "revise" pre-existing beliefs about Jesus as God's Christ through its contextual linkage to direct and frequently disharmonious developments about Jesus as the Son of Man; cf. Danove, "Son of Man and Christ," 16–34.

the smallest of seeds when sown but the largest of plants when grown (4:30), comes with/by God's power before some of Jesus' addressees die (9:1), is better to enter with one eye than, having two eyes, be cast into Gehenna (9:47), belongs to the children brought to Jesus for his touch and to those like them (10:14), is to be received as one receives a child (10:15), is entered with [how] much difficulty by those having possessions (10:23) and human beings (10:24), is entered by a rich person less easily than a camel passes through the eye of a needle (10:25), is not distant from the one recognizing the primacy of loving God and neighbor over burnt offerings and offerings (12:34), and is awaited by Joseph of Arimathea (15:43). God's reign will be where Jesus drinks the fruit of the vine after his blood is shed (14:25).

b. God's Reign as the Goal of Motion and as in Motion

God's reign is presented as the goal of motion. Entering God's reign requires prior human action to remove the impediments that cause stumbling (9:47); and entering God's reign is very difficult for those having possessions (10:23), for human beings in general (10:24), and all but impossible for the rich (10:25). Since entering God's reign and God's action of saving are presented as two perspectives on the same event (§5.1d), those who would become beneficiaries of God's saving action and so enter God's reign are required to remove all impediments and, especially, riches as the insurmountable impediment to entrance.

God's reign also is presented as in motion. God's reign has drawn near (1:15), which receives interpretation as God's reign having become present (§4.1e). It is coming with/by God's power (9:1) within the lifetime of some of Jesus' auditors. It is to be received as one receives a child (10:15), that is, in full cognizance of its demands (§5.1b). In each case, its motion is related to demands: repenting and believing in the gospel of/about God (with Jesus) (1:15); not being ashamed of Jesus and his words (8:38); and protecting and nurturing God's reign as one does a child (10:15).

These considerations clarify that both one's motion into God's reign and the motion of God's reign toward one have as prerequisite human actions and constitute two perspectives on the same event. The two perspectives are related insofar as receiving God's reign as one receives a child is the condition for entering God's reign (10:15). This event is of utmost significance to human beings because it also receives interpretation as God's action of saving ([10:27]). In light of the developments in 8:31–9:1, the requisite actions for entering and receiving God's reign and so being saved by God are the actions that make one the instrument of God's saving action for oneself.

c. God's Reign Is Compared to Seeds Growing

Emphasis also falls on the comparison of God's reign to seeds that are growing. God's reign is like the seed growing slowly and steadily until the harvest without human understanding of how it does so (4:27). Although the condition for this growth is a sower's initiating action of scattering the seed and the consequence of the growth is the sower's reaping its harvest, the growth itself is not under human control or open to human understanding. God's reign also is like the seed of the mustard plant (4:30). Although it is the smallest of seeds, it becomes the largest of plants so that birds may dwell under its shadow. These comparisons indicate that God's reign grows in a way that is unknown (and, perhaps, unknowable), offers some security and protection, and requires human action to become a direct beneficiary of it (10:15).

d. Equipping Human Beings to Enter/Receive God's Reign

The remaining attributes of God's reign receive interpretation as aids that equip one to enter and receive God's reign. The secret of God's reign equips human beings with the capacity to perceive Jesus' actions and understand his teachings as manifestations of God's reign (4:11).[10] Actual perceiving and understanding, however, require that human beings apply the secret, and those so doing are able to turn and become beneficiaries of God's action of forgiving. God's reign belongs to children and those like them, that is, those dependent and recognizing their dependence on the benevolent action of others (10:14). God's reign's static relationship of not being distant from the one recognizing God's uniqueness and the primacy of loving God and neighbor over burnt offerings and offerings (12:33-34) becomes dynamic only when one enacts the love of God and neighbor. Expectation of God's reign motivates bold action for Jesus (15:43). In this light, God's reign as the future location (14:25) of Jesus' drinking (πίνω) after he goes as was written about him (14:21) and his blood is shed (14:24) becomes the goal of the Disciples who drink (πίνω) the cup of Jesus' blood (14:23) and act as the instruments of God's saving action for themselves on the pattern of Jesus.

e. God's Reign and God's Life

The narrative coordination of God having the reign and God having [everlasting] life (*ζωή [B], §8.4) in 9:38–48 asserts a common referent for "reign" and "life" as the goal of motion. Elsewhere, both the "reign" and "life" move toward human beings: the reign draws near (1:15), comes (9:1), and is received from God (10:15), and life is inherited (10:17) and received (10:30) from God. Thus entering life and inheriting life are two perspectives on the same event just as entering the reign and receiving the reign are two perspectives on the same event. Both events require antecedent human action and are associated with God's saving action for human beings. The distinction between the two is temporal: while God's reign has drawn near (1:15) and is manifest in the lifetime of some of Jesus' auditors (9:1), God's life is associated with the coming age (10:30). Thus reception of and motion into God's reign in this age anticipates reception of and motion into life in the coming age, so that "reign" and "life" reference the same reality in the coming age. As a consequence, the requisite human action for entering and becoming the beneficiary of God's

---

10. See Matera, "Ethics," 193.

reign in the present and future is the requisite action for entering and becoming the beneficiary of God's life in the coming age.

f. God's Reign Remains Enigmatic

God's benefaction of the reign, with fourteen occurrences, is the most frequently repeated attribute of God, and the narrative coordination of "reign" and "life" offers some further clarification of its referent. Still, the nature of God's reign remains enigmatic due to the paucity of its linkages to other repeated actions and attributes of God and to other events related to God. God's reign is unrelated to any other action or attribute of God in three contexts (4:26-29, 30-32; 15:42-47). In addition to the repeated linkage of "reign" and "life," "reign" repeatedly is linked only to God (with Jesus) having/being the Topic of the gospel. This interprets the nearness of God's reign as the propitious context for belief in the gospel (1:14-15) and destroying one's life because of Jesus and the gospel as an occasion of God's reign coming with/by God's power (8:35–9:1). These associations, however, do not engender further development. The narrative coordination of "reign" and "life" asserts for them a common referent when they function as the goal of motion without providing further specification of the nature of either (9:45-47). Thus, despite its significance for life in this age and the next, God's reign and its processes remain largely unknown and, perhaps, unknowable.[11]

13. God the Agentive Benefactive

With sixty-five occurrences, God's agentive benefaction is the most frequently asserted characteristic of God in Mark. Although Mark develops these attributes in relation to their benefit for or, in the single occurrence of condemnation (κρίμα [Bb], 12:40), against human beings, not all of the entities of God's agentive benefaction receive development exclusively in relation to human beings. The following discussion considers first God's agentive benefaction of the three repeated entities and the one non-repeated entity not developed exclusively in relation to human beings and then the eight repeated and six non-repeated entities developed exclusively in relation to human beings. The discussion then considers the human beings that benefit most from God's agentive benefaction and the relationship of Jesus to the entities of God's agentive benefaction.

a. God's Agentive Benefaction Not Exclusively in Relationship to Human Beings

God's creation (*κτίσις [B], §7.3) extends beyond human beings, and God's having all possible things (*δυνατόν [B], §7.4) and not having an impossible thing (ἀδύνατον

---

11. On the impossibility of a non-ambiguous and non-paradoxical description of God's reign, see C. Clifton Black, "Mark as Historian of God's Kingdom," CBQ 71 (2009): 79–81.

[B], 10:27) extends beyond God's ability to save human beings to things not specifically for the benefit of human beings. God's reign (*βασιλεία [B], §7.12) that human beings need to enter if they are to live beyond the end of this age also extends to the Angels who do God's (with Jesus') bidding, and to the earth that brings forth fruit of itself according to a plan or arrangement unknown to human beings. Thus, while God's creation, possible things, and reign clearly benefit human beings, they appear to have their own dynamism and telos not exclusively in relation to human beings.

b. God's Agentive Benefaction Exclusively in Relation to Human Beings

God's agentive benefaction of entities exclusively in relation to human beings receives development explicitly in relation to God's people (Vineyard), Jesus' Disciples, or both.

God has God's Vineyard (*ἀμπελών [B], §7.8), God's people, and the fence (φραγμός [Bb], 12:1), winepress (ὑπολήνιον [Bb], 12:1), and tower (πύργος [Bb], 12:1) that equip God's people for productivity. God's forgiveness (*ἄφεσις [bB], §7.1) benefits God's people and all human beings satisfying the conditions for its reception. God's scripture (*γραφή [B], §7.5) predicts and necessitates (*δεῖ [vi-iB], §7.6) events, prescribes actions, and teaches information significant to God's people. God's commandments (*ἐντολή [B], §7.9)/word (λόγος [B], 7:13) govern the relationship of God's people to God and each other and do or do not permit (*ἔξεστιν [vi-iB], §7.10) specific actions on the part of God's people. Jesus God's Christ (*χριστός [B], §7.11), Beloved Son, and Heir and the Cornerstone mediates God's relationship with those set over God's people. God's condemnation (κρίμα [Bb], 12:40) is against those of God's people seeking their own aggrandizement at the expense of others and of sincere prayer to God.

God's covenant (διαθήκη [B], 14:24) confirms the constitution of the group of Disciples established by Jesus and governs the Disciples' relationships with God, Jesus, each other, and others. Jesus God's Christ (*χριστός [B], §7.11) has these Disciples. God's voice (*φωνή [B], §7.2) speaks exclusively to Jesus and his Disciples and commands Jesus' Disciples to listen to Jesus. As interpreted by Jesus, God's scripture (*γραφή [B], §7.5) predicts and necessitates (*δεῖ [vi-iB], §7.6) events and prescribes actions of significance to Jesus' Disciples. As ordered, modified, interpreted, and applied by Jesus, God's commandments (*ἐντολή [B], §7.9)/word (λόγος [B], 7:13) govern the relationship of Jesus' Disciples to God, each other, and others and do or do not permit (*ἔξεστιν [vi-iB], §7.10) specific actions on the part of Jesus' Disciples. Disciples persevering to the end and praying during the tribulation are associated with God's Elect (*ἐκλεκτός [B], §7.7). As with God's people, God's condemnation (κρίμα [Bb], 12:40) is against Disciples of Jesus seeking their own aggrandizement at the expense of others and of sincere prayer to God.

c. Fully Benefitting from God's Agentive Benefaction

Jesus' Disciples are beneficiaries of God's attributes developed in relation to them (covenant, Christ, voice, scripture and what it necessitates, commandments and word as well as what they do/do not permit, Elect) and are warned of God's potential condemnation. As those belonging to Jesus the Christ, who is also the Cornerstone of God's relationship with God's people, the Disciples become heirs of God's attributes developed exclusively in relation to God's people (the Vineyard and its fence, winepress, and tower). Jesus' Disciples also are beneficiaries of God's creation, possible things, not impossible things, reign, and forgiveness. Thus Jesus' Disciples are depicted as having the greatest potential to benefit from God's agentive benefaction.

d. God's Agentive Benefaction and Jesus

Jesus is the definitive teacher, interpreter, and focus of God's agentive benefaction. Jesus teaches about God's creation, possible things, not impossible things, reign, (with Isaiah) Vineyard and its fence, winepress, and tower, (with John) forgiveness, condemnation, and Elect. Jesus authoritatively and properly interprets the scripture and what it necessitates, (contra the Pharisees) the commandments and word and (with John and contra the Pharisees and Scribes) what they do/do not permit. Jesus is the focus of God's benefaction as Christ and of God's voice and covenant.

Chapter 8

GOD AS INNATE AND ORIGINATING BENEFACTIVE

This chapter develops the statements of God's repeated innate benefaction (Sections 1–7) and repeated originating benefaction (Sections 8–11). Sections 1–7 develop the statements for God's innate benefaction of six repeated entities and then the characteristics of these six repeated and four further non-repeated entities. Sections 8–11 develop the statements for God's originating benefaction of three repeated entities and then the characteristics of these three repeated entities and one further non-repeated entity. The discussion addresses God's repeated innate benefaction and then God's repeated originating benefaction in the order of increasing frequency of occurrence and, for entities with the same number of occurrences, in the order of their introduction. Each statement of God's repeated innate and originating benefaction includes a Heading that identifies the references to God, the contexts of their occurrence, and, where appropriate, further information that assists in interpretation, a Rehearsal of the specific narrative information associated with the references (subsection "a"), and an Elaboration of one or more salient contributions developed through repetition in the contexts of occurrences (beginning with subsection "b"). The concluding discussions for the two categories of benefaction identify commonalities and patterns of development in God's innate and originating benefaction.

God has repeated innate benefaction of a right [hand] (*δεξιά [B]), the Holy Spirit (*πνεῦμα [B]), glory (*δόξα [B]), power (*δύναμις [B]), life (*ζωή [B]), and authority (*ἐξουσία [B]) and repeated originating benefaction of the things (*τά [B]), way (*ὁδός [B]), and gospel (*εὐαγγέλιον [B/T]). Although God's originating benefaction of/being the Topic of the gospel (*εὐαγγέλιον [B/T]) receives consideration in this chapter, its statement addresses both aspects of God's relation to the gospel. For economy of presentation, the following discussion replaces "Angels/Messengers" with "Messenger" for John (1:2), "Angels" for all others, and "Angels" when referencing both John and Angels.

God's innate benefaction is deemed perennial, as is God's originating benefaction of the things. God's originating benefaction of the way is asserted in the time of Isaiah and of John and Jesus (1:3; cf. Isa 40:3 LXX) and is assumed to continue into the future; and God's originating benefaction of the gospel occurs in the present (1:14) and future (13:10). Thus the Headings of statements of God's repeated innate and originating benefaction consistently use present forms of "have."

1. God Has Glory (*δόξα [B])

God having glory (*δόξα [B], 8:38; 13:26) occurs in two contexts (8:31-9:1; 13:24-29) that are incorporated into those of God having power (*δύναμις [B], §8.3) and Angels (*ἄγγελος [B], §9.11).

a. The Attributes of God's Glory

God's glory is that with/by which Jesus the Son of Man will come at the end of this age in the company of God's Angels (8:38) and, together with God's power and in/by the clouds, Jesus the Son of Man will come at the end of this age (13:26).

b. God's Glory Is Manifest at the End in God's Saving Action

God's glory will be manifest exclusively in the end-time coming of Jesus the Son of Man. Although God's glory will be manifest to all human beings at the end, it will benefit only the Disciple (the one denying oneself, taking up one's cross, and following Jesus) who demonstrates that one is not ashamed of Jesus and his words by accepting the necessary events about to befall Jesus the Son of Man (8:31) and destroying one's life because of Jesus and the gospel (8:34-38), and the Elect who are chosen by God (13:20). The linkage of those enacting their call to discipleship and God's Elect confirms the association of Jesus' perseverant and praying Disciples and God's Elect and their specification as those whom God will save (*κολοβόω [Ap], §6.2b; *σῴζω [Ap], §6.6b).

c. God's Glory and God's Angels

God's glory will be manifest in Jesus the Son of Man's coming in the company of God's Angels (8:38) and coming with/by much power and sending of God's Angels (13:26-27).[1] Although God's Angels are attributed with no role in the former context, the latter clarifies that Jesus the Son of Man will send them in his gathering of God's Elect. This identifies Jesus the Son of Man as the instrument of God's end-time saving action and God's Angels as the instruments of Jesus the Son of Man's end-time actions.

---

1. The interpretation of "with glory" (8:38) and "with much glory" (13:26) as manner complements accommodates the proposal by Joshua E. Leim, "In the Glory of His Father: Intertextuality and the Apocalyptic Son of Man in the Gospel of Mark." *JTI* 7, no. 2 (2013): 221, that "the coming of the Son of Man is the revelation of his Father's glory." Leim's further claim that Jesus the Son of Man already shares his Father's glory in the present, however, lacks the support of the text, which directly associates Jesus the Son of Man and God's glory only in his end-time coming and never attributes Jesus with benefaction of God's glory.

d. God's Glory and God's Reign

The contextual relationship between the end-time manifestation of God's glory in the coming of Jesus the Son of Man (8:38) and proximate manifestation of God's power in the coming of God's reign (9:1) and their linkage to the definitive manifestation of God's great glory and power when Jesus the Son of Man functions as the instrument of God's end-time saving action (13:26) confirm the linkage of the motion of God's reign and God's saving action (*βασιλεία [B], §7.12b).

2. God Has a Right [Hand] (*δεξιά [B])

God having a right [hand] (*δεξιά [B], 12:36; 14:62) occurs in two contexts (12:35-37; 14:60-64). To be located at the right [hand] of God is to occupy the position of honor with respect to God and to be delegated to act by God's power (§5.3g).

a. The Attributes of God's Right [Hand]

God's right [hand] is where God the Lord will command the risen Jesus the Lord of David to sit until God places Jesus' enemies under Jesus' feet (12:36); and God the Power's right [hand] is where the Chief Priests and whole Sanhedrin will see Jesus the Son of Man sitting when he comes in the company of the clouds of heaven (14:62).

b. God's Right [Hand] Is Uniquely the Future Locale of Jesus as Lord and Son of Man

God the Lord will command the risen Jesus the Lord of David to sit at God's right [hand] where Jesus will remain until his end-time coming as Son of Man at the right [hand] of God the Power. God's right [hand] will be the locale of safety and vindication for the risen Jesus insofar as God will place Jesus' enemies under his feet. The greater context specifies these enemies as the Chief Priests, Scribes, and Elders (11:27–12:12), the false witnesses at Jesus' trial (14:56-59), the Chief Priest who accuses Jesus of blasphemy for acknowledging that he is the Christ and Son of the Blessed and stating that he is Son of Man (14:61-64), and the Chief Priests and whole Sanhedrin who condemn Jesus as worthy of death (14:64). These enemies are contrasted with David who acknowledged Jesus as his Lord (12:36-37). God's action against Jesus' enemies clarifies that those opposing Jesus set themselves in opposition to God.

3. God Has Power (*δύναμις [B])

God having power (*δύναμις [B], 9:1; 12:24; 13:26) occurs in three contexts (8:31–9:1; 12:18-27; 13:24-29) that incorporate those of God having glory (*δόξα [B],

§8.1) and that are incorporated into those of God having Angels (*ἄγγελος [B], §9.11). "The Power" functions as a designation for God (14:62).

a. The Attributes of God's Power

God's power is that with/by which God's reign is coming within the lifetime of some of Jesus' auditors (9:1) and is not known by the Sadducees to be the instrument by which the dead rise (12:24). God's great power (with God's glory) is that with/by which Jesus the Son of Man will be seen coming at the end (13:26).

b. God's Power and God's Saving Action

"See," "come," "Angels," "glory," and "power" tightly link the first (8:31–9:1) and third (13:24-29) contexts. This linkage interprets the end-time coming of Jesus the Son of Man as the definitive manifestation of God's power, glory, and reign in this age and identifies all of the associated events with God's action of saving (*δόξα [B], §8.1d). Jesus the Son of Man's end-time coming as the instrument of God's saving action for God's Elect interprets the proximate coming of God's reign with/by God's power as an occasion of God's saving action. Thus those not tasting death before they see the coming of God's reign with/by God's power have a foretaste of God's end-time saving action.

c. God's Power and the Rising of the Dead

"Rise," "Angels," and "power" tightly link the first (8:31–9:1) and second (12:18-27) contexts. The first context relates Jesus the Son of Man's suffering, being rejected, being killed, and rising (8:31) and the Disciple's destroying and saving of life as the instrument of God's saving action for oneself (8:35). This relationship interprets Jesus the Son of Man's suffering, being rejected, and being killed as the events in which Jesus acts as the instrument of God's saving action for himself and identifies the rising of Jesus the Son of Man as an instance of saving one's life. The second context's identification of God's power as the instrument of the dead's rising (12:18-27) joins with the repetition of "rise" (ἀνίστημι) that links the rising of Jesus the Son of Man (8:31) and of the dead (12:24) to propose God's power as the instrument of Jesus' rising. The first context also relates the proximate suffering, being rejected, being killed, and rising of Jesus the Son of Man (8:31) and the proximate coming of God's reign with/by God's power (9:1) and links these to the rising of the dead by God's power (12:18-37). These relationships and linkages interpret the proximate coming of God's reign with/by God's power as accomplished when Jesus the Son of Man rises.[2] They also interpret the proximate coming of

---

2. Although Michael Bird, "The Crucifixion of Jesus as the Fulfillment of Mark 9:1," *TrinJ* 24, no. 1 NS (2003): 23–36, carefully argues for Jesus' crucifixion as the coming of God's reign by God's power, he does not account for the noted repeated linkages of the coming of God's reign by God's power to the rising of Jesus and the dead.

God's reign by God's power and the rising of the dead by God's power as manifestations of God's saving action.

d. God's Power and God's Reign

The interpretation of the rising of Jesus the Son of Man by God's power as the proximate manifestation of God's reign by God's power (§8.3c) and of Jesus the Son of Man's end-time coming with much power and glory as the definitive manifestation of God's reign (§8.3b) interprets the rising of the dead by God's power as a further manifestation of God's reign.

e. The Beneficiaries and Benefit of God's Power

God's power directly benefits Jesus the Son of Man in his rising (9:1), the dead who rise (12:25-26), God's Elect (13:26-27), and, by association, the Disciple destroying one's life for the sake of Jesus and the gospel (8:35) and the one not ashamed of Jesus and his words (8:38). The second context associates these with the living who, like God's Angels (§5.3e), live forever (12:27). The first two contexts contrast these beneficiaries of God's power with the Chief Priest, Scribes, and Elders who reject Jesus the Son of Man (8:31), the one wishing to save one's life but destroying it (8:35), the one ashamed of Jesus and his words (8:38), the Sadducees who do not know God's scriptures or God's power (12:24), and the dead (12:27). If these non-beneficiaries do not rise (*λέγω [Ace], §6.4d), then the statement that the one wishing to save one's life destroys it (8:35) must be taken literally.

f. God's Power and Jesus the Son of Man's End-Time Coming

The dead who rise do so by God's power (12:24-25), and Jesus the Son of Man will come with/by God's great power at the end (13:26). These considerations accommodate the interpretation of Jesus the Son of Man's end-time coming as the context in which the resurrection of the dead by God's power will occur. Since this also is the context in which Jesus the Son of Man will send God's Angels and gather God's Elect (13:27), the Elect whom Jesus will gather apparently will include both survivors of the tribulation and the dead who will rise. This also highlights the distinction between Jesus the Son of Man who rises by God's power prior to the end and the dead who rise by God's power at the end.[3]

4. God Has Life (*ζωή [B])

God having [everlasting] life (*ζωή [B], 9:43, 45; 10:17, 30) occurs in three contexts (9:38-48; 10:17-22, 28-31). The concluding discussion develops the implications of the narrative coordination of reign (*βασιλεία [B], §7.12) and life (*ζωή [B]).

---

3. Jesus' statement, "When *they* rise from the dead ...," also proposes a distinction between Jesus the Son of Man's rising and the dead's rising.

a. The Attributes of God's [Everlasting] Life

God's [everlasting] life will be better to enter without a hand (9:43) or foot (9:45) than, having two hands or two feet, go away to or enter Gehenna, will be inherited from God by those performing specific actions (10:17), and will be received from God in the coming age by the one leaving family and possessions because of Jesus and the gospel (10:30).

b. The Conditions for Entering, Inheriting, and Receiving God's Life

Entering, inheriting, and receiving God's everlasting life has as its conditions cutting off whatever causes one to stumble (9:43, 45), keeping the commandments of God who alone is good and selling what one has, giving to the poor, and following Jesus (10:20-21), and leaving house, brothers, sisters, mother, father, children, and fields because of Jesus and the gospel (10:29-30).[4] The conditions include the fulfillment of covenantal obligations through observance of God's commandments as augmented by fulfilling the demands that Jesus places on his Disciples (*ἐντολή [B], §7.9c). The nature of this life receives development through its contrast to corruption, annihilation, or disintegration (9:42-48).

c. Further Conditions and Receiving One's Wage from God

The first two contexts develop the conditions for entering and receiving life by linking Disciple's action for the benefit of fellow Disciples (giving a drink of water to one of Jesus the Christ's own, 9:41), of oneself (cutting off a foot or hand, 9:43-45), and of others (selling what one has and giving to the poor, 10:21), and the first context interprets what one receives as one's wage (μισθός [S], 9:41) from God. The third context changes this perspective and focuses on what the Disciple will receive (a hundredfold family and possessions in this age and everlasting life in the coming age, 10:30), thereby specifying the content of this wage. This interprets the hundredfold family and possession as from both fellow Disciples who come to

---

4. Michael Peppard, "Torah for the Man Who Has Everything: 'Do Not Defraud' in Mark 10:19," *JBL* 134, no. 3 (2015): 599-603, proposes that Jesus inserts the command not to defraud into his abbreviated rehearsal of the Decalogue (10:19) because the only way for the man to have many possessions (10:22) in agrarian Palestine is by defrauding others. In this light, Jesus' command to the man to sell what he has and give to the poor (10:21) would permit the man to accomplish not only the required leaving of possessions because of Jesus and the gospel as the condition for inheriting everlasting life (10:29-30) but restitution to the victims of defrauding. As Richard Hicks, "Markan Discipleship according to Malachi: The Significance of μὴ ἀποστερήσῃς in the Story of the Rich Man (Mark 10:17-22)," *JBL* 132, no. 1 (2013): 197-8, points out, the man's defrauding does not keep God's commandments and so deprives both God and the poor of what is rightfully theirs.

constitute the Disciple's family and from God.⁵ God alone, however, will be the source of everlasting life.

d. Narrative Coordination of God's Life and God's Reign

Narrative coordination of "life" and "reign" through repetition of "if your," "causes you to stumble," "enter into," "having," "than having two," and "be cast into Gehenna" (9:45, 47) asserts for them a common referent as the goal of motion. Motion into (enter) and of (inherit, receive) God's life/reign receives interpretation as two perspectives on God's action of saving (*βασιλεία [B], §§7.12b, 7.12e). Both perspectives are linked to required antecedent actions for fellow Disciples, oneself, and others. The subsequently developed relationship between God's reign and God's power (*δύναμις [B], §8.3d) and the occurrences of the semantically parallel words "life" (*ζωή [B]) and "living" (ζῶν, 12:27) further qualify this life as for those who rise by God's power and become like God's Angels.

5. God Has the Holy Spirit (*πνεῦμα [B])

God having the [Holy] Spirit (*πνεῦμα [B], 1:8, 10, 12; 3:29; 12:36; 13:11) occurs with direct references in six contexts (1:4-8, 9-11, 12-13; 3:20-35; 12:35-37; 13:9-13) and with an indirect reference in one context (7:6-13). The contexts of direct references incorporate those of God having forgiveness (*ἄφεσις [bB], §7.1) and, through recipient benefaction, the sinful actions (*ἁμάρτημα [bB], §9.2) that require God's forgiveness. The statement that Jesus recognizes in/by his spirit (2:8) proposes that God's Holy Spirit is the locus/means of God's thinking and discerning (§4.2a).

a. The Actions and Attributes of God's Holy Spirit

God's Holy Spirit was the one by whom David spoke God's statement to Jesus David's Lord, "The Lord said to my Lord, 'Sit at my right hand until I put your enemies under your feet'" (12:36; cf. Ps 110:1) and (through an indirect reference) Isaiah prophesied God's statement, "This people honors me with their lips . . ." (7:6; cf. Isa 29:13 LXX). God's Holy Spirit is seen by Jesus when it comes down onto him

---

5. The conjunction of "mothers," "brothers," and "sisters" evokes their previous conjunction in Jesus' statement that those doing God's will constitute Jesus' family (3:35). The lack of a reference to "fathers" in both contexts is interpreted to imply that one's filial relationship is with God alone as Father. This interprets the leaving of family and possessions because of Jesus and the gospel as departure from one's biological family and the reception of a hundredfold as entrance into the community of Jesus' Disciples/those doing God's will: cf. Dan O. Via, Jr., *The Ethics of Mark's Gospel—In the Middle of Time* (Philadelphia: Fortress, 1985), 143.

like a dove after he is baptized by John (1:10), casts Jesus out into the desert where he is tested by Satan for forty days (1:12), and may be blasphemed by human beings who may never have God's forgiveness (3:29). God's Holy Spirit is the one by whom Jesus does and will baptize (1:8) and who will speak when the Twelve are led and handed over (13:11).

b. The Holy Spirit Is the Instrument of God's Forgiveness

God's Holy Spirit is the instrument of God's forgiveness that extends to all sinful actions and blasphemies. Since the Spirit's instrumental role in God's forgiveness is indispensible, anyone blaspheming and thereby rejecting God's Holy Spirit does not have God's forgiveness, and this situation may continue into the coming age. Jesus the Son of Man's authority to forgive sins on the earth assumes the prior coming of the Holy Spirit onto Jesus after his baptism (1:10). The presence of the Holy Spirit on only Jesus during the first stage in the end times (*σχίζω [Ap], §6.1) and the suggested role of the Holy Spirit in forgiving by human beings (*ἀφίημι [Apb], §6.7d) interpret Jesus' command to his Disciples to forgive whatever they hold against another (11:25) to be binding only after Jesus baptizes them by the Holy Spirit. Jesus' command also distinguishes God and Jesus the Son of Man who are able to forgive sins (covenantal debts) by the Holy Spirit from Jesus' Disciples who are able to forgive by God's Holy Spirit only what they hold against another (*ἀφίημι [Apb], §6.7d).

c. The Manner of the Holy Spirit's Presence in Time

The Holy Spirit's presence on Isaiah when he prophesied (7:6) and David when he spoke (12:36), on only Jesus from his baptism (1:10) until he expires (15:37), and on the centurion (15:39; cf. §6.11c), the Twelve (13:11), Jesus' Disciples who will forgive (§8.5b), and potentially others proposes a three-fold distinction in the manner of the Spirit's presence on human beings: in the pre-eschatological times, God's Spirit was present during prophetic utterances; in the first stage of the end times, God's Spirit is continually present on Jesus; and, in the second stage of the end times, the Spirit will be continually present on those whom Jesus will baptize by the Holy Spirit (1:8).

d. The Holy Spirit's Role in the Unfolding of the End Times

The discussions of God's tearing (*σχίζω [Ap], §6.1e) identified parallels concerning Jesus in the first stage of the end times and his Disciples in the second stage of the end times that ultimately depend on the continuing presence of the Holy Spirit first on Jesus and then on his Disciples (§8.5c). Despite these parallels, the Holy Spirit functions differently with respect to Jesus and his Disciples, as apparent in Jesus the Son of Man's ability to forgive sins (covenantal debts) and the Disciples' ability to forgive only what they hold against another (§8.5b). A further distinction concerns the fact that the Holy Spirit will speak through the Twelve in their proclamation (13:11). While acknowledging that Jesus' speaking is Spirit-filled, Jesus is not portrayed, as are the Twelve, as the instrument of the Spirit's speaking. Rather, Jesus speaks for himself by the authority that God gives to him and, as a consequence, functions as the sole reliable commentator on the Spirit and interpreter of what was and will be done and spoken by the Spirit.

e. God's Holy Spirit and Jesus God's Son/the Son of Man

The actions of God's Spirit and Jesus God's Son/the Son of Man introduce comparisons to God and contrasts with each other.

Only God/God's Holy Spirit positively transfers Jesus by sending him (9:37; 12:6)/casting him out (1:12); and only God/Jesus the Son of Man forgives sins by the Holy Spirit (2:5, 7, 9; 3:28; 4:12; 11:25b/2:10).[6] The comparisons to God, however, ultimately are dependent on God: God's Spirit casts out Jesus according to God's thinking and discernment, and Jesus the Son of Man forgives sins by God's authority and after God's Spirit comes onto him. Despite their dependence, these comparisons relate both God's Spirit and Jesus God's Beloved Son/the Son of Man to God in distinct and unique (with respect to all other characters) ways.

At the same time, Jesus and God's Spirit are uniquely related to each other. The presence of the Holy Spirit on Jesus accommodates Jesus' baptizing by the Holy Spirit. This then accommodates the presence of God's Spirit on human beings. Thus Jesus and God's Spirit are equally integral to God's saving action for and relationship with human beings.

f. The Relationships Among God, God's Spirit, and Jesus God's Son

The relationship among God, God's Spirit, and Jesus God's Son admits to further clarification. God's benefaction of the Holy Spirit is deemed intrinsic on the pattern of the intrinsic relationship assumed for Jesus and his spirit (2:8). This proposes that God *qua* God has the Holy Spirit. God's benefaction of Jesus, however, initially (1:1) is developed in terms of their reciprocal relationship (Father to Son). This proposes that God *qua* Father has Jesus God's Beloved Son. These differing relationships might be construed to propose that God's relationship with the Spirit is prior to God's relationship with Jesus as God's Son. Even initially, however, Jesus God's Son is attributed with God's face (1:2), God's way (1:2, 3) and paths (1:3), and title "Lord." In particular, Jesus' benefaction of God's face, an innate attribute of God, calls into question any priority for God's relationship with God's Spirit.

---

6. God's/God's Spirit's positively evaluated transference of Jesus contrasts with all others who transfer Jesus only in his being handed over (παραδίδωμι, 3:19; 9:31; 10:33a, 33b; 14:10, 11, 18, 21, 41, 42, 44; 15:1, 10, 15).

6. God (with Jesus, the Twelve, and Disciples) Has Authority (*ἐξουσία [B])

God (with Jesus, the Twelve, and Disciples) having authority (*ἐξουσία [B], 1:22, 27; 2:10; 3:15; 6:7; 11:28a, 28b, 29, 33; 13:34) occurs in six contexts (1:21-28; 2:4-12; 3:13-19; 6:6b-13; 11:27-33; 13:32-37).

a. The Attributes of God's (with Jesus', the Twelve's, and Disciples') Authority

God's authority is held by Jesus and apparent in Jesus' teaching (1:22), is associated with Jesus' new teaching and manifest when Jesus commands unclean spirits and they obey him (1:27), is held by Jesus the Son of Man and manifest in his forgiving sins on the earth (2:10), is to be held by the Twelve and manifest in their casting out demons (3:15), is given by Jesus to the Twelve and manifest in their control over unclean spirits when on mission (6:7), is that by which Jesus does the things that he does (11:28a, 29, 33), is given to Jesus by God and manifest in what Jesus does (11:28b), and is given by Jesus to his Disciples the Slaves, with each having an assigned task (13:34).

b. Jesus' Benefaction of God's Authority

God has innate benefaction of the authority that God gives (11:28b) to Jesus. Jesus' resulting recipient benefaction of God's authority becomes agentive when Jesus teaches (1:22, 27) and acts (11:28a, 29, 33) by this authority and, as Son of Man, forgives sins by this authority (2:10). Although there is no indication of limits on God's authority, Jesus the Son of Man's exercise of God's authority to forgive sins may be limited, if "on the earth" (2:10) is taken as exclusionary. Jesus' exercise of God's authority extends to giving it to the Twelve (6:7) and his Disciples the Slaves (13:34).

c. The Twelve's/Disciples' Benefaction of God's Authority

Jesus intends the Twelve to have authority to cast out demons (3:15), gives God's authority over unclean spirits to the Twelve (6:7), and gives God's authority to his Disciples the Slaves to carry out their assigned tasks (13:34). The Twelve's and the Disciples' resulting recipient benefaction of God's authority becomes agentive when the Twelve cast out demons (6:13) and Jesus' Disciples the Slaves do their assigned tasks. The Twelve's exercise of God's authority also extends to proclaiming (6:12), healing (6:13), and all that they do and teach (6:30) when sent by Jesus. Thus the Twelve's exercise of God's authority when on their mission is similar to that of Jesus throughout his ministry, with the limitation that only Jesus the Son of Man has the authority to forgive sins on the earth. The exercise of God's authority by the Twelve and Disciples does not extend to giving it to others, which belongs solely to God and Jesus.

d. Jesus' Ministry as a Continuous Exercise of God's Authority

The parallel between Jesus' exercise of God's authority in all that he says and does and Twelve's exercise of God's authority when on their mission interprets all of Jesus' actions in the first stage of the end times as part of his mission from God.

7. God the Innate Benefactive

Although God's innately held attributes provide a limited basis for comparing God and Jesus, they serve primarily to highlight the radical distinctiveness of God from all others. God's innate benefaction of God's right [hand] (*δεξιά [B], §8:2) and God's Spirit (*πνεῦμα [B], §8.5) finds a parallel in Jesus' innate benefaction of a right [hand] (*δεξιά, 10:37, 40; 15:27) and spirit (*πνεῦμα [B], 2:8); and God's innate benefaction of a will (θέλημα [B], 3:35), name (ὄνομα [B], 11:9), and face (πρόσωπον [B], 1:2) finds a parallel in human beings' innate benefaction of a will (through "want," θέλω, 1:40, 41; 3:13; 6:19, 22, 25, 26, 48; 7:24; 8:34, 35; 9:13, 30, 35; 10:35, 36, 43, 44, 51; 12:38; 14:7, 12; 15:9, 12), a name (ὄνομα, 5:22; 6:14; 9:37, 38, 39; 13:6, 13), and a face (πρόσωπον, 12:14; 14:65). In contrast, God's innate benefaction of glory (*δόξα [B], §8.1), power (*δύναμις [B], §8.3), life (*ζωή [B], §8.4), authority (*ἐξουσία [B], §8.6), and wisdom (σοφία [B], 6:2) is unique. The following discussion considers God's parallel innate attributes and then God's unique innate attributes and concludes with a discussion that identifies the focus of God's innate attributes.

a. God's Innate Attributes That Are Similar to Human Innate Attributes

God's innate benefaction of a right [hand], spirit, will, name, and face proposes limited comparisons to Jesus and contrasts between God and all others.

Only God (12:36) and Jesus (10:37, 40) are attributed with having a right [hand] that specifies the position of honor and delegated authority to act. The parallels end here, however, because God commands Jesus the risen Lord of David to sit at God's right hand (12:26), whereas Jesus is not able to give the position at his right to others (10:40).

Only God and Jesus are attributed with having a spirit, and the portrayal of Jesus' spirit (2:8) identifies it as the locale/means of thinking and discerning. In contrast to Jesus' spirit, God's Holy Spirit is able to act (cast out, 1:12; speak, 13:11) and functions as the instrument of the forgiveness of sins (*ἀφίημι, §6.7d). Although Jesus the Son of Man has God's authority to forgive sins, he does so only by God's Holy Spirit and authority.

God and, through "want," Jesus and human beings in general are attributed with having a will. Doing God's will makes one a member of Jesus' family (3:35) that has God as its Father. Although Jesus' hard teachings about wanting (8:34; 9:35; 10:43, 44) present opportunities to conform one's will to God's will and to enact God's will, only Jesus is portrayed as actually choosing to enact what God wants (14:36); and even on this occasion, Jesus' will initially is not conformed to God's will.

Although God, Jesus, and human beings are attributed with having a name, only God and Jesus have a name in/by which events occur.[7] Jesus' coming (ἔρχομαι) in/by God's name receives interpretation as Jesus' coming at God's behest as God's representative (§5.2a). In contrast, the many coming (ἔρχομαι) in/by Jesus' name will not do so at Jesus' behest or represent him (13:6). As a consequence, Disciples can trust Jesus' affiliation with God but will need to confirm future claims of affiliation with Jesus.

God, Jesus, and human beings are attributed with having a face, but only Jesus has co-benefaction of God's face (1:2). Thus the face of Jesus manifests the face of God to human beings.

These parallel innate attributes develop a limited basis for comparing God and Jesus, a significant basis for contrasting God and Jesus, and no basis for comparing God and human beings in general. At the same time, all of God's parallel innate attributes are of potential benefit to human beings. The position of honor at God's right hand is for Jesus the risen Lord of David and Son of Man, the instrument of God's end-time saving action for human beings. God's Holy Spirit is the instrument of God's forgiveness for human beings and enables human beings to forgive what they hold against others. Doing God's will makes one a child of God the Father. Correct recognition of the one coming in/by God's name opens the possibility for recognizing the face of God in the face of Jesus. Thus, although God's parallel innate attributes consistently distinguish God from human beings, it is precisely their distinctiveness that permits them to contribute to human salvation.

b. God's Unique Innate Attributes

God's innate benefaction of glory, power, life, authority, and wisdom is unique. God manifests God's power in the proximate coming of God's reign and definitively manifests God's glory and power in the end-time coming of Jesus the Son of Man as the instrument of God's saving action for God's Elect. Since the previous discussion (*δύναμις [B], §8.3c) identified the proximate coming of God's reign with Jesus' resurrection, all manifestations of God's glory and power are in association with Jesus. God's life is for the one cutting off the impediments for entering it and for the one leaving family and possessions for the sake of Jesus and the gospel. God gives God's authority to Jesus to do what he does. This authority extends to Jesus giving the Twelve God's authority to accomplish what they do when on their mission and to giving his Disciples the Slaves God's authority to accomplish their assigned tasks. God gives Jesus the wisdom by which he teaches, so that God's authority, power, and wisdom undergird all that Jesus does and

---

7. This discussion assumes that phrases introduced by both ἐν and ἐπί [+dative] with "name" as their object designate the same range of semantic relationships based on their use in 9:38-39, in which the Disciples tell Jesus about the one casting out demons by/with Jesus' name (ἐν τῷ ὀνόματί σου) and Jesus responds about anyone doing a powerful deed by/with his name (ἐπὶ τῷ ὀνόματί μου).

teaches. Thus all of God's unique innate attributes are placed in the service of Jesus and directly or indirectly benefit those related to God through Jesus: Jesus' Disciples and the Twelve; the one destroying one's life because of Jesus and the gospel; the one not ashamed of Jesus and his words; the one following God's commandments, selling what one has, giving to the poor and following Jesus; the one leaving family and possessions because of Jesus and the gospel; and the Elect and perseverant and praying Disciples gathered by Jesus the Son of Man in his end-time coming.

c. The Focus of God's Innate Attributes

God's parallel and unique innate attributes focus on and are primary means of God's saving action for human beings. God's parallel innate attributes present limited comparisons to those of Jesus but only contrasts to those of human beings in general, and their potential benefit for human beings resides specifically in their distinctiveness. God's unique attributes consistently receive specification in relation to Jesus in a manner that highlights their potential benefit for human beings.

8. God Has the Things (*τά [B])

God having the things (*τά [B], 8:33; 12:17b) occurs in two contexts (8:31–9:1; 12:13-17).

a. The Attributes of God's Things

God's things are not thought by Peter who, instead, thinks the things of human beings (8:33) and are to be given back to God as the things of Caesar are to be given back to Caesar (12:17b).

b. Thinking and Giving Back the Things of God

Thinking the things of God constitutes enacting one's commitment to God (§4.8d) by accepting and embracing the events predicted by God's scriptures concerning Jesus the Son of Man's necessary suffering, being rejected, being killed, and rising (8:31) and the hard teachings about Discipleship (8:34-38). Such thinking conforms one to Jesus the Son of Man whose suffering, rejection, and being killed are the condition for his rising. Such thinking recognizes that denying oneself, taking up one's cross, and following Jesus (8:34), destroying one's life because of Jesus and the gospel (8:35), that is, acting as the instrument of God's saving action for oneself, and not being ashamed of Jesus and his words (8:38) are the condition for saving one's life. Thinking the things of human beings, in contrast, constitutes enacting one's commitment to those opposed to God by rejecting both the necessary events predicted for Jesus the Son of Man and the associated hard teachings about discipleship. Such thinking conforms one to Satan who opposes both God and Jesus and to the one whose attempt to save one's life destroys it.

Giving back to God the things of God is compared to giving back to Caesar the things of Caesar (12:16). The comparison assumes that the things of Caesar, the coins bearing his image (εἰκών), rightfully belong to Caesar and so ought to be given back to Caesar. This has the potential (*ἔξεστιν [vi-iB], §7.10c) to propose that the things of God, human beings made in God's image (εἰκών, Gen 1:26), rightfully belong to God and so ought to be given back to God.

These considerations propose that thinking the things of God, that is, accepting and embracing the predicted events concerning Jesus the Son of Man and enacting Jesus' hard teachings about discipleship are the means by which one is able to give oneself back to God. In so doing, the human being made in God's image and so rightfully belonging to God conforms oneself to Jesus the Son of Man who rises and to the Disciple who becomes the instrument of God's saving action for oneself and saves one's life.

c. God's Things and the Love Commandments: A Possible Link

"Love" combines experience and agency (ἀγαπάω [Ec/Apb], §1.7a), so that loving is characterized both by an affective response to and action for another. The proximity of the two love commandments (12:29-33) to the second occurrence of the things of God (12:17b) and repetition of life (ψυχή, 8:35-36; 12:30) has the potential to evoke the linkage of thinking the things of God (experience) and giving back the things of God (action). This evocation would propose enacting one's commitment to God by destroying one's life for the sake of Jesus and the gospel of/about God (with Jesus) as an appropriate way of loving God with one's whole heart, life, mind, and strength.

9. God (with Jesus) Has the Way (*ὁδός [B])

God (with Jesus) having the way (*ὁδός [B], 1:2, 3; 12:14) occurs in two contexts (1:1-3; 12:13-17).

a. The Attributes of God's Way

God's (with Jesus') way is prepared by John the Messenger and is to be prepared by John's addressees (1:2-3) and is taught in truth by Jesus the Teacher (12:14).

b. Preparing God's (with Jesus') Way

Preparing the way of God (with Jesus) is the first action of a human being (John the Messenger, 1:2) and the first action commanded to human beings (1:3) in the present of the story time. The way and the command to prepare it are the content of what was written. Jesus' statement of what God's commandments permit

(12:14-17) indicates that preparing the way also requires the keeping of God's commandments as interpreted and applied by Jesus and giving back to God the things of God, which includes oneself as one created by God in God's image (*τά [B], §8.8b). The same commandments are compatible with giving back to Caesar what belongs to Caesar, so that preparing the way of God (with Jesus) entails fulfilling obligations to others than God and members of one's faith community. Thus the way of God (with Jesus) recognizes duties to earthly rulers (Caesar) while insisting on fulfilling the demands concerning what God's commandments, as interpreted and applied by Jesus, do and do not permit.

c. The Way That Is to Be Prepared

Preparing the way of God (with Jesus) by giving back to God the things of God evokes the relationship between giving back to God the things of God and thinking the things of God (*τά [B], 8.8b) and associates preparing the way of God (with Jesus) with accepting and embracing the predicted events concerning Jesus the Son of Man and enacting Jesus' hard teachings about discipleship. In this light, the way of God (with Jesus) is the way that leads to human salvation by making oneself the instrument of God's saving action for oneself.

d. Correctly Teaching God's (with Jesus') Way

Jesus' teaching of God's way confirms his agentive benefaction of God's way. Jesus' manner of teaching the way provides a guide to proper instruction concerning the way and further illustrates its proper preparation. Jesus, the one manifesting God's face (πρόσωπον [B], 1:2), teaches the way in truth and does not look at the face (πρόσωπον) of, that is, show partiality toward, particular human beings (12:14). The repetition of "face" contrasts Jesus with the Pharisees and Herodians who do not recognize the face of God in the face of Jesus but readily recognize the image of Caesar (12:17) and who use their speech not to teach in truth but to attempt to trap (12:13) and test (12:15) Jesus.

10. God (with Jesus) Has/Is the Topic of the Gospel (εὐαγγέλιον [B/T])

God (with Jesus) having/being the topic of the gospel (*εὐαγγέλιον [B/T], 1:1, 14, 15; 8:35; 10:29; 13:10; 14:9) occurs in six contexts (1:1-3, 14-15; 8:31–9:1; 10:28-31; 13:9-13; 14:3-9). This statement develops concurrently God and Jesus' co-benefaction of the gospel and God and Jesus as the Topic of the gospel.

a. The Attributes of the Gospel of/about God (with Jesus)

God's (with Jesus') gospel has a beginning just as was written in/by Isaiah God's Prophet (1:1-2), is proclaimed by Jesus (1:14), is to be believed in (1:15), is (with Jesus) to be the cause of destroying one's life to save it (8:35), and is (with Jesus) the cause of leaving family and possessions (10:29). God's (with Jesus') gospel must be proclaimed to all the nations by the Twelve (13:10) and will be proclaimed throughout the world with a remembrance of what the woman anointing Jesus did for him (14:9).

b. *The Gospel about God (with Jesus) Is of God (with Jesus)*

God's benefaction of the gospel is originating, and Jesus' benefaction of the gospel is agentive.[8] This is apparent in the fact that Jesus is its first proclaimer (1:14) and its only noted proclaimer in the first stage of the end times. Repetition of "proclaim" with Jesus as the subject (1:15, 38) establishes that proclaiming is the purpose for Jesus' "coming forth," which is interpreted to reference Jesus' being sent by God (*ἀποστέλλω, 9:37; 12:6).[9] In contrast, God does not proclaim the gospel. Rather, God's sending of Jesus identifies Jesus as God's delegated proclaimer of the gospel that has its origin in God. Thus Jesus' agentive benefaction of the gospel of/about God (with Jesus) is dependent on God's originating benefaction of the gospel of/about God (with Jesus).

c. *The Gospel of God (with Jesus) Is about God and Jesus*

The gospel of God (with Jesus) references specific content about both God and Jesus. The beginning of the gospel is intelligible only through references to God's agency in writing and sending (1:2), God's benefaction of Jesus God's Christ and Son (1:1), of Isaiah God's Prophet, of John God's Messenger (1:2), and (with Jesus) of God's face, way, paths, and title "Lord" (1:2-3). Jesus' proclamation of the gospel (1:14-15) references God's reign and the need for belief in the gospel. The gospel (with Jesus) as the cause of actions is set in relation to what God's scriptures necessitate (8:31), God's things (8:33), content about Jesus the Son of Man (8:31, 38), the glory and Angels of God the Father of Jesus the Son of Man (8:38), God's reign and power (9:1), what the one leaving family and property receives and will receive from God (10:29-30), and God's life (10:30). The gospel's future proclamation by the Twelve to all the nations is necessary by God's scriptures (13:10) and will exhibit God's agency in giving the Twelve what they will say and in the agency of God's Spirit speaking through them (13:11).

d. *The Gospel of/about God (with Jesus) Also Is of/about Jesus' Disciples*

Just as God sends Jesus to proclaim (1:38; cf. 9:37; 12:6), Jesus plans to (3:14) and does (6:7) send the Twelve to proclaim, and God's scriptures will necessitate that the Twelve proclaim the gospel to all the nations (13:10). This chain of sending with Jesus

---

8. Although accurate as stated, this statement receives further clarification in the discussion of God's benefaction of Jesus the Son (*υἱός [B], §9.12b).

9. Note that both "come forth" and "send" portray Jesus as in motion.

as the intermediary between God and the Twelve affirms the Twelve's future agentive benefaction of the gospel. The gospel of/about God (with Jesus) also is about Jesus' Disciples insofar as it is to function as the cause of Disciples' actions (8:35; 10:29), incorporates teachings about discipleship (8:34-37; 10:28-29), and contains a remembrance of a specific action by a woman portrayed as a Disciple (14:9).

e. Jesus Is God's Sole Intermediary in Sending to Proclaim the Gospel

There is no indication that Jesus delegates to those whom he sends to proclaim the gospel the capacity to send others to proclaim the gospel. Rather, as with God's authority (*ἐξουσία [B], §8.6c), Jesus is proposed as the sole intermediary between God and the Twelve in this matter. Thus the future sending to proclaim the gospel is to be attributed directly to Jesus.

f. The Gospel's Significance for Human Beings

The significance of the gospel of/about God (with Jesus) is apparent in the fact that Jesus commands belief only in the gospel (1:15) and God (11:22). Together with Jesus, the gospel is to be the cause of destroying one's life (8:35) and leaving family and possessions (10:29) as the condition for saving one's life (8:35) and receiving a hundredfold family and possessions in this time and everlasting life in the coming age (10:30). Thus the teachings of Jesus that are part of the content of the gospel prescribe how the one believing in God and the gospel is to act as the instrument of God's saving action for oneself and what God's saving action entails.

11. God the Originating Benefactive

God's origination benefaction of the gospel (*εὐαγγέλιον [B/T], §8.10), way (*ὁδός [B], §8.9), things (*τά [B], §8.8), and paths (τρίβος [B], 1:3) are linked in 1:1-3 (gospel, way, paths), 8:31–9:1 (things, gospel), and 12:13-17 (way, things).

The gospel of/about God (with Jesus) contains the notice that John the Messenger prepares the way of God (with Jesus) and the command to prepare the way of God (with Jesus) and make straight the paths of God (with Jesus) and is (with Jesus) to be the cause of destroying one's life as the condition for saving it. The one preparing the way, making straight the paths, and destroying one's life on the pattern of Jesus the Son of Man's necessary suffering much, being rejected, being killed, and rising saves one's life and thinks the things of God by enacting one's commitment to God.

The way (and paths) of God (with Jesus) is the way that leads to human salvation and is taught in truth by Jesus who commands giving back to God the things of God. The one so doing thinks the things of God and destroys one's life for the sake of Jesus and the gospel as the condition for saving it.

The things of God concern the necessary events about to befall Jesus the Son of Man and Jesus' hard teachings about discipleship (destroying one's life because of Jesus and the gospel and giving back to God), as commanded by Jesus who teaches the way of God (with Jesus) in truth. Giving back to God the things of God entails giving oneself, as one created in God's image, back to God and accomplishes the commanded preparation of the way of God (with Jesus) and making straight the paths of God (with Jesus).

The gospel, way, paths, and things, that is, all that God has through originating benefaction, highlight the action and thinking required of the one who would act as the instrument of God's saving action for oneself on the pattern of Jesus the Son of Man and become the beneficiary of God's saving action.[10]

---

10. The first two contexts also link God's action of writing (*γέγραπται [Ace], 1:2) about the required action of preparing the way and making straight the paths to thinking the things of God necessitated by God's scripture (*γραφή [B]) about Jesus the Son of Man's suffering much, being rejected, being killed, and rising.

Chapter 9

GOD AS RECIPIENT AND RECIPROCAL BENEFACTIVE

This chapter develops the statements of God's repeated recipient benefaction (Sections 1-8) and repeated reciprocal benefaction (Sections 9-13). Sections 1-8 develop the statements for God's recipient benefaction of seven repeated artifacts and then the characteristics of these seven repeated and four further non-repeated artifacts. Sections 9-13 develop the statements for God's reciprocal benefaction of three repeated groups of characters and one repeated character and then the characteristics of the repeated groups and character and three further occurrences of the character under different designations. The discussion addresses God's repeated recipient benefaction and then God's repeated reciprocal benefaction in the order of increasing frequency of occurrence and, for artifacts and characters with the same number of occurrences, in the order of their introduction. Each statement of God's repeated recipient and reciprocal benefaction includes a Heading that identifies the references to God, the contexts of their occurrence, and, where appropriate, further information that assists in interpretation, a Rehearsal of the specific narrative information associated with the references (subsection "a"), and an Elaboration of one or more salient contributions developed through repetition in the contexts of occurrences (beginning with subsection "b"). The concluding discussions for the two categories of benefaction identify commonalities and patterns of development in God's recipient and reciprocal benefaction.

God has repeated recipient benefaction of human sinful actions (*ἁμάρτημα [bB]), blaspheming (*βλασφημέω [acB]), blasphemies (*βλασφημία [bB]), and sins (ἁμαρτία [bB]), all of which are understood as covenantal debts owed to God by human beings (§1.2b), and of the house (*οἶκος [bB]), sanctuary (*ναός [bB]), and Temple (*ἱερόν [bB]), edifices built for God and for use by human beings. God has repeated reciprocal benefaction of Slaves (*δοῦλος [B]), Prophets (*προφήτης [B]), Messengers/Angels (*ἄγγελος [B]), and Jesus the Son (*υἱός [B]).

Since God's agency in forgiving is perennial (*ἀφίημι [Apb], §6.7), God's recipient benefaction of human blaspheming, sinful actions, blasphemies, and sins that require God's forgiveness is deemed perennial. God's recipient benefaction of the house is in the past (2:26) and present (11:17a), of the sanctuary is in the present (14:58a) and future (14:58b), and of the Temple is in the present. Thus the

Headings of statements of God's repeated recipient benefaction consistently use the present tense of "be" or "have." God's repeated reciprocal benefaction of Slaves is developed in the past (12:2-5) but is deemed to continue into the present and future (§5.3a), of Prophets is in the past (1:2) and present (6:4), of Messengers/Angels is in the past and present (1:2) and future (8:38), and of Jesus the Son is in the present (1:11) and future (13:32). Thus the Headings of these statements use present forms of "have."

Although "have" is a grammatically appropriate means for indicating God's recipient benefaction, its unqualified use with nouns designating artifacts is ambiguous because these nouns also require completion by those having agentive benefaction of the artifacts. To address this ambiguity, the Headings and Rehearsals of the following Statements associated with nouns explicitly state that God has recipient benefaction of the artifacts designated by nouns.

1. God Has (Recipient Benefaction of) Sinful Actions (*ἁμάρτημα [bB])

God having recipient benefaction of sinful actions (*ἁμάρτημα [bB], 3:28, 29) occurs in a single context (3:20-35) that is incorporated into those of God forgiving (*ἀφίημι [Apb], §6.7), having the Holy Spirit (*πνεῦμα [B], §8.5), being/not being blasphemed (*βλασφημέω [apB], §9.2), and having recipient benefaction of blasphemies (*βλασφημία [bB], §9.3).

a. The Attributes of the Sinful Actions against God

God has recipient benefaction of all sinful actions and blasphemies unless and until they are forgiven by God (3:28) and of the everlasting sinful action of the one blaspheming God's Holy Spirit (3:29).

b. God's Action of Forgiving Sinful Actions (Debts)

God has recipient benefaction and the sinner agentive benefaction of sinful actions, and, since these sinful actions cannot be undone, the sinner's only recourse is to ask God's forgiveness (§4.3d). God's action of forgiving establishes a complementary set of relationships insofar as God has agentive benefaction and the sinner recipient benefaction of God's forgiveness and neither God nor the sinner retains benefaction of the sinful action once it is forgiven.

c. The Everlasting Sin

God's action of forgiving has conditions (*ἀφίημι [Apb], §6.7b; *ἄφεσις [Bb], §7.1c), blaspheming God's Holy Spirit constitutes rejection of the instrument of God's forgiveness (§4.1b), and blaspheming God's Holy Spirit is a self-perpetuating action that renders one unable to correct the erroneous beliefs concerning God that are the basis for rejecting God's Holy Spirit (*βλασφημέω [apB], §9.2b). Thus blaspheming God's Holy Spirit makes one guilty of an everlasting sinful action not because God withholds God's forgiveness but because the erroneous belief concerning God prevents the sinner from satisfying the condition for God's forgiveness.

2. God Is/Is Not Blasphemed (*βλασφημέω [acB])

God being/not being blasphemed (*βλασφημέω [apB], 2:7; 3:28, 28) occurs in two contexts (2:1-12; 3:20-35) that incorporate that of God having recipient benefaction of sinful actions (*ἁμάρτημα [bB], §9.1).

a. The Attributes of Blaspheming/Not Blaspheming God

God is not blasphemed when Jesus tells the paralyzed man that God forgives his sins (2:7), (with others) is blasphemed by human beings (3:28), and (with Jesus and the Holy Spirit) is blasphemed by human beings (3:29).[1]

b. The Basis for Blaspheming and the Manner of Addressing It

The contexts of blaspheming God also concern the blaspheming of Jesus (2:7) and of Jesus and the Holy Spirit (3:29). In the first context, Jesus' recognition that the faith-based action of the paralyzed man and those carrying him (hereafter, the men) satisfies the condition for God to forgive the sins of the paralyzed man (*ἀφίημι [Apb], §6.7b) indicates that God is not blasphemed when Jesus affirms this fact. As a consequence, the Scribes' assertion that Jesus' statement blasphemes God, in fact, blasphemes both God who forgives the paralyzed man's sins and Jesus who accurately recognizes this fact. Both the positively evaluated action of the men and the negatively evaluated blaspheming by the Scribes are based on what they believe (content) concerning God (topic). The men's faith concerning God correctly acknowledges that Jesus is able to enact God's healing for the paralyzed man. In contrast, the Scribes' faith concerning God does not acknowledge either that Jesus is able to recognize the faith-based actions that satisfy the condition for God's forgiveness or that Jesus the Son of Man has God's authority to forgive sins (2:10). Jesus' response to the Scribes attempts to address their erroneous belief by using their apparent assumption that the man's paralysis is dependent on sin. Jesus both states and, through the healing of the man, demonstrates that he is able to enact God's healing and that, as Son of Man, he has God's authority to forgive sins

---

1. Joel F. Williams, "Foreshadowing, Echoes, and the Blasphemy at the Cross (Mark 15:29)," *JBL* 132, no. 4 (2013): 916, interprets the blaspheming of Jesus in 15:29 as blaspheming of God in that it claims that God would send a messiah who would rather save himself than others. The specific content blasphemed in 15:29, however, concerns Jesus *saying* that he would raze the sanctuary and build another in three days.

on the earth. Thus, if the Scribes acknowledge and act on this correct belief, they can satisfy the condition for God to forgive this blasphemy for them.

c. The Unforgivable Sinful Action

In the second context, Jesus' interaction with the Scribes from Jerusalem presents an example of blaspheming that never has God's forgiveness. These Scribes blaspheme Jesus by accusing him of having Beelzebul/an unclean spirit (3:22/30). The basis of the Scribes' blaspheming of Jesus is their erroneous belief concerning God that does not acknowledge that Jesus has God's Holy Spirit (1:10). As a consequence, the Scribes' blaspheming of Jesus also constitutes blaspheming of both the Holy Spirit and God who has the Holy Spirit. As in the former context, Jesus responds by attempting to correct their erroneous belief, this time through logical arguments based on the premise that a house divided against itself cannot stand. In this case, however, there is no apparent response by the Scribes. Jesus' use of arguments without an accompanying demonstrative action, as there was in the former context, highlights the dilemma of blaspheming the Holy Spirit: since Jesus' actions always and already demonstrate that he has God's Holy Spirit, there is no further action that can demonstrate this fact to the Scribes. This clarifies that blaspheming and so rejecting God's Holy Spirit is a self-perpetuating action insofar as it renders the blasphemer incapable of correction and subsequent forgiveness. Thus, although God forgives all sinful actions and blasphemies that human beings may blaspheme, the one blaspheming God's Holy Spirit rejects the instrument of God's forgiveness and remains guilty of an everlasting sinful action.

3. God Has (Recipient Benefaction of) Blasphemies (*βλασφημία [bB])

God having/not having recipient benefaction of blasphemies (*βλασφημία [bB], 3:28; 7:22; 14:64) occurs in three contexts (3:20-35; 7:17-23; 14:60-64) that incorporate that of God having recipient benefaction of sinful actions (*ἁμάρτημα [bB], §9.2). The concluding discussion considers the semantic coordination of "blaspheme" (*βλασφημέω [apB], §9.2) and "blasphemy" (*βλασφημία [bB]).

a. The Attributes of the Blasphemies Against God

God has recipient benefaction of the blasphemies that are done by human beings (3:28) and that come out of the heart and defile a human being (7:22) but not of the blasphemy inappropriately attributed by the Chief Priest to Jesus when Jesus acknowledges that he is the Christ and Son of the Blessed One (14:62).

b. God, Jesus, and the Holy Spirit Are Recipients of Blasphemy

All actual blasphemies are against God, Jesus, and the Holy Spirit. The Scribes from Jerusalem are guilty of blasphemies against God, Jesus, and the Holy Spirit

(3:22, 30) and the Chief Priest is guilty of blasphemy against God and Jesus (14:64). Their blasphemies come from the heart, defile them, and associate them with those characterized by improper thoughts, immorality, theft, murder, adultery, greed, wickedness, deceit, sensuality, envy, arrogance, and foolishness (7:21-22). Although God forgives all blasphemies that human beings may blaspheme (3:28), the Scribes from Jerusalem are guilty of blasphemy against God's Holy Spirit, the instrument of God's forgiveness, and so render themselves unable to receive God's forgiveness (3:29). The Chief Priest's blasphemy against God and Jesus may have God's forgiveness if he satisfies the conditions for its reception by correcting his erroneous belief concerning God and acting in accord with the recognition that God has Jesus the Christ and Son and that Jesus is the Son of Man who will sit at the right hand of God the Power.

c. The Semantic Coordination of "Blaspheme" and "Blasphemy"

Semantic coordination of "blaspheme" and "blasphemy" clarifies that all specific charges are directly against Jesus, that the occurrences against Jesus simultaneously are against God (2:7; 3:30; 14:64) and the Holy Spirit (3:30), and that the occurrences consistently have their basis in the perpetrators' erroneous beliefs concerning God.[2] These erroneous beliefs about God do not acknowledge that Jesus is able to evaluate when human actions satisfy the condition for God's forgiveness, that God gives to Jesus the Son of Man God's authority to forgive sins on the earth, that Jesus has God's Holy Spirit, and that Jesus is God the Blessed One's Christ and Son and the Son of Man who will sit at the right hand of God the Power when he comes. Thus all observed erroneous beliefs about God focus on Jesus and God's relationship with Jesus. Whereas those blaspheming God and Jesus have the potential to be beneficiaries of God's forgiveness if they accept and act on the correct belief concerning God, those blaspheming the Holy Spirit make themselves unable to acknowledge and act on corrected belief and so never have God's forgiveness.

4. God Has (Recipient Benefaction of) Sins (*ἁμαρτία [bB])

God having recipient benefaction of sins (*ἁμαρτία [bB], 1:4, 5; 2:5, 7, 9, 10) occurs in two contexts (1:4-8; 2:1-12). The concluding discussion considers the semantic coordination of "sinful action" (*ἁμάρτημα [bB], §9.2) and "sin" (*ἁμαρτία [bB]).

---

2. Darrell L. Bock, *Blasphemy and Exaltation in Judaism and the Final Examination of Jesus: A Philological-Historical Study of the Key Jewish Themes Impacting Mark 14:61-64* (WUNT 2/106; Tübingen: Mohr Siebeck, 1998), 187–9, discusses the manner in which the religious leaders' accusations of blasphemy against Jesus consistently are overturned to characterize the words of Jesus' opponents as blasphemy.

a. The Attributes of Sins Against God

God has recipient benefaction of the sins that God is going to forgive through the baptism of repentance proclaimed by John (1:4), that are confessed by those being baptized by John (1:5), that God forgives for the paralyzed man (2:5, 7, 9), and that Jesus the Son of Man forgives by the authority that God gives to him (2:10).

b. The Conditions for God's Forgiving Sins

The linkage of John's proclaimed baptism of repentance for God's forgiveness of sins and the faith-based action of the men that culminates in God's action of forgiving the paralyzed man's sins propose a three-stage process for God's action of forgiving. In the first stage, the future recipients of God's forgiveness satisfy the experiential component of the condition for God's forgiveness through repentance (1:4), that is, the change in mindset that accommodates the recognition of one's sins and sinfulness (§4.1b), and through faith (2:5).[3] Those repenting recognize that they are in need of God's forgiveness, and the paralyzed man and those carrying him believe that Jesus is able to enact God's healing of the paralyzed man. In the second stage, the future recipients of God's forgiveness satisfy the active component of the condition for God's forgiveness. Those repenting confess their sins (1:5), and the men carry the paralyzed man to Jesus and uncover the space over Jesus (2:3-4). The third stage of the process is God's responding action of forgiving sins. This indicates that human experience must issue in human action for one to become beneficiary of God's action of forgiving.

c. The Semantic Coordination of "Sinful Action" and "Sin"

The semantic coordination of "sinful action" and "sin" clarifies that they require the forgiveness that only God (with Jesus the Son of Man) can afford by God's Holy Spirit, the instrument of God's forgiveness. The only specific examples of sinful actions and sins are blasphemies based on erroneous faith about God that focuses on God's relationship with Jesus.

5. God Has (Recipient Benefaction of) the House (*οἶκος [bB])

God having recipient benefaction of the house (*οἶκος [bB], 2:26; 11:17a) occurs in two contexts (2:23-28; 11:15-19). The concluding discussion considers the

---

3. Repentance (μετάνοια [ecT]) and faith (*πίστις [ecT]) have the same licensing properties and so place the sinner (experiencer) in the proper relation to God (topic).

narrative coordination of "house" (*οἶκος [bB]) and "Temple" (*ἱερόν [bB], §9.7) in 11:15-19.

a. The Attributes of God's House

God had recipient benefaction of the house which David entered when he and his companions were hungry and in which David ate the bread of offering and gave it to his companions (2:26; cf. 1 Sam 21:6). God has recipient benefaction of the house to be called a house of prayer for all the nations but made a den of thieves by those buying, selling, changing money, selling doves, and carrying vessels (11:17a; cf. Isa 56:7; Jer 7:11).

b. Jesus Fulfills the Office of Chief Priest in God's House

The contexts contrast the appropriate function of God's house in the past as the locale for feeding David and his companions when they were hungry (2:26) and its inappropriate use in the present as a den of thieves (11:17). In the past, the Chief Priest acted properly in assisting David and his men by giving to them the bread that was reserved for the Priests. In the present, the Chief Priests and Scribes align themselves with those making God's house a den of thieves and plot how they might destroy Jesus. In the past, the Chief Priest interpreted and applied God's commandments in a manner that addressed human exigency. In the present, only Jesus interprets and applies what was written to address the needs of all seeking a direct communication relationship to God through prayer. Thus, in the present, only Jesus fulfills the office of Chief Priest in his actions and teachings in God's house.

c. God's House to Remain a Den of Thieves

In the present, God's house no longer fulfills its proper functions, and the Chief Priests and Scribes charged with its present management adamantly are opposed to its proper functions and to Jesus who alone demonstrates that he can provide for its proper management. The Chief Priests and Scribes (with the Elders) are complicit in Jesus' arrest (14:43-46), and the Chief Priests are complicit in convicting Jesus as worthy of death (14:55-64). Their actions are directed to ensuring that their mismanagement of God's house can continue unchallenged and that God's house remains a den of thieves.

d. The Narrative Coordination of "House" and "Temple"

Narrative coordination of "house" and "Temple" specifies the proper function of God's house/Temple as providing care for those in need and as a locale for prayer to God by all the nations, contrasts its past proper management and its present mismanagement by the Chief Priests and Scribes, and associates the past Chief Priest and Jesus as those enacting its proper management.

6. God Has (Recipient Benefaction of) the Sanctuary (*ναός [bB])

God having recipient benefaction of the sanctuary (*ναός [bB], 14:58a, [58b]; 15:29, 38) occurs in three contexts (14:55-59; 15:29-32, 37-39). Pre-existing semantic beliefs recognize "sanctuary" as a designation for the Temple (§2.4f(i)), and the repetition of "raze" (καταλύω) with respect to God's Temple (13:2) and God's sanctuary (*ναός [bB], 14:58a; 15:29) confirms their identification.

a. The Attributes of God's Sanctuary

God has recipient benefaction of the sanctuary made by hands that Jesus is falsely accused of *saying* that he is going to raze (14:58a), razed and in three days built by Jesus (15:29), and having the curtain that God tears into two from top to bottom immediately after Jesus expires (15:38). God has and will have recipient benefaction of the (other) sanctuary not made by hands that Jesus is falsely accused of *saying* that he will build over a period of three days ([14:58b]).

b. God Sets the Stage for Jesus' Razing of God's Sanctuary

Since the sole function attributed to God's sanctuary made by hands is associated with having the curtain (15:38) that separates God from human beings (*σχίζω [Ap], §6.1d), God's tearing of this curtain effectively removes the sanctuary's only specified reason for continuing. This accommodates the interpretation that God's tearing of its curtain sets the stage for Jesus' razing of this sanctuary and building the sanctuary not made by hands. The fact that God's tearing of this curtain also initiates the second stage of the end times (*σχίζω [Ap], §6.1d) is taken to indicate that, in the second stage of the end times, God intends to have recipient benefaction only of the sanctuary built by Jesus.

c. God's (Other) Sanctuary Is Built by Jesus

The contexts emphasize Jesus' building, and so agentive benefaction, of God's (other) sanctuary not made by hands ([14:58b]; 15:29). "Build" (οἰκοδομέω) positively links God who built a tower for the Vineyard (12:1) and Jesus who will build God's sanctuary ([14:58b]; 15:29) and contrasts them with the Chief Priests, Scribes, and Elders, the Ones Building (12:10) who reject (12:10) Jesus God's Beloved Son by taking him, killing him, and casting him out of God's Vineyard (12:7-8). As previously discussed (*ἀμπελών [B], §7.8e), God's dual response to the killing of God's Beloved Son by the Ones Building is coming, destroying the Chief Priests, Scribes, and Elders, and giving God's people to others (12:9) and Jesus becoming the Cornerstone (12:10). This interprets God's tearing the curtain and thereby setting the stage for Jesus' razing of the sanctuary made by hands as a further response to the killing of Jesus. As a consequence both those killing Jesus and the sanctuary made by hands are destined for destruction and will be replaced by Jesus and the sanctuary built by Jesus.

d. "This" and the "Other" Sanctuary

In the first context, the statement of those accusing Jesus contrasts "this" sanctuary made by hands that Jesus will raze from the "other" (ἄλλος) [sanctuary] not made by hands that Jesus will build (14:58). This contrast distinguishes both the manner of the construction of the sanctuary (by/not by hands) and those attributed with agentive benefaction of it (others/Jesus). The latter distinction is especially significant because the one attributed with agentive benefaction of an entity is assumed to have the capacity to act with respect to that entity.[4] Thus Jesus who builds and so has agentive benefaction of the other sanctuary has and will have the capacity to act with respect to that sanctuary and so ensure its proper management and function.

e. The Building of God's Sanctuary over/in Three Days

Repetition of "three days" (τρεῖς ἡμέραι), the period over which ([14:58b]) or in which (15:29) Jesus builds God's (other) sanctuary, recalls its three previous occurrences in predictions concerning Jesus the Son of Man being killed and rising (8:31; 9:31; 10:34) and so links Jesus' building of God's other sanctuary to the interval between Jesus the Son of Man being killed and rising.

7. God Has (Recipient Benefaction of) the Temple (*ἱερόν [bB])

God having recipient benefaction of the Temple (*ἱερόν [bB], 11:11, 15a, 15b, 16, 27; 12:35; 13:1, 3; 14:49) occurs in seven contexts (11:1-11, 15-19, 27-33; 12:35-37; 13:1-2, 3-8; 14:48-52). The concluding discussion considers the narrative coordination of "house" (*οἶκος [bB], §9.5) and "Temple" (*ἱερόν [bB]) in 11:1–11.

a. The Attributes of God's Temple

God has recipient benefaction of the Temple into which Jesus comes for inspection prior to his quick departure (11:11), which Jesus re-enters (11:15a), from which Jesus casts out those selling and buying and in which Jesus overturns the tables of the moneychangers and seats of those selling doves (11:15b), through which Jesus does not allow the carrying of vessels (11:16), in which Jesus is walking when the Chief Priests, Scribes, and Elders ask him, "By which authority do you do these things?" (11:27), in which Jesus teaches and responds to the Scribes' statement that God's Christ is David's Son (12:35), from which Jesus departs as one of his Disciples expresses admiration for the stones and buildings of the locale (13:1), opposite which Jesus is sitting when his Disciples ask him when the Temple will be destroyed (13:3), and in which Jesus teaches day after day (14:49).

---

4. Further discussion of the implications of agentive benefaction appears in Danove, "The Usages of δίδωμι in the Septuagint," 26.

b. God's Temple Is a Location

Although God's Temple receives narrative coordination with God's house (*οἶκος [bB], §9.5d) and has the same referent as God's sanctuary (*ναός [bB], §9.6), its presentation differs from these in that it consistently functions as a location in relation to which (in, into, through, from, opposite) Jesus acts; and the sole occurrence of "Temple" on the lips of Jesus specifies the Temple as the location of his teaching (14:49).[5] In contrast, Jesus explicitly speaks about God's house (11:17a, 17b) and is accused of speaking about God's sanctuary (14:58a, [58b]; 15:29) in ways that do not cast them merely as locations.

c. Jesus' Public Teaching in God's Temple

Since God's Temple is the locale of all events in 11:27–12:37, the following discussion of Jesus' public teaching in God's Temple considers all rhetorical contexts in 11:27–12:37, including those not explicitly referencing the Temple.

Jesus begins 11:27–12:37 by implicitly answering the questions by the Chief Priests, Scribes, and Elders about his authority (11:28-33), instructing them on God's Vineyard (12:1-9; cf. Isa 5:1-7), and interpreting for them God's scripture (12:10-11; cf. Ps 118:22-23), but they have no answer for Jesus' question to them (11:33) and seek to arrest Jesus (12:12). Jesus teaches God's way in truth (12:14) and properly interprets what God's commandments permit (12:17) even as the Pharisees and Herodians try but fail to ensnare Jesus in his speech (12:13-15). Jesus interprets the implications of God's statements to Moses to establish the fact of the resurrection (12:26-27; cf. Exod 3:6, 14-16) even as the Sadducees fail to use God's commandment (Deut 25:5-6) to disprove the resurrection and are shown to lack knowledge of God's scriptures and God's power and to be misled (12:18-27). Jesus answers a Scribe's question by identifying and commenting on God's first and second commandments (12:29-31; cf. Deut 6:5; Lev 19:18) and offering a statement about God's reign (12:34); but this time the Scribe posing the question responds by acknowledging that Jesus answers well and speaks in truth (12:32) and that God's first and second commandments are greater than all the burnt offerings and offerings of the Temple (12:33). This is the last statement by one of the "teachers" of God's people in God's Temple; and both the Pharisees and Herodians (12:14) and the Scribe (12:32) acknowledge that Jesus speaks in truth.

In 12:35-37, Jesus concludes his public teaching in the Temple by posing and answering his own question about what David said (12:36-37; cf. Ps 110:1), thereby correcting the Scribes' erroneous identification of God's Christ as David's Son with his correct identification of God's Christ as David's Lord.

In these contexts, the superiority of Jesus' public teaching over that of all of the recognized teachers of God's people establishes that, just as Jesus alone

---

5. The Temple consistently references arguments and adjuncts with the thematic roles Goal (11:11, 15a), Locative (11:15b, 27; 12:35; 13:3; 14:49), Source (13:1), or Path, the literal or figurative locale that entails the transition in motion (11:16).

properly executes the office of the Chief Priest in his proper management of God's house (*οἶκος [bB], §9.5b), Jesus alone properly executes the teaching office of the Chief Priests and all others in the Temple. Jesus' public teaching then establishes that he is superior even to David who first proposed building a house for God (2 Sam 7:2-5).

d. Jesus' Teachings and Actions in God's Temple

Repetition of "thief," "teach," and "Temple" tightly links 11:15-19 and 14:48-52. In the former context, the Chief Priests and Scribes respond to Jesus' actions in the Temple and to his teaching about making God's house a den of thieves by seeking how they might destroy Jesus. In the latter context, those sent by the Chief Priests, Scribes, and Elders (14:43) arrest Jesus like a thief at night instead of when he is teaching publicly in God's Temple (14:48-49). This identifies Jesus' actions and teachings in the Temple as the cause of his arrest and his destruction as its goal.

e. The Narrative Coordination of "House" and "Temple"

Narrative coordination of "house" and "Temple" complements the specification of the proper function of God's house/Temple as providing care for those in need and a locale for prayer to God by all the nations and the identification of Jesus alone as properly executing the office of Chief Priest in its proper management (*οἶκος [bB], §9.5d) by identifying Jesus alone as properly executing the teaching office of Chief Priest and all others in God's Temple.

8. God the Recipient Benefactive

This discussion develops God's recipient benefaction first of the various categories of covenantal debts and then of the house, sanctuary, and Temple and concludes by identifying which of these artifacts God intends to have.

a. God's Recipient Benefaction of Blaspheming, Sinful Actions, Blasphemies, and Sins

Human actions make God the recipient of blaspheming, sinful actions, blasphemies, sins, and the once-occurring trespasses (παράπτωμα [bB], 11:25). Jesus' statement that God forgives all sinful actions and blasphemies, and, by implication, all covenantal debts, indicates God's intent to relate to human beings not through recipient benefaction of their debts but through agentive benefaction of the debts' forgiveness. Jesus' command to his Disciples to forgive whatever they hold against another as the condition for God to forgive their trespasses (11:25) then indicates God's intent for human beings to relate to each other not through mutual recipient benefaction of debts but through mutual agentive benefaction of the debts' forgiveness. Whereas Jesus' command imposes no conditions on the others that must be fulfilled before his Disciples forgive what they hold against them, God's forgiveness has the condition that those incurring covenantal debts correct their erroneous belief that is the basis of their indebtedness and act on their corrected belief concerning God. That is, the condition for God's forgiveness is that human beings remove the basis of further covenantal indebtedness to God. This indicates that God's intent is that all such debts of human beings be forgiven, sent away, and canceled.

b. God's Recipient Benefaction of the House, Sanctuary, and Temple

Human actions make God the recipient of the house, the sanctuary made by hands, and the Temple, which ultimately have the same referent, and, through the Temple and those presently teaching in it, burnt offerings (ὁλοκαύτωμα [bB], 12:33), offerings (θυσία [bB], 12:33), and gifts (δῶρον [bB], 7:11). In the past, God's house fulfilled its proper function when its Chief Priest properly exercised his office to aid David and his companions. In the present, only Jesus exercises the management and teaching office of Chief Priest properly. Absent Jesus, God's house/Temple/sanctuary made with hands is a den of thieves, is not a house of prayer for all the nations, is mismanaged, and is populated by inferior teachers who do not know God's scriptures and are unable to interpret what has been written and what God's commandments permit. It is also the locale of burnt offerings and offerings that are inferior to observing God's commandments to love God and neighbor, and its teachers promote the use of the gift that nullifies God's commandments. In response, God's tearing of the curtain sets the stage for Jesus' razing of the sanctuary made by hands and building for God another sanctuary not made by hands.

c. God's Recipient Benefaction and What God Intends to Have

The foregoing discussions clarify that it is not God's intent to have recipient benefaction of any debts incurred by human beings but, instead, agentive benefaction of the forgiveness of debts for human beings. God's setting the stage for Jesus' razing of the present sanctuary also indicates that God does not intend to have recipient benefaction of the house/Temple/sanctuary made by hands or its attending burnt offerings, offerings, or gifts. As a consequence, God intends to have recipient benefaction of only one artifact, the sanctuary not made by hands that Jesus builds. Jesus' agentive benefaction of this sanctuary will ensure that he is able to execute the office of Chief Priest and guarantee its proper function as the place of care for those in need, the house of prayer to God for all the nations, and the locale of Jesus' teachings and the proper interpretation of God's scripture and commandments. By building this sanctuary, Jesus God's Christ and David's Lord fulfills God's promise that David's descendent will build a house for God's name and that God will establish the throne of this descendent forever (2 Sam 7:13).

9. God Has Slaves (*δοῦλος [B])

God having Slaves (*δοῦλος [B], 12:2, 4, [5a], [5b]) occurs in a single context (12:1-5) that is incorporated into those of God sending (*ἀποστέλλω [Aθg], §6.9) and God having the Vineyard (*ἀμπελών [B], §7.8).

a. The Attributes of God's Slaves

God's Slaves sent by God to the Farmers (the Chief Priests, Scribes, and Elders) at the proper time for the purpose of taking some of the fruit of the Vineyard (God's People) include one beaten by the Farmers and sent back to God without any of the fruit (12:2), another whom the Farmers beat over the head and dishonored (12:4), yet another whom the Farmers killed ([12:5a]), and many others, some of whom the Farmers beat and others of whom the Farmers killed ([12:5b]).

b. God's Slaves Were Dutiful When Sent

God's Slaves were sent by God to the Farmers so that God might take some of the Vineyard's fruit. The Slaves' attempts to carry out their mission align them with God's other dutiful emissaries, John the Messenger (1:2) and Jesus God's Beloved Son (9:37; 12:6). The Farmers' hostile responses to these attempts set them in opposition to God, God's Slaves, John the Messenger, and Jesus. The Farmers' adamant opposition to God is especially apparent in usurping God's prerogatives to send and take by taking the first Slave sent to them and sending him back empty-handed (12:2-3).

c. God's Slaves and Jesus God's Son

God sends God's Slaves and Jesus God's Beloved Son to the Farmers for the same purpose, and the Farmers respond by killing some of the Slaves and Jesus. Despite these parallels, greater emphasis falls on the distinctions between God's Slaves and Jesus. God's reciprocal benefaction of Slaves is that of owner to property, whereas God's reciprocal benefaction of Jesus is that of Father to Son and Heir (*ἀποστέλλω [Aθg], §6.9c). God responds to the Farmers' killing of God's Slaves by sending Jesus God's Beloved Son but responds to the Farmers' killing of God's Beloved Son by acting directly to destroy the Farmers (*ἀμπελών [B], §7.8d). God's sending of Slaves and John prior to the sending of Jesus joins with God's sending of John to prepare the way of God (with Jesus) to propose that God's sending of Slaves to the Farmers similarly prepares the way of God (with Jesus).

10. God Has the Prophets (*προφήτης [B])

God having the Prophets (*προφήτης [B], 1:2; 6:4, 15a, 15b; 8:28; 11:32) occurs in five contexts (1:1-3; 6:1-6a, 14-16; 8:27-30; 11:27-33).

a. The Attributes of God's Prophets

God's Prophet was Isaiah in/by whom God wrote (1:2). God's Prophets are like Jesus who is dishonored in his hometown, among his own kin, and in his own house (6:4) and include, according to some, Jesus (6:15a, 15b; 8:28) and, according to all, John (11:32).

b. Distinctions Among God's Prophets

Repetition of "Prophet" relates Isaiah (1:2), the one rejected as is Jesus (6:4), Jesus (6:15a; 8:28), all of God's Prophets (6:15b), and John (11:32). Isaiah functions as the locale/means of what was written (1:2), Jesus as the one whose teachings manifest God's wisdom and whose actions manifest God's power (6:2), and John as having a baptism that is by water (1:8) and from heaven (11:32). Whereas Isaiah was the locale/means of God's written communication, Jesus is the sole competent interpreter and applier of what Isaiah prophesied (7:6-7). Whereas John baptizes by water, Jesus who is stronger than John will baptize by God's Holy Spirit (1:7-8). These considerations propose that Jesus God's Prophet is superior to God's other Prophets.

c. God's Prophets and God's Slaves

God's sending of John (1:2), Jesus (9:37; 12:6), and Slaves (12:2, 4, 5a, [5b]), the identification of both John and Jesus as God's Prophets, and the sending of God's Slaves and Jesus for the same purpose join to associate God's Slaves with God's Prophets.

11. God Has Messengers/Angels (*ἄγγελος [B])

God having Messengers/Angels (*ἄγγελος [B], 1:2, 13; 8:38; 12:25; 13:27, 32) occurs in six contexts (1:1-3, 12-13; 8:31–9:1; 12:18-27; 13:24-29, 32-37).

a. The Attributes of God's Messengers/Angels

God's Messenger is John whom God sends before God's (with Jesus') face to prepare God's (with Jesus') way (1:2), and God's Angels minister to Jesus in the desert (1:13), are those whom the dead that rise are like (12:25), and (with Jesus the Son) do not know about the day and hour of the culminating events of this age (13:32). God's Angels will accompany Jesus the Son of Man when he comes (8:38) and will be sent by Jesus the Son of Man when he comes to gather God's Elect (13:27).

b. God's Messengers/Angels Are Sent

Repetition of "send" emphasizes God's sending of John God's Messenger (1:2) and Jesus the Son of Man's sending of God's Angels (13:27). God's sending of John is God's concluding action in the pre-eschatological times (§6.11a) and is directed to preparing God's people for the coming of God (with Jesus). Jesus' sending of God's Angels initiates God's concluding saving actions in the second stage of the end times (§6.11c) and is directed to gathering the Elect whom God will prepare for a life of abundance in the coming age. These actions of sending bracket the events of the first and second stages of the end times and so the ministries of Jesus and the Twelve that extend God's interactions to others than God's people (§6.11b) and then to all the nations (§6.11c).

c. Jesus as Intermediary in God's Actions of Sending

God sends Jesus who sends the Twelve (3:14; 6:7) and Disciples (11:1; 14:13) and who, as the Son of Man and God's eschatological agent (§5.3g), will send God's Angels (13:27). Jesus' actions of sending identify Jesus as God's intermediary in the sending of the Twelve, Disciples, and Angels and relate the Twelve, Jesus' Disciples, and God's Angels as emissaries of Jesus.

d. God's Angels Will Accompany Jesus the Son of Man When He Comes

The two statements relating Jesus and God's Angels in the future clarify the sequencing of end-time events: God's Angels will come with Jesus the Son of Man (8:38) and then he will send them (13:27). These contexts also link the one denying oneself, taking up one's cross, and following Jesus (8:33), the one destroying one's life because of Jesus and the gospel (8:34), and the one not ashamed of Jesus and his words (8:38) to God's Elect (13:27) as beneficiaries of the Son of Man's end-time coming with/sending of God's Angels. This provides a further link between Jesus' Disciples and God's Elect (*κολοβόω [Ap], §6.2b; *ἐκλεκτός [B], §7.7b).

e. Jesus Is Superior to the Angels

Repetition clarifies that Jesus is superior to God's Messengers/Angels. John the Messenger prepares the way before God (with Jesus). God's Angels minister to Jesus and will accompany Jesus the Son of Man and be sent by him. Repetition of "Angel" also links the obedient Disciple of Jesus (8:34), the one destroying one's life because of Jesus and the gospel (8:35), the one not ashamed of Jesus and his words (8:38), the dead who rise (12:25), and God's Elect (13:27) and associates them with the ones who will be like God's Angels (12:25). Despite his superiority to God's Angels and those who will be like them, Jesus remains at the service of God who sends him, sends through him, and, as Father, alone knows about the day and hour (13:32).

12. God Has Jesus the Son (*υἱός [B])

God having Jesus the Son (*υἱός [B], 1:1, 11; 3:11; 5:7; 9:7; 12:6a, 6b; 13:32; 14:61; 15:39) occurs in nine contexts (1:1-3, 9-11; 3:7-12; 5:1-13; 9:2-9; 12:6-8; 13:32-37;

14:60-64; 15:37-39) that incorporate those of God tearing (*σχίζω [Ap], §6.1), having a voice (*φωνή [B], §7.2), and loving (*ἀγαπητός [Ec], §10.5) Jesus the Son.

a. The Attributes of Jesus God's Son

God's Son Jesus is the Christ with whom God has/is the topic of the gospel (1:1), is loved and delighted in by God (1:11), is recognized as such by unclean spirits (3:11), is recognized as Son of God the Most High by Legion (5:7), is loved by God and to be listened to by his Disciples (9:7), is loved by God and is the one left for God to send to the Farmers (the Chief Priests, Scribes, and Elders) of the Vineyard (God's people) (12:6a), is to be respected by the Farmers (12:6), (with God's Angels) does not know the day or hour (13:32), is Son of God the Blessed One (14:61), and is recognized as such by the centurion upon seeing that Jesus expires as he does (15:39).

b. Jesus' Unique Co-Benefaction of God's Attributes as God's Son in 1:1-3

The present of the story world begins by asserting God's reciprocal benefaction of Jesus the Son. Interpreted from the perspective of this reciprocal relationship, Jesus' co-benefaction of God's gospel (1:1), face and way (1:2), and way and paths and Jesus' co-use of God's title "Lord" (1:3) would arise through "inheriting" these attributes and this title from God his Father as God's Heir (12:7). Although subsequent developments distinguish Jesus' agentive benefaction of the gospel (*εὐαγγέλιον [B/T], §8.10b) and the way (*ὁδός [B], §8.9c) from God's originating benefaction of them, no further developments qualify the interpretation of Jesus' co-benefaction of God's innately possessed face and God's paths and title "Lord." This encourages the interpretation that the statement by God's voice (1:11) affirms Jesus' identity as God's Beloved Son (*φωνή [B], §7.2).

c. God's Actions of Tearing and the Ministry of Jesus God's [Beloved] Son

As previously discussed (*σχίζω [Ap], §§6.1b–6.1e), God's actions of tearing occur explicitly in relation to Jesus God's Son onto whom God's Spirit moves after his baptism and from whom God's Spirit moves at his death. Thus the two stages of the end times begin specifically in relation to God, Jesus God's [Beloved] Son, and God's Spirit. God's actions of tearing bracket the entirety of Jesus' ministry and specify it as the ministry of God's [Beloved] Son. The descent of God's Spirit onto Jesus initiates God's outpouring of the Spirit onto God's people in the first stage of the end times. Jesus' expiring of God's Spirit begins Jesus' baptizing by the Holy Spirit (1:8) and identifies Jesus as the mediator of God's outpouring of the Spirit onto all flesh in the second stage of the end times. Jesus' baptizing by the Holy Spirit ensures that the Twelve (fully equipped with God's Spirit, recognition of Jesus' identity, and Jesus' teachings and actions) are able to continue the ministry of Jesus God's [Beloved] Son (*σχίζω [Ap], §6.1e).

d. God's Voice Affirms Jesus' Status and Relates Others to Jesus

God's voice affirms Jesus' status as God's Beloved Son first to Jesus (1:11) and then Peter, James, and John (9:7) and commands these Disciples to be in a direct communication relationship from Jesus (9:7). This command, God's final verbal communication to human beings in this age, establishes Jesus as sole mediator of God's communications to human beings for the remainder of this age (*γέγραπται [Ace], §6.8).

e. God's Experiential and Active Love of Jesus God's Son

God's love of Jesus is both experiential and active (§§1.2a, 1.7a). The contexts relate God's experiential love of (1:11; 9:7; 12:6) and delight in (1:11) Jesus to God's actions of tearing the sky (1:10) as the condition for God's voice to address Jesus (*σχίζω [Ap], §6.1b), to the command of God's voice to Peter, James, and John and, through them, all of Jesus' Disciples to listen to Jesus (9:7), and to God's speaking the injunction to respect Jesus (12:6). Repetition specifies God's love as the defining characteristic of God's reciprocal relationship with Jesus the Son and the basis of God's command for Disciples to be in a direct communication relationship from Jesus (*φωνή [B], §7.2d).

f. The Linkage of "God's Son" to Other Designations of Jesus

The contexts referencing Jesus God's Son provide the primary means of linking designations of Jesus. Jesus God's Son is God's Christ (1:1; 14:61), the Lord (1:3), God's Beloved (1:11; 9:7; 12:6), the Disciples' Rabbi (9:5), God's Heir (12:7), and Son of Man (14:62). These linked designations assert Jesus' reciprocal benefaction of God's people (Lord, Heir) and his Disciples (Rabbi). The use of the non-Greek "Rabbi" (ῥαββί, 9:5; 11:21; 14:45) to assert Jesus' reciprocal benefaction of his Disciples and of the non-Greek and unique "Abba" (αββα, 14:36) to specify Jesus' reciprocal benefaction of God contextualizes these relationships in the ministry of Jesus.[6]

g. The Actions of Jesus God's Son

The contexts explicitly attribute to Jesus God's Son five actions: harshly commanding unclean spirits not to make him known (3:12), saying to the unclean spirit to come out of the demoniac (5:8), asking the name of the unclean spirit (5:9), permitting Legion to enter the swine (5:13), and saying "I am he" in response

---

6. In contrast, the use of the more frequent "Teacher" (διδάσκαλος) would introduce ambiguities concerning the extent of Jesus' reciprocal benefaction, since "Teacher" in a majority of its occurrences appears on the lips of those not explicitly identified as Disciples (5:35; 9:17; 10:17, 20; 12:32; 14:14) or of those explicitly identified as opponents of Jesus (12:14, 19).

to the Chief Priest's question, "Are you the Christ, the Son of the Blessed One?" (14:61-62). Repetition links the unclean spirits and the Chief Priest and sets them in opposition to both God and Jesus God's Son.

13. God the Reciprocal Benefactive

God has repeated reciprocal benefaction of Jesus the [Beloved] Son, Prophets, Messengers/Angels, and Slaves and on three further occurrences of Jesus God's Holy One (ἅγιος [B], 1:24), Heir (κληρόνομος [B], 12:7), and the one whom God has (ἔχω [Bp], 12:6) left to send to the Farmers of the Vineyard. The following discussion develops the relationship among those reciprocally related to God and their function as instruments of God's saving action.

a. The Relationships Among Those Reciprocally Related to God

Those reciprocally related to God are related to each other in ways that highlight the uniqueness of Jesus. Although God's Slaves and Jesus God's Beloved Son are related by being sent to the Farmers for the same purpose, God's reciprocal benefaction of Jesus (Father to Son) is more intimate than that of God's Slaves (owner to property), and God responds to the killing of Slaves by sending Jesus (12:5) but to the killing of Jesus by taking direct action against the Farmers (12:9). Whereas Isaiah God's Prophet is the locale/means (1:2) and prophesier (7:6) of what was written and John God's Prophet has the baptism from heaven (11:30) by water (1:8), Jesus God's Prophet teaches by God's wisdom and acts by God's power (6:2), is the sole competent interpreter of what was written (7:6-7), is stronger than John, and will baptize by God's Holy Spirit (1:7-8). Only God (1:2) and Jesus the Son of Man (13:27) send God's Messengers/Angels, who prepare the way of God and Jesus (1:2-3), minister to Jesus (1:13), and accompany Jesus the Son of Man (8:38).

b. Those Reciprocally Related to God Are Instruments of God's Saving Action

Those reciprocally related to God function as instruments of God's saving action for human beings in three ways. First, the actions of God's Slaves in the past, Jesus God's Beloved Son in the present, and Jesus the Cornerstone in the future are directed to permitting God's people to render to God what is due to God, thereby ensuring their proper relationship with God. Second, God's Prophets were the locale/means of what was written to God's people, Jesus properly teaches, interprets, and applies what was written for God's people and his Disciples, and Jesus God's Beloved Son will be God's sole delegated instrument of God's communications to all for the remainder of this age. Third, God's Messengers/Angels summon God's people to prepare God's (with Jesus') way and paths and will be sent by Jesus the Son of Man and God's eschatological agent in his gathering of God's Elect. Thus those reciprocally related to God are instruments of God's saving actions for God's people, Jesus' Disciples, God's Elect, and potentially all human beings.

Chapter 10

GOD AS CONTENT, EXPERIENCER, GOAL, AND INSTRUMENT

This chapter develops the statements of God's repeated attributes as Content (Section 1) and Experiencer (Sections 2–8) and then considers God's non-repeated attributes as Goal (Section 9) and Instrument (Section 10). Section 1 develops the statement for God as repeated Content; and, since these are the only occurrences of God as Content, there is no separate concluding discussion. Sections 2–8 develop the statements for God's six repeated experiences and then consider the characteristics of God's six repeated and nine non-repeated experiences. The discussion addresses the repeated experiences in the order of increasing frequency of occurrence and, for those with the same number of occurrences, in the order of their introduction. Each statement of God as Content and Experiencer includes a Heading that identifies the references to God, the contexts of their occurrence, and, where appropriate, further information that assists in interpretation, a Rehearsal of the specific narrative information associated with the references (subsection "a"), and an Elaboration of one or more salient contributions developed through repetition of the contexts of occurrences or through vocabulary parallels (beginning with subsection "b"). The concluding discussion identifies commonalities and patterns of development in God's six repeated and nine non-repeated experiences. Since there is no repetition of God as Goal and Instrument, their presentations follow the format of the concluding discussions of repeated attributes.

Although the experience/action of God being loved (*ἀγαπάω [eC/apB]) and loving (*ἀγαπητός [Ec/Apb]) receives consideration in this chapter, the associated statements address both aspects of God's relation to loving.

The command to love (*ἀγαπάω [eC/apB]) God occurs in the past and present (12:30; cf. Deut 6:5) and is assumed to remain binding into the future, and the Heading of its statement uses present forms of "love." God's experiences of being given thanks (*εὐχαριστέω [acE]) and being blessed (*εὐλογέω [atE/Apb]) by Jesus, of hosanna (*ὡσαννά [aE]), and of loving (*ἀγαπητός [Ec]/Apb) Jesus the Son occur in the present, and the Headings of their statements use present verb forms. Since God's experiences of prayer (*προσευχή [E]) occur in the past and present (11:17; cf. Isa 56:7) and presumably the future and of praying (*προσεύχομαι

[acE]) occurs in the present (1:35) and future (13:18), the Headings of their statements also use present verb forms.

1. God Is to Be Loved (*ἀγαπάω [eC/apB])

God being loved (*ἀγαπάω [eC/apB], 12:30, 33) occurs in a single context (12:28-34) that is incorporated into those of God having commandments (*ἐντολή [B], §7.10), having the reign (*βασιλεία [B], §7.12), and being God (*θεός [bP], §11.3) and is coterminous with that of God being one (*εἷς [P], §11.1). Being loved (§§1.2a, 1.7a) entails being affectively responded to by another (eC) and being the beneficiary of the other's action (apB).

a. The Attributes of God Being Loved

God is to be loved by Israel (God's People) from all one's heart and from all one's life and from all one's mind and from all one's strength (12:30; cf. Deut 6:5) and from all one's heart and from all one's understanding and from all one's strength (12:33; cf. Deut 6:5).

b. God's Uniqueness

Repetition of God being one (12:29, 32) and the further assertion that there is not another than God (12:32; cf. Isa 45:21) distinguishes God who is unique and in whom the entirety of divinity is present from the neighboring peoples' gods who are multiple and in whom divinity is divided. The uniqueness and completeness of God's divinity is proposed as the basis for the commanded response to love God alone completely from all one's heart, life, mind, and strength (12:30) and from all one's heart, understanding, and strength (12:33).

c. Affectively Responding to and Acting for God

The differing statements of the command to love God highlight the totality of the required affective response to and action for God. The required affective response demands that one maintain a vigilant and continuing focus on one's relationship with God. The required action for God, however, introduces an apparently insurmountable impasse, because there is no human action that can directly benefit God. The contextually proposed solution to this impasse is found in the repeated coordination of the first commandment, to love God, and the second commandment, to love one's neighbor as oneself (12:31, 33). This double coordination proposes that the proper action for one's neighbor satisfies the commanded action for loving God.

d. Loving God and Neighbor

Loving God "from all one's life" (ψυχή, 12:30) and "from all one's heart" (καρδία, 12:30, 33) poses significant challenges to fulfilling the commands to love God and neighbor. Repetition of life (ψυχή) clarifies that loving God from all one's life requires doing good and saving life rather than doing evil and killing (3:4), destroying one's life for the sake of Jesus and the gospel rather than futilely attempting to save it (8:35-37), and doing what God wants rather than what one wants even in circumstances that make one's life sad to the point of death (14:34; cf. Ps 42:6, 12; 43:5) and requires of Jesus the Son of Man that he give his life as a ransom for many (10:45). Repetition of heart (καρδία) emphasizes the special difficulty of satisfying the commanded love of God through loving one's neighbor. Elsewhere the heart is portrayed as the seat of deliberations against Jesus (2:6, 8), hardened to prefer doing evil and killing rather than doing good and saving life (3:4-5), hardened not to understand about the bread (6:52), being far distant from God (7:6; cf. Isa 29:13 LXX), the goal into which unclean food does not enter (7:19), the source from which a host of unclean things and evils exit (7:21-22), hardened not to perceive or understand (8:17), and the locale where faith is to reside (11:23). Six of these eight occurrences receive negative evaluation, and half focus on improper responses to other human beings (2:6, 8; 3:4-5; 7:21-22). Thus satisfying the commanded loving action for God through loving action for one's neighbor demands orienting one's heart properly toward one's neighbor as the prerequisite for loving God.

e. Loving God and Neighbor as Oneself

Although direct actions against one's own physical integrity are restricted to those possessed by unclean spirits (1:26; 5:5; 9:22, 26), the repetition of "life" and "heart" also clarify that improper thinking and wanting can lead to actions that are to one's detriment: the Pharisees and Scribes' commitment to the traditions of the Elders situates their hearts far from God (7:6-7), Peter's thinking the things of human beings leads him to rebuke Jesus (8:32-33), and the one wanting to save one's life will destroy it (8:35). Thus satisfying the commanded loving action for God through a loving experience and action for one's neighbor demands not only that one orient one's heart properly toward one's neighbor but, at the same time, that one orient one's heart, thinking, and desires to one's own benefit.

f. Loving God and Neighbor Is Greater Than All Other Commandments

Jesus' identification of the love of God as the first commandment and the love of neighbor as the second commandment relegates all other commandments to tertiary status. The Scribe's further statement that the first and second commandments are greater than all burnt offerings and offerings then specifically highlights the tertiary status of Temple sacrifices (12:33). As previously discussed (§9.8c), God does not intend to have recipient benefaction of these Temple sacrifices once Jesus builds the sanctuary not made by hands. Repetition of "heart" also evokes Jesus' declaration of all foods as clean (7:19). These considerations are taken to indicate that God does not intend to maintain benefaction of the commandments governing Temple sacrifices and foods specifically because the distinctions that they introduce among human beings hinder fulfillment of the commandments to love God and neighbor. As a consequence, the determination of which tertiary commandments God intends to maintain is to be governed by their potential to contribute to the love of God and neighbor. At this point, the repetition of "life" contributes that the interpretation and application of those tertiary commandments are to be directed to doing good and saving life.

g. Loving God and Neighbor and God's Reign

The one understanding that God is one and that loving God and loving neighbor are greater than all burnt offerings and offerings is not far from God's reign (12:34). While proximity to God's reign is better than distance from God's reign, only dynamic motion into God's reign or motion of God's reign toward oneself results in the reception of life in the coming age (*βασιλεία [B], §7.12e). To participate in this life-giving dynamic, the Scribe will need to move beyond understanding the significance of the commandments to love God and to love neighbor and actually fulfill these commandments.

h. A Potential Reciprocal Relationship with God

Jesus' rehearsal of the first commandment begins, "Hear, O Israel, the Lord our God is one Lord" (12:29; cf. Deut 6:4). The original context of this statement (Deut 6:1-4) interprets the relationship introduced by "our God" as one of artifact (Israel) to artisan (God), identifies fostering fear of the Lord as the purpose of observing God's commandments, and proposes this fear as the means of converting the relationship between artifact and artisan into a reciprocal relationship between God's people and God. In this light, the one fulfilling the commandments to love God and to love neighbor becomes faithful to God on the pattern of those already in a reciprocal relationship with God (Jesus God's Beloved Son and God's Slaves, Prophets, Messengers/Angels, §9.13) and enters a reciprocal relationship with God. Such a relationship is not limited to faithful Israel but is possible for anyone fulfilling the commands to love God and to love one's neighbor as oneself.

2. God Is Given Thanks (*εὐχαριστέω [acE]) by Jesus

God being given thanks (*εὐχαριστέω [acE], 8:6; 14:23) by Jesus occurs in two contexts (8:1-9; 14:22-26) that are incorporated into those of God being blessed (*εὐλογέω [aE], §10.6).

a. The Attributes of God Being Given Thanks

God is given thanks by Jesus for the seven loaves of bread that Jesus takes, breaks, and gives to his Disciples to distribute to the four thousand to eat (8:6) and for the cup that Jesus gives to his Disciples/the Twelve (14:14/14:17), and that Jesus says is his blood of the covenant and shed for many, and from which the Disciples/Twelve drink (14:23).

b. Two Eucharistic Meals

Repetition of "eat" (8:1, 2, 8; 14:22) and "bread" (8:4, 5, 6; 14:22) and of Jesus' actions of taking (8:6; 14:22a, 23), giving thanks (8:6; 14:23), breaking (8:6; 14:22), giving (8:6; 14:22; 23), and blessing (8:7; 14:22) tightly links the feeding of the four thousand and Jesus' last meal with the Disciples/Twelve. Jesus' statements that the bread is his body (14:22) and that the cup is of his blood (14:24) join his action of giving thanks (14:23) and his reference to the covenant (14:24) to identify the latter meal as a Eucharistic meal.[1] At this point, the noted repetition of linking words and presence of "give thanks" in both contexts interpret the feeding of the four thousand as a Eucharistic meal. The locations of these Eucharistic meals, the Decapolis (7:31) and Jerusalem (11:27), propose both Gentiles and Jews as appropriate participants in Eucharistic meals.

c. The Conditions for the Eucharistic Meals

The contexts propose Jesus' actions of taking the bread, thanking God for the bread, breaking the bread, giving the bread to his Disciples (8:6), and blessing God for the fish (8:7) as the condition for the multiplication of the bread and fish (8:8), Jesus' actions of taking the bread, blessing God for the bread, breaking the bread, and giving the bread to the Disciples/Twelve as the condition for the bread becoming Jesus' body (14:22), and Jesus' actions of taking the cup, thanking God for the cup, and giving the cup to his Disciples/the Twelve (14:23) as the condition for the contents of the cup becoming Jesus' blood (14:24). These observations indicate that only Jesus properly thanks/blesses God in the context of Eucharistic meals. The latter context proposes Jesus' blood as the instrument for establishing God's covenant (14:24) that will govern the relationship between God and Jesus' Disciples and the Eucharistic meal as the context for recalling the establishment of this covenant.

d. A Meal That Looks Backward and Forward

Repetition of "drink" (πίνω), first with the Disciples/Twelve (14:23) and then with Jesus (14:25), indicates that those drinking from the cup of Jesus' blood at the Eucharistic meal are related to Jesus who will drink it new in God's reign (14:25). In this way, the Eucharistic meal replaces the Passover meal's looking back to God's

---

1. Note the association of break (κλάω), bread (ἄρτος), body (σῶμα), cup (ποτήριον), blood (αἷμα), give thanks (εὐχαριστέω), and covenant (διαθήκη) in Matt 26:26-28, Luke 22:17-20, and 1 Cor 11:23-28 and the reference to this meal as the table of the Lord (1 Cor 10:21).

saving action in the Passover and forward to God's saving action in bringing God's people to the promised land with looking back to Jesus' miraculous feeding of the four thousand and Jesus' giving his body and the cup of his blood—the instrument of establishing God's covenant with Jesus' Disciples—and looking forward to drinking with Jesus in God's reign.

3. God Is the Experiencer of Prayer (*προσευχή [E])

God experiencing prayer (*προσευχή [E], 9:29; 11:17) occurs in two contexts (9:28-29; 11:15-19).

a. The Attributes of God Being the Experiencer of Prayer

God experiences the prayer by which specific kinds of spirits, such as the one making a man mute and deaf, are cast out (9:29; cf. 9:25) and is to experience the prayer of all the nations (11:17; cf. Isa 56:7).

b. Direct Communication Relationships

"Cast out" (ἐκβάλλω) links the spirit making the man mute and deaf (9:18, 28) and those selling and buying in the Temple and making the Temple a den of thieves (11:15). Jesus' expulsion of the spirit restores the man's ability to speak and hear, and Jesus' expulsion of those making the Temple a den of thieves restores the Temple's ability to function as a house of prayer for all the nations. As a consequence, Jesus' actions open the possibility for direct communication relationships from the man to other human beings and from all the nations to God. Jesus' actions indicate that God intends all human beings to be in a direct communication relationship to other human beings and in a direct communication relationship of prayer to God.

4. God Is the Experiencer of Hosanna (*ὡσαννά [aE])

God experiencing "hosanna" (*ὡσαννά [aE], 11:9, 10) occurs in a single context (11:1-11) that is incorporated into those of God having the Temple (*ἱερόν [bB], §9.7). "Hosanna" receives interpretation as an acclamation of praise addressed to God (§2.4a).

a. The Attributes of God as Experiencer of Hosanna

God experiences "hosanna" in the context of the blessing of Jesus as coming in/by the name of God the Lord (11:9; cf. Ps 118:26) and of the blessing of David's coming reign (11:10).

b. Proper and Improper Praise of God

The context juxtaposes the proper praise of God concerning Jesus who comes in/by the name of God the Lord (11:9; cf. Ps 118:26) and the improper praise of God concerning the reign of David which is not associated with the coming of Jesus and is not coming (11:10). This juxtaposition indicates that those preceding and following Jesus do not properly understand Jesus' relationship with David, David's reign, and God. Although a descendent of David (10:47, 48), Jesus does not come to restore the reign of David. Rather, repetition of "highest" (ὕψιστος, 11:10) recalls that Jesus is the Son of God the Most High (5:7), and repetition of "reign" recalls that Jesus proclaims the reign of God (*βασιλεία [B], §7.13) and not the reign of David. This context indicates that even acclamations of praise directed to God can be inappropriate when one does not understand properly God's relationships with Jesus, people, and events.

c. God's Locale Is the Highest [Heavens]

"Highest" (ὕψιστος) links God the Most High (5:7) and the most high [heavens] (11:10) and clarifies that God's locale, previously established as in the heavens (*φωνή [B], §7.2c), in fact, is the highest of the heavens.

5. God Loves (*ἀγαπητός [Ec]/Apb) Jesus the Son

God loving Jesus the Son (*ἀγαπητός [Ec/Apb], 1:11; 9:7; 12:6) occurs in three contexts (1:9-11; 9:2-9; 12:6-8) that incorporate those of God having a voice (*φωνή [B], §7.2) and that are incorporated into those of God having Jesus the Son (*υἱός [B], §9.12). Love (§§1.2a, 1.7a) entails affectively responding to another (Ec) and acting for another (Apb).

a. The Attributes of God's Love of Jesus

God loving Jesus the Son is communicated by God's voice prior to the statement that God delights in Jesus (1:11) and prior to God's command to Peter, James, and John to listen to Jesus (9:7) and is said by God in a statement enjoining the Farmers (Chief Priests, Scribes, and Elders) to respect Jesus (12:6).

b. God's Voice Affirms and Communicates God's Love of Jesus the Son

God's voice affirms that God loves Jesus God's Son to Jesus (1:11) and to Peter, James, and John (9:7), and God's statement affirms that God loves Jesus God's Son to the implied reader (12:6). God's voice and statement establish direct communication relationships from God to Jesus, to Peter, James, and John and, through these Disciples, all of Jesus' Disciples (*φωνή [B], §7.2), and to the implied reader (*λέγω [Ace], §6.4). The two statements of God's voice, which are God's last two oral communications in this age, and God's direct statement indicate God's intent that human beings know that God loves Jesus. The command to Peter, James, and John to listen to Jesus also clarifies that, going forward, Jesus' Disciples are to remain in a direct communication relationship not from God but from Jesus, the mediator of God's communications to human beings (*γέγραπται [Ace], §6.8d). The contexts propose God's love of and delight in Jesus as the basis of Jesus' enduring role as sole mediator of God's future communications to human beings.

c. God's Experiential and Active Love of Jesus

The contexts relate God's experiential and active love of Jesus, and repetition links these related events. The first context relates God's experiential love of and delight in Jesus (1:11) to God's action of tearing the sky (1:10), the condition for the coming of God's Spirit onto Jesus and God's voice to address Jesus (*σχίζω [Ap], §6.1b). The second context relates God's experiential love of Jesus to God's command to Peter, James, and John and, through them, all of Jesus' Disciples to listen to Jesus (9:7). The third context continues this pattern by relating God's experiential love of Jesus to God's injunction (interpreted only by the implied reader) that the Farmers respect Jesus.

d. God's Loving Actions for Jesus Also Are Loving Actions for Others

God's tearing the sky accommodates the coming onto Jesus of God's Spirit (1:10) by which Jesus is going to baptize human beings (1:8). God then commands Jesus' Disciples to listen to Jesus (9:7) and enjoins on the Farmers (and implied reader) respect for Jesus. These communications relate their interpreters, Jesus, Jesus' Disciples, and the implied reader. The one obeying God's command and heeding God's injunction places oneself in the appropriate experiential (listen, respect) relationship with Jesus and acts according to what one hears from Jesus and out of one's respect for Jesus. These related experiences and actions receive interpretation as manifesting one's love for Jesus. Thus God's tearing, commanding, and enjoining for Jesus the Son whom God loves also establish the possibility for those baptized by Jesus, listening to Jesus, and respecting Jesus to love Jesus.

6. God Is Blessed (*εὐλογέω [atE]) by Jesus

God being blessed (*εὐλογέω [atE], 6:41; 8:7; 14:22) occurs in three contexts (6:35-44; 8:1-9; 14:22-26) that incorporate those of God being given thanks (*εὐχαριστέω [atE], §10.2). The following Elaboration avoids redundancies by assuming and referencing the content of the statement of God being thanked (*εὐχαριστέω [acE], §10.2) by Jesus and focusing on the contribution of the new context (6:35-44).

a. The Attributes of God Being Blessed

God is blessed by Jesus for the five loaves of bread that Jesus takes, breaks, and gives to his Disciples to distribute to the five thousand men (6:41), for the few fish that Jesus says his Disciples are to distribute to the four thousand to eat (8:7), and for the bread that Jesus takes, breaks, and gives to his Disciples/the Twelve (14:14/14:17) and that Jesus says is his body (14:22).

b. Three Eucharistic Meals

The further repetition of "eat" (6:36, 37, 42, 44) and "bread" (6:37, 38, 41a, 41b, 44) and Jesus' actions of taking (6:41), blessing (6:41), and giving (6:41) tightly link the feedings of the five thousand men and four thousand and Jesus' last meal (*εὐχαριστέω [acE], §10.2b). This linkage interprets the feeding of the five thousand men as a Eucharistic meal on the pattern of the feeding of the four thousand and Jesus' last meal. The locations of these Eucharistic meals, opposite Bethsaida (6:45), the Decapolis (7:31), and Jerusalem (11:27), confirm both Jews and Gentiles as appropriate participants in Eucharistic meals.

c. Thanking/Blessing God as a Condition for the Eucharistic Meal

As with the previously considered Eucharistic meals (*εὐχαριστέω [acE], §10.2c), Jesus' actions of taking the bread, blessing God for the bread, breaking the bread, and giving the bread to his Disciples and Jesus' blessing the fish (6:41) receive interpretation as the condition for the multiplication of the bread and fish (6:42). These observations indicate that blessing God for the bread (6:41; 14:22) and thanking God for the bread (8:6) constitute the same action in the context of a Eucharistic meal and that only Jesus properly thanks/blesses God in the context of Eucharistic meals.[2]

d. A Meal That Looks Backward and Forward

These Eucharistic meals look back to Jesus' miraculous feeding of the five thousand men and four thousand and Jesus' giving his body and the cup of his blood by which God establishes God's covenant with Jesus' Disciples, and they look forward to drinking with Jesus in God's reign (*εὐχαριστέω [acE], §10.2d).

7. God Is Prayed To (*προσεύχομαι [acE])

God being prayed to (*προσεύχομαι [acE], 1:35; 6:46; 11:24, 25; 12:40; 13:18; 14:32, 35, 38, 39) occurs in six contexts (1:35-38; 6:45-52; 11:20-25; 12:38-40; 13:18-20;

---

2. Eugene LaVerdiere, *The Beginning of the Gospel: Introducing the Gospel According to Mark, Vol. 1: Mark 1–8:21* (Collegeville, MN: Liturgical, 1999), 175–6, notes that thanking and blessing have the same meaning and are addressed to God.

14:32-42) that incorporate that of God shortening (*κολοβόω [Ap], §6.2) the days. The concluding discussion develops the implications of the semantic coordination of God's experience of prayer (*προσευχή [E], §10.3) and of God being prayed to (*προσεύχομαι [acE]).

a. *The Attributes of God Being Prayed to*

God is prayed to by Jesus in a deserted place (1:35), on the mountain (6:46), and at Gethsemane (14:32) that this hour may pass by him (14:35, 39) and by Pharisees who do so at length as a pretext and will receive God's greater condemnation (12:40). God is to be prayed to by Jesus' Disciples who are to believe that they receive what they ask of God (11:24), who are to forgive what they have against another as the condition for God their Father in the Heavens to forgive for them their trespasses (11:25), and who are to ask that they not come into testing (14:38). In the future, God is to be prayed to by Jesus' Disciples that the tribulation not occur in winter (13:18).

b. *The Appropriate Circumstances and Conduct for Praying to God*

Jesus' words and actions clarify the appropriate circumstances and conduct for praying. Jesus' praying to God alone in the desert (1:35), alone on a mountain (6:46), and apart from his Disciples in a garden (14:35, 39) verifies the propriety of solitary prayer. These occurrences present Jesus praying to God after healing many and casting out many demons (1:34) and before going elsewhere to proclaim (1:38), after feeding the five thousand men (6:41-44) and before walking on the sea (6:48-50), and after his final instruction to his Disciples (14:27-31) and before his arrest (14:43-49). These considerations identify praying as an appropriate interlude between significant events. Jesus' teachings (11:24, 25) and commands (13:18; 14:38) to his Disciples to pray to God using plural verbs verify the propriety of group or communal prayer. Jesus' condemnation of the Scribes (12:40) highlights the impropriety of ostentation when praying to God. Jesus' command to his Disciples to pray to God that the tribulation not occur in winter (13:18) and his own prayer to God before his arrest (14:32, 35, 39) indicate the propriety of praying to God in times of crisis.

c. *Qualifications of Praying to God*

Jesus explicitly sets in parallel praying (*προσεύχομαι [acE], 1:35; 6:46; 11:24) to God and asking (αἰτέω [acE], 11:24) of God, and what is prayed to God, when specified, consistently is constituted by or incorporates a request: that, if possible, this hour might pass by Jesus (14:39), that Disciples not come into testing (14:38), and that the tribulation not happen in winter (13:18). Praying to God also is the context for forgiving what one holds against another as the condition for God to forgive trespasses (11:25). The general condition for receiving that for which one prays to God is believing concerning God that God acts as requested (*ἀφίημι [Apb], §6.7b).[3]

d. A Format for Praying to God

The only explicit statement of what is prayed to God appears in Jesus' prayer in the garden (14:36), and the implied repetition of this prayer (14:39) grants emphasis to its format. Jesus' prayer resolves into an initial acknowledgment of Jesus' intimate but dependent relationship to God (Abba Father), an acclamation of God's unique capacity to grant good things (all possible things are yours), a simple and sincere statement of what is requested (take this cup from me), and a concluding affirmation to abide by God's will (but not what I want but what you [want]). Conspicuous here are the non-elaboration of designations for God, the genuine recognition of God's capacity to act, the direct statement of the request (contra the ostentatious Scribes who pray at length), and the commitment to do what God wants without any pretense of wanting the same thing.

e. Praying and Not Receiving

Despite Jesus' statement to Disciples, "All things for which you pray and ask, believe that you receive, and it will be yours" (11:24), Jesus does not receive what he prays for, that this hour pass him by (14:35). Jesus' non-reception of what he requests of God clarifies that God who has all possible things is willing to enact only those possible things that serve human salvation (*δυνατόν [B], §7.4b). This augments the condition for reception in Jesus' statement, "believe that you have [it]," by the further condition, "if it serves human salvation."

f. The Semantic Coordination of "Prayer" and "Pray"

The semantic coordination of "prayer" (*προσευχή [E], §10.3) and "pray" (*προσεύχομαι [acE]) makes one contribution to the discussion of praying and one contribution to the discussion of prayer. The statement that God's house is to be called a house of prayer for all the nations (11:17a) supports the propriety of group or communal prayer (§10.7b) and—since the present house of God, the Temple, is to remain a den of thieves (*οἶκος [bB], §9.5c)—proposes the sanctuary built by Jesus as the venue for such group or communal prayer. The discussion of praying also fills a lacuna in Jesus' discussion of what is required to drive out particular kinds of spirits (9:29). Although Jesus states that this kind of spirit can be cast out only by prayer, Jesus is not portrayed as praying when he drives out the spirit. This is taken to indicate that Jesus' statement is not focusing on the prayer

---

3. Dowd, *Reading Mark*, 151–2, proposes that Jesus' boldness in praying to God to take away his predicted passion recommends similar boldness in praying on the part of Jesus' believing Disciples.

that may occur at the moment of exorcism but on the continuity and quality of the exorcist's communication relationship of prayer to God. In this regard, Jesus differs from his Disciples and all others in being continually at prayer to God in the interludes between events.[4] This interprets the character of Jesus' direct communication relationship to God, rather than what he prays at a particular moment, as what enables him to cast out this kind of spirit.

8. God the Experiencer

God is attributed both with experience as the subject of verbs and verbal adjectives and with experiencing communications and other actions. As the subject of verbs and verbal adjectives, God repeatedly is attributed with loving (*ἀγαπητός [Ec/Apb], §10.5) and on one occasion each with delighting in (εὐδοκέω [Ec], 1:11), being merciful (ἐλεέω [Eb], 5:19), knowing (οἶδα [Et], 13:32), and wanting (θέλω [Ec], [14:36]). God repeatedly experiences communications with "give thanks" (*εὐχαριστέω [acE], §10.2), "prayer" (*προσευχή [E], §10.3), "hosanna" (*ὡσαννά [aE], §10.4), "bless" (*εὐλογέω [atE], §10.6), and "pray" (*προσεύχομαι [acE], §10.7) and once with "ask" (αἰτέω [acE], 11:24) and "sing" (ὑμνέω [acE], 14:26). God's only noted experiences of other human actions occur with "glorify" (δοξάζω [aE], 2:12), "worship" (σέβομαι [aE], 7:7), and "honor" (τιμάω [aE], 7:6). The following discussion considers these three categories of God's experience and then identifies the focus of God's experience.

a. God's Experience as the Subject of Verbs and Verbal Adjectives

God's sole repeated experience is loving (1:11; 9:7; 12:6) Jesus the Son, and this experience is augmented by God's delight in (1:11) Jesus God's Beloved Son. God's affective response of loving and delighting in Jesus is related to God's actions of tearing the sky (1:10) as the condition for the coming of God's Spirit onto Jesus and God's voice to address Jesus (*σχίζω [Ap], §6.1), of commanding Peter, James, and John and, through them, all of Jesus' Disciples to listen to Jesus (9:7), and of enjoining the Farmers (Chief Priests, Scribes, and Elders) and the implied reader to respect Jesus. God's only other explicitly narrated direct experience of a human being, (with Jesus) being merciful (5:19) to the demoniac, also is coordinated with a statement of the action that God (with Jesus) does (*ποιέω [Ap], 5:19) for the demoniac. This coordination interprets God (with Jesus) being merciful to and acting for the demoniac as God (with Jesus) loving the demoniac. The interpretation

---

4. In this regard, the alternative statement of the instrument by which the kind of spirit is driven out (prayer and fasting) better captures the need for regular and repeated action; cf. Metzger, *Textual Commentary*, 101, for a discussion of the proposed reason for excluding "and fasting" in 9:29 despite its extensive manuscript support.

of all that God does as merciful actions (*ποιέω [Ap], §6.3e) then interprets God's action of making (*ποιέω [Ap], 10:6) human beings male and female and God acting (*ποιέω [Ap], 12:9) by coming, destroying the Farmers, and giving the Vineyard (God's people) to others as God's loving action for human beings and God's people. God's experience of things rather than human beings is limited to not wanting ([14:36]) to take away this cup from Jesus and alone knowing (13:32) about the day and hour of the end of this age. The apparent reason for God not wanting to take the cup from Jesus (*δυνατόν [B], §7.4b) is that doing so would take away Jesus the Son of Man's passion and death and so the necessary condition for his rising (8:31). Thus God is not willing to act to the detriment of Jesus the Son of Man. God alone knowing the day and hour distinguishes God's complete knowledge of all things from that of the Angels and even Jesus the Son. In this light, Jesus' choice of what God wants over what Jesus wants is a tacit confirmation that God who knows all knows best.

b. God's Experience of Communications

This discussion considers first God's actual experience of communications, then God's potential experiences of communications, and draws conclusions concerning the communications that God does and will welcome. God is assumed to experience all communications addressed to God, whether or not there is an explicitly noted response by God.

Among God's actual communication experiences, God's approval of the content of communication is manifest in God's actions through and for Jesus and others. God's approving responses to Jesus' actions of giving thanks is apparent in the miraculous multiplication of the fish for the four thousand (8:7) and in the contents of the cup becoming Jesus' blood (14:23-24). God's approving response to Jesus' actions of blessing God are apparent in the miraculous multiplication of the bread and fish for the five thousand men (6:41) and bread for the four thousand (8:6) and in the bread becoming Jesus' body (14:22). God approvingly responds to Jesus' praying (1:35; 6:46) by enabling Jesus to order out a kind of spirit that can only come out by prayer (9:25). In contrast, God's response to the ostentatious praying of the Scribes will be their greater condemnation (12:40) and to Jesus' request for this cup to pass him by is inaction (14:35). Although no response is indicated, God is assumed to approve of the exclamation of praise that properly identifies Jesus as the one coming in/by God's name (11:9) and the singing of the hymn (14:26) but not to approve the exclamation of praise that improperly associates Jesus and David's reign (11:10).

Among God's potential communication experiences, God will respond approvingly to the nations' prayer (11:17) insofar as it is according to God's intent (Isa 56:7), the praying by Jesus' Disciples who believe that they receive what they ask (11:24) of God, forgive what they have against another so that God their Father in the Heavens may forgive for them their trespasses (11:25), and ask that the tribulation not occur in winter (13:18) and that they not come into testing (14:38).

These observations clarify that God actually experiences communications from Jesus (*εὐχαριστέω [acE], *προσευχή [E], *εὐλογέω [aE], and *προσεύχομαι [acE]), those preceding and following Jesus into Jerusalem (*ὡσαννά [aE]), the Scribes (*προσεύχομαι [acE]), and Jesus and the Twelve (ὑμνέω [acE]). Among these, all communications receiving God's approval are initiated by Jesus or a group containing Jesus or concern God's relationship with Jesus. Inappropriate communications inaccurately associate Jesus with David's reign, are ostentatious, or request something to the ultimate detriment of Jesus the Son of Man. Appropriate potential communications are to be enacted by all the nations and Jesus' Disciples believing that they receive what they ask, forgiving what they hold against another, requesting that they not come into testing, and asking that the tribulation not occur in winter. Jesus' example indicates that God will respond positively to communications that request what is beneficial to human salvation (*δυνατόν [B], §7.4b).

c. God's Experience of Human Actions

God is attributed with three experiences of human action. Those in the synagogue appropriately glorify (2:12) God when they recognize the manifestation of God's authority in Jesus' healing of the paralyzed man. The Pharisees and Scribes, in contrast, inappropriately honor (7:6) and worship (σέβομαι [aE], 7:7) God when they nullify God's commandments so that their tradition might stand. These considerations indicate that God approvingly experiences actions by human beings who glorify God for actions by God's authority that benefit human beings and who honor and worship God by keeping God's commandments.

d. The Focus of God's Experience

God's experience has a primary focus on Jesus and a secondary focus on Jesus' Disciples. God loves and delights in Jesus, responds approvingly to Jesus' giving thanks, blessing, and prayer and, in all but one context, to Jesus' praying, and approves of the singing by Jesus and his Disciples. God's secondary and as yet unrealized focus of experience will come from Jesus' praying Disciples and all the nations.

9. God the Goal

God is the one to whom the Farmers (Chief Priests, Scribes, and Elders) sent (ἀποστέλλω [aθG], 12:3) God's Slave without any of the fruit of the Vineyard (God's people) and the one to whom the things of God are to be given back (ἀποδίδωμι [aθG], 12:17). In the former occurrence, the Farmers do not render what is owed to God; and, in the second, the Pharisees and Herodians are commanded to give back to God but are not depicted as doing so. Thus neither the Farmers nor the Pharisees and Herodians act properly in relation to God; and God never receives what is due to God.

10. God the Instrument

The sole attempt by a character to make God the instrument of another's action appears in Legion's statement, "I make you swear (ὁρκίζω [aec-I], 5:7) by God that you (Jesus) not torment me." Since Jesus is not portrayed as swearing and the subsequent drowning of the pigs admits to interpretation as torment for Legion (§2.6), God never functions as the instrument of another's action.

Chapter 11

GOD AS PATIENT, SOURCE, THEME, AND TOPIC: PROPOSALS AND CONCLUSION

This chapter develops the statements of God's repeated attributes as Patient (Sections 1–4), Source (Sections 5–7), and Topic (Sections 9–10) and God's non-repeated attribute as Theme (Section 8) and offers concluding considerations (Sections 11–12). Sections 1–4 develop the statements for God's three repeated Patient attributes and then consider the characteristics of God's three repeated and three non-repeated Patient attributes. Sections 5–7 develop the statements for God's two repeated Source attributes and then consider the characteristics of God's two repeated and five non-repeated Source attributes. Section 8 considers the characteristics of God's four non-repeated Theme attributes. Sections 9–10 develop the statements for God's two repeated Topic attributes; and, since these are the only occurrences of God as Topic and are semantically coordinated, there is no separate concluding discussion. The discussion addresses the repeated Patient, Source, and Topic attributes in the order of increasing frequency of occurrence and, for those with the same number of occurrences, in the order of their introduction. Each statement of God's Patient, Source, and Topic repeated attributes includes a Heading that identifies the references to God, the contexts of their occurrence, and, where appropriate, further information that assists in interpretation, a Rehearsal of the specific narrative information associated with the references (subsection "a"); and an Elaboration of one or more salient contributions developed through repetition of the contexts of occurrences (beginning with subsection "b"). The concluding discussions for God as Patient and Source identify commonalities and patterns of development in God's repeated and non-repeated attributes. Section 11 offers four proposals for augmenting the Theological Study, and Section 12 provides a concluding review of the study.

Since God is One and God in the past and present (12:29-30; cf. Deut 6:4-5) and presumably in the future and God is Father in the present (14:36) and future (8:38), the Headings of the statements for God's repeated Patient attributes use the present tense of "be." God as the Source of signs is confined to the present (8:11), God as the Source from whom one receives is applicable in the present (11:24) and future (10:30), and the Headings of these statements use present forms of verbs. Jesus' commands for Disciples to have faith concerning God (11:22) and to believe concerning God (11:23) are deemed to be applicable in the present and future; and the Headings of the statements of these repeated attributes use the present forms of verbs.

1. God Is One (*εἷς [P])

God being one (*εἷς [P], 12:29, 32; cf. Deut 6:4) occurs in a single context (12:28-34) that is incorporated into those of God having commandments (*ἐντολή [B], §7.10), having the reign (*βασιλεία [B], §7.13), and being God (*θεός [bP], §11.3) and coterminous with that of God being loved (*ἀγαπάω [eC/apB], 12:30, 33).

a. The Attributes of God as One

God the Lord is one (12:29) and is one, there being no other than he (12:32).

b. God's Uniqueness as the Basis for a Complete Loving Response

Repetition of God being one (12:29, 33) and the further assertion that there is not another than God (12:33; cf. Isa 45:21) distinguish God who is unique and in whom the entirety of divinity is present from the neighboring peoples' gods who are multiple and in whom divinity is divided (*ἀγαπάω [eC/apB], §10.1b). God's uniqueness and completeness is proposed as the basis for the commanded love of God from all one's heart, life, mind, and strength (12:30) and from all one's heart, understanding, and strength (12:33).

c. The Lord Our God Is One Lord

The statement that God is one (12:29) twice references God as Lord, which identifies "Lord" as the designation *par excellence* for evoking God's uniqueness and possession of all divinity. The use of "Lord" to designate Jesus (1:3) in the context of his identification as God's Son (1:1) and his benefaction of God's face (1:2), way (1:2, 3), and paths (1:3) proposes that Jesus as God's Son participates in or inherits (*υἱός [B], §9.12b) God's uniqueness and completeness of divinity.

2. God Is Father (*πατήρ [bP])

God being Father (*πατήρ [bP], 8:38; 11:25; 14:36) occurs in three contexts (8:31–9:1; 11:20-25; 14:32-42).

a. The Attributes of God as Father

God is the Father in the Heavens of Jesus' Disciples, especially in the context of their forgiving what they hold against another and God forgiving their trespasses (11:25), and Jesus' Abba Father for whom all things are able [to be done]/possible

(14:36). God will be the Father of Jesus the Son of Man in his end-time coming with/by God's power in the company of God's holy Angels (8:38).

b. God Is Father of Jesus and Those Related to God Through Jesus

The attribution of "praying" to Jesus' Disciples (11:25) and Jesus (14:32, 35, 39) emphasizes that God is Father to those in a direct communication relationship to God. Semantic coordination of "will" (θέλημα [B], 3:35) and "want" (θέλω [Ec], 14:36) also clarifies that Jesus who accedes to what God wants affirms his filial relationship with God his Abba Father (14:36) and that those doing God's will become Jesus' brother, sister, and mother (3:35). The consequent familial relationship with God as Father for those doing God's will is remarkable in that it makes one Jesus' brother, sister, and mother without a commensurate expectation that one is acquainted with Jesus' teaching or receives from Jesus an explicit call to discipleship.[1] Whereas God is Abba Father of Jesus and will be Father of Jesus the Son of Man, God's reciprocal relationship as Father with all others is only potential and depends on doing God's will and remaining in a direct communication relationship of prayer to God and forgiving what one holds against another.

c. The Saving Actions and Attributes of God as Father

God as Father has the glory with/by which Jesus the Son of Man will come (8:38), as Father in the Heavens forgives the trespasses of Jesus' Disciples who forgive what they hold against another in the context of praying to God (11:25), and as Abba Father of Jesus has all possible things (14:36). The coming of Jesus the Son of Man with/by God's glory is the context of God's definitive end-time saving action for human beings (*δόξα [B], §8.1b); God's forgiving sins is a saving action that cancels all covenantal debts owed to God (*ἀφίημι [Apb], §6.7); and, since the possible thing that God alone can do is save ([10:27]), God Jesus' Abba Father does not take away the opportunity for Jesus to act as the instrument of God's saving action for himself (*δυνατόν [B], §7.4b). Thus all of God's actions and attributes as Father contribute to human salvation.

d. God as Father in the Present and Future

The first context relates the present suffering, being rejected, being killed, and rising of Jesus the Son of Man (8:31) to his end-time coming with/by the glory of his Father (8:38) and makes the Disciple denying oneself, taking up one's cross, and following Jesus, destroying one's life because of Jesus and the gospel, and not being ashamed of Jesus and his words (8:34-38) the beneficiary of Jesus the Son of Man's end-time coming. As a consequence, God who is the Abba Father of Jesus and

---

1. Donahue, "The Revelation of God," 167.

becomes the Father in the Heavens of the Disciple praying and forgiving what is held against another will remain the Father of Jesus the Son of Man in his end-time coming and of the Disciple enacting Jesus' hard teachings.

3. God Is God (*θεός [bP])

God being God (*θεός [bP], 12:26b, 26c, 26d, 27a, [27b], 29, 30; 15:34a, 34b) occurs in three contexts (12:18-27, 28-34; 15:33-36) that incorporate that of God being loved (*ἀγαπάω [eC/apB], §10.1) and of God being one (*εἷς [P], §11.1).

a. The Attributes of God as God

God is the God of Abraham (12:26b), Isaac (12:26c), and Jacob (12:26d) and the living ([12:27b]) but not the dead (12:27a), of Israel (God's people, 12:29), Jesus (12:29), and Israel (12:30), and of Jesus (15:34a, 34b).

b. God Is the God of the Living

The first context identifies God as God of the living, that is, the dead who rise and are like Angels. Being like God's Angels implies living forever in relation to God (§5.3e). The second context identifies God as the God of Jesus and God's people who affirm that God is one and of God's people who, on the pattern of Jesus, love God their Lord with all their heart, life, mind, and strength and love their neighbor as themselves. Those fulfilling these commandments move toward God's reign (*ἀγαπάω [eC/apB], §10.1g) and enter into God's life (*ζωή [B], §8.4d). The third context twice identifies God as God of Jesus who, before his final cry and expiring, addresses God, questioning why God has abandoned him (15:34). Thus, even in his experience of complete abandonment by God, Jesus ends his life in a direct communication to God and so in the proper relationship with God and in fidelity to the demands of the command to love God with all his life (*ἀγαπάω [eC/apB], §10.1c). These characteristics associate with Jesus the living who will rise and be like God's Angels, those who enter God's life, and those who enact the love commandments and enter God's reign.

c. God Is Not the God of the Dead

Although no one is specified as remaining among the dead, some place themselves in opposition to God and open the possibility of remaining among the dead. Not knowing the scripture and the power of God leads one into error (12:24) and is especially inappropriate for those like the Sadducees who are entrusted with teaching God's people. Graver still is the situation of the one recognizing that the love of God and neighbor is paramount (12:33) but not enacting these commandments. The gravest situation, however, attends those who, like Jesus, commit to serve and love God and neighbor but, unlike Jesus, do not persevere to the end. Only Jesus is presented as actually persevering to the end. These three scenarios present dangers at three stages in one's relationship with God as God: in the beginning, not knowing or doing; in the middle, knowing but not doing; and, at the end, knowing and doing but not persevering. Failure at any stage places one in opposition to God and opens the possibility of being among the dead whom God does not have.

d. Reciprocal Benefaction of God as God

Only Jesus who rises (16:7) and the living ([12:17b]), including Abraham, Isaac, and Jacob who remain alive in the time of Moses (12:26), are portrayed as already having benefaction of God as God. For all others, such a relationship remains only potential and is dependent on maintaining a direct communication relationship to God and enacting the commandments to love God and neighbor.

4. God the Patient

Repetition highlights God as one (*εἷς [P], §11.1), Father (*πατήρ [bP], §11.2), and God (*θεός [bP], §11.3), and God's non-repeated attributes identify God as good (ἀγαθός [P], 10:18), Lord (κύριος [bP], 12:9) of the Vineyard (God's people), he (αὐτός [P], 12:32) other than whom there is no god, and Most High (ὕψιστος [P], 5:7).

Contextually related are God being one, God, and he (12:28-34). God is one, God, he, Most High (5:7), and good (10:18) whether or not God is in a relationship with another. God being Father and Lord, in contrast, identifies God specifically in terms of God's reciprocal relationships with Jesus the Beloved Son and the Vineyard.

In the present, God affirms God's reciprocal benefaction of Jesus God's Beloved Son (1:11), and Jesus affirms his reciprocal benefaction of God his Abba Father (14:36). God will continue to be the Father of Jesus the Son of Man at his end-time coming (8:38). God's people and all others have the potential to enter a relationship with God as God by maintaining a communication relationship to God and fulfilling the commandments to love God and neighbor, and Jesus' Disciples also have the potential to enter a reciprocal relationship with God as Father in the Heavens by praying and forgiving what they hold against another.

Two attributes further clarify the uniqueness of Jesus' relationship with God. Since God alone is good (10:18), the one recognizing Jesus as good recognizes Jesus' likeness to God (§5.1c). God who is one (*εἷς [P], §11.1) has one Beloved Son, Jesus (12:6).

5. God Is the Source of the Sign (*σημεῖον [S])

God being the source of the sign (*σημεῖον [S], 8:11, 12a, 12b) occurs in a single context (8:11-14) that is incorporated into those of God giving (*δίδωμι [Aθg], §6.10).

a. The Attributes of God's Sign

God is the source of the sign that the Pharisees seek from Jesus, testing him, and to which Jesus responds with a sigh (8:11), that this generation seeks (8:12a), and that God does not give to this generation (8:12b).

b. No Further Authenticating Sign from God for the Pharisees

God is the one from whom comes the sign authenticating Jesus' words and actions, but this sign is not provided on demand to the Pharisees who do not recognize Jesus' previous teachings (2:17, 25-28; 3:4; 7:6-13) and actions (2:16; 3:5) in their presence as God's validating signs (*δίδωμι [Aθg], 6.10d).[2] Instead, they respond to Jesus' teaching and healing by plotting to destroy Jesus (3:6). Their response to Jesus renders a further sign from God pointless and associates them with "this generation" that is adulterous and sinful (8:38), unbelieving (9:19), and not passing away until Jesus' predictions concerning the end time happen (13:30).[3] The circumstance of the Pharisees in this context evokes that of the Scribes from Jerusalem (3:20-35) whose judgments concerning Jesus and his previous actions prevent them from perceiving the implications of a possible further action of Jesus (*βλασφημέω [apB], §9.1b).

6. God Is the Source from Whom One Receives (*λαμβάνω [gθS])

God being the source from whom one receives (*λαμβάνω [gθS], 10:30; 11:24; 12:40) occurs in three contexts (10:28-31; 11:20-25; 12:38-40).

a. The Attributes of God from Whom One Receives

God is the source from whom the one leaving family and possessions because of Jesus and the gospel receives in this time a hundredfold houses, brothers, sisters, mothers, children, and fields and in the coming age life everlasting (10:30), from whom Disciples receive what they pray for and ask of God on the condition that they believe that they have it (11:24), and from whom the Scribes—wanting to

---

2. That Jesus is not in principle averse to offering validating signs is apparent in his first direct encounter with the Scribes (2:1-12), where the healing of the paralytic is his proffered sign that the paralytic's sins are forgiven. Jeffrey Gibson, "Jesus' Refusal to Produce a 'Sign' (MK 8:11-13)," *JSNT* 38 (1990): 37–66, proposes that the sign "from heaven" (ἀπὸ τοῦ οὐρανοῦ) has as its reference a sign of salvation (45), liberation from enemies (47), and freedom from domination (50) and establishes that the story of the healing of the paralytic (2:1-12) contains the salient characteristics of scriptural signs (38–42). The Pharisees' demand for a sign in 8:11, however, is not their initial direct encounter with Jesus.

3. This interpretation receives further development in William L. Lane, *The Gospel of Mark* (NICNT; Grand Rapids, MI: Eerdmans, 1974), 277, and Moloney, *Mark*, 159.

walk around in robes, greetings in markets, the first seats in synagogues, and seats of honor at dinners and devouring the houses of widows—receive greater condemnation (12:40).

b. God Is the Source of What Jesus' Disciples and the Scribes Receive

In the present and future, Disciples who believe that they have what they pray for and ask of God receive it (11:25), who pray and forgive what they hold against another have God's forgiveness (11:24), and who leave family and possessions because of Jesus and the gospel receive a hundredfold from both God and fellow Disciples and in the coming age everlasting life from God (10:30). In contrast, the Scribes praying to God at length and for show and devouring the houses of widows receive from God nothing in the present and greater condemnation at the end of this age (12:40). Thus those characterized by belief, sincere prayer to God, forgiveness of what they hold against another, and abandonment of family and possessions because of Jesus and the gospel are recipients of good things from God in this age and the next.

c. Receiving From God as God's Response to "Letting Go"

Repetition of "leave/forgive" (ἀφίημι, 10:28, 29; 11:25) in the context of receiving from God clarifies that the one letting go of/sending away (the basic meaning of ἀφίημι) what one holds against another and family and possessions is the condition for God letting go of/sending away one's trespasses and for receiving from God forgiveness, family, and possessions among Jesus' Disciples, and everlasting life in the coming age. Repetition of "leave/forgive" also links holding onto the debts of others, biological family, and possessions, pretense in praying, and desires for human praise, honor, and property to receiving God's condemnation.

7. God the Source

Repetition highlights God as the one from whom the Pharisees do not receive a sign (*σημεῖον [S], §11.5) but Jesus' Disciples receive what they pray for and ask with faith, family and possessions in the community of Disciples, and everlasting life in the coming age (*λαμβάνω [gθS], §11.6). God also is the one from whom the Pharisees and Scribes are distant (ἀπέχω [θS], 7:6) when they cling to the tradition of the elders, from whom the one doing God's commandments and fulfilling the demands of discipleship inherits (κληρονομέω [gθS], 10:17) everlasting life, and from whom come John's baptism (βάπτισμα [S], 11:30), Jesus' inheritance (κληρονομία [S], 12:7), that is, the Vineyard (God's people), and one's wage (μισθός [S], 9:41).

a. Receiving and Not Receiving from God: Clarifications

Linkages among the contexts further distinguish those receiving and those not receiving from God and clarify what is required to receive good things from God.

"From heaven" and "give" link the Pharisees seeking but not given a sign (8:11-12) and the Chief Priests, Scribes, and Elders not acknowledging John's baptism as from God and not recognizing the source of Jesus' authority (11:28-31). This linkage clarifies that repeated failure to recognize what is from God both diminishes one's capacity to recognize what is from God and places one in opposition to God.

"Everlasting life" contrasts the man not selling his possessions, giving to the poor, and following Jesus and so not inheriting everlasting life from God (10:17) and the Disciple of Jesus leaving family and possessions for the sake of Jesus and the gospel and receiving everlasting life from God (10:30). Jesus' statement that the one selling possessions, giving to the poor, and following him has treasure in heaven identifies everlasting life as the content of this treasure.

Semantic coordination of "inherit" (10:17) and "inheritance" (12:7) links the man having many possessions who does not fulfill what is required to inherit everlasting life and the Farmers who have no rightful claim to the Vineyard as an inheritance. The man's inaction prevents him from becoming Jesus' Disciple, and the Farmers' action against Jesus sets them in opposition to God who will destroy them and give the Vineyard to others. Thus both improper action and the lack of proper action can set one in opposition to God (and Jesus).

These comparisons and contrasts receive explanation in the contextual repetition of "forgive/leave" (ἀφίημι, 10:28, 29; 11:25a, 25b) which specifies the need to forgive or let go of what one has against another as the condition for God's forgiveness and the need to leave or let go of the family and possessions that keep one from following Jesus. The one letting go sets oneself in the proper relationship with God and with those indebted to one, receives a new extended family of those in the proper relationship with God, and disposes oneself to receive from God what is necessary for discipleship and life in the coming age.

b. Only Those Reciprocally Related to God Receive Good Things from God

God has reciprocal benefaction of Jesus God's Beloved Son and Heir (*υἱός [B], §9.12) who has the Vineyard as an inheritance (12:7) and of Jesus' Disciples (*πατήρ [bP], §11.2) who receive what they ask of God (11:24), will receive a hundredfold and everlasting life from God (10:30), and do not destroy their wage from God (9:41). These are the only noted recipients of good things from God. All others related to God as source oppose God: the Pharisees do not have God's sign (*σημεῖον [S], §11.5), the Pharisees and Scribes remain distant from God (7:6), the man does not inherit everlasting life (10:17), John's baptism does not benefit the Chief Priests, Scribes, and Elders (11:30), and the Scribes praying insincerely receive God's greater condemnation (12:40). The common characteristic of those opposed to God is that they have every reason to assume that they are in a proper relationship with God. What is lacking in each case is a proper recognition of the role of Jesus in their relationship to God. Such faulty assumptions are not restricted to the religious authorities and those declining Jesus' invitation to follow. As the teaching on the wage clarifies, the one earning one's wage from God and so presumably in the proper relationship with God can destroy this wage and relationship through unsympathetic action for others who are of Jesus the Christ (9:41).

8. God the Theme

God is portrayed as in motion or located in a place. God left on a journey (ἀποδημέω [Θg], 12:1) after establishing the Vineyard (God's people) and leasing it to Farmers (Chief Priests, Scribes, and Elders) and is received (δέχομαι [gΘs], 9:37d) by the one receiving Jesus. God the Disciples' Father is in (ἐν [Θl], 11:25) the heavens, and God the Lord of the Vineyard will come (ἔρχομαι [Θg], 12:9), destroy the Farmers, and give the Vineyard to others. The following discussion considers God's motion to and from the Vineyard, God's location, and the reception of God.

God's past motion from the Vineyard followed God's actions in establishing the Vineyard, and God's future motion to the Vineyard will precede God's concluding actions concerning the Vineyard in this age. God's motion from and to the Vineyard highlights God's continuing care for and commitment to God's people.

God the Disciples' Father being in the heavens (11:25) coheres with the heavens as God's assumed locale when not in motion. Elsewhere the heavens are the locale of God's tearing (1:10), voice (1:11), Angels (12:25; 13:32), and the treasure of the one inheriting everlasting life from God (10:21), the locale to which Jesus looks when giving thanks to God (6:41) and when performing a healing (7:34), and the locale from which God's sign would come (8:11) and John's baptism does come (11:30, 31).

Jesus' statement that the one receiving a child in reference to Jesus' name receives Jesus and, through Jesus, God (9:37) is exceptional in providing the only noted way for human beings to receive God who is in the heavens.

9. God Is the Topic of Faith (*πίστις [ecT])

God being the Topic of faith (*πίστις [ecT], 2:5; 4:40; 5:34; 10:52; 11:22) occurs in five contexts (2:1-12; 4:35-41; 5:25-34; 10:46-52; 11:20-25).

a. The Attributes of God as Topic of Faith

God is the topic of faith of the paralyzed man and those carrying him who believe that Jesus is able to enact God's healing of the paralyzed man (2:5), of the woman with the flow of blood who believes that God is able to save her from her affliction through Jesus (5:34), and of blind Bartimaeus who believes that God is able to save him from his blindness through Jesus the Son of David (10:52). God is to be the topic of faith of Jesus' Disciples who are to believe that they receive from God what they pray for and ask and that God acts for believers just as God acts for Jesus in his injunction that no one ever eat of the fig tree's fruit (11:14) by having the fig tree wither (11:22). God is not the topic of faith of Jesus' Disciples who do not believe that God is able to command even the wind and the sea through Jesus (4:40)

b. The Content of Faith Concerning God References Both God and Jesus

The content of faith concerning God consistently references both God and Jesus. Repetition emphasizes the content of faith that God (through Jesus) is able to heal the man's paralysis (2:5), the woman's flow of blood (5:34), and Bartimaeus' blindness (10:52) and to command the wind and sea (4:40). God also grants what is prayed for and asked by believing Disciples just as God acts for Jesus (11:21) if what is prayed for and asked serves human salvation (*προσεύχομαι [acE], §10.7e). Thus what one believes about God and God's actions for human beings references Jesus either as God's instrument or as the model for asking.

c. Faith That God Acts through Humans as Instrument For Others

Faith concerning God recognizes that God works through Jesus as instrument for others (paralyzed man, bleeding woman, blind Bartimaeus) and for a group containing Jesus (Jesus and his Disciples in a storm). This proposes that God's granting of what Disciples pray for and ask applies especially when Disciples pray for and ask what is for the benefit of others or a group containing themselves and, on the pattern of Jesus, offer themselves as the instrument through whom God works.

d. Faith Concerning God Motivates and Is Apparent in Actions

Faith concerning God motivates and is apparent in the actions of those carrying the paralyzed man to Jesus and digging through the roof above Jesus (2:3-5), the woman with the flow of blood coming to and touching Jesus' garments (5:27-28), and Bartimaeus calling out to Jesus despite opposition and going to Jesus (10:47-51). These actions demonstrate the propriety of turning to God by seeking out Jesus, the instrument of God's healing and saving action. In contrast, Jesus' Disciples lack faith concerning God when they turn to Jesus in a cowardly manner and accuse him of not being concerned about them (4:38-40). These considerations interpret Jesus' command to his Disciples to have faith concerning God as an invitation for them to turn to God courageously in prayer in situations of need and offer themselves as the instruments through whom God acts.

10. God Is to Be Believed In (*πιστεύω [ecT])

God being believed in (*πιστεύω [ecT], 5:36; 9:23, 24; 11:23, 24) occurs in three contexts (5:35-43; 9:14-27; 11:20-25). Since all occurrences of God as topic are associated with "faith" and "believe," the concluding elaboration of their semantic coordination constitutes the discussion of God as topic.

a. The Attributes of God Who Is to Be Believed In

God is to be believed in by Jairus that God is able to save his daughter through Jesus (5:36), by the man that God is able to cast the unspeaking spirit from his son through Jesus (9:23, 24), and by Jesus' Disciple that what the Disciple speaks happens for the Disciple (11:23) and that Disciples receive what they pray for and ask of God and that it is theirs (11:24).

b. Believing That God Acts through Humans as Instrument For Others

God works through Jesus as instrument for the benefit of Jairus and his daughter (5:36) and the man and his son having an unspeaking spirit (9:23, 24). Thus what is believed concerning God is that God acts through Jesus as instrument for the benefit of others. This interprets Jesus' command to his Disciples to believe that they have what they say (11:23) and pray for (11:24) to God as especially applicable when they say or pray for what is for the benefit of others and, on the pattern of Jesus, offer themselves as the instrument through whom God works.

c. Believing In/Concerning God that God Raises the Dead through Jesus

The first two contexts relate believing in/concerning God and the apparent death of those in need. At the announcement that Jairus' daughter is dead (ἀποθνῄσκω), Jesus commands Jairus not to fear but to believe (5:35-36); and after ordering the unspeaking spirit out of the man's son, those present assume that the son is dead (ἀποθνῄσκω). In the former case, Jesus goes to Jairus' daughter and, grasping her hand (κρατήσας τῆς χειρὸς), commands her to rise (ἐγείρω, 5:41), and she rises (ἀνίστημι, 5:42); and, in the latter case, Jesus, grasping the son's hand (κρατήσας τῆς χειρὸς), raises (ἐγείρω) him, and he rises (ἀνίστημι, 9:27). Repetition of the noted words and phrase tightly links these contexts and highlights believing in/concerning God that God is able to raise those assumed dead through Jesus as instrument. Although the third context lacks the noted repeated vocabulary, its linkage with the previous contexts indicates the propriety of Jesus' Disciples saying and praying to God to raise the dead through Jesus as instrument.

d. The Extent of God's Ability to Act through Human Beings as Instrument

The second context contrasts the inability of Jesus' Disciples to cast out the unspeaking spirit from the man's son (9:18) and Jesus' ability to do so (9:25-26). The Disciples are unable to do so, even though Jesus gives the Twelve God's authority to cast out unclean demons/unclean spirits (3:14-15/6:7) and this authority apparently also extends to healing (6:13). Jesus' statement that this kind of spirit comes out only by prayer (9:29) attributes the Disciples' inability to cast out the unspeaking spirit not to the absence of members of the Twelve but to the Disciples' lack of prayer. These considerations indicate that God's ability to act through Jesus' Disciples as instrument is limited by the quality of their direct communication relationship of prayer to God (*προσεύχομαι [acE], §10.7f), which develops the significance of Disciples praying to God and believing that what they pray for and ask of God is theirs (11:23-24).

e. The Semantic Coordination of "Faith" and "Believe"

The semantic coordination of "faith" (*πίστις [ecT], §10.8) and "believe" (*πιστεύω [ecT]) encompasses all occurrences of God as topic, and these words are contextually related in 5:25-34 and 11:20-25. Semantic coordination clarifies that one's faith/believing concerning God is that God acts through Jesus as instrument to heal or save human beings from physical infirmities, to command the wind and sea, to cast out demons, and to raise those assumed to be dead, that God acts for Jesus' Disciples as God acts for Jesus, and that what believing Disciples say and pray for to God is theirs, if it serves human salvation. God also is able to act through Jesus' Disciples who offer themselves as the instruments of God's actions for others and for groups containing themselves. The discussion of "believe" cautions that the quality of the Disciples' direct communication relationship of prayer to God determines the extent to which God is able to act through Disciples. Thus faith and what is believed concerning God come to contain claims about God, Jesus, and Jesus' Disciples.

11. Proposals for Further Developing the Theological Study

The Theological Study's statements of God's fifty-six repeated actions and attributes rely on a coherent set of semantic/narrative/rhetorical methods and their application to identify the 314 semantically and narratively justified direct and indirect references to God within 1:1–16:8. As a consequence, the statements of God's repeated actions and attributes and concluding summaries of categories of God's actions and attributes provide a secure basis for articulating Mark's Theology. At the same time, none of the statements of God's repeated actions and attributes exhaust the potential for development afforded by their rhetorical contexts; the rigorous semantic and narrative criteria for identifying direct and indirect references to God exclude many possible candidates for reference; and primary reliance on the interpretive potential afforded by predicator repetition frames, secondary use of other categories of semantic, narrative, and rhetorical frames, and the limited engagement with other methods of analysis primarily in the footnotes indicate that the Theological Study is open to further development. The following discussion proposes four avenues for developing the Theological Study, three using the potentialities of the semantic/narrative/rhetorical methods and one from unrelated methods.

a. Further Development of the Content Already Available

As previously discussed (§3.10b), the statements of God's repeated actions and attributes and especially those associated with more frequently occurring predicators remain open to development. This receives illustration in relation to

God's (with Jesus') benefaction of the way (*ὁδός [B], §8.9) and God's love (*ἀγαπητός [Ec/Apb], §10.5) of Jesus the Son.

Although the statement of God's (with Jesus') benefaction of the way provides salient observations about the way, the two contexts of its occurrence (1:1-3; 12:13-17) provide only limited content for its development. The method accommodates its further development through an examination of its scriptural antecedents, which associate the way of the Lord most frequently with love and service of God and keeping God's commandments and, on five occasions (Deut 10:12; 11:22; 19:9; 30:16; Josh 22:5), relates these.

The careful rhetorical organization of contextual content concerning God's love (*ἀγαπητός [Ec/Apb], 1:11; 9:7; 12:6) of Jesus the Son accommodates significant further development of God's relationship with Jesus. These contexts (1:9-11; 9:2-9; 12:6-8) incorporate those of God having a voice (*φωνή [B], 1:11; 9:7) and that of God speaking (*λέγω [Ace], 12:6) and link the only oral communications from God in the first stage of the end times, which constitute God's last direct communications to those on earth in this age, place them in the service of affirming God's love for Jesus the Son, and command Jesus' Disciples to listen to (ἀκούετε) and so remain in a direct communication relationship from Jesus (9:7) and enjoin respect for Jesus (12:7). At this point, predicator repetition frames would permit the expansion of the statements of God's love of Jesus (*ἀγαπητός [Ec/Apb]. §10.5) and benefaction of Jesus the Son (*υἱός [B], §9.12) through a specification of the linked content associated with Jesus' commands to listen (ἀκούετε). This would clarify that God's command to listen to Jesus extends to Jesus' teachings about the sowing of the seeds/word (4:3, 9), what is hidden being revealed and God's end-time evaluation based on how one measures out (4:24), nothing entering from the outside defiling one (7:15), and God being one and the greatest commandments (12:29). That is, God intends Jesus' Disciples to listen to Jesus God's Beloved Son concerning their mission, God's judgment, the removal of distinctions between Jews and Gentiles, and the primacy of loving God and neighbor.

b. Augmentation through the Use of Other Categories of Frames

Although the Theological Study addresses at least briefly every occurrence of semantic and narrative coordination in which God references the same or parallel arguments of the predicators, it did not develop instances of such coordination when both predicators do not satisfy the requirements for identifying references to God. Additionally, the repetition of words other than those providing references to God in the contexts on which the statements of repeated actions and attributes depend received only limited consideration. Further consideration of such occurrences has the potential to provide further content concerning God.

Further investigation of the semantic coordination of "live" (ζάω, 5:23; 12:27) and "life" (*ζωή [B], §8.4) would reveal that the contexts of the occurrences of "live" link Jesus' action of placing his hand on Jairus' daughter so that (result) she may live (5:23) and those rising by God's power and so (result) those living (12:27). This would associate Jesus and God's power as instruments of God's saving action for human beings.

The discussion of the Vineyard (*ἀμπελών [B], §7.8) briefly developed implications of its three continuous contexts (12:1-5, 6-8, 9-12) presenting the greatest density of God's actions and its second context presenting the greatest density of God's reciprocal benefaction of Jesus the Son. Since the same contexts present the greatest density of God's agentive benefaction (*ἀμπελών [B], 12:1; φραγμός [Bb], 12:1; ὑπολήνιον [Bb], 12:1; πύργος [Bb], 12:1; *ἀμπελών [B], 12:2, 8, 9a, 9b) and reciprocal benefaction (*δοῦλος [B], 12:2, 4, [5a], [5b]; ἔχω [Bp], 12:6; *υἱός [B], 12:6a, 6b; κληρόνομος [B], 12:7; κληρονομία [S], 12:7; κύριος [bP], 12:9), further investigation would clarify the relationship between what and whom God has through agentive and reciprocal benefaction and expand the claim (§8.7c) that God's unique innate attributes consistently receive specification in relation to Jesus in a manner that highlights their potential benefit for human beings.

c. Expansion through Inclusion of Oblique References to God

The study of Mark's Theology may be expanded through modification of the methods to identify and address references to God that do not qualify as direct or indirect. Such oblique references could be associated with either a single or multiple occurrences of a predicator.

As previously discussed (§2.4c(ii) n. 33), Jesus' statement, "Sitting at my right and left is not mine to give but is for those for whom it has been prepared" (10:40), was excluded from consideration because preparing elsewhere is a delegated task. Although God is the most probable referent of the one issuing the command to prepare these positions, this reference is twice removed from a direct semantic relation to "prepare" and so is excluded from the Theological Study.

At times, the excluded oblique references are repeated, and some of these repeated oblique references are significant. For example, Jesus' statements to the Sadducees (12:24-27) are interpreted to indicate that the dead rise (ἀνίστημι) by God's power (*δύναμις [B]); and the context narratively coordinates two verbs of rising (ἀνίστημι and ἐγείρω). Since "by the power of God" functions as an unrealized adjunct of these verbs, the method excludes both from direct investigation. Inclusion of the verbs and the recognition that both are repeated when designating the resurrection would introduce two new repeated attributes for God, "God has the power by which the dead rise (ἀνίστημι, 5:42; 8:31; 9:9, 10, 27, 31; 10:34; 12:23, 25 / (ἐγείρω, 5:41; 6:14, 16; 9:27; 12:26; 14:28; 16:6)," with the former also permitting the consideration of the semantic coordination of "rise" (ἀνίστημι, 5:42; 8:31; 9:9, 10, 27, 31; 10:34; 12:23, 25) and "resurrection" (ἀνάστασις, 12:18). Finally, recognition that those living do so by God's power would provide for a direct address of the semantic coordination of "life" (*ζωή [B], §8.4) and "living" (ζάω, 5:23; 12:27).

d. Inclusion of Content from Other Methods

Incorporation of content derived from alternate methodological approaches presents the opportunity to augment specific statements of actions and attributes and to fill in gaps in their formulations but requires an initial evaluation to ensure that the proposed content does not introduce contradictions into otherwise coherent narrative developments.

Within the Theological Study, information derived from other methodological approaches played a crucial role in offering a series of clarifications concerning the implications of the dead who rise becoming like God's Angels (*δύναμις [B], §8.3e) and the risen Jesus the Lord of David who is to sit at God's right (*δεξιά [B], §8.2b). In general, such coherent information has great potential for strengthening and otherwise augmenting the statements of God's repeated actions and attributes.

Caution, however, is required when content from other methodological approaches introduces inconsistencies or contradicts otherwise coherent narrative developments. Such is apparent when studies of antecedent and contemporary apocalyptic literature serve as the basis for interpreting "be necessary" (*δεῖ [vi-iB], §7.6) to have God's will or plan as the referent of its Instrument.[4] The same holds for those who attempt an uncritical retrieval of God's plan or will from the scriptures.[5] These proposals contradict the otherwise coherent development apparent in the repetition of "suffer much" that links what is necessary (8:31) and what is written (9:12) concerning Jesus the Son of Man. They also fail to recognize that what was written is attributed only with predictive potential (*γέγραπται [Ace], §6.8b) and that, although attributed with predictive, didactic, and prescriptive potential, God's scripture has no mechanism to effect what its commandments require (*γραφή [B], 7.5d).

While what was written concerning God's sending of God's Messenger (Mal 3:1) reflects God's intent insofar as God does the sending (1:2), the second occurrence of what is written concerns the Pharisees and Scribes honoring God only with their lips (7:6; cf. Isa 29:13 LXX), something clearly at odds with God's intent for the Pharisees and Scribes. Again, interpreting "be necessary" to indicate God's will or plan introduces a contradiction insofar as Jesus' Disciples, in fact, will see the abominating desolation standing where it is necessary that he not [stand] (13:14; cf. Dan 9:27; 11:31; 12:11). Thus, if God's plan or will necessitates that this not happen, this plan or will ultimately will be thwarted, something clearly at odds with the tenets of apocalyptic literature. In contrast, the narratively guided interpretation of God's scripture as necessitating events presents a coherent development with respect to its predictive (*γραφή [B], §7.5d) and prescriptive (*δεῖ [vi-iB], §7.6d) potential and the predictive potential of specific antecedent prophetic texts (9:11; cf. Mal 3:1; 4:5) or group of prophetic texts (8:31; 13:7, 10; 14:31), whether or not they reflect God's intent.

---

4. As in Grundmann, "δεῖ, δέον ἐστί," 23–4; Collins, *Mark: A Commentary*, 403–4; France, *Mark*, 334; and D. E. Nineham, *The Gospel of St. Mark* (PNTC; Harmondsworth, Middlesex: Penguin, 1963), 225.

5. As in Stein, *Mark*, 401; Hooker, *The Gospel According to Saint Mark*, 205; Boring, *Mark*, 240; Gundry, *Mark*, 428; John Painter, *Mark's Gospel: Worlds in Conflict* (London and New York: Routledge, 1997), 125; Augustine Stock, *The Method and Message of Mark* (Wilmington, DE: Michael Glazier, 1989), 236; Harrington, *Mark*, 128; and Lane, *The Gospel of Mark*, 301.

12. Conclusion

This study began with the goals of providing narrative biblical scholars with a methodological approach that guides the interpretation of biblical narratives from the semantic surface structure of a text to the formulation of statements of characters' actions and attributes, demonstrating the application of this methodological approach in the specification of the repeated and non-repeated actions and attributes of God in the Gospel of Mark, and formatting and articulating the statements of God's repeated actions and attributes in a manner that readily is usable both by students of the bible and by theologians. To this end, the Methodological Study proposed and illustrated the application of a set of complementary semantic, narrative, and rhetorical methods for investigating characterization (Chapters 1–3). The Exegetical Study succinctly re-presented the narrative and narratively interpreted semantic content of the contexts containing the 314 references to the character God within Mark 1:1–16:8 (Chapters 4–5). The Theological Study then developed statements of God's fifty-six repeated actions and attributes (Chapters 6–11.10) and indicated the manner in which the study of God's actions and attributes might be made more comprehensive (Chapter 11.11).

The study presented much that already is accepted concerning Mark's presentation of God. It also uncovered much that is new. The rigorous application of strictly conceived semantic and narrative criteria isolated no less than 314 direct and indirect references to God in a text frequently noted for the paucity of such references. The Exegetical Study revealed that there are references to God in over half of the rhetorical contexts of Mark and clarified that specific actions and attributes of God repeatedly appear in the same relationships. The Theological Study demonstrated that the rhetorical linkage of God's actions and attributes opens productive and frequently novel avenues of elaboration and development and points to further such opportunities.

In 1991, Nils Dahl recommended an address of the neglect of God in New Testament Theology through a "careful, analytic description of words and phrases and of their use within sentences and larger units of speech" and concluded with the observation that such a study of God "will have important implications for the systematician as well."[6] The forgoing study attempted such a project. It is my hope that the Methodological Study provides useful tools for biblical scholars engaged in narrative and rhetorical studies and that the Theological Study contributes to addressing the neglect of God in New Testament studies in a manner that proves to be accessible and useful for both Biblical Studies and Systematic Theology.

---

6. Nils Alstrup Dahl, "The Neglected Factor in New Testament Theology," in *Jesus the Christ: The Historical Origins of Christological Doctrine*, ed. Donald H. Juel (Minneapolis, MN: Fortress, 1991), 157, 162.

APPENDICES

A. Definitions: Thematic Roles

1. Thematic Roles Directly Pertaining to the Characterization of God

Agent (A): the animate entity that actively instigates an action and/or is the ultimate cause of a change in another entity
Benefactive (B): the ultimate entity for which an action is performed or for which literally or figuratively something happens or exists
Content (C): the content of a mental or psychological state, event, or activity
Event (V): the complete circumstantial scene of an action or event
Experiencer (E): the animate being that is the locus of a mental or psychological state, event, or activity
Goal (G): the literal or figurative entity towards which something moves
Instrument (I): the means by which an action is performed or something happens
Locative (L): the literal or figurative place in which an entity is situated or an event occurs
Patient (P): the entity undergoing an action or object of predication
Source (S): the literal or figurative entity from which something moves
Theme (Θ): the entity literally or figuratively moving from one place to another or located in a place
Topic (T): the topic of focus of a mental or psychological state, event, or activity

2. Other Thematic Roles

Cause (Cau): the circumstantial motivation for an action or event
Condition (Cnd): the entity or event required for another event to occur
Manner (Man): the circumstantial qualification of an action or event
Purpose (Pur): the goal of a complete event
Result (Res): the consequence of a complete event

B. References to God by Thematic Role

(314 References—56 Repeated—62 Non-Repeated)

B1. Direct References to God by Thematic Role (301—54 Repeated—61 Non-Repeated)

Agent (62 references—10 repeated—17 non-repeated)
take up (αἴρω [Aθs], 4:25)
destroy (ἀπόλλυμι [Ap], 12:9)
send (*ἀποστέλλω [Aθg], 1:2; 9:37; 12:2, 4, 5a, [5b], 6)
forgive (*ἀφίημι [Apb], 2:5, 7, 9; 3:28; 4:12; 11:25b)
write (*γέγραπται [Ace], 1:2; 7:6; 9:12, 13; 11:17; 14:21, 27)
come to be (*γίνομαι [pA], 2:27a, [27b]; 6:2b; 12:11)
give (*δίδωμι [Aθg], 4:11, 25; 6:2; 8:12; 11:28; 12:9; 13:11)
abandon (ἐγκαταλείπω [Ap], 15:34)
lease (ἐκδίδομαι [Aθg], 12:1)
choose (ἐκλέγομαι [Ap], 13:20)
shorten (*κολοβόω [Ap], 13:20a, 20b)
create (κτίζω [Ap], 13:19)
take (λαμβάνω [Aθs], 12:2)
say (*λέγω [Ace], 12:6, 26a, 36)
measure (μετρέω [Aθg], 4:24)
build (οἰκοδομέω [Ap], 12:1)
dig (ὀρύσσω [Ap], 12:1)
[not] take away (παραφέρω [Aθs], 14:36)
strike (πατάσσω [Ap], 14:27)
put around (περιτίθημι [Ap], 12:1)
do/make/act (*ποιέω [Ap], 5:19; 10:6; 12:9)
add (προστίθημι [Aθg], 4:24)
join (συζεύγνυμι [Apg], 10:9)
tear (*σχίζω [Ap], 1:10; 15:38)
save (*σῴζω [Ap], 8:35b; [10:27]; 13:13, 20)
put (τίθημι [Aθg], 12:36)
plant (φυτεύω [Ap], 12:1)

Benefactive (160 references—30 repeated—19 non-repeated)
angel/messenger (*ἄγγελος [B], 1:2, 13; 8:38; 12:25; 13:27, 32)
holy one (ἅγιος [B], 1:24)
[not] impossible thing (ἀδύνατον [B], 10:27)
sinful action (*ἁμάρτημα [bB], 3:28, 29)
sin (*ἁμαρτία [bB], 1:4, 5; 2:5, 7, 9, 10)
vineyard (*ἀμπελών [B], 12:1, 2, 8, 9a, 9b)
forgiveness (*ἄφεσις [Bb], 1:4; 3:29)
reign (*βασιλεία [B], 1:15; 4:11, 26, 30; 9:1, 47; 10:14, 15, 23, 24, 25; 12:34; 14:25; 15:43)

blaspheme (*βλασφημέω [apB], 2:7; 3:28, 29)
blasphemy (*βλασφημία [bB], 3:28; 7:22; 14:64)
scripture (*γραφή [B], 12:10, 24; 14:49)
right [hand] (*δεξιά [B], 12:36; 14:62)
covenant (διαθήκη [B], 14:24)
glory (*δόξα [B], 8:38; 13:26)
slave (*δοῦλος [B], 12:2, 4, [5a], [5b])
power (*δύναμις [B], 9:1; 12:24; 13:26)
thing able [to be done]/possible thing (*δυνατόν [B], 10:27; 14:36)
gift (δῶρον [bB], 7:11)
elect (*ἐκλεκτός [B], 13:20, 22, 27)
commandment (*ἐντολή [B], 7:8, 9; 10:19; 12:28, [29], [31a], 31b)
authority (*ἐξουσία [B], 1:22, 27; 2:10; 3:15; 6:7; 11:28a, 28b, 29, 33; 13:34)
gospel (*εὐαγγέλιον [B/T], 1:1, 14, 15; 8:35; 10:29; 13:10; 14:9)
have (ἔχω [Bp], 12:6)
life (*ζωή [B], 9:43, 45; 10:17, 30)
will (θέλημα [B], 3:35)
offering (θυσία [bB], 12:33)
Temple (*ἱερόν [bB], 11:11, 15a, 15b, 16, 27; 12:35; 13:1, 3; 14:49)
heir (κληρόνομος [B], 12:7)
condemnation (κρίμα [Bb], 12:40)
creation (*κτίσις [B], 10:6; 13:19)
word (λόγος [B], 7:13)
sanctuary (*ναός [bB], 14:58a, [58b]; 15:29, 38)
way (*ὁδός [B], 1:2, 3; 12:14)
house (*οἶκος [bB], 2:26; 11:17a)
burnt offering (ὁλοκαύτωμα [bB], 12:33)
name (ὄνομα [B], 11:9)
trespass (παράπτωμα [bB], 11:25)
spirit (*πνεῦμα [B], 1:8, 10, 12; 3:29; 12:36; 13:11)
face (πρόσωπον [B], 1:2)
prophet (*προφήτης [B], 1:2; 6:4, 15a, 15b; 8:28; 11:32)
tower (πύργος [Bb], 12:1)
wisdom (σοφία [B], 6:2)
things (*τά [B], 8:33; 12:17b)
path (τρίβος [B], 1:3)
son (*υἱός [B], 1:1, 11; 3:11; 5:7; 9:7; 12:6a, 6b; 13:32; 14:61; 15:39)
winepress (ὑπολήνιον [Bb], 12:1)
fence (φραγμός [Bb], 12:1)
voice (*φωνή [B], 1:11; 9:7)
Christ/Anointed (*χριστός [B], 1:1; 8:29; 9:41; 12:35; 13:21; 14:61; 15:32)

Content (2 references—1 repeated—0 non-repeated)
love (*ἀγαπάω [eC/apB], 12:30, 33)

Experiencer (31 references—6 repeated—9 non-repeated)
beloved (*ἀγαπητός [Ec/Apb], 1:11; 9:7; 12:6)
ask (αἰτέω [acE], 11:24)
glorify (δοξάζω [aE], 2:12)
be merciful (ἐλεέω [Eb], 5:19)
delight [in] (εὐδοκέω [Ec], 1:11)
bless (*εὐλογέω [aE], 6:41; 8:7; 14:22)
give thanks (*εὐχαριστέω [acE], 8:6; 14:23)
want (θέλω [Ec], [14:36])
know (οἶδα [Et], 13:32)
prayer (*προσευχή [E], 9:29; 11:17)
pray (*προσεύχομαι [acE], 1:35; 6:46; 11:24, 25; 12:40; 13:18; 14:32, 35, 38, 39)
worship (σέβομαι [aE], 7:7)
honor (τιμάω [aE], 7:6)
sing (ὑμνέω [acE], 14:26)
hosanna (*ὡσαννά [aE], 11:9, 10)

Goal (2 references—0 repeated—2 non-repeated)
give back (ἀποδίδωμι [aθG], 12:17)
send (ἀποστέλλω [aθG], 12:3)

Instrument (1 reference—0 repeated—1 non-repeated)
compel to swear (ὁρκίζω [aec-I], 5:7)

Patient (18 references—3 repeated—4 non-repeated)
good (ἀγαθός [P], 10:18)
he (αὐτός [P], 12:32)
one (*εἷς [P], 12:29, 32)
God (*θεός [bP], 12:26b, 26c, 26d, 27a, [27b], 29, 30; 15:34a, 34b)
lord (κύριος [bP], 12:9)
father (*πατήρ [bP], 8:38; 11:25; 14:36)
most high (ὕψιστος [P], 5:7)

Source (11 references—2 repeated—5 non-repeated)
be distant (ἀπέχω [θS], 7:6)
baptism (βάπτισμα [S], 11:30)
inherit (κληρονομέω [gθS], 10:17)
inheritance (κληρονομία [S], 12:7)
receive (*λαμβάνω [gθS], 10:30; 11:24; 12:40)
wage (μισθός [S], 9:41)
sign (*σημεῖον [S], 8:11, 12a, 12b)

Theme (4 references—0 repeated—4 non-repeated)
go on a journey (ἀποδημέω [Θg], 12:1)
receive (δέχομαι [gΘs], 9:37d)

in (ἐν [Θl], 11:25)
come (ἔρχομαι [Θg], 12:9)

Topic (10 references—2 repeated—0 non-repeated)
believe (*πιστεύω [ecT], 5:36; 9:23, 24; 11:23, 24)
faith (*πίστις [ecT], 2:5; 4:40; 5:34; 10:52; 11:22)

B2. *Indirect references to God by Thematic Role (13 References—2 Repeated—1 Non-Repeated)*

Benefactive (13 references—2 repeated—1 non-repeated)
be necessary (*δεῖ [vi-iB], 8:31; 9:11; 13:7, 10, 14; 14:31) (cf. *γέγραπται [Ace])
be permitted (*ἔξεστιν [vi-iB], 2:24, 26; 3:4; 6:18; 10:2; 12:14) (cf. *ἐντολή [B])
prophesy (προφητεύω [aci-iB], 7:6) (cf. *πνεῦμα [B])

C. Rhetorical Contexts with References

1:1-3 (§4.1a), *εὐαγγέλιον [B/T], 1:1; *χριστός [B], 1:1; *υἱός [B], 1:1; *γέγραπται [Ace], 1:2; *προφήτης [B], 1:2; *ἀποστέλλω [Aθg], 1:2; *ἄγγελος [B], 1:2; πρόσωπον [B], 1:2; *ὁδός [B], 1:2, 3; τρίβος [B], 1:3
1:4-8 (§4.1b), *ἄφεσις [Bb], 1:4; *ἁμαρτία [bB], 1:4, 5; *πνεῦμα [B], 1:8
1:9-11 (§4.1c), *σχίζω [Ap], 1:10; *πνεῦμα [B], 1:10; *φωνή [B], 1:11; *υἱός [B], 1:11; *ἀγαπητός [Ec/Apb], 1:11; εὐδοκέω [Ec], 1:11
1:12-13 (§4.1d), *πνεῦμα [B], 1:12; *ἄγγελος [B], 1:13
1:14-15 (§4.1e), *εὐαγγέλιον [B/T], 1:14; *βασιλεία [B], 1:15; *εὐαγγέλιον [B/T], 1:15
1:21-28 (§4.1f), *ἐξουσία [B], 1:22; ἅγιος [B], 1:24; *ἐξουσία [B], 1:27
1:35-38 (§4.1g), *προσεύχομαι [acE], 1:35
2:1-12 (§4.2a), *πίστις [ecT], 2:5; *ἀφίημι [Apb], 2:5; *ἁμαρτία [bB], 2:5; *βλασφημέω [apB], 2:7; *ἀφίημι [Apb], 2:7; *ἁμαρτία [bB], 2:7; *ἀφίημι [Apb], 2:9; *ἁμαρτία [bB], 2:9; *ἐξουσία [B], 2:10; *ἁμαρτία [bB], 2:10; δοξάζω [aE], 2:12
2:23-28 (§4.2b), *ἔξεστιν [vi-iB], 2:24; *οἶκος [bB], 2:26; *ἔξεστιν [vi-iB], 2:26; *γίνομαι [pA], 2:27a, [27b]
3:1-6 (§4.3a), *ἔξεστιν [vi-iB], 3:4
3:7-12 (§4.3b), *υἱός [B], 3:11
3:13-19 (§4.3c), *ἐξουσία [B], 3:15
3:20-35 (§4.3d), *ἀφίημι [Apb], 3:28; *ἁμάρτημα [bB], 3:28; *βλασφημία [bB], 3:28; *βλασφημέω [apB], 3:28, 29; *πνεῦμα [B], 3:29; *ἄφεσις [Bb], 3:29; *ἁμάρτημα [bB], 3:29; θέλημα [B], 3:35
4:10-12 (§4.4a), *δίδωμι [Aθg], 4:11; *βασιλεία [B], 4:11; *ἀφίημι [Apb], 4:12
4:24-25 (§4.4b), μετρέω [Aθg], 4:24; προστίθημι [Aθg], 4:24; *δίδωμι [Aθg], 4:25; αἴρω [Aθs], 4:25
4:26-29 (§4.4c), *βασιλεία [B], 4:26

4:30–32 (§4.4d), *βασιλεία [Β], 4:30
4:35–41 (§4.4e), *πίστις [ecT], 4:40
5:1–13 (§4.5a), *υἱός [Β], 5:7; ὕψιστος [Ρ], 5:7; ὁρκίζω [aec-I], 5:7
5:18–20 (§4.5b), *ποιέω [Ap], 5:19; ἐλεέω [Eb], 5:19
5:25–34 (§4.5c), *πίστις [ecT], 5:34
5:35–43 (§4.5d), *πιστεύω [ecT], 5:36
6:1–6a (§4.6a), σοφία [Β], 6:2; *δίδωμι [Αθg], 6:2; *γίνομαι [pA], 6:2b; *προφήτης [Β], 6:4
6:6b–13 (§4.6b), *ἐξουσία [Β], 6:7
6:14–16 (§4.6c), *προφήτης [Β], 6:15a, 15b
6:17–20 (§4.6d), *ἔξεστιν [vi-iB], 6:18
6:35–44 (§4.6e), *εὐλογέω [aE], 6:41
6:45–52 (§4.6f), *προσεύχομαι [acE], 6:46
7:6–13 (§4.7a), προφητεύω [aci-iB], 7:6; *γέγραπται [Ace], 7:6; τιμάω [aE], 7:6; ἀπέχω [θS], 7:6; σέβομαι [aE], 7:7; *ἐντολή [Β], 7:8, 9; δῶρον [bB], 7:11; λόγος [Β], 7:13
7:17–23 (§4.7b), *βλασφημία [bB], 7:22
8:1–9 (§4.8a), *εὐχαριστέω [acE], 8:6; *εὐλογέω [aE], 8:7
8:11–14 (§4.8b), *σημεῖον [S], 8:11, 12a; *δίδωμι [Αθg], 8:12; *σημεῖον [S], 8:12b
8:27–30 (§4.8c), *προφήτης [Β], 8:28; *χριστός [Β], 8:29
8:31—9:1 (§4.8d), *δεῖ [vi-iB], 8:31; *τά [Β], 8:33; *σῴζω [Ap], 8:35b; *εὐαγγέλιον [Β/Τ], 8:35; *δόξα [Β], 8:38; *πατήρ [bP], 8:38; *ἄγγελος [Β], 8:38; *βασιλεία [Β], 9:1; *δύναμις [Β], 9:1
9:2–9 (§4.9a), *φωνή [Β], 9:7; *υἱός [Β], 9:7; *ἀγαπητός [Ec/Apb], 9:7
9:11–13 (§4.9b), *δεῖ [vi-iB], 9:11; *γέγραπται [Ace], 9:12, 13
9:14–27 (§4.9c), *πιστεύω [ecT], 9:23, 24
9:28–29 (§4.9d), *προσευχή [Ε], 9:29
9:33–37 (§4.9e), δέχομαι [gΘs], 9:37d; *ἀποστέλλω [Αθg], 9:37
9:38–48 (§4.9f), *χριστός [Β], 9:41; μισθός [S], 9:41, *ζωή [Β], 9:43, 45; *βασιλεία [Β], 9:47
10:1–9 (§5.1a), *ἔξεστιν [vi-iB], 10:2; *κτίσις [Β], 10:6; *ποιέω [Ap], 10:6; συζεύγνυμι [Apg], 10:9
10:13–16 (§5.1b), *βασιλεία [Β], 10:14, 15
10:17–22 (§5.1c), κληρονομέω [gθS], 10:17; *ζωή [Β], 10:17; ἀγαθός [Ρ], 10:18; *ἐντολή [Β], 10:19
10:23–27 (§5.1d), *βασιλεία [Β], 10:23, 24, 25; ἀδύνατον [Β], 10:27; *δυνατόν [Β], 10:27; *σῴζω [Ap], [10:27]
10:28–31 (§5.1e), *εὐαγγέλιον [Β/Τ], 10:29; *λαμβάνω [gθS], 10:30; *ζωή [Β], 10:30
10:46–52 (§5.1f), *πίστις [ecT], 10:52
11:1–11 (§5.2a), *ὡσαννά [aE], 11:9; ὄνομα [Β], 11:9; *ὡσαννά [aE], 11:10; *ἱερόν [bB], 11:11
11:15–19 (§5.2b), *ἱερόν [bB], 11:15a, 15b, 16; *γέγραπται [Ace], 11:17; *οἶκος [bB], 11:17a; *προσευχή [Ε], 11:17
11:20–25 (§5.2c), *πίστις [ecT], 11:22; *πιστεύω [ecT], 11:23; *προσεύχομαι [acE], 11:24; αἰτέω [acE], 11:24; *πιστεύω [ecT], 11:24; *λαμβάνω [gθS], 11:24;

*προσεύχομαι [acE], 11:25; *πατήρ [bP], 11:25; ἐν [Θl], 11:25; *ἀφίημι [Apb], 11:25b; παράπτωμα [bB], 11:25

11:27-33 (§5.2d), *ἱερόν [bB], 11:27; *ἐξουσία [B], 11:28a; *δίδωμι [Aθg], 11:28; *ἐξουσία [B], 11:28b, 29; βάπτισμα [S], 11:30; *προφήτης [B], 11:32; *ἐξουσία [B], 11:33

12:1-5 (§5.3a), φυτεύω [Ap], 12:1; *ἀμπελών [B], 12:1; περιτίθημι [Ap], 12:1; φραγμός [Bb], 12:1; ὀρύσσω [Ap], 12:1; ὑπολήνιον [Bb], 12:1; οἰκοδομέω [Ap], 12:1; πύργος [Bb], 12:1; ἐκδίδομαι [Aθg], 12:1; ἀποδημέω [Θg], 12:1; *ἀποστέλλω [Aθg], 12:2; *δοῦλος [B], 12:2; λαμβάνω [Aθs], 12:2; *ἀμπελών [B], 12:2; ἀποστέλλω [aθG], 12:3; *ἀποστέλλω [Aθg], 12:4; *δοῦλος [B], 12:4; *ἀποστέλλω [Aθg], 12:5a; *δοῦλος [B], [12:5a]; *ἀποστέλλω [Aθg], [12:5b]; *δοῦλος [B], [12:5b]

12:6-8 (§5.3b), ἔχω [Bp], 12:6; *υἱός [B], 12:6a; *ἀγαπητός [Ec/Apb], 12:6; *ἀποστέλλω [Aθg], 12:6; *λέγω [Ace], 12:6; *υἱός [B], 12:6b; κληρόνομος [B], 12:7; κληρονομία [S], 12:7; *ἀμπελών [B], 12:8

12:9-12 (§5.3c), κύριος [bP], 12:9a; ἀμπελών [B], 12:9a; *ποιέω [Ap], 12:9; ἔρχομαι [Θg], 12:9; ἀπόλλυμι [Ap], 12:9; *δίδωμι [Aθg], 12:9; *ἀμπελών [B], 12:9b; *γραφή [B], 12:10; *γίνομαι [pA], 12:11

12:13-17 (§5.3d), *ὁδός [B], 12:14; *ἔξεστιν [vi-iB], 12:14; ἀποδίδωμι [aθG], 12:17; *τά [B], 12:17b

12:18-27 (§5.3e), *γραφή [B], 12:24; *δύναμις [B], 12:24; *ἄγγελος [B], 12:25; *λέγω [Ace], 12:26a; *θεός [bP], 12:26b, 26c, 26d, 27a, [27b]

12:28-34 (§5.3f), *ἐντολή [B], 12:28, [29]; *θεός [bP], 12:29; *εἷς [P], 12:29; *ἀγαπάω [eC/apB], 12:30; *θεός [bP], 12:30; *ἐντολή [B], [12:31a], 31b; *εἷς [P], 12:32; αὐτός [P], 12:32; *ἀγαπάω [eC/apB], 12:33; ὁλοκαύτωμα [bB], 12:33; θυσία [bB], 12:33; *βασιλεία [B], 12:34

12:35-37 (§5.3g), *ἱερόν [bB], 12:35; *χριστός [B], 12:35; *πνεῦμα [B], 12:36; *λέγω [Ace], 12:36; *δεξιά [B], 12:36; τίθημι [Aθg], 12:36

12:38-40 (§5.3h), *προσεύχομαι [acE], 12:40; *λαμβάνω [gθS], 12:40; κρίμα [Bb], 12:40

13:1-2 (§5.4a), *ἱερόν [bB], 13:1

13:3-8 (§5.4b), *ἱερόν [bB], 13:3; *δεῖ [vi-iB], 13:7

13:9-13 (§5.4c), *δεῖ [vi-iB], 13:10; *εὐαγγέλιον [B/T], 13:10; *δίδωμι [Aθg], 13:11; *πνεῦμα [B], 13:11; *σῴζω [Ap], 13:13

13:14-17 (§5.4d), *δεῖ [vi-iB], 13:14

13:18-20 (§5.4e), *προσεύχομαι [acE], 13:18; *κτίσις [B], 13:19; κτίζω [Ap], 13:19; *κολοβόω [Ap], 13:20a; *σῴζω [Ap], 13:20; *ἐκλεκτός [B], 13:20; ἐκλέγομαι [Ap], 13:20; *κολοβόω [Ap], 13:20b

13:21-23 (§5.4f), *χριστός [B], 13:21; *ἐκλεκτός [B], 13:22

13:24-29 (§5.4g), *δύναμις [B], 13:26; *δόξα [B], 13:26; *ἄγγελος [B], 13:27; *ἐκλεκτός [B], 13:27

13:32-37 (§5.4h), οἶδα [Et], 13:32; *ἄγγελος [B], 13:32; *υἱός [B], 13:32; *ἐξουσία [B], 13:34

14:3-9 (§5.5a), *εὐαγγέλιον [B/T], 14:9

14:17-21 (§5.5b), *γέγραπται [Ace], 14:21

14:22-26 (§5.5c), *εὐλογέω [aE], 14:22; *εὐχαριστέω [acE], 14:23; διαθήκη [B], 14:24; *βασιλεία [B], 14:25; ὑμνέω [acE], 14:26

14:27-31 (§5.4d), *γέγραπται [Ace], 14:27; πατάσσω [Ap], 14:27; *δεῖ [vi-iB], 14:31

14:32-42 (§5.5e), *προσεύχομαι [acE], 14:32, 35; *πατήρ [bP], 14:36; *δυνατόν [B], 14:36; παραφέρω [Aθs], 14:36; θέλω [Ec], [14:36]; *προσεύχομαι [acE], 14:38, 39

14:48-52 (§5.5f), *ἱερόν [bB], 14:49; *γραφή [B], 14:49

14:55-59 (§5.5g), *ναός [bB], 14:58a, [58b]

14:60-64 (§5.5h), *χριστός [B], 14:61; *υἱός [B], 14:61; *δεξιά [B], 14:62; *βλασφημία [bB], 14:64

15:29-32 (§5.6a), *ναός [bB], 15:29; *χριστός [B], 15:32

15:33-36 (§5.6b), *θεός [bP], 15:34a, 34b; ἐγκαταλείπω [Ap], 15:34

15:37-39 (§5.6c), *ναός [bB], 15:38; *σχίζω [Ap], 15:38; *υἱός [B], 15:39

15:42-47 (§5.6d), *βασιλεία [B], 15:43

BIBLIOGRAPHY

Abbott, H. Porter. *The Cambridge Introduction to Narrative*, 2nd edn. Cambridge: Cambridge University Press, 2008.

Ackerman, Farrell, and John Moore. "Valence and the Semantics of Causativization." *BLS* 20 (1994): 1–13.

Aguilar Chiu, José Enrique. "A Theological Reading of ἐξέπνευσεν in Mark 15:37, 39." *CBQ* 78, no. 4 (2016): 682–705.

Aland, Barbara, Kurt Aland, Johannes Karavidopoulos, Carlo M. Martini, and Bruce M. Metzger (eds.). *The Greek New Testament*, 4th rev. edn. Stuttgart: Biblia-Druck, 1993.

Aland, Kurt. "Bemerkungen zum Schluss des Markusevangeliums." In *Neotestamentica et Semitica: Studies in Honour of Matthew Black*, edited by E. Earle Ellis and Max Wilcox, 157–80. Edinburgh: T&T Clark, 1969.

Allan, Keith. *Linguistic Meaning* 2 vols. London: Routledge & Keegan Paul, 1986.

Allerton, D. J. *Valency and the English Verb*. London and New York: Academic Press, 1982.

Alter, Robert. *The Pleasures of Reading in an Ideological Age*. New York: Simon and Schuster, 1989.

Ambrozic, Aloysius M. *The Hidden Kingdom: A Redaction-Critical Study of the References to the Kingdom of God in Mark's Gospel*. CBQMS 2; Washington, D.C.: Catholic University of America Press, 1972.

Anderson, Hugh. *The Gospel of Mark*. NCB; London: Oliphants, 1976.

Best, Ernest. "Mark's Readers: A Profile." In *The Four Gospels*, edited by F. Van Segbroeck, C. M. Tuckett, G. van Belle, and J. Verherden, 839–55. Vol. 2. Leuven: Leuven University Press, 1992.

Beyer, Hermann Wolfgang. "βλασφημία." *TDNT* 1:621–25.

———. "εὐλογέω and εὐλογία." *TDNT* 2:754–65.

Bird, Michael. "The Crucifixion of Jesus as the Fulfillment of Mark 9:1." *TrinJ* 24, no. 1 NS (2003): 23–36.

Black, C. Clifton. *Mark*. ANTC; Nashville, TN: Abingdon, 2011.

———. "Mark as Historian of God's Kingdom." *CBQ* 71 (2009): 64–83.

Blass, Friedrich, Albert Debrunner and Robert W. Funk. *A Greek Grammar of the New Testament and Other Early Christian Literature*. Cambridge: Cambridge University Press, 1961.

Bock, Darrell L. *Blasphemy and Exaltation in Judaism and the Final Examination of Jesus: A Philological-Historical Study of the Key Jewish Themes Impacting Mark 14:61–64*. WUNT 2/106; Tübingen: Mohr Siebeck, 1998.

———. *Mark*. NCBC; Cambridge: Cambridge University Press, 2015.

Boomershine, Thomas E., and Gilbert L. Bartholomew. "The Narrative Technique of Mark 16:8." *JBL* 100, no. 2 (1981): 213–23.

Booth, Wayne C. *The Rhetoric of Fiction*, 2nd edn. Chicago: University of Chicago Press, 1983.

Boring, M. Eugene. *Mark: A Commentary*. TNTL; Louisville, KY: Westminster John Knox, 2006.

———. "Markan Christology: God-Language for Jesus?" *NTS* 45 (1999): 451–71.

Botner, Max. "The Messiah Is 'the Holy One': ὁ ἅγιος τοῦ θεοῦ as a Messianic Title in Mark 1:24." *JBL* 136, no. 2 (2017): 417–33.
Brinton, Laurel J. *The Structure of Modern English: A Linguistic Introduction*. Amsterdam/Philadelphia: Benjamins, 2000.
Brower, Kent. "Mark 9:1: Seeing the Kingdom in Power." *JSNT* 6 (1980): 17–41.
Brown, Raymond E. *The Death of the Messiah: From Gethsemane to the Grave*, 2 vols. New York: Doubleday, 1994.
Brown, Russell. "Theme." In *Encyclopedia of Contemporary Literary Theory: Approaches, Scholars, Terms*, edited by Irena R. Makaryk, 643. Toronto: University of Toronto Press, 1993.
Bultmann, Rudolf. *The History of the Synoptic Tradition*, translated by John Marsh. Rev edn. New York: Harper & Row, 1968.
Chafe, Wallace L. *Meaning and the Structure of Language*. Chicago: University of Chicago Press, 1970.
Chatman, Seymour. *Story and Discourse: Narrative Structure in Fiction and Film*. Ithaca, NY: Cornell University Press, 1978.
Chronis, Harry L. "The Torn Veil: Cultus and Christology in Mark 15:37-39." *JBL* 101, no. 1 (1982): 97–114.
Collins, Adela Yarbro. "The Charge of Blasphemy in Mark 14.64." *JSNT* 26, no. 4 (2004): 379–401.
———. *Is Mark's Gospel a Life of Jesus?: The Question of Genre*. Milwaukee, WI: Marquette University Press, 1990.
———. *Mark: A Commentary*, edited by Harold W. Attridge. Minneapolis, MN: Hermeneia; Augsburg: Fortress, 2007.
Conzelmann, Hans. "εὐχαριστέω, εὐχαριστία, εὐχάριστος." *TDNT* 9:401–15.
Cook, Walter A. "A Case Grammar Matrix." *Languages and Linguistics: Working Papers* 6 (1972): 15–47.
Cousar, Charles B. "Eschatology and Mark's Theologia Crucis: A Critical Analysis of Mark 13." *Interpretation* 24, no. 3 (1970): 321–35.
Cranfield, C. E. B. *The Gospel According to St. Mark*. CGTC; Cambridge: Cambridge University Press, 1959.
Culpepper, R. Alan. *Mark*. S&HBC; Macon, GA: Smyth & Helwys, 2007.
Dahl, Nils Alstrup. "The Neglected Factor in New Testament Theology." In *Jesus the Christ: The Historical Origins of Christological Doctrine*, edited by Donald H. Juel, 153–63. Minneapolis, MN: Fortress, 1991.
Danove, Paul L. "The Action of Forgiving in the New Testament." In *Forgiveness: Selected Papers from the 2008 Annual Conference of the Villanova University Theology Institute*, edited by Darlene Fozard Weaver and Jeffrey S. Mayer, 41–66. Villanova, PA: Villanova University Press, 2008.
———. "A Comparison of the Usages of δίδωμι and δίδωμι Compounds in the Septuagint and New Testament." In *The Language of the New Testament: Context, History, and Development*, edited by Stanley E. Porter and Andrew W. Pitts, 365–400. LBS 6; Leiden: Brill, 2013.
———. *The End of Mark's Story: A Methodological Study*. BIS 3; Leiden: Brill, 1993.
———. *Grammatical and Exegetical Study of New Testament Verbs of Transference: A Case Frame Guide to Interpretation and Translation*. SNTG 13; LNTS 329; London: T&T Clark, 2009.
———. "Λέγω Melding in the Septuagint and New Testament." *FN* 16 (2003): 19–31.

———. *Linguistics and Exegesis in the Gospel of Mark: Applications of a Case Frame Analysis and Lexicon*. JSNTSup 218; SNTG 10; Sheffield: Sheffield Academic Press, 2001.
———. "Mark 1,1–15 as Introduction to Characterization." In *Greeks, Jews, and Christians: Historical, Religious and Philological Studies in Honor of Jesús Peláez del Rosal*, edited by Lautaro Roig Lanzillotta and Israel Muñoz Gallarte, 127–48. Córdoba: El Almendro, 2013.
———. "The Narrative Function of Mark's Characterization of God." *NovT* XLIII, no. 1 (2001): 12–30.
———. *New Testament Verbs of Communication: A Case Frame and Exegetical Study*. LNTS 520; London: Bloomsbury, 2015.
———. *The Rhetoric of the Characterization of God, Jesus, and Jesus' Disciples in the Gospel of Mark*. JSNTSup 290; New York: T&T Clark, 2005.
———. "The Rhetoric of the Characterization of Jesus as the Son of Man and Christ in Mark." *Bib* 84 (2003): 16–34.
———. "The Usages of δίδωμι in the Septuagint: Its Interpretation and Translation". *BIOSCS* 43 (2010): 23–40.
———. "Verbs of Transference and Their Derivatives of Motion and State in the New Testament: A Study of Focus and Perspective." *FN* 19 (2006): 53–72.
Dirven, René and Marjolijn Verspoor (eds.). *Cognitive Exploration of Language and Linguistics*. Amsterdam/Philadelphia: Benjamins, 1998.
Docherty, Thomas. *Reading (Absent) Character: Towards a Theory of Characterization in Fiction*. Oxford: Clarendon, 1983.
Donahue, John R. *Are You the Christ? The Trial Narrative in the Gospel of Mark*. SBLDS 10; Missoula, MT: Scholars, 1973.
———. "A Neglected Factor in the Theology of Mark." *JBL* 101, no. 4 (1982): 563–94.
———. "The Revelation of God in the Gospel of Mark." In *Modern Biblical Scholarship: Its Impact on Theology and Proclamation*, edited by Francis A. Eigo, 157–83. Villanova, PA: Villanova University Press, 1984.
Donahue, John R. and Daniel J. Harrington. *The Gospel of Mark*. SPS 2; Collegeville, MN: Liturgical, 2002.
Dowd, Sharyn Echols. *Prayer, Power, and the Problem of Suffering: Mark 11:22-25 in the Context of Markan Theology*. SBLDS 105; Atlanta: Scholars, 1988.
———. *Reading Mark: A Literary and Theological Commentary on the Second Gospel*. Macon, GA: Smyth & Helwys, 2000.
Dowty, David R. "On the Semantic Content of the Notion 'Thematic Role'." In *Properties, Types and Meaning*, edited by Gennaro Chierchia, Barbara H. Partee, and Raymond Turner, 69–130, 2 vols. Dordrecht: Kluwer, 1989.
———. "Thematic Proto-Roles and Argument Selection." *Language* 67, no. 3 (1991): 547–619.
———. "Thematic Roles and Semantics." *BLS* 12 (1986): 340–54.
Driggers, Ira Brent. "God as Healer of Creation in the Gospel of Mark." In *Character Studies and the Gospel of Mark*, edited by Christopher W. Skinner and Matthew Ryan Hauge, 81–106. JSNTSup 483; London: Bloomsbury, 2014.
Eco, Umberto. *The Role of the Reader: Explorations in the Semiotics of Texts*. Bloomington, IN: Indiana University Press, 1979.
Fackre, Gabriel. "Narrative Theology: An Overview." *Interpretation* 37, no. 4 (1983): 340–52.

Fillmore, Charles J. "The Case for Case." In *Universals in Linguistic Theory*, edited by Emmon Bach and Robert T. Harms, 1–88. New York: Holt, Reinhart and Winston, 1968.
———. "Frames and the Semantics of Understanding." *QS* 6, no. 2 (1985): 222–54.
———. "The Need for Frame Semantics Within Linguistics." In *Statistical Methods in Linguistics*, edited by Hans Karlgren, 5–29. Stockholm: Scriptor, 1977.
———. "Pragmatically Controlled Zero Anaphora." *BLS* 12 (1986): 95–107.
———. "Topics in Lexical Semantics." In *Current Issues in Linguistic Theory*, edited by Roger W. Cole, 76–138. Bloomington, IN: Indiana University Press, 1977.
Fillmore, Charles J., and Paul Kay. *Construction Grammar*. Stanford: CSLI, 1999.
Foerster, Werner. "ἔξεστιν." *TDNT* 2:560–1.
Fowler, Robert M. *Loaves And Fishes: The Function of the Feeding Stories in the Gospel of Mark*. SBLDS 54; Chico, CA: Scholars Press, 1981.
France, R. T. *The Gospel of Mark: A Commentary on the Greek Text*. Grand Rapids, MI: Eerdmans, 2002.
Fraser, Bruce, and John Robert Ross. "Idioms and Unspecified N[oun] P[hrase] Deletion." *LInq* 1, no. 2 (1970): 264–95.
Friedrich, Gerhard. "Prophets and Prophecies in the New Testament." *TDNT* 6:828–56.
Geddert, Timothy J. *Watchwords: Mark 13 in Markan Eschatology*. JSNTSSup 26; Sheffield: Sheffield Academic Press, 1989.
Gibson, Jeffrey. "Jesus' Refusal to Produce a 'Sign' (MK 8:11-13)." *JSNT* 38 (1990): 37–66.
Givón, Talmy *Syntax: A Functional-Typological Introduction*, 2 vols. Amsterdam/Philadelphia: Benjamins, 1984.
Gray, Timothy C. *The Temple in the Gospel of Mark: A Study in Its Narrative Role*. Grand Rapids, MI: Baker Academic, 2008.
Gruber, Jeffrey S. *Lexical Structures in Syntax and Semantics*. Amsterdam: North-Holland, 1976.
Grundmann, Walter. "δεῖ, δέον ἐστί." *TDNT* 2:22–25.
———. "δεξιός." *TDNT* 2:37–40.
Guelich, Robert A. *Mark 1–8:26*. WBC 34A; Dallas: Word Books, 1989.
Gundry, Robert H. *Mark: A Commentary on His Apology for the Cross*. Grand Rapids, MI: Eerdmans, 1993.
Gurtner, Daniel M. "The Rending of the Veil and Markan Christology: 'Unveiling' the ΥΙΟΣ ΘΕΟΥ' (Mark 15:38-39)." *BibInt* 15 (2007): 292–306.
Hare, Douglas R. A. *Mark*. WeBC; Louisville, KY: Westminster John Knox, 1996.
Harrington, Wilfrid. *Mark*. Wilmington, DE: Michael Glazier, 1979.
Harris, Randy Allen. *The Linguistics Wars*. New York: Oxford University Press, 1993.
Healy, Mary. *The Gospel of Mark*. CCSS; Grand Rapids, MI: Baker Academic, 2008.
Heil, John Paul. *The Gospel of Mark as Model for Action: A Reader-Response Commentary*. New York/Mahwah, NJ: Paulist, 1992.
Henderson, Suzanne Watts. *Christology and Discipleship in the Gospel of Mark*. SNTSMS 135; Cambridge: Cambridge University Press, 2006.
Hicks, Richard. "Markan Discipleship according to Malachi: The Significance of μὴ ἀποστερήσῃς in the Story of the Rich Man (Mark 10:17-22)." *JBL* 132, no. 1 (2013): 179–99.
Hooker, Morna D. *The Gospel According to Saint Mark*. Peabody, MA: Hendrickson, 2005.
———. *The Message of Mark*. London: Epworth, 1983.
Humphrey, Hugh M. *"He Is Risen!": A New Reading of Mark's Gospel*. New York/Mahwah, NJ: Paulist, 1992.
Hurtado, Larry W. *Mark*. GNC; Cambridge: Harper & Row, 1983.

Jackendoff, Ray S. *Semantic Interpretation in Generative Grammar*. Cambridge, MA: MIT Press, 1972.
———. *Semantic Structures*. CSL, 18; Cambridge, MA: MIT Press, 1990.
Jackson, Howard M. "The Death of Jesus in Mark and the Miracle from the Cross." *NTS* 33, no. 1 (1987): 16–37.
Jauss, Hans Robert. *Toward an Aesthetic of Reception*, translated by Timothy Bahti. Minneapolis, MN: University of Minnesota, 1982.
Jeremias, Joachim. *New Testament Theology: The Proclamation of Jesus*, translated by John Bowden. New York: Scribner, 1971.
———. *The Parables of Jesus*, translated by S. H. Hook. London: SCM, 1955; rev. edn, New York: Scribner, 1963.
Johansson, Daniel. "*Kyrios* in the Gospel of Mark." *JSNT* 33, no. 1 (2010): 101–24.
Johnson, Sherman E. *A Commentary on the Gospel according to St. Mark*. London: Adam & Charles Black, 1960.
Juel, Donald. *Messiah and Temple: The Trial of Jesus in the Gospel of Mark*. SBLDS 31; Missoula, MT: Scholars, 1977.
Keegan, Terrence, J. *A Commentary on the Gospel of Mark*. New York: Paulist, 1981.
Kelber, Werner H. *The Kingdom in Mark: A New Place and a New Time*. Philadelphia: Fortress, 1974.
Kingsbury, Jack Dean. "'God' within the Narrative World of Mark." In *The Forgotten God: Perspectives in Biblical Theology*, edited by A. Andrew Das and Frank J. Matera, 75–89. Louisville, KY: Westminster John Knox, 2002.
Kittilä, Seppo and Fernando Zúñiga. "Introduction: Benefaction and Malefaction from a Cross-linguistic Perspective." In *Benefactives and Malefactives: Typological Perspectives and Case Studies*, edited by Fernando Zúñiga and Seppo Kittilä, 1–28. TSL 92; Amsterdam/Philadelphia: Benjamins, 2010.
Klauck, Hans-Josef. *Vorspiel im Himmel? Erzähltechnik und Theologie im Markusprolog*. B-TS 32; Neukirchen: Neukirchener, 1997.
Lane, William L. *The Gospel of Mark: The English Text with Introduction, Exposition, and Notes*. Grand Rapids, MI: Eerdmans, 1974.
———. *The Gospel According to Mark*. NICNT; Grand Rapids, MI: Eerdmans, 1974.
Lategan, Bernard C. "Coming to Grips with the Reader in Biblical Literature." *Semeia* 48 (1989): 3–17.
LaVerdiere, Eugene. *The Beginning of the Gospel: Introducing the Gospel According to Mark, Vol. 1: Mark 1–8:21*. Collegeville, MN: Liturgical, 1999.
Leim, Joshua E. "In the Glory of His Father: Intertextuality and the Apocalyptic Son of Man in the Gospel of Mark." *JTI* 7, no. 2 (2013): 213–32.
Leroux, Neil R. "Repetition, Progression, and Persuasion in Scripture." *Neot* 29, no. 1 (1995): 1–25.
Linton, Olof. "The Demand for a Sign from Heaven (Mk 8,11-12 and Parallels)." *ST* 19 (1965): 112–29.
Louw, Johannes P. and Eugene A. Nida. *Greek–English Lexicon of the New Testament Based on Semantic Domains*, vol. 1, 2nd edn. New York: UBS, 1988.
Lövestam, Evald. *Jesus and 'this Generation': A New Testament Study*, translated by Moira Linnarud. CBNT 25; Stockholm: Almqvist & Wiksell, 1995.
Malbon, Elizabeth Struthers. "History, Theology, Story: Re-Contextualizing Mark's 'Messianic Secret' as Characterization." In *Character Studies and the Gospel of Mark*, edited by Christopher W. Skinner and Matthew Ryan Hauge, 35–56. JSNTSup 483; London: Bloomsbury, 2014.

———. "Narrative Criticism: How Does the Story Mean?" In *Mark & Method: New Approaches in Biblical Studies*, edited by Janice Capel Anderson and Stephen D. Moore, 23–49. Minneapolis, MN: Fortress, 1992.

Marcus, Joel, *Mark 1–8: A New Translation with Introduction and Commentary*. AB 27A; New York: Doubleday, 2000.

———. *Mark 8–16: A New Translation with Introduction and Commentary*. AB 27B; New Haven and London: Yale University Press, 2009.

Martin, George. *The Gospel According to Mark: Meaning and Message*. Chicago: Loyola, 2005.

Matera, Frank J. "Ethics for the Kingdom of God: The Gospel According to Mark." *Louvain Studies* 20 (1995): 187–200.

———. *The Kingship of Jesus: Composition and Theology in Mark 15*. SBLDS 66; Chico, CA: Scholars, 1982.

Matthews, Peter Hugoe. *Syntax*. Cambridge: Cambridge University Press, 1981.

McCawley, James D. *Grammar and Meaning: Papers on Syntactic and Semantic Topics*. New York: Academic Press, 1976.

Metzger, Bruce M. *A Textual Commentary on the Greek New Testament*. Stuttgart: Biblia-Druck, 1975.

Michel, O. "ναός." *TDNT* 4:880–90.

Mittwoch, Anita. "Idioms and Unspecified N[oun] P[hrase] Deletion." *LInq* 2, no. 2 (1971): 255–9.

Moloney, Francis J. *The Gospel of Mark: A Commentary*. Peabody, MA: Hendrickson, 2002.

Moore, Stephen D. *Literary Criticism and the Gospels: The Theoretical Challenge*. New Haven, CT: Yale University Press, 1989.

Motyer, S. "The Rending of the Veil: A Markan Pentecost?" *NTS* 33, no. 1 (1987): 155–7.

Myers, Ched. *Binding the Strong Man: A Political Reading of Mark's Story of Jesus*. Maryknoll, NY: Orbis, 1988.

Neville, David J. "Moral Vision and Eschatology in Mark's Gospel: Coherence or Conflict?" *JBL* 127, no. 2 (2008): 359–84.

Newmeyer, Frederick J. *Linguistic Theory in America: The First Quarter-Century of Transformational Generative Grammar*. New York: Academic Press, 1980.

Nineham, D. E. *The Gospel of St. Mark*. PNTC; Harmondsworth, Middlesex: Penguin, 1963.

Painter, John. *Mark's Gospel: Worlds in Conflict*. London and New York: Routledge, 1997.

Pascut, Beniamin. "The So-Called *Passivum Divinum* in Mark's Gospel." *NovT* 54 (2012): 313–33.

Peppard, Michael. "Torah for the Man Who Has Everything: 'Do Not Defraud' in Mark 10:19." *JBL* 134, no. 3 (2015): 595–604.

Perelman, Chaïm. *The Realm of Rhetoric*, translated by William Kluback. Notre Dame, IN: University of Notre Dame Press, 1982.

Perry, Menakhem. "Literary Dynamics: How the Order of a Text Creates Its Meaning." *Poetics Today* 1, no. 1–2 (1979): 35–64, 311–61.

Pesch, Rudolf. *Das Markusevangelium*, 2 vols. HtKNT II/1–2; Freiburg: Herder, 1976–7.

Petersen, Norman R. "'Point of View' in Mark's Narrative." *Semeia* 12 (1978): 97–121.

Platt, John T. *Grammatical Form and Grammatical Meaning: A Tagmemic View of Fillmore's Deep Structure Case Concepts*. Amsterdam: North-Holland, 1971.

Prince, Gerald. *Narrative as Theme: Studies in French Fiction*. Lincoln, NE: University of Nebraska Press, 1992.

Pryke, E. J. *Redactional Style in the Marcan Gospel: A Study of Syntax and Vocabulary as Guides to Redaction in Mark*. Cambridge: Cambridge University Press, 1978.
Puig i Tàrrech, Armand. "The Glory on the Mountain: The Episode of the Transfiguration of Jesus." *NTS* 58, no. 2 (2012): 151–72.
Rabinowitz, Peter J. *Before Reading: Narrative Conventions and the Politics of Interpretation*. Ithaca, NY: Cornell University Press, 1987.
———. "Truth in Fiction: A Reexamination of Audiences." *Critical Inquiry* 4, no. 1 (1977): 121–41.
Rahlfs, Alfred (ed.). *Septuaginta*. Stuttgart: Deutsche Bibelstiftung, 1935.
Rengstorf, Karl Heinrich. "ἁμαρτωλός." *TDNT* 1:317–33.
———. "σημεῖον." *TDNT* 7:200–61.
Rhoads, David. *Reading Mark, Engaging the Gospel*. Minneapolis, MN: Fortress, 2004.
Rhoads, David and Donald Michie. *Mark as Story: An Introduction to the Narrative of a Gospel*. Philadelphia: Fortress, 1982.
Rhoads, David, Joanna Dewey, and Donald Michie. *Mark as Story: An Introduction to the Narrative of a Gospel* 2nd rev. edn. Minneapolis, MN: Fortress, 1999.
Saeed, John I. *Semantics*. Oxford: Blackwell, 1997.
Sag, Ivan A. and Jorge Hankamer. "Toward a Theory of Anaphoric Processing." *L&P* 7, no. 3 (1984): 325–45.
Santos, Narry F. "Jesus' Paradoxical Teaching in Mark 8:35; 9:35; and 10:43–44." *BibSac* 157 (2000): 15–25.
Schmidt, Frederick W. "Loyal Opposition and the Law in the Teaching of Jesus: The Ethics of a Restorative and Utopian Eschatology." *ATJ* 56, no. 1 (2001): 31–44.
Schrenk, Gottlob. "γράφω." *TDNT* 1:742–49.
———. "δίκαιος." *TDNT* 2:182–91.
Senior, Donald. "The Death of God's Son and the Beginning of the New Age (Matthew 27:51–54)." In *The Language of the Cross*, edited by Aelred Lacomara, 29–51. Chicago: Franciscan Herald, 1977.
———. *The Passion of Jesus in the Gospel of Mark*. Passion Series 2; Wilmington, DE: Michael Glazier, 1984.
Shively, Elizabeth E. "Recognizing Penguins: Audience Expectation, Cognitive Genre Theory, and the Ending of Mark's Gospel." *CBQ* 80, no. 2 (2018): 273–92.
Smith, C. Drew. "'This Is My Beloved Son; Listen to Him:' Theology and Christology in the Gospel of Mark." *HBT* 24 (2002): 53–86.
Smyth, Herbert Weir. *A Greek Grammar for Colleges*. New York: American Book, 1920.
Spitaler, Peter. "Welcoming a Child as a Metaphor for Welcoming God's Kingdom: A Close Reading of Mark 10.13-16." *JSNT* 31, no. 4 (2009): 423–46.
Stählin, Gustav. "The Linguistic Usage and History of ἁμαρτάνω, ἁμάρτημα and ἁμαρτία before and in the NT." *TDNT* 1:293–6.
Stählin, Gustav and Walter Grundmann. "The Concept of Sin in Judaism." *TDNT* 1:289–93.
Stauffer, Ethelbert. "ἀγαπάω." *TDNT* 1:21–55.
Stein, Robert H. *Mark*. BECNT; Grand Rapids, MI: Baker Academic, 2008.
Stern, David. "Jesus' Parables from the Perspective of Rabbinic Literature: The Example of the Wicked Husbandmen." In *Parable and Story in Judaism and Christianity*, edited by Clemens Thoma and Michael Wyschogrod, 42–80. New York: Paulist, 1989.
Sternberg, Meir. *The Poetics of Biblical Narrative: Ideological Literature and the Drama of Reading*. Bloomington, IN: Indiana University Press, 1985.
Stock, Augustine. *The Method and Message of Mark*. Wilmington, DE: Michael Glazier, 1989.

Tannehill, Robert C. "The Disciples in Mark: The Function of a Narrative Role." *JR* 57, no. 4 (1977): 386–405.

———. *The Sword of His Mouth*. Philadelphia: Fortress, 1975.

Telford, W. R. *The Theology of the Gospel of Mark*. Cambridge: Cambridge University Press, 1999.

Thayer, Joseph H. *Thayer's Greek-English Lexicon of the New Testament*. Peabody, MA: Hendrickson, 1996.

Thiessen, Matthew. "A Buried Pentateuchal Allusion to the Resurrection in Mark 12:25." *CBQ* 76, no. 2 (2014): 273–90.

Tolbert, Mary Ann. *Sowing the Gospel: Mark's World in a Literary-Historical Perspective*. Minneapolis, MN: Fortress, 1989.

Traub, Helmut. "οὐρανός." *TDNT* 5:497–536.

Trick, Bradley R. "Death, Covenants, and the Proof of Resurrection in Mark 12:18-27." *NovT* 49, no. 3 (2007): 232–56.

Ulansey, David. "The Heavenly Veil Torn: Mark's Cosmic *Inclusio*." *JBL* 110, no. 1 (1991): 123–5.

van Dijk, Teun A. "Semantic Macro-Structures and Knowledge Frames in Discourse Comprehension." In *Cognitive Processes in Comprehension*, edited by Marcel Adam Just and Patricia A. Carpenter, 3–32. Hillsdale, NJ: Lawrence Erlbaum Associates, 1977.

van Iersel, Bastiaan M. F. "Locality, Structure, and Meaning in Mark." *LB* 53 (1983): 45–54.

———. *Mark: A Reader-Response Commentary*, translated by W. H. Bisscheroux. JSNTSup 164; Sheffield: Sheffield Academic Press, 1998.

———. "The Reader of Mark as Operator of a System of Connotations." *Semeia* 48 (1989): 83–114.

van Iersel, Bastiaan M. F. and A. J. M. Linmans. "The Storm on the Lake, Mk iv 35–41 and Mt viii 18–27 in the Light of Form-Criticism, 'Redaktionsgeschichte' and Structural Analysis." In *Miscellanea Neotestamentica*, edited by T. Baarda, A. F. J. Klijn, and W. C. van Unnik, 17–48, vol. 2. NovTSup; Leiden: Brill, 1978.

Via, Dan O. Jr. *The Ethics of Mark's Gospel—In the Middle of Time*. Philadelphia: Fortress, 1985.

———. *Kerygma and Comedy in the New Testament: A Structuralist Approach to Hermeneutic*. Philadelphia: Fortress, 1975.

Wasserman, Tommy. "The 'Son of God' Was in the Beginning (Mark 1:1)." *JTS* (NS) 62, no. 1 (April 2011): 20–50.

Watts, Rikki E. *Isaiah's New Exodus and Mark*. WUNT 2:88; Tübingen: Mohr Siebeck, 1997.

Wheaton, Gerald. "Thinking the Things of God? The Translation and Meaning of Mark 8:33c." *NovT* 57 (2015): 42–56.

Williams, Joel F. "Foreshadowing, Echoes, and the Blasphemy at the Cross (Mark 15:29)." *JBL* 132, no. 4 (2013): 913–33.

Witherington, Ben III. *The Gospel of Mark: A Socio-Rhetorical Commentary*. Grand Rapids, MI: Eerdmans, 2001.

Wong, Simon S. M. *A Classification of Semantic Case-Relations in the Pauline Epistles*. New York: Peter Lang, 1997.

Wright, N. T. *Jesus and the Victory of God*. COQG 2; Minneapolis, MN: Fortress, 1996.

INDEX

Abba 18, 96, 102, 183, 183n.6, 202–5
Abraham 89, 108–9, 132, 204–5
Adam 107
Agent
   cognate verbs for 127
   and default benefactive
      relationships 13
   and God as 27, 37, 51, 76
   and Jesus 84
   and narrative frames 22
   semantic analysis and description
      16–18
   of sending 48
   and the Sabbath 68
   of writing 63, 78, 85, 95, 112–13, 127
agentive benefaction 146–47, 177–78, 214
all possible things 131
Andrew 92
Angels/Messengers
   attributes of 180–81
   and God's agentive benefaction 147
   and God's Glory 150–51, 150n.1
   and God's innate benefaction 149–50
   and God's power 76–77, 89–90, 94, 203
   and God's preparatory actions 124–25
   and Jesus 122, 181
   and living forever 153, 204
   and narrative coordination 155
   and reciprocal benefaction 109,
      167–68, 184
   and rhetorical contexts 53
   and the rising of the dead 152, 215
   specific actions of 50
argument 31–32
authority 149, 158–59

Bartimaeus 209–10
Beelzebul/unclean spirit 170
beliefs
   cultivated 5
   evoked 5
   pre-existing 5

benefactive relationships
   default 13–14, 14n.24–25
   and God's agency 35, 82
   innate and originating 15–17
   of Jesus 22, 27, 72
   reciprocal 184
Bethsaida 193
Bird, Michael 152, 152n.2
blasphemies 33, 69, 74, 111–12, 120–21,
      167–70, 169n.1, 171, 177
'blood of the covenant' 95
Bock, Darrell L. 171, 171n.2
bread 95, 141, 173, 193, 197
building 174
Bultmann, Rudolf 65, 65n.7

Caesar 88, 141, 161–63
case frames
   forgive 17
   has been written/be necessary/be
      permitted 17–18
   love 17
'cast out' 190
cause 44, 81–83, 89
census tax 88, 141
centurion 104, 123
character frame analysis
   actions and attributes of God 38–40
   clarifications 40–41
   convergence 33–37
   designation of God 26–27
   interpretive conventions 27–31
   narrative beliefs 41–42, 41n.47,
      42n.51
   narrative retrieval 31–32
   references to God 23
   scriptural parallels 24–26
Chief Priest(s)
   as Agent handing over Jesus 95
   agentive benefactive 37
   among the enemies 138
   and authority 175–76

and blasphemies 170–71
and building 174
and David 173, 178
eating the bread 68
execution of the office of 177
giving the secret of God's reign 118
and God's power 153
and God's right hand 151
and God's scripture 132–34
and God's sending 115–16
and Jesus 97–98, 108–9, 177, 184
and John's baptism 208
and rejection of the Son of Man 75
seeking to destroy Jesus 85–86, 121
children 82–83, 144
claims 40–41
Collins, Adela Yarbro 31, 31n.31, 33, 33n.35
commandments, the 8, 88, 111, 119, 127, 135, 139–42, 162–63, 178, 187
communication model 4–5
condition 82
content 17–18, 27, 37, 72, 75, 85
contextual retrieval 27
corban 34, 42
Cornerstone 123–24, 132–33, 138–39, 148, 184
covenant, the 95, 147
covenantal debts 7, 112
creation 127, 130

David
  and Christ 143, 151, 175–76, 197, 209
  coming reign of 190–91
  descendent of 178
  eating the bread of offering 67
  and God's commandments 141
  and God's right hand 151, 159–60
  and the Holy Spirit 155–56
  and the house 173, 177
  Jesus, the Lord of 108–9, 138
  Jesus, the Son of 84
  reign of 198
  sitting at God's right 215
dead 204, 211, 215
debts 177–78
Decapolis 193
demoniac 196

den of thieves 177–78
description introduction 3
Disciples, the
  admiration for stones and buildings 175
  authority to accomplish their assigned tasks 160–61
  and everlasting life 154
  exegesis of the rhetorical contexts 91–96
  and God as Agent 114–18, 121, 123–24
  and God as Agentive benefactive 136–38, 141–42, 147–48
  and God the father 203, 209
  and God not the topic of faith of 209–10
  and God as the source 207
  and God's attributes 188–89
  and God's authority 157
  and God's elect 150, 181
  and God's forgiveness 178
  and God's Tearing of the Heavens 102
  and God's voice and statement 191
  hard teachings about 161
  and the Holy Spirit 156
  inability to cast out unspeaking spirit 211–12
  instruments of God's saving for themselves 111
  Jesus bids farewell to 73
  and Jesus as God's intermediary 181–83
  Jesus takes and breaks bread for 193
  Jesus's commands to have faith 201–2
  Jesus's hard teachings about 76
  and narrative coordination 155
  part of Jesus 79, 192, 196, 213
  and potential communications 198
  praying to God 194, 197
  receiving what they pray for 211
  and the rising of the dead 152
  singing of 198
  the topic of the faith 85
  a woman portrayed as 165
divorce 32, 140
doves 175

Elaboration 58–59, 101, 127, 149, 167,
    185, 192
Elders
    actions of those with swords and
        clubs 97
    and authority 175–76
    and building 174, 177
    commitment to the traditions of 187
    destruction of 108–9
    God as Agent 115–18
    God as Agentive benefactive 132–34,
        138–39
    and God's power 153
    and John's baptism 208
    and the questioning of Jesus 86
    Son of Man rejected by 75
Elect, the
    beneficiaries of Son of Man's end-time
        181
    chosen by God 93, 111, 150
    and God's agentive benefaction 127,
        131, 134–36, 147–48
    and instrument of God's saving
        action 160
    and Jesus, Son of Man 180–81
    rhetorical frames 44
    shortening the days 105–6, 124–25
    whom Jesus will gather 153
Elijah 31, 78, 102, 113, 119, 121, 134, 136
end times 119–20, 122–24, 138, 156, 160,
    181–82
Eucharistic meals 189, 189n.1, 193
Event 12, 18
everlasting life 82, 153–54
evil 187
Exegetical Study
    extent of 56, 59
    format of 55–56
    Mark 1 63–67
    Mark 2 67–68
    Mark 3 68–69
    Mark 4 69–71
    Mark 5 71–72
    Mark 6 72–73
    Mark 7 73–74
    Mark 8 74–77, 75n.23, 77n.29–30
    Mark 9 77–78
    Mark 10 81–84, 83n.4
    Mark 11 84–86

Mark 12 86–91
Mark 13 91–94, 93n.19
Mark 14 94–98
    order of presentation of 56
    prelude 55
    scholarly resources for 56
Experiencers 17–18, 22, 27–28, 35, 39, 46,
    85, 190, 196

faith 210
false prophet 28, 28n.20
Farmers
    destruction of 123, 197
    and God's Slaves 179, 198
    and reciprocal benefaction 184
    and respect of Jesus 191–92, 196
    and the Vineyard 86–88, 107, 109,
        114–16, 118–21, 137–39, 182,
        208–9
fig tree(s) 85, 209
Fillmore, Charles J. 16n.27
fish 193, 197
food 187, 189
forgiveness 33, 112, 127–29, 167

Gehenna 79, 125, 144, 154–55
gentiles 37, 193, 213
Gethsemane 194
glory 149, 150
goal 39, 48, 54, 144
God
    as Agent 101–21, 104n.3
    as Agentive Benefactive 127–48,
        133n.6, 143n.9
    as content, experiencer, goal and
        instrument 185–99
    exegetical study (Mark 1-9) 63–77
    exegetical study (Mark 10-15) 81, 98
    innate benefaction of 149–66,
        160nn.7,10
    narrative analysis 19–41
    as Patient, Source, Topic and Theme
        201–16
    recipient, reciprocal benefaction
        167–84
    rhetorical analysis 43–56
    and semantic analysis 3–18
gospel, the 94, 124, 131, 161, 163–66, 181,
    187

Head of the Household 94
healing 67, 72, 84, 158, 169, 172, 194, 206, 209–10
Healy, Mary 68, 68n.13
Herod 88, 141, 163
Herodians 176, 198
Herodias 141
Holy Spirit
    and blasphemies 112, 170–71
    a designation for God's Spirit 28–29, 28n.21
    future speaking of through the Twelve 117
    and God as Agent 102–5
    and God in possession of 64, 68–69, 73–74, 92
    and God's forgiveness 128, 155–56, 156n.5
    and innate benefaction of a right hand 149
    instrument of the forgiveness of sins 159–60
    and Jesus 120, 123, 157, 170, 182, 184
    and John 180
hosanna 185, 190
house 167, 170, 172–73, 175, 177–78
human beings
    actions of 178, 198
    agentive benefaction of 89, 130–32, 136–37, 140–42, 144–47
    baptizing of 192
    and blasphemy 169–71
    as Goal 54
    God's ability to act through as Instrument 211
    and God's Agency 109–10, 118–21, 124
    and God's saving 93, 106–7
    and the Holy Spirit 156, 160
    innate benefaction of 159
    know that God loves Jesus 192
    made in God's image 162
    and Peter 187
    saving of 83, 212
    sinful actions of 167
husband 89

inherit/inheritance 208
innate benefaction/attributes 159–61
Instrument(s) 18, 37, 51, 69, 71–72, 77, 199, 211
Isaac 89, 108–9, 132, 204–5
Isaiah 42, 113, 119, 155, 164, 180, 184
Israel 86, 90, 119, 139, 143, 186, 188, 204

Jacob 89, 108–9, 204–5
Jairus 72, 211
James 77–78, 96, 102, 114, 129–30, 182, 191, 196
Jerusalem 171, 193, 198, 206
Jesus
    and exegesis of rhetorical contexts (Mark 1-9) 63–77
    and exegesis of rhetorical contexts (Mark 10-15) 81–98
    with God, as content, experiencer, goal and instrument 185–99
    and God as Agentive Benefactive 127–48
    and God as Patient, Source, Topic and Theme 201–16
    God and repeated reciprocal benefaction 167–84
    as God's Beloved Son 101–25, 116n.12, 122n.16
    and God's innate benefaction 149–66, 154n.4
    and narrative analysis method 19–41
    and rhetorical analysis method 43–56
    and semantic analysis method 3–18
Jews 213
John the Baptist
    baptism of 86, 172, 209
    and the baptism of repentance 37, 64–65
    command to listen to Jesus 192, 196
    and God's Agency in Writing 113–14
    and God's agentive benefaction 127–30, 134–36, 141
    God's command to 191
    and God's Holy Spirit 156
    and God's Prophets 180
    and Jesus 183
    as the referent of 'messenger' 42
John the Messenger
    and God's actions of writing 113–15, 115n.11

and God's final pre-eschatological
    action 119, 125
and God's innate benefaction 149, 164
and God's Scripture 134
and God's sending of 50, 58, 63,
    63n.1, 121
and God's Slaves 179
placing in Elijah's clothing 102
preparation of God's way 162
and rhetorical frames 45, 48
Joseph of Arimathea 98, 144
Judea 92, 135

Legion 40–41, 41, 71, 182, 199
Leim, Joshua E. 150, 150n.1
Levirite regulation 135, 135n.10
Linguistics and Exegesis (Danove) 12–13
Lord of the Vineyard 22, 25–26, 86–88,
    88n.11
love 6, 185–86

main clause 38–40
markets 91, 207
marriage 73, 81, 89–90, 141
moneychangers 85, 175
Mosaic covenant 6
Moses 74, 78, 81–82, 89, 108, 121, 131–33,
    176, 205

narrative coordination 155, 167
narrative frames
    characters 22–23
    communication 19–20
    contextual 21
    coordination 52–53
    overlay 21
    scriptural 20–21, 31
neighbor(s) 140, 186–88

paralyzed man 67, 111–12, 120–21, 169,
    198, 209
Passover meals 189–90
Patient(s) 12–13, 17, 37, 39, 201
Peppard, Michael 154, 154n.4
Perelman, Chaïm 41, 41n.47
Peter
    and God's command to 191–92, 196
    and God's scriptures 75, 134–35
    and God's voice 77–78, 102, 129–30

and human beings 161
and Jesus 76, 114, 182
thinking the things of human beings
    187
and topic of the gospel 92
Pharisees
    commitment to the traditions of the
        Elders 187
    and the face of God 163
    and God the Source 207–8
    and God's commandments 74, 139
    and God's condemnation 194
    God's withholding of further action
        for 121
    honoring God only with their lips 215
    inappropriate worshipping of God 198
    and Jesus 75, 88, 113–14, 117–18, 176
    Priests and eating the bread 68
    and question about the permissibility
        of divorce 81
    remaining distant from God 208
    and the sign 206
Pilate 98
prayer 27, 185–86, 190, 193–96, 195n.3,
    196n.4
pre-eschatological actions 118
predicators 23–24, 24n.8, 38, 40, 46, 49
    cognate 52–53, 52n.7
    rhetorical frames 59
Prophets 33, 72–75, 110, 134–37, 143,
    167–68, 179–80, 184
Puig i Tàrrech, Armand 130, 130n.2

Rabbis 183
reciprocal benefaction 35, 78, 87–88, 90,
    96, 108–9, 115, 182–84, 214
rehearsals 58, 101, 127, 149, 168
Rejected Stone 132–33, 138–39
repentance 64, 127, 172, 172n.3
repetition 118, 187, 210
Resurrection, the 90, 121, 132
rhetorical frames
    Beliefs concerning God 55
    clarifications 51–53
    content of 45–47
    Exegetical Study (Part II) 55–56
    linkages and emphases 47–49
    model of communication 43–45
    organized Content about God 49–51

predicator repetition 47, 47n.5, 53–54
Theological Study (Part III) 56–60, 60n.10
right hand 143, 151, 155, 159–60, 171

Sabbath 34, 44, 67–68, 109–10, 110, 119, 141
Sadducees 89, 108, 121, 133, 135, 151, 153
sanctuary 97–98, 167, 174–75, 178
Sanhedrin 97, 151
Satan 66, 66–67, 162
Save 37, 50–51
Schmidt, Frederick W. 81
Schrenk, Gottlob 28, 28n.19
Scribes
   and authority 175, 176
   and blasphemy 169–71
   and building 174
   commitment to the traditions of the Elders 187
   and God as Agentive Benefactive 132–34, 138–39, 142
   and God the Source 91, 207
   and God's Agency 113–18, 121
   and God's first and second commandments 176, 187
   and God's house 173
   and God's power 153
   and God's scriptures 75
   and God's word 74
   honoring God only with their lips 215
   inappropriate worshipping of God 198
   and Jesus 37, 85, 108–9, 176–77, 194, 198
   and John's baptism 86, 208
   judgments of 206–7
   remaining distant from God 208
scriptures 89, 92, 97, 113, 127, 132, 134–35, 176
semantic analysis
   clarifications 13–17
   frame content 6–8
   frames 3–6, 9–12, 9n.17, 51–53
   introduction 3
   predicators 12–13
semantic beliefs, pre-existing 18
semantic coordination 212

Sending 114–15
Septuagint (LXX) 20–21
seven brothers 90
sheep 95–96, 113–14
Shepherd 95–96, 96, 96n.24–6, 121
shortening the days 105–6, 110, 130–31, 136
signs 117, 205–6, 206n.2
sin 29, 29n.22, 120–21, 159, 167–69, 171–72, 177
Slaves
   attributes of 179
   authority to accomplish their assigned tasks 160
   and the Farmers 86–88, 198
   and God as Agentive benefactive 138
   and God's Agency 114–16, 118–19, 121
   and God's authority 158
   and God's Prophets 180
   and God's sending 48, 50, 58
   and Jesus 94
   and reciprocal benefaction 167–68, 184
Son of Man
   and the coming suffering 46
   giving life as a ransom 187
   and God as Agent 113–14, 121–25, 122n.16
   God as Agentive benefactive 131, 133–37, 143
   and God, Father of Jesus 203
   and God's Angels 180
   and God's authority to forgive 169–70
   and God's Glory 150–53, 152n.2
   and God's right hand 160–61
   and the Gospel of God 164
   and the Holy Spirit 156–57
   and instrument of God's saving action 160
   and Jesus 8, 50–51, 75–78, 92–95, 94n.21, 97, 165–66, 171–72, 184, 198
   and the rising of the dead 152
Source 16, 35, 40, 74–75, 83, 87, 116, 201, 206–7
Spirit 135, 182, 192, 196
synagogues 91, 117, 198, 207

teachers 183, 183n.6
tearing

of the curtain 98, 174, 178
and God as Agentive benefactive 138
God's action of 49
and God's Agency 34, 36, 101, 122–23, 125
in relation to Jesus 182
the sky 192
tearing of the heavens 16, 34, 65, 65n.5, 101–2, 119–20, 209
Temple, the
  attributes of 175
  a den of thieves 190
  destruction of 175
  and God as Agent 113–14, 121
  and God as recipient and reciprocal benefactive 167, 173
  and Jesus 84, 86, 91–92, 176–77
  'sanctuary' as a designation for 174, 178
  status of sacrifices 187–88
thematic roles 10–11, 10n.20, 16
Theme(s) 39, 201, 209
Topic 85, 94, 149, 201, 210
Topic of Faith 209–10
trespasses 85, 85n.7, 112
tribulation 136

unclean spirits 182

verbs
  and non-verb predicators 49
  predicators 13, 16–17, 49–50
  of transference 15–16
Vineyard, the
  claim of the Farmers 208
  establishing of 209
  giving to others 197
  and God 86–87, 107
  and God as Agent 109–10, 114–21, 123–24
  and God as Agentive benefactive 127–28, 133, 137–39
  God as innate and originating benefactive 147–48
  and God's Slaves 179
  and God's tower 174
  implications of its three continuous contexts 214
  Lord of the 205
voice 129–30

wife 12, 73, 81, 89–90, 132–33, 140–41
Williams, Joel F. 169, 169n.1